W9-CRR-298

Ethical Life

Ethical Life

The Past and Present of Ethical Cultures

Harry Redner

ROWMAN & LITTLEFIELD PUBLISHERS, INC.
Lanham • Boulder • New York • Oxford

ROWMAN & LITTLEFIELD PUBLISHERS, INC.

Published in the United States of America
by Rowman & Littlefield Publishers, Inc.
4720 Boston Way, Lanham, Maryland 20706
www.rowmanlittlefield.com

12 Hid's Copse Road
Cumnor Hill, Oxford OX2 9JJ, England

British Library Cataloging in Publication Information Available

Library of Congress Cataloging-in-Publication Data

Redner, Harry.
    Ethical life : the past and present of ethical cultures / Harry Redner.
       p.   cm.
    Includes bibliographical references and index.
    ISBN 0-7425-1232-0 (alk. paper)—ISBN 0-7425-1233-9 (pbk.: alk. paper)
    1. Social ethics.   2. Social values.
  HM665 .R43   2002
  303.3'72—dc21   2001041699

Printed in the United States of America

♾ ™ The paper used in this publication meets the minimum requirements of American National Standard for Information Sciences—Permanence of Paper for Printed Library Materials, ANSI/NISO Z39.48-1992.

Contents

~

Preface

This book does not stand by itself alone. It is an integral part of a comprehensive theory of human culture. In fact, it is the second in a quartet of books on this subject, the first of which was *A New Science of Representation: toward an integrated theory of representation in science, politics and art* (1994). The fourth work in this sequence is also now complete and is provisionally entitled *The Triumph of Technics: global culture and its local alternatives*. The third book, which is in an advanced state of preparation, is a companion volume to this one, dealing with the arts and aesthetic culture in general, to be called *Aesthetic Life: the past and present of artistic cultures*.

The four books follow the general thesis, briefly set out at the start of chapter 1, that cultural life consists of three fundamental aspects: representation, ethos and technics. The first of the books in the quartet deals with representation, the last with technics; ethos, the whole domain of values, has two diverse constituents, the ethical and the aesthetic, hence it requires two distinct works. The comparison between ethics and aesthetics is briefly spelled out in chapter 4 of this work.

As the title of the fourth and last book intimates, the ultimate conclusion of present relevance of all these works is that the contemporary global culture that is sweeping the world apparently without resistance is marked by the triumph of technics over representation and ethos. This is as much as to say that techniques of all kinds take preponderance over symbolic meanings and values, and this reflects itself in the ethical dimension as in every other. The countless details of the case presented in this work substantiate this thesis. However, as the subtitle of the last work also intimates, global culture is not the only extant one, there are all kinds of surviving competitors and other possible alternatives to it. The battle between global culture and these usually local alternatives is the coming *Kulturkampf* of our time, on which the outcome depends not only the state of our societies and the world as a whole, but, as it were, the salvation of our souls.

This battle, as it is being fought out in ethics, is recorded in this work. It is a struggle taking place not among philosophers about this or that feature of abstract ethical theory or among professional ethicists over this or that practicality of law, usually a dispute on some development deriving from novel technologies, but an engagement concerning the tenor of the whole of ethical life. Ethical life is the comprehensive term for the domain of ethical practices whose study stands between abstract theory and applied ethics, the two kinds of approaches that have academic currency at present in all the universities of the world. I use the term in line with the work of my friend Gernot Böhme whose work, originally published in German, is now to appear in English translation entitled *Ethics in Context.* Since completing my own work I have been delighted to discover that "ethical life", or "lived morality" as he calls it, is used in the same sense by Richard Stivers in his ground-breaking but sadly neglected work, *The Culture of Cynicism: American Morality in Decline.* I found this book by serependipitous chance, unfortunately too late to make any use of it in this text, for it bears out my main argument. Nothing else in the extant literature known to me so complements my own study as these two works, apart from, in quite other respects, the classical sociological work on religious ethics by Max Weber.

Though this book does not stand by itself alone, it can be read and understood independently of any of my other works. In fact, apart from thoughtful attention and a little good will, it makes few demands on any reader with a broad and general education. For this is not a book only for academics or specialists, nor is it intended for study purposes alone, rather it is designed to be of some use to anyone who wishes to lead an ethical life. Hence it is addressed to all those who are serious about ethics. Compared to that agreement in basic orientation, all other disagreements on this or that point of fact or interpretation are relatively minor matters of disputation.

I know that there will be many to whom this book will appear as merely a dispiriting gospel of bad news. I also know how difficult it is to confront real ethical problems in one's life. I wish I could have written something more comforting or even uplifting, but in these hard times that would have been a self-deceiving illusion, another life-lie to add to the many already in circulation. It seems to me to be far better to confront the grim truth about ethics in our time, for only then is it possible to do something about it. And just as the test of a pudding is in the eating, so the test of a book on ethics is ultimately in the living, that is, whether it can make some difference in ethical life. So I relinquish this book to the public domain in the hope that it will be of as much use to others in reading as it has been to me in writing.

~

Acknowledgments

First and foremost I wish to thank my friend Arye Botwinick for reading and reviewing this work and for his interest in my works in general over many years past. Secondly, on the publishing side of this endeavour, my thanks go to Christa Acampora, who saw the values of this work before others.

This book was written over many years under various circumstances and postings for which I wish to express my appreciation to a number of people and organizations who made these possible. It was begun in Haifa, in fact on the very Mount Carmel where the prophet Elijah once engaged the priests of Baal in a contest over the true God and so by implication also over ethical truth. For giving me the opportunity to take up the gauntlet again in a contemporary context, I thank Yael Yishai and Abram Brichta of Haifa University. However, most of it was thought out and written in Darmstadt, the home-town of the playwright Büchner whose work was an ethical challenge to the Baal-worshipers of his time. For that good fortune I am grateful to the beneficence of Alcatel-SEL and their Managing Director, Dr Dieter Klumpp, for endowing a chair at the Darmstadt Technisches Universität; and for appointing me to it I thank Prof. Dr. Ing. Johann-Dietrich Wörner, President, Prof. Hans Seidler, Chancellor, and their gracious and diligent assistant, Frau Elizabeth Sundermann.

Last, but not least, I wish to express my sincere appreciation to Lynette Carter who has laboured on my barely legible manuscripts for many years. I am glad that I have this opportunity to publicly acknowledge all that I owe to her skill, care and concern and the soothing spell of her never-failing cheerfulness of spirit.

INTRODUCTION

◠

Problems and Paradoxes of Ethics

Standing on the threshold of a new millennium, there are crucial questions about the present state and condition of ethics to be asked. The ethical norms, beliefs, practices, and institutions we have inherited from the past, and according to which we still profess to live, are not much older than those two millennia. Certainly, the two-thousand-year span coincides exactly with the history of Christian morality, the most important ethical system in the West during this time and now throughout the world. What has now become of Christian morality?

What has happened in the East to Confucian ethics, to Buddhist morality, and to the Hindu codes of dharma? Islam, as we all know from the daily papers, is undergoing a fundamentalist revival, but can such a medieval ethic of Koranic law function in any kind of technically advanced society? What will become of it once the new wave of religious enthusiasm recedes? What is left in the West of the various medieval ethics, such as that of knightly chivalry? What will become of the Protestant ethic once the spirit of capitalism has left it and become global? Where are now the various humanist ethics of the Enlightenment and their nineteenth-century successors, the ethics of the various "isms"?

Perhaps the most crucial historical question is what has happened to ethics in the course of the twentieth century, the period of so much change and disruption in all the traditional forms of culture. A century ago ethics seemed unassailable. Most people assumed then that civilization is impossible without ethical norms; to be civilized, civil, and ethical seemed almost synonymous. The opposite was barbarism and anarchy, and that, it seemed, could not happen under modern conditions; it was almost unthinkable. In the course of the tumults of the twentieth century, we have now learned to know better. Having lived through some of the worst barbarisms of history, we can

1

no longer believe that civilization depends on ethics. Certainly, a modern technological civilization can proceed without much of an ethical basis. Everywhere such markers of civilization as industrial production, social organization, political order, general education, and scientific knowledge have advanced to new levels of attainment, despite all the ethical setbacks of wars, revolutions, and totalitarian dictatorships. Civilization has advanced apace and spread all over the globe even as all the traditional ethics have seemed to falter.

A century ago it was generally believed that ethical improvement would keep pace with civilizational advance. Only a few daring and pessimistic thinkers entertained the notion that something could go wrong with ethics. Nietzsche was one such who raised the horrendous possibility that morality might become devalued and collapse. He considered himself an immoralist and actively worked for this to come about; he cried out longingly, "Where are the barbarians of the twentieth century?"[1] George Eliot, an avowed moralist whom he detested, also entertained similar apocalyptic thoughts but with the opposite attitude. She warned of the dangers to come: "There is no general doctrine that is not capable of eating out our morality if unchecked by the deep-seated habit of direct fellow-feeling with individual fellow men."[2] Her warning was prescient. Those general doctrines of the nineteenth century, become the "isms" of the twentieth, proved themselves well capable of eating out our morality. They consumed far more than that, of course, and might also have swallowed most of our culture if they had not encountered some opposition on the way. Above all, these were the political "isms," such as Bolshevism, Fascism, Nazism, but there were also the unpolitical ones, such as statism, bureaucratism, economism, technologism, scientism, and ultimately even capitalism and liberalism themselves insofar as they remained unchecked by deep-seated habits of feeling.

Morality, even more so than any other type of ethics, depends precisely on such "habits of direct fellow-feeling with individual fellow men." It is more than anything a direct response to others in difficult predicaments—that is, situations demanding moral intervention—such as, for example, when one feels immediate and almost instinctive ire if one witnesses someone being inhumanely mistreated. Once such habits of direct fellow-feeling have been corrupted by the currents of the world or not even inculcated by society in the first place, then morality is degraded and is in danger of disappearing as a social practice. We seem to have come quite close at times to this outcome.

We might ask in general, where does ethics stand at present? This is the same as asking, where do people stand in regard to ethics? Do they worry about having done or said the right things in public or private life? Do they get indignant when wrong is done to others? Do they blame the wrong-doers and offer sympathy and support to the victims? Are they stirred up and motivated by burning ethical passions for just or ideal causes? Are they scrupulous about their obligations or duties? Putting it all in a nutshell, do people at the end of the twentieth century still affirm an ethical stand in all important and serious matters, in the way that people at the end of the nineteenth century claimed or, at least, pretended to be doing?

In making such a comparison between the two *fins de siècle*, it soon becomes apparent that the answer to such a catch-all question will be extremely ambivalent. It all depends on what is being examined and how this is done. Ethical matters look very different when seen in terms of whole societies or when examined through the lives of individuals. Both points of view ought to be consonant with each other—for what are societies but collections of individuals?—but *prima facie* they seem not to be so.

Looked at in terms of societies, it seems incontrovertible that social conditions are much better now than a century ago, at least in Western or advanced countries. One might assert this not only on material, but precisely on ethical, grounds. There is much more social freedom and political stability now than there was then. Nobody is killed wantonly without serious repercussions or carelessly allowed to die from lack of food or essential medical attention, as was often the case in many countries a century ago. Personal freedoms, such as those of speech, religion, marriage, domicile, and work, are guaranteed almost throughout the world. Equality before the law has been generally attained and draconian punishments for minor offenses mostly abolished. Slavery has been almost eliminated and serfdom much curtailed throughout the world. At least in Western societies, destitution has been diminished through social welfare provisions. In these and in most other countries some measure of political participation through democratic institutions is now prevalent. Secret police terror is almost nonexistent except in a few isolated instances. Literacy is widespread, information and knowledge are freely available almost everywhere. The constant threat of war has been lifted, there is almost peace on earth, or at least more so than ever before in human history. Except that lurking behind this façade of tranquility is the still ever present danger of total nuclear annihilation.

Thus one might say that the traditional universal Christmas message of hope: peace on earth, good will to all men, has been almost attained. But there is ambivalence in both respects, for just as peace is uncertain, so is good will restricted. There is a kind of impersonal good will exercised by public agencies and welfare institutions. But as for personal good will, the "direct fellow-feeling with individual fellow men" that George Eliot speaks of, that is no longer much in evidence.

None of the law and order or social welfare provisions previously mentioned rely much on personal good will. As Adam Smith put it at the very start of these modern developments, "It is not from the personal benevolence of the butcher, the brewer, or the baker, that we expect our dinner, but from their regard to their own interest . . . it is by treaty, by barter and by purchase, that we obtain from one another the greater part of those mutual good offices which we stand in need of."[3] And as we turn to the market to supply our daily wants, so we look to the state and its agencies to protect us from the travails of fortune or the vagaries of the market in case we fall ill or fall into unemployment. Good will plays no part in any of it. Anymore than the baker bakes the bread or the candlestick maker made candles out of good will, does the social worker succor widows and waifs, or the teacher instruct children, or the lawyer defend the indigent, or the administrator dispense largesse, or the policeman guard the weak, and so on for all those in the so-called helping professions. For to benefit from their services, one has to prove eligibility and entitlement by the official criteria, otherwise nothing is forthcoming. Anyone who has to rely on the personal discretion of good will can expect to find it wanting. Hence, nobody any longer relies on it.

In some quarters of our societies there is now a considerable increase of bad will and rage of a kind that was not so openly displayed a century ago. The levels of crimes of all kinds are growing. Murders, muggings, rapes, and other acts of violence are now prevalent in some areas of all big cities. Cries from victims for help are often ignored by bystanders, for they have come to believe it is none of their business; it is a matter for the professionals to handle. Good Samaritans are rare. As a result, trust between people, even neighbors living together, is no longer there. And, in any case, what does it now mean to be a neighbor in anonymous building-blocks or housing estates or bedroom outer-suburbs of urban conglomerations? Trust even among friends and family members is breaking down. Parents cannot depend on their young children not to succumb to peer pressure and take drugs or indulge in premature sex or shop-lifting. Children cannot depend on their parents to stay married or provide them a secure home. Newlyweds secure their own separate possessions by prenuptial contracts on the assumption—backed by statistical probability—that they will divorce before too long. So what trust is left in marriage? In friendship there is often none at all.

And what is true of trust holds also for respect, honor, integrity, dignity, and even honesty or any of the other basic ethical virtues. There is little respect for teachers or regard for pupils at any educational level. Education is a service provided like any other; nobody need be beholden or grateful to a caring teacher. So why should teachers care? People in positions of responsibility or authority are no longer held in any honor and so feel themselves absolved of the need for honorable conduct. Politicians are among the least honored or honorable. They need evince no integrity or dignity, and even their honesty is highly questionable where the law does not strictly stipulate that they are forbidden to lie. Lying in ordinary transactions is now commonplace and no longer strongly reproved, for as Samuel Goldwyn's cynical malapropism puts it, a verbal agreement is not worth the paper it is written on. In a society driven by market forces, career and status ambitions, and general greed, people prey on each other in all sorts of ways and get away with it where the law is blind. There is no ethical community to call them to account. In general, people feel themselves to be less ethically bound to each other than perhaps ever before.

In this sense people have become ethically worse than a century ago. Yet the society they constitute is at the same time ethically better. This is a strange paradox: How can people as individuals be worse than the society in which they live together? To fully plumb the depth of this paradox will require the full extent of this book; it lies at the heart of our whole endeavor. Here we shall merely begin exploring it with a few initial observations. As we shall show, the issue must be looked at historically as a process of ethical bifurcation, a split that has gradually opened up over the last century or so between the state of ethics in society and for the individual. For as society has gradually achieved its main ethical goals, mainly through the political and legal means of reform movements and ameliorating legislative enactments, so individuals have felt themselves absolved from much of what they would have previously considered their ethical responsibilities. Why should one put oneself out and sacrifice one's own means for that which society is obliged to see to or provide anyway? So gradually, as the social and bureaucratic agencies and institutions that concern themselves with general ethical matters were established, individuals have learned to distance themselves and withdraw from ethical responsibilities, especially the moral ones that are personally so onerous.

It is true that some people had to be committed to ethical causes in the first place to achieve those social goals of reform. Some individuals had to devote enormous good will and frequently make personal sacrifices in the political battles and other social struggles necessary to achieve anything ethically worthwhile. Many virtues had to be displayed by those involved at the forefront of such endeavors. Such people had to be ethically motivated to an intense degree, usually over the course of a whole lifetime. They would invariably begin as young idealists devoted to altruistic causes but, unfortunately, some would end up as self-righteous fanatics. During the nineteenth and early part of the twentieth century, there were many such individuals given to public causes. Today there are few left, partly because the need for them is no longer there in the so-called advanced societies, but largely because such societies are no longer capable of producing such people. The few that do emerge tend to turn to Third World countries, where the need for them is greater than ever. There they are usually joined by heroic indigenous reformers who are also desperately struggling for the social justice and freedom already achieved in the West. Their success is bound to be partial for it is doubtful whether the flood of corruption with which these countries are inundated can be sufficiently drained to permit impartial public institutions to function effectively, at least in the near future.

In the West the mood for idealism is long past. The last resurgence of it during the student movement of the late 1960s and early 1970s proved to be purely ephemeral. There was something phony about it from the start, and it soon fizzled out. What it left behind was a legacy of failure and cynicism that fed into the contrary mood of selfishness that became subsequently predominant, especially among the young. In economic conditions of intensified market competition, getting and keeping a job became the first priority. Apart from that, a withdrawal into privacy has supervened. Narcissistic preoccupations with one's own body, its vigor, health, and beauty, play a more prominent part than any concern with others. Personal success is valued above everything. Ethics takes a back seat in the onward drive for wealth, power, status, or simply personal pleasure and satisfaction.

We can illustrate this whole historical process whereby ethics is rendered redundant by reference to one key example: the cardinal virtue of charity. We can demonstrate very clearly the inverse relation between the prevalence of social and personal charity. Charity or *caritas*, as its etymology reminds us, is the basic principle of Christian morality. St. Paul's ringing injunction to the Corinthians is still heard often from the pulpit: "Though I speak with the tongues of men and of angels, and have not charity, I am become as sounding brass, or a tinkling cymbal." What it means today is no more than rhetorical. In the past it meant very much more than that. Traditionally, what it amounted to was very real and practical, indeed, for it imposed a wide range of duties and helping activities upon each individual Christian. Taken together, these constituted a whole network of eleemosynary provisions, especially for the poor. But to enable the virtue of charity to be fully exercised, a constant supply of these had also always to be available, as, indeed, Christ's pronouncement promised, "The poor you have always with you." Thus, in the Christian moral scheme of things, the apparent ineradicability of poverty in the fallen world was to be compensated for by the saving grace of charity.

But all this changed with the economic success of capitalism. As bakers and candlestick makers became more and more proficient at producing bread and light at less and less cost, so ever greater numbers could afford their products. Eventually, nobody need lack for bread or remain in darkness. But the very success of the capitalism that economists from Adam Smith to Milton Friedman have extolled spelled the death of charity and much of Christian morality with it. It brought material riches and ethical impoverishment, at once. The reasons for this are inherent in the very nature of capitalism as a rational economic system functioning in a purely impersonal way. As Max Weber explained it already a long time ago:

> It is impossible to control a universe of objective rational business activities by charitable appeals to particular individuals. The functionalized material world of capitalism certainly offers no support whatever for any such charitable orientation. In this rationalized economic world of capitalism, not only do the requirements of religious charity founder against the refractoriness and unreliability of particular individuals which happens in all systems, but they actually lose their meaning altogether.[4]

The fact that charity has lost its meaning was perhaps not as obvious in Weber's day as it has become since. Now it is fully apparent.

But for this to happen in such a thorough way, the moral erosion produced by capitalism had to be seconded by the state. The state entered the field of charitable endeavors precisely to mitigate and make up for the apparently callous heartlessness of capitalism. With its welfare provisions the state sought to provide compensations to the victims of capitalism, the unemployed, sick, and dependent. But it was no longer to be seen as charity, but as social welfare that came as of right to those who needed it. Thus at once the duty and burden of dispensing charity were removed from the shoulders of the rich, and the stigma of receiving it was taken away from the poor and needy. Charity was no more; it had lost its meaning.

Nobody wanted charity anymore in any shape or form. Anything that smacked of it got a bad name, so gradually it was converted from a cardinal virtue to a kind of vice, for those who persisted in personal charitable exertions came to be looked on askance as do-gooders, meddling busybodies who only want to make themselves feel good. The charitable impulse was interpreted as a kind of psychological self-gratification that was really selfishness masquerading as morality.

This reconception of charity generalized itself and spread to much of moral life. The aversion to charity on the part of givers and receivers infused itself to any kind of giving or receiving of help. The asking for help in any respect and the giving it tended to be shunned. To ask for help means to admit weakness or defeat and that nobody wants to do, for it risks being regarded as a loser. To offer help is to be looked on with suspicion, for as Adorno noted already long ago, "Not to be 'after something' is almost suspect: no help to others in the rat-race is acknowledged unless legitimized by counter-claims."[5] Those who persist in offering help to others *gratis* where no exchange relation is involved risk worse than ingratitude or rebuff, for they are considered "suckers" from whom anything can be extracted without compunction. If someone is so desperate as to have to turn for help, this can only be sought from those whose professional work it is, the exponents of the so-called helping professions. For then the help can be accepted as a right and not as charity beholden to someone's good will. It can simply be seen as a service like any other that is publicly provided.

The consequences for the whole of moral life in this transformation of charity from a personal virtue to a civic right go very deep. Not only is the whole notion of help and helpfulness altered, but all relations of mutuality give way to those of impersonality. There emerges a hesitancy in freely giving or receiving anything. Not needing or asking for any kind of assistance or offering it to others becomes the hallmark of personal independence. This shades into all the responses that one person makes to another. Thus freely offered approval, emotional support in need, commiseration on loss, solidarity in defeat, none of these expressions of fellow-feeling is now as prevalent as it used to be. Everyone withdraws into himself or herself and avoids reaching out to others in need. Obviously, there are many interacting causes for such a change in bearing, mood, and manner; eschewing charity is but one of these. But not being charitable goes very deep into the whole fabric of moral life.

Many of these transformations take the general form of a change from relying on personal good will to demanding rights and entitlements—that is, roughly expressed, a transition from a personal to an institutional basis, or, in short, from ethics to law. Law now plays a preponderant role in regulating all behavior in contemporary societies. It is the legal system that endows individuals with all their rights and entitlements and demands from them in return obligations and duties. The law protects and provides, as well as punishes any breach of itself. But at the same time the law makes otiose any other ethics except that which is encapsulated in law. Morality, in particular, tends to receive no legal recognition. A moral claim that is not legally secured does not stand anyone in good stead. Hence, as we shall show, law and ethics in this way also stand in an inverse relation to each other: the more laws there are, the less the need for ethics.

The growth and expansion of the state, which is the source and guardian of our laws, play a leading role in this. The refinement and multiplication of laws have been steadily taking place as the state increased in power and scope, taking under its administrative charge ever greater domains of social life. These it regulates and rules with an ever more extensive and diversified network of legal measures. Laws governing all aspects of human life are promulgated, such that in theory at least there should be nothing taking place between people that cannot be legally adjudicated. There are codes of laws for how people must treat each other in nearly every imaginable circumstance. There are laws concerning what people are entitled to from the state and all other organizations and institutions, and correlative laws as to what services they are obliged to render; there are laws governing every conceivable kind of contract and personal arrangement freely entered into by anyone with anyone else; there are laws protecting peoples' dignity, honor, pride, and any kind of standing they might be entitled to by law; there are all manner of legally specified rights, from the most basic human rights to the special rights accrued by those with privileges or entitlements. In short, nothing but a thick legal textbook of many volumes can exhaust the extensive juristic framework in which people are enmeshed and in a sense also trapped. For laws are inescapable, backed as they are by the state's full coercive power.

With all these laws in place, what need is there for ethical discretion or for moral scruple? A hundred years ago morality was precisely that which was not legally instituted or enforced coercively. As Max Horkheimer writes, "What was called moral during the past century were forms of conduct which had once been guaranteed by religion and were socially desirable and indeed essential in the enlightened, liberal era *but not enforced by law*. Important among these were good faith in business and private matters, and faithfulness in marriage, love, friendship and even towards strangers."[6] Such moral norms can only exist precisely when they are not enforced by law, when they are the free expressions of a person's will and character. Something similar holds for much of ethics. To act honorably, to be charitable, to keep to one's freely given promises, to give of oneself for the public good—all such ethical acts are conditional on not being made compulsory, for once this happens they soon cease being ethical and become merely legal instead. For once juridified, that is, rendered obligatory for fear of punishment, an ethical mode of action changes its character and meaning. In most people's minds its legal compulsion will soon outweigh its ethical imperative—they do it because it is the law, not because their conscience tells them it ought to be done. If the law were to change and forbid what was previously required, most people would go along and comply with the new impositions, for the initial ethical "ought" would have been eroded and lost by then. The complete juridification of ethics would be a dangerous procedure—even were it possible. In respect of much of ethical conduct and the corresponding relations between people it is not even possible, for the fine play of scruple and discretion that is often invoked in ethical judgments cannot be reduced to rules or promulgated as unambiguous laws. Where the law attempts to do this, it often only succeeds in rendering the original ethical norm into a crude regulation that can have the opposite effect to that intended.

There are many examples of this in contemporary society; a topical case occurs in current family law. In a divorce situation, it is one thing to care for one's children to the best of one's ability out of a moral sense of love and responsibility, another to be obliged by law to pay a stipulated amount as maintenance. The law can impose the latter but not the former. And where it compels the latter, then often the former is weakened and lost. For many parents, especially fathers, compelled by law to pay, even if they do not resent this, come to feel their duty done. Over a period of time fathers come to accept that there is no more required of them in caring for their children than that which the law prescribes. Ethics falls into desuetude in such matters and is eventually disregarded. There is no denying that there are obvious immediate advantages in legislating such financial protection of children; and possibly children are better off materially in our society, where divorce is so common and any sense of parental love and responsibility uncertain. If people were brought up to accept their ethical obligations to their children as a matter of course, then no such laws would be necessary. But then the rate of divorce would very likely not be as high as it is now. Family ethics is all of a piece; the bond of marriage and that of parent and child are interconnected, so that as the one falters, so does the other.

The laws regarding maintenance seem to be correcting a problematic situation for children; they seem to be making up for the character deficiencies of parents. Looked at from a short-term perspective, this is undoubtedly true, but in the long term it is far from the case. For the law only seconds and consolidates the avoidance of ethics and makes the predicament of children worse. For just as the law of divorce opens up the possibility of separation at will without any moral blame attached to anyone, so it also opens up the possibility of the abandonment of children at will, also without incurring any moral censure. In such a general situation of freedom from ethical restraint in family matters—where one can do what one pleases without shame or guilt, only provided it is within the law—the whole ethical dimension in relations between family members is destroyed. The love of parents for children and vice versa changes its basic character; it, too, becomes a matter of personal predilection, for it is no longer morally mandatory and so not cultivated as an obligatory part of family life. Thus in the long run the multiplication of laws on family matters—frequently undertaken for good, but shortsighted, ethical reasons—threatens to destroy what is left of family ethics. Here, as in so many other spheres of life, law and ethics are in an inverse relation to each other—the more there is of the one, the less of the other.

Another example of this phenomenon is the spate of "politically correct" legislation designed to make up for the weakening of ethical norms in relations between the sexes. Many of these are designed to restrain men, and as such have been welcomed by feminists who prefer the certainty of legal protection to the uncertainty of ethical discretion. Women should be protected by law, they insist, rather than demeaned by delicacies of behavior toward the "weaker sex." But the attempt to enforce decency in sexual relations by law, rather than through personal character formation, has had the opposite effect to that of ameliorating regard for women, as those who have lived through the predatoriness of the so-called "sexual revolution" can testify. Now the prevalence of sexual harrassment cases in the courts involving high-placed personages has made such matters the stuff of serialized mass entertainment and has not only discredited these laws but threatens to make a legal mockery of normal sexual relations. Clearly, the law is an ass when it intrudes into domains such as the bedroom, where it is too clumsy and does not possess the delicacy required to cope with the tender vagaries of human behavior. In such matters there is no way of compensating for an absence of ethics by means of law.

On the contrary, the multiplication of laws only furthers the elimination of ethics. In a highly legalized society, the officially approved-of need for ethics is diminished, as it no longer serves the essential function of controlling conduct it used to have; so it retreats to a twilight-zone of disused traditions that are still recognized and acknowledged but no longer fully upheld or relied on. For what is not legally guaranteed cannot be depended on or rued when it does not take place. There is thus an inverse relation between law and conscience. This was already recognized long ago by Emerson when he said, "Wild liberty develops iron conscience. Want of liberty, by strengthening law and decorum, stupefies conscience."[7] The antinomian conclusions he drew from this, that "the less government we have the better—the fewer laws and less confided power,"[8] are far too utopian for us now. Nevertheless, his main point is still valid: Too much law stifles conscience and decreases personal liberty. This is a view shared even now by some outstanding jurists. Thus Learned Hand, the greatest American judge of the 1950s, declared as follows: "I often wonder whether we do not rest our hopes too much upon constitution, upon laws and upon courts. These are false hopes: believe me, these are false hopes."[9]

These are the false hopes of people who no longer trust themselves and prefer to rely on legal machinery to keep each other in check. They no longer look to the ethical character of those with whom they deal, but only to the state's forces of restraint. This is symptomatic of a fundamental change in mentality that has all kinds of social consequences. People without a well-formed ethical character become much greater conformists, for all they are concerned with is to obey the law. Except for the delinquent few who turn to crime, they have no moral strength to resist or to turn against the law even when it is morally wrong. Though many are inclined to skate on the thin edge of the law, especially if they can afford clever lawyers to get them off if they happen to stray beyond it. For one need not be a criminal to take full advantage of the law; it is simply a more sophisticated form of prudence in our society.

The choice to be ethical and do more than the law requires or do it in a different, more generous spirit has come to be seen as a purely personal matter about which people are free to differ and to please themselves. Some people still prefer to behave morally, just as some still like to attend church or concerts of classical music. Others prefer football matches and rock concerts and do not choose to be bound by morality in their dealings. They prefer to behave in a "liberated" fashion, free from the traditional restraints and unwilling to feel guilt or bother their conscience with anything that they might have done. People are more or less "emancipated" in such matters. Nobody thinks it his or her business to advise or blame other people as to how they lead their private lives. It is only if the law is breached that blame is attached and then the police are usually called.

In a society where the state is overpowering, the law all-embracing, and people less given to the promptings of conscience or other ethical feelings, a condition of demoralization ensues with unforeseeable social consequences. Politically, it could lead to regimes akin to totalitarianism if the legislative power of the state were to fall into the wrong hands. This happened in Germany during Nazi times, for there most people were too law-abiding out of respect for authority to oppose the immoral laws of the state, even if they found them abhorrent or their conscience rankled and most were vaguely troubled by them. Within a liberal democracy such an eventuality is unlikely to arise, but there the juridification and over-regulation of society can lead to chronic personal problems. Ties of mutuality and interdependence, whether in the intimacy of family life or in the wider network of social relations, are weakened and broken so that the individual is left isolated and helpless when confronted by the power of the state or of the other major agencies of society, such as market forces in the guise of the large business corporations.

The corporations and the market they serve are as ethically ambivalent and as conducive to demoralization in the long run as is the state and its laws. The "laws" of the market have also no regard for ethical norms, and corporations have no consciences. Of course, it has to be acknowledged that a capitalist system of economy, freed from ethical restraints and so all the more efficient, has delivered untold wealth at least to the so-called advanced societies, where it has largely solved the problems of scarcity that ethics was previously designed to ameliorate. As we have already shown by reference to Christian morality, this has led to a virtual dispensing with the need for charity and a consequent disregard of any ethical responsibility with regard to material poverty or need in general.

Unfortunately, poverty and need as such have not been thereby eliminated; they have simply taken new guises, and for these there are now no appropriate ethical measures of redress. In every wealthy society there are those whom one might call the new "affluent poor," the denizens of the slums and ghettos, those whom the market has turned against because they lack the necessary salable skills to succeed in a time of rapid technological change. Even when they suffer no basic material shortages, when food is abundant, and there is even low-paid work, such people are nevertheless impoverished in other ways. This is the social and spiritual poverty of a deprived and alienated existence, with its family breakdowns, drug addictions, and pervasive insecurities due to violence and crime. In many ways this is worse than the merely material poverty of Third World countries where the social fabric is intact. Yet there is now no "charity" to help these "affluent poor." The old-style charity is certainly of no use to them, for what they want is not succor, but the high-status goods and brand-name products that the advertising of the market culture has convinced them is the only thing worth having. Of what use is ethics to people such as these?

At the other end of the social scale, among the very wealthy, ethics also makes little sense. These are the people who can afford whatever it is they desire. They can allow themselves to indulge in all the illicit pleasures that are too dangerous for everybody else, secure in the knowledge that they can fend off the law if caught and avoid any repercussions. Forbidden fruit to tempt them does not exist, for everything is available and nothing is banned. Even a little crime can be tasted now and then to provide the necessary frisson of perverse excitement so necessary in relieving the boredom of their lives, and criminals are looked on as boon companions to consort with. For such people, too, ethics is without any significance.

Thus at both ends of the social scale, among the very rich and the very poor, ethics has diminished and individual ethical decisions are no longer expected or required. What has to be decided is frequently done for such people by expert professionals who make it their career or business to manage the lives of the very poor or the very rich. For the very poor there are the social workers, paid for by the state, who make nearly all the crucial decisions for their so-called clients. And they do so "nonjudgmentally," that is, without any ethical considerations but solely according to utility, practicality, and the bureaucratic regulations they administer. These poor are thus held in a state of paternalistic tutelage, constantly advised in what to do, not responsible for anything, and not helped to assume responsibility, which they are mostly unwilling to do anyway, for they prefer that someone else with knowledge and resources take care of them. To take an independent ethical stand for personal autonomy is almost an impossibility under these conditions.

For the very rich it is analogous, but for the opposite reasons. They choose to make no decisions, for they hire paid advisers with the necessary knowledge and expertise to do it for them. Thus lawyers see to their personal problems, accountants handle their financial affairs, doctors monitor their health and advise on the regimen of activities for their style of living, and psychoanalysts, those modern *directeurs d'âme*, take care of their psyche for want of a soul. There need be nothing for which a personally responsible ethical decision is called, nothing to feel guilty about or to anguish their conscience or disturb the equanimity of their self-indulgence and self-satisfaction. Of shame there is no question, for the only shameful thing is to fail and that they would do everything to avoid, regardless of ethics.

The role of experts of all kinds, who are continually multiplying in our society, is also crucial in accounting for the decay of ethics. Such experts are generally trained and indoctrinated not to take ethical issues into account. Theirs is a supposedly scientific value-free methodology of decision-making and policy-implementation that is only concerned with pragmatic results, not with ethical judgments. And even if there are ethical consequences attendant on what they decide, they need take no responsibility and need not fear being blamed since they mostly work within a division of functions and a hierarchy of authority where no personal accountability can ever be demanded from any specific individual. Experts and officials working for government agencies, large companies, or public institutions of any kind need only keep to their sphere of competence and the set letter of the law; any other eventualities are not their business. And even if the law is breached, as it sometimes is by business corporations, the issue is handled in a purely legal manner, usually to be settled by monetary compensation out of court.

Bureaucracy in general can be looked on as a system of organization designed to absolve people from personal ethical responsibility. We can see this very clearly in the widespread bureaucratization of education that has been taking place in all societies at all levels, from primary child care to the highest university studies. For instead of each single teacher taking charge of and being responsible for one pupil or for one class at a time, there is now a vast educational apparatus that collectively manages the learning of all children in a given country or province. This system is comprised of a task force of general experts at the top that sets methods and standards of teaching, of others who train teachers to implement these in the classroom, still others who supervise and test the results of this process at every stage, and, finally, there are the teachers who do the actual work but are treated as the small cogs in the teaching machine.

In some countries all children are compulsorily consigned by law to be processed by this machine; in all others, most people lack the means necessary to avoid it. The results are all too apparent, with many children unable to read or write fluently even after ten years in such institutions and most others having but the barest smattering of any kind of knowledge. Ethics or morals have, of course, no place in such an approach, which at best approximates to technical training. New developments in educational technology are even more certain to produce such outcomes, for teachers are now coming to be dispensed with, replaced by computers, television monitors, teaching machines, and other gadgets of all kinds. There is also a supplementary system of other experts, such as psychologists, child counselors, and therapists, to deal with those children who do not respond to or cannot put up with the system and who cause disciplinary problems; these are usually dealt with medically, utilizing the well-known behavior modification therapies, backed up with a pharmacopeia of drugs. The aim is to turn them into well-behaved passive recipients of the routine. The gross dereliction of public trust that all this entails cannot be laid to anyone's door; there is nobody responsible and so there is nobody to blame. Only the most resolute of parents will stand up against the apparatus and the laws backing it. Those who completely opt out and choose to educate their children themselves are treated as criminals in some countries, such as Germany, and in all others are regarded as deluded eccentrics, liable to be hounded by the education inspectors.

Bureaucracies manned by cadres of professional experts are administering and taking over more and more aspects of ordinary living. Undoubtedly, there is often a positive side to all this. It provides control and care where previously there might have been neglect. Thus in a society where children are sent early to work, it is ethically better to provide them with some schooling rather than with none at all. In liberal democratic societies where the laws are generally just and the institutions in principle benign, there are considerable improvements in most aspects of social life, as compared with earlier stages of the same society or with not so advanced societies. But these ameliorations have usually come at a cost that has to be paid for in ethical coin.

A sense of the scale of this cost can be grasped in noting a peculiar paradox operating in relation to education in general: That as the educational levels and qualifications attained, on average, are raised, the standards of learning, culture, even of literacy and numeracy are lowered. Simple statistics demonstrate that an ever-increasing percentage of young people in advanced societies is completing at least twelve years of schooling, that between a third to half go on to tertiary institutions, that many of these obtain university degrees and not an inconsiderable fraction even doctorates. But these same people, as judged by other less formal criteria, seem to be showing an ever lower level of knowledge, culture, mathematics, and even basic reading ability. Judged by the content of the mass consumption of newspapers and magazines, not to speak of cinema, television, and the other entertainment media, it would appear that education only serves to make people stupid. The decline in standards in these respects, as compared to a century ago, is all too evident. This is even more pronounced when judged by book reading and theater and concert attendance, where now the best-seller and box-office hits predominate almost to the exclusion of everything else. Ever-decreasing levels of intelligence and increasing stupefaction are revealing themselves in a process that is sometimes consciously manipulated for commercial reasons and colloquially known as "dumbing down."

Part of the cause of this inverse relation between education and intelligence and culture is undoubtedly due to the lack of ethics. For as education is pursued for purely pragmatic considerations and frequently solely for material advantage, it loses its ethical character or personal value. It becomes a means to ends that have nothing to do with knowledge or culture. Qualifications serve as the necessary means of certification to enable people to be fitted into jobs. So learning is not undertaken for any of the old ethical goals it used to have, such as the development of awareness and knowledge, the sharpening of critical intelligence, attainment of maturity and sophistication, the growth of personal character, and the promotion of ethical integrity and a sound outlook on life. Now it is more a matter of discrete skills rather than of comprehensive virtues. Thus having lost its ethical and intellectual worth, education is valued as technical training that is a means to a career providing social status and wealth.

Being educated has in many ways become counterproductive of any love of learning. Those who have gone through the educational mills—even at the costliest and so, presumably, the best schools and universities—are ground small and dry; any regard for learning has been squeezed out of them, at best what they value is useful information. This is ethically disastrous, for it means that no ethical knowledge can be imparted and no maturing of character occurs. Instead, cynicism and demoralization follow such educational experiences, which often cannot be reversed by anything later in life. The prevalence of cynicism is an oft remarked on feature of our age; the initial causes of it must be looked for in our educational regimen and what it does to any love of learning.

This paradox of education is closely related to another that has been even more dangerous for the past century: that of the prevalence of lies where the truth is known. As the old saying goes, a little learning is a dangerous thing, and where that little is not even ethically informed, it is all the more pernicious for it leaves people open to the enticements of all the lies to which our century has been prone. This has been, and in many ways continues to be, the age of mass indoctrination, of mass propaganda, of disinformation of the masses for political and ideological purposes, and even of mass advertising for commercially self-serving ends. We now know that advertising works, that the propaganda lie often enough repeated will be accepted as truth, that the ideological distortion can have the power to cancel out the most obvious facts and common-sense perceptions, that the illusions of the media will be taken for reality, that virtual realities can be concocted that will prove convincing, and so on, for all the forms of deceit that have been so widespread and so effective of the course of the last century. Even a cursory reading of the voluminous literature on these subjects will show how pervasive lies have been in our time and how deeply they have penetrated social consciousness.[10] Intellectual and academic lies are no less prominent than the more popular varieties. These are the ideological lies of pseudo-science, of opinion dressed up as fact, of discredited theories and illusory worldviews and of the intellectual tyranny of the latest fads and fashions. Intellectuals and academics have been ever more prone to spawn such lies and to endow them with the official imprimatur of their institutions, thereby making them available for the propagandists and hucksters to use to dupe the masses.

We know that all these are lies because there is also a critical literature that exposes them as such. Hence the paradox of our century, that perhaps never before has the truth been so freely available, yet the lie so prevalent. For never before have critical faculties of systematic doubt, distrust, skepticism, and reluctance to accept anything on faith or authority been so developed, and yet most people have proved themselves gullible and credulous. Intellectuals and scientists have devised a whole panoply of rigorous testing and investigative procedures of any proposed verity, but they themselves have proved all too easy to convince of whatever it is that their political masters have wished them to accept. Whole new critical methods for the exposure of falsehood and deceit have been elaborated but have not helped in making truth prevail; among these are ideology critique, demythologization, analysis of ideas and language, the psychoanalysis of rationalizations, and many more. Thus the truth is known—there are libraries filled with books of impeccable honesty and veracity on all subject matters. But, unfortunately, it is generally not credited—if it is available, it tends to be overlooked; if seen, it is ignored; and if noted, it is usually too late to do any good.

To a large degree the causes of this perverse situation are due to a failure of ethics. For the sake of advantage or out of conviction, frequently in pursuit of ideal utopian goals, so many in the just concluded century were prepared to lie or to countenance the so-called "necessary lies" of others. Few have had the moral courage to stand up against these falsehoods, especially when they were backed by the pressure of large numbers or money or have had the institutional support of states, parties, or corporations. Hence, to refuse to accede to the lie in whatever shape or form is perhaps the most fundamental and essential of all the ethical commandments of our time. But it is an extremely difficult one to fulfill, because often the personal costs are prohibitive. If one is willing and able to resist the lies on offer, then one has the correlative duty to refute them by seeking for the truth, which is even more difficult and daunting. But it is not impossible, for the necessary truth is generally available, if only one knows where to look for it and is unafraid to do so. In the last resort, truth is largely a matter of courage.

Thus the paradoxes of ethics in our time are many and varied, though interrelated. They point to the ethically ambivalent and even frequently contradictory nature of most of the social, political, and cultural developments of this last century, including those dubbed "progressive." To their proponents they all seemed initially good and were frequently enthusiastically hailed both by the intellectual elites and the masses, for otherwise they would not have succeeded. But once having gained support and won out and become institutionalized as common practices and permanent fixtures of social life, they soon revealed themselves to be other than what they first appeared to be and displayed the negative facets that proved later so disastrous. Among these, ethical failings have usually been particularly pronounced. This is bound up with the paradox with which we began: that as our standard of living rises, there is a correlative decline in the ethical quality of our lives. Or putting it in simple terms, we are worse people living in better societies.

But how long can this process go on? Does it mean that if society were to improve even more, then ethics, at least as a personal moral matter, would decline further and perhaps eventually even disappear? Can such a society, for example, dispense with morality altogether? Has our global technological civilization entered a stage of cultural development where there is no longer a social function for ethics apart from its instantiation in law? Is it no longer necessary to control, limit, and direct conduct by such old-fashioned ethical means as inner conscience, refinement of feelings, and molding of character? In short, is civilization about to enter a post-ethical stage as once it had been in a pre-ethical one? Or, putting it in the current intellectual jargon, does postmodernism also entail post-moralism?

There are now many thinkers willing to answer these questions in the affirmative. They hold that morality has come to an end much in the way that Nietzsche predicted it would just over a century ago. Intellectuals are not alone in this belief; moralizing has a bad name even in popular parlance. It is only a step from this to argue that no kind of ethics is necessary except that enshrined in law. If the kinds of developments previously outlined, leading to the displacement of ethics by law, were to prevail, then in the strict sense of the term an unethical civilization would ensue.

This outcome is not impossible in theory, for civilization does not necessarily depend on ethics. The early civilizations had an ethos that cannot be called ethical in the same sense as that which ensued later with the rise of universal religions and philosophies. Thus it can be argued that just as there was a pre-ethical stage of civilization so, too, there might eventuate a post-ethical stage. We seem to be moving toward such an ethos, one where ethics does not play a major role. This ethos has some of the features of a pre-ethical state of culture. As in polytheistic societies, where men worshiped many different and opposed deities, so, too, in contemporary society, life is ruled by many incompatible values. Max Weber, at the start of this century, spoke in this sense of a "struggle of gods": "many old gods ascend from their graves; they are disenchanted and hence take the form of impersonal forces."[11] Instead of the "one thing needful" of Christian morality, there are now many conflicting values battling for supremacy: "our civilization destines us to realize more clearly these struggles again, after our eyes have been blinded for a thousand years—blinded by the alleged or presumably exclusive orientation towards the grandiose moral fervour of Christian ethics."[12] According to Weber, we seem to have returned to a pre-moral stage but one that is disenchanted, intellectualized, and rationalized in the midst of a technically advanced civilization. The barbarians beyond good and evil of the twentieth century, whom Nietzsche called for, might not have been as far away as he imagined.

Since Nietzsche's time there have been many kinds of barbarisms and primitive revivals, as well as other throwbacks to pre-ethical stages of ethos. The closest analogy to this unusual cultural development has occurred in the arts, where there has been a selective return to all kinds of primitive styles in what one might consider a process of intellectual re-barbarization, which also has distinct complements in ethical life. This began in the early years of the twentieth century in the avant-garde styles of Modernism, most notably in the work of Picasso, Stravinsky, and many other outstanding artists. It also took a popular form, particularly so in music, where the syncopated rhythmic beat of jazz and rock-and-roll and the associated styles of neo-tribal dancing are now all pervasive. Together with these art forms have also come fashions for simpler styles of living. A neo-primitivist ethos is pronounced in various twentieth-century cults, most recently in those of the flower-children of the 1960s who preached a neo-tribal collectivity and later in the extreme feminist cults of witches and Goddess worship. All these are in revolt against the main Western ethical traditions, which they accuse of being patriarchal and repressive. At present, such artifically revived historical fragments function as modes of living for occasional purposes, mainly as weekend relaxations from the stresses of the contemporary competitive struggle for advancement. None of them can constitute a substitute for a coherent ethical life. It is hard to know how seriously to take all this, but it does add to the prevailing confusion in ethics.

The ethical confusion of such revivals has been compounded by the survivals in many parts of the world of fragments of indigenous cultures and ethos of every imaginable kind. In a highly truncated and reduced state, non-Western ethics have survived in various parts of Asia, particularly aspects of Hinduism, Buddhism, and Confucianism. These are also having a desultory influence in the West, where, for example, a cult of Japanese Zen Buddhism has long been popular among avant-garde intellectuals and artists, such as the so-called Beats and their followers. In Africa and Oceania there are still remaining elements of a pre-ethical tribal ethos. These, too, have found echoes in other parts of the world, where returning tourists have brought back a smattering of a largely concocted "negritude" just as they bring back made-for-the-market carvings. All such flotsam and jetsam of ethos are deposited all over the world, and people pick them up and dabble in them out of curiosity or need, a little like the diverse modes of cuisine found in all major cities, among which one can choose whether to dine Chinese, Indian, Algerian, or whatever on any given evening. It all fuses into the melting-pot of styles of life from which one can select any item, such as a tasty dish or exotic article of clothing, for every special occasion.

It is now impossible to tell from anyone's outer garb and bearing or style of self-presentation what ethics, if any, that person lives by or subscribes to. For even if a person declares that he or she is ethnically a such-and-such, it is often impossible to know with what seriousness to take such an avowal or how it reflects itself in overall comportment and relationships with others. This makes it difficult to establish anyone's ethical identity and thereby to be able to tell from this what can and cannot be expected from that person or what he or she will or will not scruple to do. Even how a given person understands basic ethical principles is now frequently uncertain: What do people from different cultural and ethical backgrounds mean by telling the truth, keeping promises, or being faithful? Such ethical uncertainties make personal relations very difficult for they are fraught with hesitations, tensions, and ambivalences that make for distrust.

Into all this ethical confusion that is the prevailing spirit of the times, some intellectuals have now intruded their declarations that ethics is at an end, just as others pronounce art to be at an end. Ordinary people are baffled by such talk. They find themselves particularly puzzled when this is celebrated as some kind of liberation. Thus there are Parisian intellectuals who rejoice at the overthrow of the categorical imperative just as they hail the demise of representation in art. Theorists such as Foucault and Barthes, who attacked representation of every kind indiscriminately, were no less determined opponents of morality. Their so-called anti-humanism—resounding in Foucault's ringing declaration that Man is dead—combines a rejection of representation and morality in a radical revolutionary orientation directed against all traditional forms and standards. This chimed in with the movement of revolutionary radicalism that the students promulgated during the late 1960s and early 1970s. That wave has now long passed, but its attacks on morality and ethics in general have left behind a permanent scum of cynicism with which we now have to contend. This cynicism is the acid that the general doctrines that have been eating out morality have deposited in our culture, as George Eliot foresaw and feared over a century ago.

It is the mood that matters and not the doctrines with their spurious intellectual arguments that might have given rise to it. Here we shall not be concerned with general theoretical discussions about ethics, either in attack or rebuttal. Our main concern is practical, not theoretical, and even though the question "Why be ethical?" will be raised, it is meant as a real existential issue of living rather than a speculative problem. On the whole, our main preoccupation is with actual developments in ethics as these are found in social practices and cultural ideas that are historically given.

Nevertheless, we are not merely concerned with what has been or is happening now but also with future possibilities insofar as these can be extrapolated from present trends. If ethics continues to taper off and becomes increasingly more inconsequential, then this could conceivably lead to a future post-ethical society. It would be one spanning the earth, a global society of mere law and order that might be envisaged as a Hobbesian post-state state of nature. With the diminution of the sovereign state, law and order would be enforced by numerous supra-state agencies, perhaps much enlarged and strengthened arms of the United Nations Organization. Such a society would demand from its people complete adjustment and integration to the prevailing values and conformity to the acceptable roles. Its quality of life might be the opposite of solitary, poor, nasty, brutish, and short; it might become gregarious, affluent, pleasant, humane, and long—very long and very boring. But such a life need be ethnically no better than its opposite.

A post-ethical world or some close approximation to it is a distinct possibility, but no more than that. It is not inevitable. Other, ethically more appealing, possibilities can also be entertained on the basis of present trends. Ultimately, what will eventuate will depend on people's reactions to the life in store for them, which are now unpredictable. However, if one conceives of oneself as a responsible ethical agent and a moral being to boot, then one must even now work for an outcome that will give rise to some kind of ethical society. One must strive for an ethical life within the limited possibilities, usually in the margins of society, that are still open to one; one must raise one's children accordingly; one must urge others to do likewise.

But why should anyone try to be ethical? What point is there in this endeavor? This book might be considered, on a basic level, as an extended attempt to answer this simple question. It holds that it is both possible and necessary to justify ethics as a way of life. Later in the book it will be argued that the ethical life is better than its opposite, in that it is more conducive to a meaningful and serious existence and that only in the context of such a life can the individual develop into a self-directed and autonomous being. Thus the ethical person is better as a human being than the unethical, for such a person has a better grasp of the sense of life as a whole. Correlatively, an ethical society is better than one that does not cultivate ethics in respect of the quality of life it affords its people. In this respect ethics is like art; just like the individual, society can get along with a minimum of either, but in doing so it impoverishes the lives of its people. Those who have little appreciation or understanding of any kind of aesthetic phenomenon, who see neither beauty nor sublimity, have no sense of humor or pathos, and do not respond to form or design, such people are stunted in the spiritual core of their being. With ethics it is even more urgent, for those who have no ethical sense of right and wrong, no moral conscience to speak of, who simply live by law and the rules, even if they never do anything wrong, cannot properly relate to others and develop themselves in such relations; they, too, are spiritually stunted beings capable of the worst excesses if the circumstances warrant.

However, this book aims to offer more than just a justification of ethics, it also seeks to provide the knowledge about it essential for any comprehensive ethical education. Ethical education and the culture of ethical discourse that goes with it are not well developed at present. That this is so is also one of the symptoms of the diminution and shrinkage that ethics has suffered in this century. Young people are no longer taught much about ethics. It is not even a recognized subject in their curriculum. This book sets itself to remedy this situation. It might be read as part of a proposal for the institution in schools of higher learning of a new type of ethnical subject, one that might be called comparative studies of ethics, analogous to the already existing comparative studies of religion with which it could work in tandem. In this respect it differs from most of the current literature on ethics, whose view of ethnical knowledge is either as philosophical theories or empirical investigations of practices and beliefs.

Providing people, especially the young, with extensive ethical knowledge is in itself of some importance. It might not make them any better as people, at least in the short run, but it will make them more aware of what ethics is about and why it matters for social, as well as personal, reasons. It might also serve a useful subsidiary function in helping to overcome ethnocentric prejudices that result in narrow self-righteousness and promote a more tolerant attitude toward traditions other than one's own, especially those emanating from different cultures. For just as the study of comparative religion need not necessarily be conducive to religious faith and practice, but it is helpful for mutual religious understanding, so a study of comparative ethics need not promote good deeds, but, nevertheless, it is an essential part of the educative process that, if nothing else, helps to make people more intelligent about such matters.

Hence this book does not preach any specific ethical doctrine nor does it take sides in any of the current ethical controversies. Putting it bluntly, it does not try to tell people what is right and wrong. But this does not mean that it is some kind of scientific value-free neutral investigation or some mode of philosophic meta-ethical analysis, neither of which is really satisfactory except for the most narrowly circumscribed study of one small aspect of the subject, for little else can be done within such artificial self-imposed restrictions. This book does assume a general evaluative standpoint that might be termed enlightened pluralism. It sets itself against adherence to one set of exclusive principles in ethics and in favor of a variety of ethical values, for that alone will be adequate to the complexities of life; and these are bound to result in tensions that continually have to be resolved as and when they arise. But this is part of the very nature of ethics. Ethics is not a static system of norms, like an extended version of the Ten Commandments, given once and for all, but an ongoing process of transformation, adjustment, and accommodation. Opposition, conflict, and contradiction are inescapable features of ethical life. Thus ethics sets the stage for tragedy. Any approach that disregards or fails to account for the potential for tragic conflict in ethics is not adequate to the subject.

At the same time, without lapsing into any sham objectivity, the book seeks to be as rational as possible in its approach to ethics. It eschews any resort to "existential choices" or arbitrary "commitments" in its discussion of ethical judgments and decisions. Ethical disputation calls for rational justification and judiciousness in reasoning.

Thus even though this book does not pretend to preach, it does offer to guide those who are perplexed about ethics. Since there is less assurance than a century ago on all ethical matters, a guide such as this is perhaps far more indispensable now than it was then. A century ago it could be assumed that at least educated people had a sound knowledge of their own ethical traditions. Now this is no longer so. Traditions have become a matter of history, and anyone who wishes to know them has to delve into the past. This is the reason that so much of the book is preoccupied with historical issues.

The book is divided into two major parts, which can be read to some extent independently of each other. Readers might begin with either one first. Those without much historical knowledge or curiosity might be well advised to skip part I and get straight into part II, which deals with contemporary matters and problems. But on concluding what is in effect the ending of the story of ethics, they will find that to understand it properly they will need to know what happened before, what was the sequence of events that led to this end. For without a knowledge of their historical antecedents and sources, it is doubtful whether any of the contemporary problems can be fully grasped. On the other hand, readers whose interests are primarily historical, scholars of various types, are urged to persevere into part II, for only by reference to the analysis of the present situation can the rationale for the historical presentation be given. In this sense, as Croce said, all history is contemporary history and this holds as much for the history of ethics as for any other.

PART I

THE PAST

Preamble

The word *ethics* can be read both in the singular and plural at once. This is a grammatical felicity that is indicative of the nature of the subject. For there are many ethics, but ethics is also one. Historically considered, quite a number of distinct ethical systems have emerged at different times in different localities. This number, however, was initially quite small and can be analytically reduced to a few basic types, with some sub-type variants in some of them. We shall restrict ourselves to just four: religious moralities, the civic ethics, the ethics of duty, and the ethics of honor. Of these, only the civic ethics is exclusively Western in origin, having begun in the Greek polis; the ethics of duty and the ethics of honor had Eastern origins in China and Persia, respectively; while morality appears almost simultaneously in the West and East in the Judaic and Buddhist religions. Thus, though there are many ethics, there are far fewer distinct types. This tells decisively against relativistic assumptions that there are as many ethics as there are cultures or even that every social group has its own ethics. For not everything that is the ethos of a society can be taken as an ethics.

This is the reason that ethics is also one, for only those cultural practices of various ethos that have specific essential features in common can be called ethics. What these features are becomes apparent from a study of the origins of the different ethics. They all emerged out of a fundamental civilizational transformation that produced the universal world religions and philosophies, which began during the so-called Axial Age, roughly 700–300 B.C.; these are those that assumed a universal scope and have continued ever since; they are the religions and philosophies associated with the earliest saviors and sages of world history. It was only then that notions of a higher transcendent reality, either a supreme Power or Order, were developed, which led to ethics being formulated on this basis. From this derive the factors, such as reference to transcendence, universality, and rationality, that ethics have in common and that separate them from all earlier types of cultural ethos.

Any proper historical account or theory must strive to be true to both the singularity and plurality of ethics. Ethics is both one and many, and neither aspect should be allowed to obscure the other. Thus the idea that ethics is one must not lead to the assumption that there is but a single universal ethics true for all times and places. The contrary, and equally valid, idea that there is a plurality of ethics counts against this and means that the basic types cannot be brought to complete unity in a common agreement on principles and so reduced to one. But this plurality cannot be indefinitely multiplied and taken to the extreme of supposing that there are as many ethics as separate societies.

The history of ethics reflects both of these aspects: the pluralism in conflict and the unity in attempts at reconciliation. Conflict is endemic to the history of all ethics, since clashes are inevitable as the basic types contradict and oppose each other in most respects. This is the tragedy of ethics, the constantly replayed tragic drama of history that has caused such an inordinate amount of human suffering and misery. But this same conflict has led to ever renewed attempts at unification, which have brought about syntheses and syncretisms resulting in ethics of ever-wider scope and universal application. Yet this is no Hegelian dialectic of contradictions leading to *Aufhebungen* on the march to ever-higher stages of progress. Rather, it is a series of contingent processes of transformation brought about by all kinds of forces for change whose course is by no means "rational" and whose outcome is often paradoxical.

We are now the heirs of over two millennia of such changes, which might be called ethical development, but that has not placed us at any apogee of ethical progress. Somewhat to the contrary, any unprejudiced assessment of the main trends of ethics in the twentieth century must lead to the opposite conclusion, for ethics has entered into very difficult times, perhaps even unethical times. Ethics is now under great threat, in some respects greater than ever before in its history. Some well-known thinkers even now foresee a coming end to ethics. Whether they mourn this passing as a cultural disaster or greet it with glee as a liberation from the burdens of the past depends on their view of the nature and functions of ethics. Here we shall not assume that it is all over with ethics, believing that current reports of the death of ethics are somewhat exaggerated, as Mark Twain put it in a different context. Ethics, we hold, is not so far gone as to be beyond recovery. This, however, still leaves the question open: What of past ethics should be recovered and what is best left buried in the past? This problem will concern us most in part II of this work.

In part I we shall be more intent on studying the record of the past, focusing mainly on origins and processes of change. The two initial chapters divide roughly along these lines: the first deals with the beginnings and earliest formations of the four basic types; the second outlines their later developments, especially those where they enter into interaction with each other. Thus the first is concerned with basic structures, the second with transformations; or, putting it in the now *passé* jargon of Structuralism, the first is synchronic and the second diachronic. But this, of course, is not seriously meant as a theoretical distinction, for the separation of structure and process is a purely analytic expedient undertaken for heuristic reasons to facilitate the exposition of complex historical forms and their formations and transformations.

Thus the first chapter outlines the basic forms of each of the four types of ethics and concludes with a comparative study of their differences. The second chapter examines the processes of change and development that they have undergone in the course of history. These processes are adaptation, conservation, syncretism, purism or puritanism, rationalization (in Weber's sense), secularization, and demoralization. Most of them can be found in all ethical traditions. However, we shall restrict ourselves mainly to the Western tradition of morality, with particular attention to the changes in Christian morality over its two-thousand year span, for this forms the main historical background to the ethics of our own time.

Part I concludes with a brief historical account of the problems of ethics in our time, which leads directly into part II where these problems are analyzed in greater detail and depth. Part I begins with an introductory section that raises some very basic questions about ethics and ethos and how they differ. These are largely matters of definition. But definition is not a matter of an arbitrary stipulation of verbal usages; it concerns the formulation of concepts adequate to the historical reality of the subject.

∽

CHAPTER 1

The Four Pure Types

Ethos and Ethics

We begin with the simplest question of all: What is ethics? But before we can undertake to answer that, we must first tackle an even more basic question: What is an ethos? For, as we shall show, an ethics is simply an ethos that has undergone certain highly differentiating processes of historical transformation. Or, putting it in crude terms, an ethics in a refined and specialized ethos. But that only forces us back to the question: What is an ethos?

The term *ethos* is a basic anthropological concept of universal provenance. An ethos is present in every society since it is a fundamental aspect of culture. It is that portion of the culture of a society concerned with everything to do with conduct and behavior and, in general, with what can be called the style of life. It is everything that is involved in the actions and interactions of people insofar as they are judged or valued in respect of socially binding rules, conventions, laws, and norms determining what is permissible or not, what is obligatory or arbitrary, what is valid or illicit; it is everything that is involved in judging or valuing goods, services, and people in terms of their worth, according to standards of social superiority or inferiority, nobility or unworthiness, demeaning or virtuous qualities, and in general according to standards of social discrimination; it is everything concerned with ranking in this way the aims, goals, and aspirations of activities that people pursue that are socially induced, encouraged, and even enforced; it is everything to do with assessing the feelings, beliefs, and ideas insofar as they are involved in motivating such social activities; and, finally, it concerns the qualities of personality that express themselves in all of the previous. An ethos is thus not the whole of a culture but only that which marks it off as a way of life.

The complete culture of a society has many aspects, of which the ethos is only one. One can distinguish at least two others that are different: the symbolic system of representations and the whole repertoire of techniques. Thus an ethos might also be specified by the negative method of separating it from that in culture which it is not, that which belongs to representation or technique. Thus the ways a people have of working, fighting, exercising, cooking, playing games, building, experimenting, and so on, even in some respects of making love and worshiping, belong to their techniques, not to their ethos. Their modes of representing, in all the possible senses of this word, are also not part of the ethos; this includes their symbolic representations of reality through description or depiction in language, action, art, or any medium whatsoever, as well as their representative arrangements by way of delegation, agency, authority, or any other such social means.[1] As we have argued elsewhere, language *per se* belongs to none of these specifically cultural aspects and is something else again.[2]

The whole complex of culture is thus composed of three distinguishable aspects: ethos, representation, and technique. But this does not mean that these are separable objects. There are some things that, seen in isolation, belong predominantly to one or another of these. But any complex activity will involve all three at once, for it will be bound by the regulations and values of the ethos that govern its character; it will have a symbolic meaning determined by its representational role and features; and it will employ an ensemble of techniques. There are few activities that are wholly one or other of these; most have something of all three aspects.

Thus ethos does not necessarily entail ethics in the more specialized sense. All societies have an ethos; only a few managed to attain to an ethics in the course of history. Primitive or tribal societies have an ethos that is pre-ethical, one that has not as yet undergone the civilizational processes necessary to bring it within reach of ethics. Such an ethos does not operate with ethical norms or ethical standards of judgment or valuation but the far more basic ones of taboos, customary codes, traditional values, notions of the sacred or blessed, propitiatory or ill-starred activities, simple standards of worth based on heroic virtues, magical powers, and other such cruder qualities of character. In a modern ethos such judgments and valuations are branded as superstitious and are generally disdained, though many have still survived.

But it must not be supposed that a modern ethos completely overcomes and surpasses its original historical beginnings in primitive ethos. Something of the latter still remains, even in highly civilized societies. And what does so are not merely the archaic superstitions that unenlightened people still cling to, like fortune telling, but also necessary and universally observed taboos, such as the prohibitions of incest and cannibalism. Many other types of taboos are still prevalent; for example, nearly every society observes some kind of food prohibitions, whether it be against the eating of pork or beef or horse-flesh or kangaroo or something else. Thus there is always a primitive residue left, no matter how civilized or modernized an ethos becomes. We do not completely outgrow our origins and always retain something of our savage past.

Many transitional stages intervene between a primitive and a modern ethos. To account for the origin of ethics, we must trace the most crucial of these, that which is the necessary precondition for any subsequent ethical development: the transition from a primitive to a civilized ethos. It is obvious that we cannot speak of ethics before civilization. Behavior and all its attendant relationships must first become civilized or civil before it can become ethical. That is to say, we must first specify what is a civil ethos before we can define what is an ethical one. And insofar as civilization precedes ethics, it will inevitably be the case that there are civil ethos that are not ethical ones, for not all civilizations were productive of ethics, as we shall presently show. In fact, those that were so constitute a small and unique minority, a mere handful of favorable cases around which the whole history of ethics revolves. There were many autonomous or distinct civilizations in world history, arising at different times in various parts of the globe, perhaps as many as twenty-one according to Arnold Toynbee, though that figure is debatable. Each of them developed a distinctive civil ethos, which varied from case to case. In no two cases is it completely alike, anymore than their styles of art or politics or science are the same. Hence what is considered appropriate or civil behavior by the standards of one ethos will not be so by those of another. There are no universal standards that hold for all.

Nevertheless, it is a constantly recurring preconception or prejudice to be found in every civilization that its particular kind of civil ethos is the defining one for all of humanity and that it almost invariably identifies with what it means to be truly human. All those who fall outside for whatever reason, either because they are foreigners or because they cannot quite cope with its demands, are considered somehow less than fully human. This is as true of recent secular European conceptions of what it is to be civilized as it is of traditional Javanese religious assumptions, as Clifford Geertz reports:

> It is a cluster of sacred symbols, woven into some sort of ordered whole, which makes up a religious system. For those who are committed to it, such a religious system seems to mediate genuine knowledge, knowledge of the essential conditions in terms of which life must, of necessity, be lived. Particularly, where these symbols

are uncriticized, historically or philosophically, as they are in most of the world's cultures, individuals who ignore the moral-aesthetic norms the symbols formulate, who follow a discordant style of life, are regarded not so much as evil as stupid, insensitive, unlearned, or in the case of extreme dereliction as mad. In Java, where I have done field work, small children, simpletons, boors, the insane, and the flagrantly immoral are all said to be "not yet Javenese," and, not yet Javanese, not yet human. Unethical behaviour is referred to as "uncustomary," the most serious crimes (incest, sorcery, murder) are commonly accounted for by an assumed lapse of reason, the less serious ones by a comment that the culprit "does not know order," and the word for "religion" and for "science" are the same. Morality has the air of simple realism, of practical wisdom; religion supports proper conduct by picturing a world in which such conduct is only common sense. It is only common sense because between ethos and world view, between the approved style of life and the assumed structures of reality, there is conceived to be a simple and fundamental congruence such that they complete one another and lend one another meaning.[3]

We have quoted this passage at length because it is illustrative of much of our discussion till this point. The final comment on ethos and worldview matches precisely our initial distinction between ethos and symbolic system of representations or, as Geertz puts it, "between the approved style of life and the assumed structure of reality." The point of Geertz's account is, of course, to show that the two are inherently congruent and bound up with each other as aspects of the one culture. This culture of traditional Java is obviously civilized but seems to be pre-ethical, for its symbols and codes, as Geertz allows, are without self-criticism, either "philosophically or historically" or in any other way that would make for the critical self-consciousness of a real ethic. This seems to be merely a civil ethos for which terms such as *ethics* and *morality*, which Geertz invokes, seem not strictly appropriate, at least not without further argument that an ethical mode of thought is also present, even if only to a minimal degree. The main point of the passage, that those within the ethos regard those outside as less than human, holds regardless.

Like the Javanese, all civilized people tend to consider their own ethos as the hallmark of humanity. This is the ethnocentric bias of civilization. Thus in Hindu culture all foreign forms of civility were held to be *mlechha dharma* or the impure practices of the barbarians. The Greeks, who coined this term, held the neighboring Persians to be Asiatic barbarians, though otherwise noble and refined. What the Persians thought of the Greeks has not so clearly come down to us, but it must have been some variant of such a term. Closer to our own time, we know that as late as the nineteenth century, the Chinese held the Europeans to be no more than boorish "sea barbarians," and the Europeans reciprocated the compliment by calling the Chinese inscrutable "Oriental barbarians." The Other who is outside the civil ethos tends to be held to be a barbarian, pagan, or heathen. When two civilizations encounter each other, it is differences in ethos that are most obtrusive for these are felt to lie at the very heart of what it means to be human.

However, despite such clashes in encountering each other, civilizations have also much in common. They all cultivate in some form or other the four fundamental institutions of civility, those associated with the temple, the court, the city, and the state. The temple or church is the seat of religion; it is where the various kinds of religious functionaries reside. The court is the symbolic center of authority and power, where usually a monarch surrounded by courtiers resides. The city is the civic arena where citizens or burghers pursue a polite way of life and the activities of civil society. The state is the practical apparatus of rule and administration, usually carried out by a corps of service officials and soldiers. Obviously, these four functionally distinct institutions of civilization are interrelated in various ways. Sometimes they involve quite distinct groups of people; at other times the same personnel can carry out two or more of them at once. Such factors are crucial to the nature of a given civilization.

All civilizations developed some version or other of these basic social formations at least during some periods, usually from the very beginning. The transition from a pre-civilized tribal state to a civilized one is largely the formation of these four institutional bases of the higher cultures. However, in different civilizations this happens to varying degrees of differentiation. Civilizations also differ in the prominence and preponderance of some of these over others. In some cases, this can be so great as to reduce the others to a vestigial role and virtually abolish them. This play of dominance and recession evolves over time. In the Hellenic period of the classical civilization, the preponderance of the city was so great that the court ceased to function and the temple assumed a subsidiary place; a proper state apparatus never even developed. In Hellenistic times all this was partially reversed as the court once more came into its own. Alternatively, the temple or court can become so powerful as to repress the city and deprive it of all autonomy, as happened in ancient Egypt or in India during its various conquests when the capital city repeatedly changed at the whim of its rulers. City and court can be co-present but function independently of each other, as was often the case in medieval Europe, or they can fuse, as was often the case in the Muslim world, when the city was no more than an extension of the citadel. And the same kinds of diverse relations can also obtain between court and temple or church. Thus, for example, in the Christian West during the early Middle

Ages it was the Church that asserted its authority over court and city and took the lead in building a rural monastic Christian civilization. Even a body of state officials might assert itself in this way and assume civilizational preeminence, as happened in traditional China where the mandarins or Confucian scholars became the defining group in the whole civilizational ethos; they became independent of both city and temple and even partly autonomous from the imperial court itself, as they successfully withstood repeated challenges from all these quarters.

The varieties and variations of the four basic social formations as they are found in different civilizations throughout history are very numerous. It is best to conceive of them as four civilizing functions that are everywhere present but carried out in different ways. This reveals itself in the characteristic forms of schooling, producing specific styles of life marked by cultivated deportment, bearing, and character, which each civilization tends to favor. A civilization based primarily on temple or church cults, where religious schooling is all important, will result in the civility of priests or monks, characterized by ascetic and devotional practices, ritual ceremonial behavior, a devout and pious bearing expressive of humility, and reverence and fear of the gods and authorities. Such an ethos we even now can find in the Vatican City, of course, but also in some Buddhist societies, where it is prevalent not only among monks and nuns who exemplify it best, but also to lesser degrees among lay people of various classes. Civilizations based primarily on cities will have some kind of schooling in *paedeia*, giving rise to a civility of urbanity and politeness characteristic of the citizen or burgher who is worldly wise, practically proficient in dealing with others, and who mixes easily and freely in the convivial society of both friends and strangers. We can find this type almost throughout the whole historic span of the Western city, from the Athenian *asteios aner* (town bred) onward. A civilization of royal courts and castles will school its people in some form of courtesy, usually the decorous and mannered bearing of courtiers and aristocrats in general, producing cultivated and exquisitely refined personalities whose elegant bodies evince beautiful souls. This is a ubiquitous type present in nearly all cultures and still in evidence to some limited extent even now almost throughout the world, despite the virtual abolition of monarchies. Finally, a civilization of state officials will promote a schooling in competence and technical ability to suit the required capacities of servants of the state power in the way that this is traditionally exercised in various regimes. This will tend to produce a highly disciplined personality, self-controlled and dutiful, able to subjugate itself to its official role and carry it out dispassionately, *sine ira cum studio*.

To some extent our modern bureaucratic officials conform to this model, though in a characteristically simplified and reduced form.

Even though there is no one universal model of civilization or one kind of civil ethos that characterizes all civilized people, there is much in common between different civilizations, no matter how far they might be separated in time and space. Thus, it is a most remarkable social fact, one that does not cease to astonish whenever it is encountered anew, that the four analogous social formations even in widely scattered civilizations evince considerable similarities in ethos; they breathe, as it were, a common spirit. Court civility is somehow alike in all times and places. "The courtier is a phenomenon of aristocratic society in general," writes Stephen Jaeger, the historian of early medieval society in Germany; and he goes on to add that "the social ideals of the figure are to some extent constants of that society." These constants, such as "charm, nobility, gentleness, affability, physical beauty, learning and judgement, are qualities that inhere in the social situation of the advisor to an autocratic ruler. The court advisor of an Arabic or Chinese court will have embodied these same virtues, but with wide variations of detail," as will one from a medieval Ottonian-Salic or Renaissance court, according to Jaeger.[4]

This goes some way to explaining the surprising observation made by courtiers at all times that when they traveled, usually as ambassadors, from the court of one civilization to that of another, despite all the differences of language and culture, they nevertheless felt almost at home and were often accepted as near equals by their hosts. It is not inconceivable that if a noble from the court of Ikhnaten, the sun-god worshiping Pharaoh of ancient Egypt, were able to travel through time and space to the court of Louis XIV, the *roi-soleil* at Versailles, he would not feel himself out of place and, barring language problems, unable to adjust. One could make a similar case for a lady at the court of the Japanese Heian emperor at the time of the Lady Murasaki at one end of the globe and a lady at the Byzantine court of the emperor Alexis I at the almost contemporaneous period of Anna Comnena at the other end of the globe. This kind of commonality is by no means restricted to courtiers and aristocrats; it also holds for priests, for monks and religious teachers, for officials and bureaucrats, and to a lesser extent even for burghers and citizens of cities. The monks of different faiths, though doctrinally bitterly opposed to each other, yet understand and appreciate each other, for they lead a common religious way of life. It is not inconceivable that an Irish monk from the monastery of St. Columba on the isle of Iona off the western coast of Scotland would not have been at a loss were he miraculously transported to a Japanese Buddhist monastery at the other end of the then known world. The debates between representatives of these two religions carried out at the Mongol court of the Great Khan show that they had no trouble understanding each other.

Going on this basis, it is possible to abstract from the many different societies in all kinds of civilizations something like concentrated images of complete styles of life, developing on the brief sketches that we previously provided. These will be ideal-types, in Weber's sense, of the four modes of civilized behavior or what we have called the forms of civility. These are not intended as historical universals or meant to be ideals to which people must aspire at all times and places. Nevertheless, any ethos that considers itself to be civilized will be bound to instantiate at least some version of these ideal-types.

Court societies are structured hierarchically with a monarch or some other kind of autocratic ruler at the apex of the social pyramid; his companions, retainers, and courtiers in general at the next highest ring; and a surrounding aristocracy at the base of the ruling elite. The higher one ascends, the higher the social status and so, too, the more pure, intense, and concentrated the ethos of courtly manners. Proper behavior is ultimately only to be acquired at court in the highest levels and the most refined circles. Refinement is the key to this ethos, the cultivation of exquisite courtesies, ceremonial decorum, and fine feelings of great delicacy. At its most refined, the ethos produces noble souls who are like living works of art; the aesthetic perfection of the objects with which such people surround themselves also stamps its character on the owners themselves. Fine words and fine deeds, the *beau geste* of nobility, are the ways in which they express their inner nature. Of course, seen with the jaundiced eyes of sociology, the social purpose of courtly civility is to preserve the exclusivity of its bearers and maintain their social status and political dominance. But this should not lead to the cynical conclusion that it is a mere hypocritical pretense and that its nobility of manner and beauty of bearing is an insincere mask merely hiding a drive for power. Even if this were true of the class as a whole, it certainly would not be true of the individuals within it.

A religious civility is almost the opposite of a courtly one and frequently tends to be at odds with it. The priests of a temple, the mystagogues of a cult, monks, preachers, and other such religious devotees tend to promote an ethos of ascetic self-denial and self-sacrifice. Their lives are dedicated to the god, savior, or prophet according to whose dictates or example they live. Most frequently in literate cultures how they are supposed to order their lives is spelled out in inscriptions and holy books, which all such religions possess. Within these, the religious ethos is embodied in myths and sacred histories, which, of course, differ from religion to religion. But all of them tend to specify some exemplary life course that it then becomes the obligation of the adherents to translate into mundane terms and re-enact in their own lives to the best of their abilities. Any such religious way of life tends, therefore, to distinguish between those on whom the full burden of the obligatory falls and those of whom lesser demands are made, generally the distinction between the sacred priesthood and profane following or the clerical and lay. The former are bound by all kinds of rules, regulations, ritual, and ceremonial requirements, which frequently make it impossible for them to do anything else but lead a religious life; the latter are guided by a restricted range of these or weaker forms that are compatible with other courses in life and other socially necessary activities. Thus the burden of a religious ethos is differentially and unevenly distributed throughout a society.

The civic ethos of a city is, by contrast, in principle common to all full members of an urban community, the citizens or burghers. However, the nature and extent of membership in such a community differs from one type of city to another and has varied considerably throughout the recorded history of the city in different civilizations. To whom the laws apply and who has rights and obligations in respect of them depends on the particular political structure under which it is ruled or whether the city is an independent entity. The ethos of citizenship in its fully realized form was only characteristic of some kinds of Western cities; it began with the Greek polis, which stamped the form on all later Western city cultures; in a weakened and modified way on Roman cities; and later still, this became the burgher ethos of the city communes of medieval Europe. In such a civic ethos of citizenship, what counts is participation in the public affairs of the city, which in the case of the polis meant full and equal share of political rule but in the later cases much less than that, for the city had lost its political independence. In non-Western cities, such as those of the Middle East, India, or China, the civic ethos was never one of citizenship but a much weaker sense of constituting a city community of families living together, engaging in common activities, and managing their joint affairs in consultation with each other. In such cases the civic ethos was far less cohesive and civic unity was sustained in other ways: through religious means, such as joint worship of the city god and participation in his cult, or political means, such as the siting of a court or royal garrison as the ruling body within the city. Nevertheless, to some degree there was always an ethos of city dwellers, especially among the prominent denizens, usually a property-owning merchant class or proto-bourgeoisie. Its way of life tended to be characterized by conspicuous consumption and display and by the cultivation of those arts and graces that have always been the hallmarks of city sophistication. It is this that has continued to attract people to city life throughout the ages.

Within the city, but not restricted to it, there has usually also been found a social stratum with a quite distinctive ethos of its own, that of officialdom. Under different names and with somewhat different functions, this stratum has existed since the origins of civilization, more or less distinct from other strata. Such were the scribes, overseers, retainers, and couriers present from the beginning in all the great Near Eastern civilizations and still active in biblical times; such, too, were the publicans and *caesariani* of the Roman period; as were the chaplains and clerks and later servants of the king of Christian Europe; resembling them were those brahmans of India who served as advisers to the ruling *kshatriya* nobles; somewhat different were the Confucian scholars who were mandarins in China; and different again were the bourgeois members of the *noblesse de robe,* who bought their offices from the French monarchy under the *ancien regime*; and, finally, today there are the bureaucratic officials of all varieties all over the world. Generally their function has been administratively political; in one sense or another they have been servants of the crown, the staff of the ruling power in whatever form that came. Thus they can best be identified with the state authority even though they do not exercise political domination, which usually is in the hands of a monarch and a court aristocracy. Though usually subordinate to the ruling class, these state officials have tended to distinguish themselves from the ruling stratum above them by cultivating a distinctive ethos of their own. The mode of civility of officials is based on educational qualifications—that is, on the certification of one kind or another by which positions and promotions are acquired as a matter of right in the administrative apparatus. This ethos is thus inculcated through formal schooling of men—women were never in question till very recently—whose origins and previous backgrounds are of no great concern. What this educational process stresses are the character qualities of discipline and obedience, of self-abnegation and self-restraint in serving the powers that be and devoting oneself to the task in hand. It is an ethos of expertise and impersonality, one in which pride is taken in the objective exercise of skills and a matter-of-fact emotional detachment in carrying out one's official duties.

It is this ethos that has become the dominant temper of civility in contemporary societies. All affairs are now managed by officials of one type or another, as every kind of activity has become bureaucratized. Not only the administrative affairs of the state apparatus, which has grown to gigantic proportions, but also those of the equally enormous big business organizations and of educational, scientific, artistic, even religious institutions are all now in the hands of cadres of officials. Hence, their characteristic attitudes to work, to leisure, and to life in general are now widespread and inescapable, for no other ethos can stand against it. This holds throughout the world, for bureaucratization is ubiquitous. The official is now the predominant type in all international dealings and meetings, and so his manners, attitudes, and mode of bearing are obligatory for everyone on the world stage and its forums. Hence, this is the standard form of civility of our global civilization.

For all kinds of historic reasons that we will later examine, every other form of civility has been weakened almost to the point of obsolescence. Thus as monarchical power has disappeared and courts have ceased to function as foci for aristocratic life, so the ethos of nobility has now become purely vestigial, maintained by some surviving aristocratic families together with their traditional inheritance as a kind of heirloom of exclusivity, but of little consequence in society. So, too, the civic ethos of citizenship and bourgeois life has been attenuated to the point of extinction. Citizenship involves little in the way of civic participation, and the city no longer functions as a civic community of burghers; it has assumed a purely administrative role whose arrangements conform to its functional division into a commercial center, manufacturing quarters, and dormitory suburbs. Only the religious ethos still seems to be visible and viable, at least to the extent that churches or their institutional equivalents in the various religions are still prominent and the religious bodies that serve them still maintain something of a traditional religious life and the ethos that goes with it. However, as we shall see, the spirit behind it has subtly changed and continues to do so, despite the periodic upsurge of fundamentalist movements intended to reassert the traditional faiths and practices. Thus court, city, and church have lost much of their exemplary role, so only the state is left. As we shall go on to show, this recession in every kind of ethos, except that of officials, is one of the sources of the ethical problems of our time. But to understand this development, it is first necessary to explain what ethics has to do with ethos.

Ethos and ethics both derive from the same Greek etymological origins, yet the two words now mean something very different, or, at least, we propose to use them in different ways. An ethos is not in itself an ethics; it need not contain one, not even if it is a civil ethos such as we previously described. Only in a few rare cases has such an ethos given rise to an ethic, for historical reasons that will become evident as we go on. It is on these cases that we shall concentrate, and we shall study them intensively in what follows.

An ethic can only arise out of a pre-existing civil ethos, namely, in the context of a civilization, when that has undergone a very special form of historical development. This has tended to happen in those civilizations where either church or court or city or state were predominant, for, as we shall see, each of these gave rise to its own unique type of ethics. On its own, such an ethos is not sufficient to constitute an ethics. A fundamental cultural transformation has to occur before an ethos reconstitutes itself as also an ethics. Historically, such transformations took place in but a few civilizations in the course of the rise of what are now considered to be the great universal religions and philosophies of the world. This occurred almost simultaneously in widely divergent regions during what Karl Jaspers has called the Axial Age, the short historical span between 700 and 300 B.C.

During this Axial Age in Persia, Greece, India, China, and Israel, there took place those fundamental cultural revolutions that were among the most momentous events in human history. Ethical systems arose only in the context of the transformations of these civilizations and nowhere else, in no other civilized ethos. Indeed, a historical definition of ethics is to consider it as one or another of these Axial Age models of the good, right, and proper ways of life. Such ideals of living have ever since been considered as classical or canonic in their respective cultural spheres of the world, and their adherents still look back to these origins as definitive beginnings of their traditions. Frequently, these beginnings are associated with individual personalities, who were undoubtedly real people even though their lives later assumed a legendary semi-mythical status. Such were the prophets Zoroaster, the Buddah, Deutero-Isaiah, and some of the other Old Testament prophets; the philosophers Confucius, Lao-tzu, Pythagoras, Parmenides, and Heraklitus; and lawgivers such as Solon in Greece. Oddly enough, most of these were near contemporaries, if the conventional datings of their lifetimes are accepted, but there is much controversy about that. Of course, they were not themselves the originators of the Axial Age cultural revolutions but part of them; these general cultural upheavals threw up outstanding individuals and also much else of consequence for the origin of ethics. The start of ethics involved a general transformation of mentality that could only take place together with new social and political structures, new styles of art and other such representational innovations, new ways of thought, and above all new modes of literacy. It is hardly conceivable that an Axial Age could have been possible without the alphabet and the difference that it made to general literacy and the rise of texts.[5] China, the sole exception to this, managed an expanded literacy through the invention of new writing materials, such as brush, ink, and paper. This had a profound effect on ethics, which has to rely on texts, for without texts the purity of the ethical message would not have endured for long; it would soon have become corrupted. The study of the relation of texts to ethics is itself a special aspect of our subject.

We now come to the crucial point of our preliminary investigation; we can once more put the question: What distinguishes an ethics from an ethos? We shall answer this question historically by examining how an ethic arises out of a pre-existing civilized ethos. This tends to happen when the traditionally accepted and unquestioned codes of civility—the divinely sanctioned laws, the mores and customs, the manners, the conventional duties, the praiseworthy virtues, and so on, for all the features of civilized style of life—become subject to higher critical standards and are systematically revised. Usually, these standards are based on a reformulated worldview involving a new transcendent conception of Truth or Reality and a new sense of community. Men's minds are directed toward a higher Order or Power, and their relations to each other and their traditionally conventional manners and mores are revised and re-ordered in terms of the new sense of reality and new social bonds. Of course, this does not change everything in the pre-established ethos, but it does transform it in the direction of greater systematicity, rationality, and subjectivity through the application of over-arching general principles, more coherent norms and values, and a greater emphasis on the individual self or soul. In short, an ethic arises when a pre-existing civilized ethos is transformed in these ways, which might be called the process of ethicization.

This process can take many distinct forms in various cultures, and it undergoes many vicissitudes in the course of its different histories; nowhere is it exactly alike. However, there is enough in common to its different manifestations, and each constitutes such an analogous alteration in what precede it, that they can all collectively be designated by the same term, *ethics*. Thus, for example, one of the salient features that they all share is that each conceives of an ideal form of Man: that is, of how one ideally ought to behave and bear oneself, what one ought to aspire to and value, what feelings to cultivate, what to believe, and, in general, how to live the good life. This ideal of Man is made universally mandatory, so that irrespective of all other differences in race, language, society, culture, and in some cases even religion, all men are required to live up to it to the best of their ability. This is the source of the notion of universality in subsequent conceptions of ethics. But, as we shall soon see, since there are a number of different ideals of Man, each claiming universal validity, ethical conflict becomes unavoidable.

This is the reason that we previously spoke of the tragedy of ethics. Prior to ethics, in a pre-ethical stage of ethos, it was not necessary to enter into disputes with others about how they lived their lives in their own separate and distinct cultures, since each society or civilization could follow its own ethos, just as it could worship its own gods, oblivious to all others in a kind of tolerance or mutual indifference. But the rise of ethics, with its claims to universality, made that impossible. Hence, it led to heightened levels of conflict in all respects, intellectual as well as violent. This was so almost from the start of the process of ethicization. Wherever it occurred, there ensued a struggle with the older pre-ethical ethos, sometimes as a battle against the old gods, sometimes against the old mores, or laws. The ethicizing forces did not always win out, and in some cases they were forced to so compromise their initial ethical message as to render it only barely distinguishable from the prevalent ethos, as we shall show was the case in Persia. It is worth noting that one of the earliest attempts at an ethical revolution was in fact defeated by the forces of conservatism.

Around 1400 B.C., the pharaoh Amenhotep IV, who renamed himself Ikhnaten, tried to abolish all the minor gods of Egypt and abandoned the old religious priestly center, Thebes, home of the main god Amon, in favor of a new capital, Akhetaten, where the worship of the one universal sun-god, Aten, was instituted. Toynbee writes that he "stood for a revolution in every important sphere of cultural and spiritual life: in literature, in art and, above all, in religion,"⁶ which means, of course, in ethics as well. As is now well known, he was defeated by the adherents of the old religious order and ethos, who not only blackened his memory but successfully extirpated his name from Egyptian history; it was only rediscovered by modern archaeologists. Nevertheless, something of the spirit of Ikhnaten's revolution remained; Amon, the restored god, assumed some of the attributes of Aten, and the proto-ethics of conscience he introduced, of individual sin, humility, and contrition, resurfaced again in Egyptian consciousness in subsequent times, as the *Book of the Dead* reveals.

Only many hundreds of years after this premature attempt, which failed in Egypt, did the ethicizing process successfully get under way in history during the Axial Age revolutions, which happened almost simultaneously in a handful of the then established cultures, mostly in peripheral regions outside the old established centers of civilization. We shall not consider here why this was so or attempt any general explanation of how it took place; we shall merely concentrate on indicating what difference it made to how people lived.⁷

Before ethics, life was, relatively speaking, free, in that most of what one did was of no special consequence. There was an obligatory set of duties, according to one's station in life, that could not be deviated from but left considerable scope for personal initiative. After ethics, there was but one righteous path, one correct way of living, excluding all others, imposed on everyone. The ethical law is much more demanding than any other; that there is also freedom within this law is a paradox that only the ethical mind can appreciate. But inordinately more demands are placed on the ethical agent, who is no longer free to let his or her life run haphazardly but must strive for a higher sense of self. Thus a new sense of individuality arose, as each person was expected to assume those commitments that we now consider ethical—that is, to live rightly and follow the right way, to live in and by the new Truth. This entailed a completely new sense of individual responsibility and individual agency. Crimes or wrongdoings or other such misdemeanors could no longer be expiated by magical, ritual, or ceremonial performances; nor could they be indemnified by monetary payments or services. And nothing was considered an ethical wrong unless it was done intentionally with malice aforethought; the mere occurrence of the act was not in itself enough. A moral wrong, seen as a sin, had to be expiated with deep contrition or at least sincere regret. Ethics thus deepened the subjective aspects of action, stressing motives and intentions rather than objective results or consequences; not the act in itself was culpable, but the agent's state of mind, the bad will, desires, goals, thoughts, and feelings with which it was done.

All this was in keeping with new requirements for higher standards of rationality of action. This in turn came together with the imposition of much more rational law and judicial procedure. Wrongdoing became subject to rational judicial criteria of culpability, justification, and excusing. In Greece in particular, novel trial procedures arose, requiring rational proof through demonstrable evidence. This was obviously linked to the new norms of reason elaborated in philosophy and science, especially the medical sciences. In China, law was also rationalized through the hands of the philosophical school of so-called Legists, acting at the behest of the imperial authorities from the time of unification under Shi Huang-ti. Legal codification and the comprehensive reform of law through ethical critique also took place in Israel through the work of the Torah Levites, who were responsible for elaborating the *Pentateuch*. In India such codifications can be read in the Rock and Pillar Edicts of the Buddhist emperor Ashoka.

The new systems of ethics that arose during the Axial Age in the various different localities can be compared and contrasted with each other in numerous ways, which we shall undertake to do more thoroughly at the end of the chapter after they have first been separately presented. Here we will merely begin with a few simple differences of comparative categorization. The most obvious one of all is that between religious and secular ethics. This, however, soon proves itself to be a very misleading criterion, one that is usually invoked with a preconceived idea of what is religion and what is not. In one sense, all the ethics are religious, insofar as they are based on transcendent notions. It were better to consider the differences in the kind of transcendence involved. Thus, in a very rough way, it is possible to distinguish those ethics that are based on a conception of a higher Power, in which the prophet plays a major role, from those based on a conception of a higher Order, in which the sage or philosopher is the key figure.

Into the first category fall the ethics of Israel, the Buddhist ethics, and perhaps also that of the early history of Persia. The Powers in whose name these ethics were promulgated are very different. For the Israelites it was the one transcendent deity, Yahwe, ruler of the universe, who eventually in Christianity took human form as the Christ, the Savior of mankind. For Buddhism, such a universal Savior had sway over all the gods, for his power reduced them to insignificance. For the early Persians, supreme power was divided: a god of righteousness, Ahura Mazda, was engaged in a cosmic combat against an equal adversary, the lord of lies, Ahriman. This ethic has not survived in its original form, though its dualism of good and evil has had a profound historical influence ever since, and its effects can be felt in other ethics. We propose to call all these ethics "moralities," for reasons that will become clearer later and have mainly to do with their inner-directed subjectivity or conscience. The German word *Moral* captures this meaning better than the ordinary usage of the English word *moral*, which is very loose and for all intents and purposes synonymous with *ethical*. In our stricter sense, there are but two historically continuous traditions of morality, the Western, based on Judaism, and the Eastern, based on Buddhism.

In contraposition to the moralities based on conceptions of transcendent Power, there are the other ethics based on those of transcendent Order. Once again, these take very different Western and Eastern forms. The Western one is that which emerged from the ethos of the Greek polis and involved the notions of *cosmos* and *nomos*, *logos* and *dike*, and all the other order-sanctioning terms of Greek literature that were taken up and transcendentalized in later Greek philosophy. The Chinese had analogous conceptions of an order of Heaven and the *Tao* that were also given philosophical elaborations and referred to social and ethical issues. In both Greece and China, ethics assumed a legal-political form, as the transcendent conceptions of a higher Order were assumed to reflect themselves in the law and order of human societies. However, the law and politics of Greece and China were almost diametrically opposed to each other. The former was that of a polis constitution with an independent citizenry autonomously determining the mode of government and the nature of the laws. The latter was an imperial system, with rule and law dictated from above under the direction of a cadre of scholars who acted as an empowered group of professional officials. Hence the two ethics that emerged under these contrary circumstances were also opposed to each other. The former we shall call a civic ethic, the latter an ethic of duty.

On examining the social sources of each of the previously referred to ethics during the Axial Age, it becomes clear that each arose in quite varied cultural settings, formed very different ethical communities, and was carried by very diverse social groups. In fact, each one of the ethics arose in societies where one or another of the main institutions of civilization predominated. One or another of the four key loci of a civil ethos, namely, court, temple or church, city, and state, produced an ethic during the Axial Age and continued to do so at later periods. The city ethos in its most developed and autonomous form, that of the Greek polis, gave rise to the civic ethics, in a once and never to be independently repeated occurrence. The state administrative officialdom in imperial China produced the very first of the ethics of duty, that of Confucianism; but subsequently two other analogous ethics of this type were to arise independently of each other, among the Krishna-worshiping *brahmin* ritual advisers of the ruling *kshatriya* stratum in the Hindu kingdoms that arose after the collapse of the Maurya empire, and a little later among the Roman officials of the imperial period who were inclined to Stoicism. The religious ethos of Israel and India also produced ethics almost simultaneously, and these we have called moralities: the former was the creation of Torah priests and prophets and it gave rise to all Western moralities; the latter arose among groups of wandering ascetics and took the form of the Jain and Buddhist ethics, out of which all Eastern moralities developed.

The only civilizational ethos that seems not to have produced a readily identifiable ethics is the culture of court societies and their aristocratic entourages. Yet we know that among aristocrats, there is such a thing as an ethics of honor. This is precisely the term that Montesquieu uses in defining what he calls the "ruling principle" of monarchical government, which is in effect the basic ethos of a courtly aristocratic society. He described it as follows: "Here one sees and always hears three things: that a certain nobility must be put in the virtues, a certain frankness in the mores, and a certain politeness in the manners."[8] From this, it is clear that this ethos also contains an ethics. In Western Europe this began in the early Middle Ages as the ethics of chivalry, one that is quite different to any of the ethics we have so far mentioned. It is neither a morality, nor a civic ethics, nor an ethics of duty; it has no distinctive transcendent beliefs behind it and it is not carried by any ethically inclined social formation, such as those that maintained the other ethics, rather by a ruling aristocratic elite that is not otherwise ethically propitious.

In what follows in this chapter we shall try to show that despite appearances, this ethics, too, originally had a transcendent basis in a religion of the Axial Age. We shall seek to trace its origins back to the court culture of the Achaemenenian monarchy of ancient Persia, which was heavily influenced by Zoroastrianism, especially in its later forms when that religion became infused with indigenous Persian pagan beliefs and lost its initial moral purity. In between this original appearance and its much later reemergence in medieval Christian Europe, there took place a series of transmissions and transformations along a historical route stretching through its various revivals in Persia and traveling along the entire length of the Muslim *eucumene* among Turkic and Arab intermediaries, until it finally reached the borders of Europe at a number of points. What eventually emerged in Europe, from these and other influences in combination, was an unusual ethics, one with such peculiar characteristics that it has generally not been recognized as an ethics at all. Apart from brief mentions, such as that in Montesquieu, it has not received the historical recognition that its importance deserves or any extensive theoretical treatment. This we shall seek to remedy later in this chapter.

Our basic typology of ethics is now complete. We have distinguished altogether four basic types: morality, in both its Western and Eastern forms, and three other kinds, a civic ethics, an ethics of duty, and an ethics of honor. In what follows in this chapter we shall first discuss each of these individually in separate sections and then in a final one go on to compare them. The brief comparisons we have already made were in terms of their contrasting ideal and real bases—that is, the kinds of system of belief they invoke and the social forces and communities that carry them. Thus we have shown in a brief provisional manner that moralities justify themselves according to strictly religious transcendent principles, usually soteriological doctrines of salvation, whereas the other ethics appeal to more secularly inclined principles of transcendence, usually of a philosophical or literary nature. The second, more sociologically realistic, way of treating them produces an analogous distinction. Thus if we look at them in terms of the civil ethos out of which each emerges—that is, at the institutions of temple or church, court, city, or state—then it is obvious that moralities derive from religious sources and the other ethics from the more secularly inclined ones. The significance of this for the nature of these ethics will emerge more clearly in our comparative studies.

Moralities

Morality is the ethic of love. The initial and most basic principle of Western morality is clearly stated in the Torah: "Thou shalt love thy neighbor as thyself" (Leviticus 19:18). A following verse, Leviticus 19:34, makes explicit that this applies to all people, since it expressly includes "the stranger that lives in the land." The commandment to love the stranger is repeated in Deuteronomy 10:19, where it is linked to other moral injunctions, such as care for widows and orphans—that is, all the weaker members of society who are to be protected. Love of one's neighbor stands only next to love of God: "Thou shalt love thy God with all thy heart" (Deuteronomy 6:5).

Love of God and love of one's neighbor are not to be dissociated in this ethics. For loving God means keeping his commandments, the principal one of which is to love one's neighbor. The prophets, who expound the same moral message, are insistent that loving God is inescapable from doing what is morally right, being just, kind, merciful, and charitable, and that not being so is abandoning God. In other words, being wicked is a form of apostasy. Lindblom, in his extensive treatment of the prophetic literature, is clear on this point:

> In the view of those prophets moral depradation was a consequence of religious apostasy. If the people had kept to Yahwe, they would have understood what Yahwe's will was and would have obeyed His ethical commands. It is often said by the prophets that these people had despised *mispat,* the Hebrew word for the sum of all obligations which were incumbent upon the people by virtue of the covenant. Mispat includes moral demands *and* religious obligations, obedience to ethical precepts as well as the right attitude to Yahwe. The two belong together and are not strictly distinguished in Hebrew thought, ethical requirements being regarded as ultimately prescribed by Yahwe, and fear of Yahwe and love of Him providing the impulse to act according to His will.[9]

As we shall see in the historical account that follows, the love of neighbor and the love of God—that is to say, morality and religion—remained inseparable till the modern period in the West, the Age of Enlightenment, when a secularization of morality ensued. We are still in the midst of this historical process of trying to develop a purely secular morality, and the outcome is still uncertain. Dostoyevsky's warning "if God is dead all is permitted" is answered by Nietzsche's strident rejoinder "God is dead, we must become like gods ourselves." Both are extreme responses to the problem of morality without religion. But it remains an unsolved problem. Whether morality can be completely secularized must still remain in doubt, despite the many outstanding individuals who led exemplary moral lives without any religious supports. However, at this point we must not prejudge the issue one way or another.

When we assert that morality is the ethic of love, this must be understood in a very special sense of the term *love*, as is evident from the religious meaning of this multifaceted word. Love is a human universal, and some form or other of it must be found in every ethos, and, in turn, one expression or another of that will be valorized in the corresponding ethics. Whether it be love of gods or men or women or family or friends or city or country or state or abstract qualities or ideals, something or other is bound to be pre-scribed as worthy of love and that will determine ethical conduct. The bibli-cal "love of one's neighbor" is a very special form of love, a unique development of the Judaic religion and unlike any to be encountered outside it. It is a supremely altruistic love, for to love one's neighbor as oneself means always to put oneself in his place and to act on his behalf as one would naturally and selfishly act on one's own.

Furthermore, one's neighbor is always a specific individual who can be anybody. Loving one's neighbor is, therefore, not like loving a special collec-tivity or group and everyone who belongs to it; it is not loving "my people" or even "people who are like me." For insofar as it includes the stranger, it also includes those who are strange and utterly "unlike me." Eventually, in Christianity it would be extended to include even those who are enemies, those who are hostile and "hate me." It is these features of the concept of loving one's neighbor that distinguish Judeo-Christian morality from every other ethics, including Eastern morality.

Complementary to this concept of "love," as its opposite negative pole, is a concept of "sin," which has also a very special meaning, for eventually it develops into a concept of moral conscience, the *syneidis* or *conscientia* of later terminology. It is disputable whether there is such a later concept in the Hebrew Bible itself, but a reconception of sin had already occurred that would prepare the ground for the eventual emergence of a fully fledged con-science and without which the latter is unthinkable. Conscience is a unique elaboration and refinement of the feeling of guilt, which otherwise, in all kinds of diffuse forms, is universally prevalent and is part of the very defini-tion of human being, for no socialized psyche can be without it.

Even the very conception of sin is already a further historical development on the most primitive feelings of guilt, such as those involved in the breaking of taboo. This can take an extremely physical form and can be tantamount to a self-imposed sentence of death, as used to be the case among Australian aboriginals. Sin in its earliest historical manifestations also took a physical and quasi-objective form. It was felt and seen as pollution or impurity in the offending body itself. Only purification or catharsis could remove the indelible stain and render the body pure and clean. Such is the Greek archaic conception of *miasma,* which was feared as a contagion that can be passed on from body to body much in the way we now fear infectious diseases. Thus Oedipus, in Sophocles' play of that name, becomes a polluted outcast whom "neither the earth nor the holy rain nor the sunlight can accept."[10] Pollution and purification played a leading role in the religion of ancient Egypt, as continual references to both in the *Book of the Dead* exemplify, such as the following: "I am pure. My breast is pure, my after-part is clean, my middle is in the well of *Maat.* I am pure of mouth and pure of hands. My purity is the purity of the Great Phoenix that is in Herakleopolis. . . ."[11] All ancient religions manifested such a dread of pollution, and Hinduism is to this day obsessed by it, especially as caste pollution. It is present in the Hebrew Bible as well and must be accounted for not only as an archaic survival from its oldest strata but as a continuing preoccupation of its priestly code, which passed over into its rabbinic form and is still present in strictly Orthodox Judaism.

Sin as moral guilt is very different from sin as pollution. E. R. Dodds explains the difference as follows: "The distinction between the two situations is, of course, that sin is a condition of will, a disease of man's inner consciousness, whereas pollution as the automatic consequence of an action, belongs to the world of external events and operates with the same ruthless indifference to motive as a typhoid germ."[12] A historic move toward the later conception of sin manifests itself very early; it is already incipiently present in the curious Egyptian eschatology of judgment, when in the afterlife the heart of the dead person is weighed by the infernal deities. But this material conception of sin was accompanied by a more moral notion, for the heart was "both capable of, and disposed to, acting as an independent witness against its owner at his trial after death."[13] But this view of the heart, which evinced "a deepening moral sensitivity," always coexisted with a cruder view of its role in the judgment of the dead.[14] It was the same in Greek ethical development, where there was also a continuing coexistence of early and late beliefs of pollution and sinfulness. Dodds notes that "the transference of the notion of purity from the magical to the moral sphere was a similar late development: not until the closing years of the fifth century do we encounter explicit statements that clean hands are not enough—the heart must be clean also."[15] The full transformation of a primitive sense of guilt into a sense of sin that can be referred to as conscience took place later still, as a "phenomenon which appears late and uncertain in the Hellenic world, and does not become common until long after secular law had begun to recognize the importance of motive."[16]

In the Hebrew Bible the move from the sense of sin as pollution to that of moral guilt is chiefly reflected in the prophetic writings. Right from the start, with Amos and Hosea, they fulminate against those who believe that sins can be expunged through ritual proprieties, such as sacrifices and offerings. Purification is of no use either, "though you wash yourself with lye and use much soap, your guilt would stand fully in my sight," speaks Yahwe through the mouth of Jeremiah (2:22). Only sincerely meant repentance can earn atonement through God's forgiveness. Thus Yahwe exhorts a sinning humanity: "Remove the evil of your doings from before My eyes; cease to do evil, learn to do good. Seek justice . . ." (Isaiah 1:16). The moral message of the Psalms, though expressed somewhat differently, is essentially the same. Here the terminology is that of the right "way" and the "direction" to be followed. According to Psalm 25, as interpreted by Martin Buber, "to 'direct' means to show the way which men should 'choose' and the means to teach each man to distinguish this way, the right way, from the other, the wrong ways."[17] Sinning is missing the mark or the way; repenting is finding it again.

According to Buber, a conception of sin in its full moral depth and psychological subtlety is inherent in the story of Cain and Abel, in itself an early myth but presented in a much later version that it is now impossible to date. What is involved in this is a moral "knowledge of good and evil" given by "man's self-exposure to the opposites inherent in existence within the world, but now in its ethical mould. From quite general opposites, embracing good and evil as well as good and ill and good and bad, we have arrived at the circumscribed area peculiar to man, in which only good and evil confront each other."[18] The passage from the Torah that Buber interprets in this sense is where God speaks to Cain at the start of the story: "if thou purposest good bear it aloft, but if thou dost not purpose good—sin before the door, a beast lying in wait, unto thee his desire, but prevail thou over him" (in Buber's own idiosyncratic translation). We cannot follow all the twists and turns of Buber's convoluted interpretation, nor can we take issue with him here. However, if there is anything in what he has to say, it shows that the Hebrew Bible is already aware of the psychological intricacies of sin and conscience, what Buber calls "the true dynamic of the soul as it is given by the 'knowledge of good and evil.' "[19]

To what extent the Hebrew Bible already disposes of a concept of conscience as an inner call (sineidis, conscientia) is still a moot point in scholarly literature. Certainly, this is present in later rabbinic writing, but to what extent it was influenced by Hellenistic thought is also in dispute. The issue is whether the demand to do the morally right thing is to be understood as an inner voice speaking within Man or as an outer voice, that of God's commandment, speaking to Man's inwardness. We cannot debate this highly technical interpretative moral-theological issue here.[20]

As we have already noted, the origins of morality and the various early stages through which it passed are extremely difficult to date or even to disentangle analytically from their embeddedness in other kinds of ethos. The Hebrew Bible is a document that was worked and reworked continuously for many centuries. It contains strata and even sentences lumped together that belong to quite different periods and reflect utterly divergent mentalities. Hence, even though the basic moral principle of "love thy neighbor as thyself" is already stated in Leviticus and Deuteronomy, yet both books of the Torah are replete with all kinds of other prescriptions and laws, and these are also treated as divine commandments in no way to be distinguished from the moral law; mostly they are rules of ritual propriety and social lore. It is all regarded as an undifferentiated expression of God's will and so to be obeyed indiscriminately with equal devotion. In this respect the Torah is no different from earlier pre-ethical guides of conduct such as the laws of Hammurabi or the Babylonian sin registers or the Egyptian *Book of the Dead*, all of which are formulations of an ethos of civility rather than an ethics in the full sense.

Nevertheless, a pronounced ethics does already appear in the Torah, for as Weber puts it, "without doubt the 'ethical' Decalogue owes its most important characteristics above all to its separation from both ritualistic and welfare prescriptions to its public."[21] Among all these ancient documents, the Decalogue is ethically unique, as Weber makes clear:

> Despite all similarities in detail in one important respect Israelite ethic was opposed to Egyptian as well as Babylonian ethic. It was rationally systematized to a far reaching extent. The mere existence of the ethical Decalogue and of other similar compositions indicates the contrast to the quite unsystematic registers of sins in Egypt and Babylonia.[22]

Apart from this key feature of rationalization, Weber goes on to add, "nothing is transmitted from both these culture areas which would equal or merely resemble a systematic ethical religious exhortation of the kind of *Deuteronomy*."[23] He means, of course, such commandments as "thou shalt love thy neighbor as thyself."[24] Thus he concludes decisively that "unlike pre-exilic Israel, Babylon and Egypt knew no unified, religiously substructured ethic. . . ."[25] That is to say, in our terms, they knew no morality.

Morality, as first registered in the Hebrew Bible, was the joint creation of the Levites and the prophets. According to Weber:

> In Israel this ethic was the product of the ethical Torah of the Levites continued for many generations, and of prophecy. Prophecy did not so much influence the content—which it rather accepted as given—rather it promoted systematic unification, by relating the people's life as a whole and the life of each individual to the fulfillment of Yahwe's positive commandments. Moreover, it eliminated the predominance of ritual in favour of ethics.[26]

We are reminded here of the numerous exhortations to be found in the prophets from Amos onward that what Yahwe demands is not burnt offerings but only purity of heart, justice, and charity. Hence morality is not in the hands of the priests or only of those religiously qualified but in the hearts of anyone who harkens to the will of Yahwe, as revealed through the mouths of those whom He calls on to be his prophets, and this might be anyone at all, even a humble shepherd, as in the case of Amos: "Surely the Lord God will do nothing, but he revealeth his secret unto his servants the prophets. The lion hath roared, who will not fear? The Lord God hath spoken, who will not prophesy?" (Amos 3:7–8). Thus, as Weber concludes, the Levites and the prophets "jointly imparted to the ethic its simultaneous plebeian and rationally systematic character."[27] This has been a leading feature of Western morality ever since.

The practical expression of the basic moral injunction to love one's neighbor as expounded by the prophets is charity or good deeds in general. The prophetic writings as well as the Torah, especially Deuteronomy, are full of exhortations to charitable endeavors. The most general expression of this is the demand to give freely stated in Deuteronomy (15:11): "Thou shalt open thy hand wide." The passive complement to charity in dealing with one's neighbor is the avoidance of doing any kind of harm or perpetrating mistreatment or injustice. Thus there is an explicit injunction in Leviticus (19:18) against hatred and vindictiveness and to resort only to open and candid discussion in settling differences.

Charity is the key feature of Western morality. Though it remained constant as an ideal moral norm throughout its history, its practical realization underwent numerous mutations and transformation. Thus rabbinic *tzadakah* is quite different from the *agape* or *caritas*, the love of fellow men, of the early Christian communities or of the institutionalized good works of the Roman Church later. Protestant Christianity took a quite different view again of individual and of organized charitable endeavors. This much more self-responsible and individualistic attitude is expressed in the popular saying "Charity begins at home." The entry of the state into welfare provisioning in the modern period altered the moral character of charity altogether and brought it back to what it had been at a pre-ethical stage in some of the ancient empires. This has brought about the moral crisis of charity that we discussed in the introduction.

However, charity is by no means a unique feature of Western morality. It is to be found in other ethics as well. In particular, the Eastern moralities of Jainism and Buddhism also make it a cardinal virtue. But, as Weber explains, Indian charity derived from a different conception to Western charity:

> Indian charity rested on the conception of all life as a unity. This was reinforced by the belief in *Samsara*. Indian charity, as expressed also in the Decalogues of the Buddhists, soon adopted a formal and almost purely ritualistic character.[28]

It is true that Western charity, both in the later rabbinic Judaism as in the Christianity of the various Churches, also became a set of fixed and ritualistic requirements for socially prescribed and canonically sanctioned good deeds. But the love of one's neighbor and the call to be charitable never ceased in the West to produce more extensive and revolutionary moral demands, such as those for social justice in general. Social welfare provisions are also not new; they are to be found in Egyptian charity prescriptions that predate Israelite moral charity by a millennium or more. However, as Weber makes clear, "in Egypt charity was strongly influenced by the bureaucratic structure of the state and the economy."[29] Thus it was more akin to the social welfare provisions of the modern state, the fulfillment of which is also in the hands of authorized officials acting on prescribed laws and regulations. This is unlike the specifically religious injunctions placed on individuals as moral beings that the prophets proclaim. The fact that some of these individuals might be kings or officials of kings is not morally relevant; they, too are bound, just like all others, by God's moral law, which is indifferent to status and position. The prophets had no hesitation in bringing a king to brook if he had strayed by being uncharitable.

In this way, one by one the basic features of a rigorous and systematic moral code fell into place to constitute the first thoroughgoing and coherent instance of ethical rationalization in history. According to Weber, there were but two decisive instances of ethical rationalization, prophetic Judaism and puritan Protestantism; what took place between these crucial termini he sees as rationally compromised. The intermediate period covers rabbinic Judaism as well as ancient and medieval Christianity. We shall have more to say about these in the next chapter when we examine the various kinds of processes of adaptation and adjustment that they underwent. Here we shall merely sketch a few salient aspects of their development.

The post-prophetic development of morality within Judaism took place in various ways within the different sects, among which the Pharisees (*perushim*) were initially the most important, for out of them derived both of the main later trends of rabbinic Judaism and Christianity, though the latter was very likely also influenced by the Essenes and their ascetic creeds. The Pharisees constituted an order or brotherhood (*chavurah*) that required of its adherents a strict obedience to morality and ritual purity prescriptions. Thus, as Weber puts it, "the charisma of the priest was deprecated in favour of personal religious qualification as proven through conduct."[30] The Pharisees derived out of the lofty but quite unspecific general moral pronouncements of the Torah and prophets a detailed ethic of everyday life that they made incumbent on all pious Jews; those who failed to live up to this strict regimen were castigated as "peasants" (*am ha-aretz*, those too ignorant to know or observe the law). In order to make the law known to all, they instituted synagogue worship, with its regular weekly reading of the Torah, a key feature of moral instruction in Judaism ever since.

Rabbinic Judaism—which originated after the destruction of the Second Temple and has continued till now—took off from the main moral emphases of the Pharisees. It has mainly been concerned with practical everyday matters, which it addresses through a process of deliberation in the form of casuistic discussion, sometimes extremely hairsplitting, in which different points of view are opposed, as is characteristic of the contentious issues debated by the various schools of rabbis in the Talmud. This has not meant that general moral principles were overlooked; these were continually also invoked as, for example, in Rabbi Hillel's pronouncement of the Golden Rule, "Do not do unto others as ye would not wish them to do unto you." However, no attempt was made in the rabbinic literature to provide any rational justification or grounding for such moral norms. On the contrary, in a reaction against Hellenistic philosophy, rational proofs and demonstrations were shunned. The law was not to be questioned but observed, for "fear of sin surpasses wisdom." Thus we encounter here, perhaps more explicitly than ever before, the apparent paradox of a highly rational ethic that is averse to rational discourse and rational thought.

In the history of early Christianity an opposite development ensues: the ethical discourse becomes increasingly more rationalized but the morality, at least as imposed on lay believers, less so. The reason for this is that Christian ethical discourse becomes theological as it takes over more and more of the forms of thought of Greek philosophy, but, at the same time, the moral code becomes less demanding as Christian morality adapts and adjusts to the prevailing ethical standards of the Roman empire. In the next chapter we shall study this historical process of transformation, which eventually gave rise to the syncretist ethics of later Christianity. Here we shall merely consider the main intellectual stages of the process in the moral thought of Jesus, St. Paul, and St. Augustine. We shall focus explicitly and solely on the prime principle of morality, love of one's neighbor or charity (*caritas, agape*). This, as we shall try to show, changes its meaning and significance from one stage to the next in the evolution of Christianity. It begins with Jesus as a basically practical moral injunction; it is spiritualized by St. Paul into a theological virtue; finally, it is intellectualized by St. Augustine into a philosophical state of being, in keeping with the then established view of philosophy as an ethical form of life.

It is difficult now to establish exactly what was Jesus' own original moral position, for contradictory statements are ascribed to him, but everything in the Synoptic Gospels points to the fact that charity as love of one's neighbor was the key to it. The Catholic theologian Hans Küng puts it as follows:

> Apart from the formulation of the chief commandment, drawn from the Old Testament, Jesus in the Synoptic Gospels uses the words "love" and "loving" in the sense of love of "neighbour" itself, very sparingly. Nevertheless, love of one's fellow man is present everywhere in Jesus' proclamation. Evidently, where love is concerned, actions speak louder than words. It is not talk, but action, which makes clear the nature of love. Practice is the criterion.[31]

This attitude is totally in keeping with the Judaic approach to morality and contrasts with that of the later apostles and Church Fathers. As Küng makes clear, Jesus "came to fulfill the law by making God's will prevail"; "according to Jesus, love is essentially love of both God and man."[32] As we have seen, this is essentially the moral message of the Torah and the prophets, and Küng agrees that "Judaism had already spoken sporadically of love in this dual sense."[33] Also, in keeping with Judaism, "it is typical of Jesus that love thus becomes the criterion of piety and of a person's whole conduct."[34]

However, Jesus goes further than rabbinic Judaism in his gospel of love, in that he refers all commandments back to the primal "indissoluble unity" of love of God and love of Man.[35] He also extends it to embrace literally all men, including one's enemies and those who hate one. Thus the Sermon on the Mount declares: "But I say to you, 'Love your enemies and pray for them that persecute you.'" This unrestricted interpretation of the love of one's neighbor is the hallmark of Christian morality. However, practicing that degree of forbearance is a mark of sainthood and does not reflect the moral realities of ordinary people in the Christian community. Hence, it can only be held up as an ideal to which the great majority of Christian mankind can only aspire, not as an attainable virtue.

The ideal and spiritual, rather than practical, nature of the Christian interpretation of the love of neighbor becomes more pronounced in St. Paul. St. Paul links charity (*caritas*) with faith and hope, which are not matters of action but states of the soul (*pneuma*) or spiritual attainments. If love of neighbor is like faith and hope then it, too, loses its immediate practical stress and becomes more of a pneumatic matter, a state of one's inner being. St. Paul explicitly detaches it from practical action: "And though I bestow all my goods to feed the poor and though I give my body to be burned, and have not charity, it profiteth me nothing" (Corinthians I, 13:3). The sense of that seems to be that no matter what one does for one's neighbor, one might still be lacking in charity. Charity then is a kind of love that goes beyond any practical realization, and together with faith and hope, which it surpasses, it must be seen as a state of grace, a form of inner perfection that presumably only the Christian can attain. For if the Christian alone has true faith and hope, then charity must be reserved only for the Christian as well. Which removes it from practical morality, for that is open to all, as, indeed, Judaism recognizes in acknowledging righteous gentiles.

We move even further from practical morality when we come to St. Augustine's interpretation of love of neighbor, which took off directly from St. Paul's but extended it in a philosophical direction, one not present in the latter's religious theology. St. Augustine theorized the concept of "love" on the basis of the metaphysical doctrines of Plato and the neo-Platonists, particularly Plotinus. Love is no longer a purely human sentiment or a practical issue but is treated as ultimately a metaphysical principle governing the universe. All things are bound by love. Thus, in St. Augustine, Christian philosophy takes its first decisive step toward its eventual core metaphysical doctrine that God is Love.

St. Augustine's treatment of love as a moral issue falls into three aspects: love of God, love of self, and love of neighbor. Of the three, love of neighbor has least independence and force. It is more or less subsumed into true love of self, which in turn is taken up into love of God. Putting it crudely, one might say that God and self are far more real for St. Augustine than the neighbor. This seems to be the upshot of an extensive treatment of St. Augustine's doctrine of love in Hannah Arendt's thesis, which she wrote as a young student under Heidegger and Jaspers and subsequently revised a decade or so before her death, though she never saw to its publication. It would be all too easy to impute one's own meaning into a work that is extraordinarily difficult to read, especially in translation. However, there is no doubt that the one and only critical comment, a long footnote inserted in the later revision, seems to support the case we are making here.[36]

With that, we conclude our initial treatment of Western morality, whose further developments we shall study later. Even in its widest extension in Christianity, this morality was always limited in one key respect: it was bound to love of neighbor where this neighbor can be only a fellow human being. Despite its lofty metaphysical vision, as in St. Augustine, and despite its universal affirmation that God is Love, in a practical sense there was never any call to love animals and the rest of sentient Nature. Perhaps some of the mystical sentiments about Nature and God's creatures expressed by St. Francis might be read as the almost sole exception. Certainly, there was never any concerted call in the West to stop the slaughter of animals for food, for animals were always seen as serving the human purpose for which God made them and not as existing autonomously in their own right. In this respect Western morality has preached and practiced a more exclusive conception of love. Because it was based on a much more inclusive conception of the living unity of all living creatures, Eastern morality took a quite different view of love and a very different approach to the killing of animals.

Eastern morality is as much an ethic of love as is Western. In its historically most important version, Buddhism, love is also propounded as the basis of all moral action. However, Buddhistic *maitri* is very different from Christian *caritas*. An earlier commentator, Washburn Hopkins, expresses the difference as follows:

> It differs from the aggressive love which inspires the Christian missionary; but it is philanthrophic enough to send the Buddhist missionary over the earth to preach the new gospel. Later Buddhism, reflecting the Buddha's own sacrifice of immediate felicity to save the world, made for itself a similar ideal and imitated Buddha in copying his self-sacrificing spirit. But this did not affect the general Buddhist conception of all-embracing "love" (real kindness) as a means of reaching perfection.[37]

The opposite of love, namely hatred, must be completely eschewed, as must desire in general. Instead kindly feeling is to be sought, full of meditative calm and patience.

The practical expression of love in Buddhism is the willingness to sacrifice oneself for others—all others irrespective of caste, rank, or power. The famous Buddhist legend of King Siri tells of how he gave his eyes to a blind beggar. This active sense of devotion to all beings is morally even more distinctive than the doctrine and practice of non-injury, which is not unique to Buddhism alone but is prefigured in earlier Brahmanism and taken to an extreme by the coeval Jain cult, for which even the killing of insects is forbidden.

The crowning moral achievement of Buddhism—in which respect it seems to be unique among all the early religions and can be deemed on this one point morally superior to all Western creeds—is that it preached tolerance for other religions and ethics. Thus King Ashoka records in his Rock and Pillar Edicts the following statement:

> His Majesty does reverance to men of all sects . . . by donation and other modes of reverence. . . . A man should not do reverence to his own sect by disparaging that of another man for trivial reasons. . . . The sects of other people deserve reverence. By respecting another's sect one exalts one's own sect. . . . by acting contrariwise one hurts one's own sect.[38]

Such a sentiment is not to be found in any Western ethics till the liberal Enlightenment; it would have been abhorrent to every Judaic morality, including Christianity. No Western king or ruler, no matter how otherwise pious, would have been capable of or have been required to publicly express his sorrow and regret over victory in war leading to the conquest of a heathen people and, presumably, their conversion, as Ashoka did:

> His majesty feels remorse on account of this conquest of the Kalingas. . . . Because of the slaughter caused, death, and the taking away of the people. He feels sorrow and regret. . . . Though one should do him an injury His Majesty now holds that it must be patiently born, so far as it can possibly be born.[39]

The contrast between Western and Eastern morality is one major theme that preoccupied Max Weber in his various writings. His main intent is to establish differences, not to draw parallels, for his thesis of the rise of economic rationalism out of a religious ethic in the West—but not in the East, where any such tendencies were blocked—predisposes him to see contrasts and not likenesses. Thus it is possible to criticize him on this score, as we shall see some contemporary scholars doing. Nevertheless, his remarks constitute an indispensable introduction to any comparative study of morality.

Weber's initial contrast focuses on the quality of love as found in Buddhism and the Judaic religions, particularly Christianity:

The concept of neighbourly love, at least in the sense of the great Christian virtu-osi of brotherliness, is unknown [in Buddhism]. . . . The mystic, acosmic love of Buddhism *(maitri, meta)* is psychologically conditioned through the euphoria of apathetic ecstasy. This love and "unbounded feeling" for men and animals like that of a mother for her child gives the holy man a magical soul-compelling power over his enemies as well. His temper remains cool and aloof in this.[40]

According to Weber, love in Buddhism is cultivated not as an active emo-tional drive, as an outer-directed impulse to moral action, but rather as an inward state of bliss and perfection, a kind of state of grace: "The Buddhistic caritas is characterised by the same impersonality and matter-of-factness as Jainism and, in another manner, also that of Puritanism. . . . the personal *certitudo salutis* not the welfare of the neighbour is at issue."[41] The aim of Buddhistic love is thus to free the monk who seeks salvation—"always a personal act of the single individual," as Weber reminds us—from involve-ment with the mundane world, rather than to compel him to inner-worldly activity:

The *arhat* who has reached the goal of the methodical, contemplative ecstasy is *karma-free* and feels himself replete with a strong and delicate (objectless and de-sireless) love, free from earthly pride and Philistine self-righteousness, but pos-sessed by an unshakeable self-confidence which guarantees a lasting state of grace, free from fear, sin and deception, free from yearning for the world and—above all—for life in the hereafter.[42]

From this basic opposition in their conception of love follow all the other differences separating Eastern from Western moralities. Thus we are told by Weber that "the love of enemies is necessarily quite foreign to Buddhism. Its quietism could not stand such virtuoso powers of self-domination, but only the equanimity of not hating one's enemies. . . ."[43] But in the light of King Ashoka's regard for the Kalingas, his enemies, it would not appear that the contrast drawn has much significance in practical affairs. Similarly, we are told that "Buddhism knows of no consistent concept of 'conscience' and cannot know it because of the *karma* doctrine substructuring the Buddhistic denial of the idea of personality."[44] But this, too, is undercut by Weber's admission that Buddhism does have a sense of sin, though he explicitly dis-tinguishes it from the Christian sense of sin:

A concept of sin based on an ethic of intentions is as little congenial to Buddhism as it was for Hinduism in general. Certainly there were sins for Buddhist monks, even deadly sins which excluded the offender forever from fellowship. And there were sins which only required penance.[45]

Unless one were to read the phrase "a concept of sin based on an ethic of intention" in a particularly restrictive sense as referring only to Christianity, it would not appear possible to deny to Buddhism a sense of sin constitutive of conscience any more than to Judaism.

Weber is intent on denying Buddhist morality the capacity to develop an embracing social ethic and thereby to order all of social life in a rational way:

> A sense of "social" responsibility resting on a social ethic which operates with the idea of the "infinite" value of the individual human "soul" must be as remote as possible from a salvation doctrine, which, in any value emphasis upon the "soul" could discern only the grand and pernicious basic illusion. Also the specific form of Buddhist "altruism," universal compassion, is merely one of the stages which sensitivity passes when seeing through the nonsense of the struggle for existence of all individuals in the wheel of life, a sign of progressive intellectual enlightenment, not, however, an expression of active brotherliness.[46]

Hence Weber concludes disparagingly that "unlike later Christian ethic, Buddhistic monastic ethic simply does not represent a rational ethical endeavour supported by special gifts of grace to surpass 'inner-worldly' ethical conduct as channelled in the social order, but it takes precisely the opposite direction, principally an asocial course."[47] But somewhat in contradiction to this conclusion, Weber has to allow that out of Buddhist morality, King Ashoka developed what looks exactly like a social ethic—in fact, one of the most pronounced examples of the ethic of a social welfare state in history: "with this pacificistic-religious turn from the traditional kingly *dharma* came, as could not be otherwise, the development toward a patriarchal ethical and charitable ideal of a welfare state."[48] In other words, a "sense of social responsibility resting on a social ethic" could just as well originate from Buddhistic as from any other morality, provided that the social and political conditions were appropriate.

As is well known and needs no elaboration here, Weber's whole thesis regarding ethics and religion is to counterpose East and West somewhat in line with the fundamental predisposition of his time. Though, of course, Weber is as above crude prejudices as it is possible for an intellectual to be, nevertheless a basic feeling that "East is East and West is West and never the twain will meet" can be detected in his determination to distinguish the two moralities. The main basis for this distinction is his separation of the two kinds of prophecies: ethical and exemplary. The terms of this in themselves seem to be denying ethical prophecy to the East. This, as we have shown, works itself out in his account of Buddhist morality.

Weber's contraposition of Eastern and Western moralities has been criticized by contemporary scholars, especially by exponents of Buddhism, such as Gananath Obeyesekere. He is particularly insistent that Buddhism is not just a religion of personal salvation but also a morality of love, precisely of love of one's neighbor and even love of one's enemy, which is what Weber explicitly denies it.[49] Obeyesekere does not deny that a personal *certitudo salutis* is crucial in Buddhism, but he insists that this is not at the expense of love of neighbor. If, indeed, it is the primary object of the religious devotee, there is, nevertheless, also a secondary one of nearly equal importance: spreading the faith in saving others and the institution of a lay community of mutual help and support. It is arguable whether this is enough to constitute love of neighbor in the Western moral sense, but it is sufficient to show that the differences are not as large as Weber supposed.

As opposed to Weber, Obeyesekere is more intent on affirming the likenesses and not the differences between Western and Eastern morality. He does, of course, recognize the obvious contrasts. The Judaic prophets and the Indian prophets—above all, the Buddha—distinguish themselves from each other in terms of the transcendent basis of their moral mission, the former speaking in the name of the one true God, the latter being indifferent to the gods and enunciating a self-declared path to salvation. Nevertheless, the ethical reformist zeal of both was the same. Both strove to carry through a process of ethicization so as to critically revise a priestly cultic traditional religion in terms of a new moral awareness. In both, there occurred "ein Prozess in welchem die Sozialmoral unauflösbar mit der religiösen Moral verkoppelt wird."[50] The key aspect in the formulation of such a social morality was the interrelation, always a particularly close one, between the community of monks and the lay society. The moral demands made on the former were much more stringent than on the latter, but, nevertheless, practical moral requirements were imposed on lay people as well, such as the five commandments of Buddhism. As in all the great Western moral religions, so, too, in Buddhism "ist das moralische Leben der Gesellschaft systematisch in die Religion einbezogen, so dass jede Verletzung eines soziales Gebots gleichzeitig die Verletzung eines religiösen Gebots bedeutet und für das Individuum 'Sünde' ist."[51] Such a process of ethicization is part and parcel of the ever-more embracing process of rationalization in Weber's sense.

This disagreement between Weber and Obeyesekere is many faceted; it is both conceptual and historical. Both are agreed that the two concepts of Christian and Buddhistic love, *caritas* and *maitri*, differ in quality, but just what this difference amounted to in practice at various periods is in dispute. For our purposes, it is not necessary to follow it through further. It is typical of all such contentions between Weber and contemporary specialists. Weber might have overemphasized some things and might have got some details wrong, but the specialists are unable to allow that such corrections do not touch the overall validity of his theory. It is also a failing of contemporary academic specialization that it has led to the virtually total neglect of Weber as an ethical thinker. What Weber has to say about ethics, which is extremely extensive and important, has generally been discounted, especially by ethical philosophers, because it has been consigned to the department of sociology where he is located by academic convention. And the sociologists themselves are not interested enough in ethics to make proper use of his work in this regard.

Weber's own ethical orientation tends toward a secularized version of a puritan ethics of vocation, which we can view as a late and sophisticated version of an ethics of duty. He himself defends what he calls the "ethics of responsibility," which he opposes to the "ethics of absolute ends." Both these "ethics" are intended by Weber as formal Kantian principles governing the relationship between ends, means, and consequences, such that the ethic of absolute ends places priority on the rightness of ends and means and disregards consequences, whereas the ethic of responsibility takes consequences into account and is prepared to compromise to some extent the purity of ends and means. Seen from a purely formal point of view, this does not necessarily privilege any one substantive ethics over any other. Nevertheless, the way that Weber invokes it in practice tends to go against a specifically moral point of view in both its original religious and subsequent secular manifestations. Weber's espousal of a multiplicity of fundamental values, which he calls the new "polytheism" of gods and demons, at the expense of "the one thing needful" of Christian morality, also reveals a tendency to be critical of morality.[52] In this respect he was following Nietzsche, whose influence he acknowledged.

Nietzsche was the most implacable and intemperate critic of morality in the whole history of Western thought, Machiavelli notwithstanding. His criticisms have been extremely influential on intellectuals and artists ever since. From Thomas Mann and D. H. Lawrence to Michel Foucault and Gilles Deleuze, a whole line of writers has been touched by them. However, of even more serious consequence was the impact of his "immoralist" doctrines on the extremist political movements of Fascism and Nazism; he was Hitler's favorite philosopher and the most influential thinker within the Nazi ideological dispensation. Nietzsche's attack on the morality of Jews and Christians and his so-called "genealogy of morals" thesis was the anticipatory intellectual expression of the revolt against the whole Western moral tradition that has had such fatal consequences in this last century.

Some of the central points of Nietzsche's genealogy thesis are, indeed, quite correct; there is a crucial distinction to be drawn between morality and other ethical systems; but, unfortunately, Nietzsche has tendentiously misinterpreted the real difference by casting it as the opposition between a supposed slave morality and a master morality, rather than presenting it neutrally as that between different kinds of ethics. Nietzsche is also correct in seeing morality, his so-called slave morality, as having both a Western Judeo-Christian version and an Eastern Buddhist one; in this he was following a lead given by Schopenhauer. But as opposed to his philosophical mentor, he turns against both kinds of morality, though against the latter with nowhere near as much fury and venom as against the former. In opposition to Judeo-Christian slave morality, he wishes to resurrect what he calls "master morality." This is very poorly defined and consists of an indiscriminate assortment of principles and practices derived from many heterogenous sources: from the civic ethics, the aristocratic ethics of honor and soldierly ethics of duty, as well as elements drawn from the heroic ethos of all kinds of people—above all, the Homeric Greeks. What all these have in common, at best, is that they exemplify the ethos of ruling elites or "masters" in Nietzsche's terminology. But that in itself is not enough to constitute any kind of coherent type.

His critique of morality is, however, worth taking more seriously. His supposition that morality is an ethic of slaves or pariah people or even exclusively of subordinate strata is historically insupportable. The Jews were initially in no such position, at least in their own land, and rarely, if at all, even in exile. The Christians drew support from the start from all levels of Roman society. Hence Nietzsche's idea that morality is the outcome of the *ressentiment* of slaves against their masters is without historical foundation. The idea of *ressentiment* leading to an inversion of values—such that the slave morality's "evil" is formed by inverting the master morality's "good"—is also without historical basis.[53] The concept of "evil" is there in Genesis at the very start of the biblical narrative, as Buber has shown. It is defined in terms of the disobedience of divine sanctions or transgression of autonomous norms that is quite distinct from and indifferent to any exterior conceptions of good. Nietzsche's notion that so-called slave morality is parasitic on master morality is his own interpretative concoction designed to discredit morality. Morality is no more dependent on other ethics than they are dependent on it. Nietzsche asserts a half-truth when he intemperately declares that "morality is in Europe today herd-animal morality—that is to say, as we understand the thing, only *one* kind of human morality beside which, before which, and after which many other, above all higher moralities, are possible or ought to be possible."[54] He is quite correct in insisting that morality is only one extant ethic, beside which, before which, and perhaps even after which other ethics are also possible (whether these rate as higher or lower is a dubious issue). But it is not true that morality is any more "herd-animal" than any other ethic, for all are equally social codes for the control and guidance of individual conduct.

Nietzsche's hatred of morality is prompted above all by his aversion to guilt and conscience. He wishes to restore humanity to a state of innocence, the innocence of paganism before the fall into monotheistic religion. The main source of moral guilt, according to Nietzsche, is a feeling of indebtedness (here he etymologically plays on the literal meaning of the German *Schuld*) toward God, which grows, as if it were a capital debt, by compound interest. It increases as the one God supplants all other gods and becomes more exclusive. Eventually, "the advent of the Christian God as the maximal god yet achieved, thus also brought about the appearance of the greatest feeling of guilt on earth."[55] The only release from this accumulated burden of guilt is atheism:

> we should be justified in deducing, with no little probability, that there is, even now, a considerable decline in the consciousness of human guilt; indeed the possibility cannot be rejected out of hand that the complete and definitive victory of atheism might release humanity from this whole feeling of being indebted towards its beginnings, its *causa prima*. Atheism and a sort of second innocence belong together.[56]

Once again, it is evident that there is something right about this account of the intrinsic connection between morality and guilt but also much that is completely misconceived. It is true that morality does induce guilt, the special moral guilt called conscience, but it is not the source of guilt, which is a basic human emotion having nothing to do with indebtedness toward a god. Hence, the elimination of moral guilt or conscience—which is, indeed, very possible and has been precipitously taking place since Nietzsche's time—does not remove guilt as such or inaugurate any second state of innocence for humanity. Guilt simply assumes other forms. When people no longer have a bad conscience over moral failings, they feel guilty over other far less consequential breaches. The Nazis, who, in Nietzsche's name, sought to extirpate the guilt of Christian morality only succeeded in re-awakening the guilt of group-conformity provoked by any failure to live up to their ideological ethos of hardness and brutality.

It is, of course, undeniable that there are such things as pathologies of guilt, as there are of any other emotion. An excess of bad conscience, which can be induced by some practices of Christian morality, is indeed a harmful psychological condition that can reach extremes of psychic and even physical debilitation. The critics of morality tend to focus on such problems of guilt-consciousness. Thus the anthropologist Ruth Benedict writes as follows of the effect of Puritan morality as inculcated by New England divines:

> A sense of guilt as extreme as they portrayed and demanded both in their own conversion experiences and in those of their converts is found in a slightly saner civilization only in institutions for mental diseases. They admitted no salvation without a conviction of sin that prostrated the victim, sometimes for years, with remorse and terrible anguish. It was the duty of the minister to put the fear of hell into the heart of even the youngest child, and to exact of every convert emotional acceptance of his damnation if God saw fit to damn him.[57]

Certainly, when moral guilt reaches this pitch, it has taken a pathological turn and any kind of release is desirable. But this does not mean that all sense of moral guilt or conscience has to be extirpated or that it is possible to return to a pre-moral state of innocence, such as that in which the Samoan Polynesians were assumed to be by Margaret Mead. Such anthropological fantasies of a return to the Garden of Eden in the tropical islands have played havoc with all our inherited moral motions. They have now become the commercialized enticements of tourism to exotic places.

Almost in line with Nietzsche's prescription, the elimination of moral guilt has become a constant preoccupation of many of the therapeutic agencies of contemporary society. The psychological clinicians, beginning with the psychoanalysts, treat their patients as if they were all suffering from extreme Puritan guilt-complexes and encourage them to believe that guilt is only part of their disease. The social care agencies avoid moral blame or the making of moral demands altogether, so that moral responsibility is not called for and criminals are considered victims of their bad social circumstances.

Whether morality can survive these and many other kinds of contemporary onslaughts is uncertain. It is possible that a complete demoralization will eventually ensue. It is also possible, as Nietzsche hoped, that another type of ethics might supplant it. One thing is clear, however: that a return to anything like Nietzsche's master morality is highly unlikely. Anything sound in it was largely modeled on the classical Greek civic ethics. The disasters that the all-too-recent attempts to realize such a model in practice have proved themselves to be, for the Fascist and Nazi "experiments" in ethics are still green in memory, make it improbable that such a thing will be tried again so soon.

The civic ethics in other, less militant, forms still survives in a fragmentary state. It is an aspect of the Western classical heritage. Once upon a time it was of crucial importance, for next to morality it was the key component of Western ethics. For two thousand years it entered into all kinds of relations with morality, sometimes of conflict and sometimes of complementarity. To understand the reasons for this, we must establish its basic character by undertaking a kind of Nietzschean genealogical study of its origins.

The Civic Ethics

The civic ethics is a specifically Western ethics. It had a unique origin in the Greek polis and from there its influence spread to all other cities that were heirs to the traditions of Greek classicism. The time of its widest extent was during the Hellenistic and early Roman eras. During the later part of the Roman imperial period, it was challenged by many "Oriental" religious ethics, the foremost of which was Christian morality. The struggle between the two constitutes a large part of Western ethical history. In one form or another, the civic ethics survived and maintained itself throughout Western history, as did so much else of the classical heritage. It could always be appealed to by those who were averse to morality. In this section we shall disregard its later manifestations and concentrate solely on its original form in the polis.

In its original polis form it is an ethic of devotion to one's native city. The highest virtue was readiness to die for one's city and to sacrifice everything for its welfare and glory. This is typified by the apocryphal saying attributed to Spartan mothers, who told their sons leaving for war: "Either come back with your shield or upon it"—the point being that a hoplite fleeing from the field of battle would be likely to dispose of his shield. Roman mothers and fathers were no less severe in legend with their sons; death is preferable to disgrace, and many are the tales of fathers condemning their own sons to death because they had failed in some particular the cause of the city. Death is also redeeming, hence the Roman saying, "dulce et decorum est pro patria mori." In Athens, Pericles' great funeral oration puts the point in a more moderate way. *Philopolis* is the greatest value. Those who have proven it by dying for their city are excused all other failings. The dead are all glorified in death, provided their death was glorious. These same sentiments, we must remember, were repeated by Abraham Lincoln in his Gettysburg address, which goes to show just how persistent they were in the Western classical tradition of ethical discourse. It is a tradition dedicated to glorious death.

In later expressions of the civic ethics, the love of one's city features as the more general virtue of patriotism, the love of one's country, regardless of whether one is in it or not. *Philopolis* was much more specific and only held for as long as one was an active citizen in one particular city, almost invariably the city of one's birth. In Greek there was no need for such a special term as *patriotism*, for it was simply taken for granted that every citizen was completely bound to his city and at its disposal with all his means. The supreme proof of that was readiness to die for one's city.

The obverse side of this total devotion to the city as long as one was in it and of it was the readiness to go against it and betray it as soon as one was out of it. This was especially so if one lost one's citizenship through ostracism or for some other such reason had to flee one's city, for there was no requirement or expectation that one will continue to love one's city once one has been forced to abandon it and lives in exile from it. As the Roman legend of Coriolanus exemplifies, those who were exiled could turn to the enemies of their city and plot and fight against it. The reality behind the legend is the actual behavior of many ostricized leaders, including some of the greatest from Athens and even Sparta, such as Themistocles and Pausanias. The ethic applies only as long as one is, so to speak, on "active duty"; otherwise, it lapses. In this respect the civic ethics contrasts with morality, for it is always conditional and city-specific, as it were, whereas morality is unconditional and universal; it holds forever under all circumstances.

There are many other fundamental differences between the civic ethics and morality that need to be brought out. Morality is based on presumed-to-be-eternal sacred norms that are unalterable. There is nothing sacrosanct about the civic ethics. It requires absolute obedience to laws, but these are alterable in every respect, provided the proper constitutional forms are followed—that is, if the citizens agree in common. That is the gist of the Roman adage "vox populi, vox dei." In fact, the gods are hardly involved at all. Whatever favor they enjoy, they owe to the laws that oblige the citizens to participate formally in the required official city cults. Apart from this, the citizens are not bound by the civic religion; their consciences are free and they are at liberty to follow their own private religions and the appropriate ethics these entail. Conscience only plays a part in the civic ethics in a largely formal sense, in that guilt was incurred by breaches of the law. A deep sense of guilt in transgression, a sense of sin of this anguished kind, was not inculcated.

What was above all inculcated was adhesion to the unique polis way of life, which the civic ethic was designed to uphold. This is what was meant by teaching devotion to the city. To induce the sentiments of this way of living, a very intense educational regimen, *paideia*, was instituted. Its burden was to instill the main precepts of the civic ethics and the rudiments of civic virtue. As Plato puts it in his *Laws*, *paideia* is "the education from childhood in virtue, that makes one desire and love to become a perfect citizen who knows how to rule and be ruled with justice."[58] As we shall soon see, the notions of "law," "justice," and "ruling," and to some extent even those of "desire" and "love," are key features of this ethics, which might, therefore, be considered predominantly a political ethic, as opposed to morality, which is religious. Indeed, it is only the elevated, sublimated, and rational nature of these conceptions that is decisive in defining this as an ethics rather than simply a civic ethos. As we shall soon show, each of these notions was to receive a highly abstract philosophical conceptualization in the context of treatises that we cannot but regard as ethical. Seen etymologically, the term does not properly apply to anything else.

Paideia was not only concerned with ethical virtues, it dealt with all the aspects of the art of living in a polis. Much of it emphasized physical prowess, through hunting, athletic exercises and games, and artistic capabilities, especially in music, poetry, and drama. Rhetoric played a key part in preparation for an eventual inevitable political role. To what extent homoerotic love was involved is a contentious issue among scholars that it is unnecessary to raise here. Certainly, *paideia* also required teaching of the appropriate social roles, among these that of the relation of older to younger men. But above all, it was concerned with educating young men to eventually take their part in city life as full citizens and assume the duties of military and political life and thereby the full burden of the city laws.

The fundamental feature of the civic ethics is obedience to city law (*nomos*). There are many sayings that attest to the recognition of this, such as Heraklitus' dictum that "the people must fight for law as for a rampart" and the lines from Pindar: "Law, sure foundation stone of cities, dwells with Justice and Peace, dispenser of wealth to man." Herodotus relates the story that on being asked by the Persian king who is the ruler of his people, a Spartan answers "law, which they fear more than thy people fear thee." Simonides' couplet eulogizing the Spartans under Leonidas who fell at Thermopylae bears this out:

> O stranger, bear this message to the Spartans:
> We lie here in obedience to their law.

The conception of law was not, however, the same in all cities; it had undergone a gradual evolution from that of Sparta to that of Athens and later to that of imperial Rome. In Sparta there was a highly traditionalistic and semi-sacred attitude to the polis constitution, which was supposedly the creation of a semi-divine mythical law-giver, Lykurgus. The deliberative decisions of the political authorities, the assembly of citizens and the "kings," so-called, also commanded total obedience. In archaic Rome, even right down to late Republican times, there was an analogous attitude. In Athens, however, this began to change at least from the time of Solon and would continue changing from then on, partly also under the impact of the new philosophies that became influential at the time of Pericles. On this view, law is no longer based simply on the charismatic enunciation of an authority figure, a law-giver, but on principles of justice and wisdom. Solon distinguishes between *disnomia* and *eunomia* and asserts that "*eunomia* makes everything orderly and as it should be, and often fetters the unjust."[59] Thus, in the Athenian conception, the law that commands obedience is the just and wise law, not the law as such. This is reflected in Sophocles' play *Antigone,* where Creon, the ruler who insists that his word is law and that it must be obeyed regardless—"You must obey the ruler whom the city sets/Above you, even in little things, just and unjust"—is clearly shown up as displaying the attitude of a tyrant. A Hobbsian view of law as the deliverance of the Sovereign will, though perhaps already mooted by one or another of the Sophists, was not acceptable to conservative Athenians such as Sophocles.

There are, of course, many different forms of law and civic law is only one among these, differing fundamentally from sacred law, common law, royal statute law, and legislative state law, such as we have at present. According to Max Weber, civic law was an important stage in the process of rationalization of law making and judicial procedure. It evolved from a charismatic conception of law as issuing from a legislator, such as Lykurgus or even Solon, to the far more rational one of law as the deliberative decision of the assembly of citizens. This stage was reached when the demos captured power in Athens and allied cities and set about democratizing law-making. Weber describes the change that ensued as follows:

> Correlated therewith was a changed concept of the nature of law. The law was transformed into institutionalized form applying to the burghers and inhabitants of the city area as such. . . . Simultaneously it increasingly became a rational statute-law rather than an irrational charismatic judicature. . . . But soon the new creation of permanent laws was accepted. In fact new legislation by the *ecclesia* became so usual as to produce a state of continuous flux. . . . The creation of law reached such a fluid state that eventually in Athens the question was directed yearly to the people whether existing laws should be maintained. Thus it became

an accepted premise that the law is artificially created and that it should be based upon the approval of those to whom it will apply.[60]

As Weber is careful to point out, "this conception did not become omnipotent in classical antiquity." Even in Athens at the height of democracy, "not every decision (*psephisma*) of the *demos* was law (*nomos*) even if it contained general rules."[61] Such decisions could always be appealed by citizens before a jury. Nevertheless, the general tenor of the development is toward rational law-making. It is the people, rather than the gods—that is, ancient traditions—who decide what is the law. In other words, the citizens determine what is to be the content of the civic ethics. And as the laws will differ from city to city, so the content of the ethic—that is, what is right or wrong, what ought to be done—will also differ. What alone is constant is the injunction that the law must be obeyed.

But even in that respect there were evolving changes. At first in the earliest period, as in Sparta, the law could not even be questioned or doubted. But later, as in Athens, the issue begins to be raised whether the existing laws are just or unjust. Thus the question of justice stands next to law as the fundamental issue of the civic ethics.

All the leading poets and thinkers who express this ethic, from Tyrtaeus to Aristotle, are preoccupied with justice. We are told by Dodds that "the proverbial saying popular in that age, that 'all virtue is comprehended in justice,' applies no less to gods than to men."[62] The chief of the gods, Zeus, became "an embodiment of cosmic justice."[63] Justice was the main theme of Athenian drama, most notably at the conclusion of Aeschylus' trilogy, in the *Eumenides*, where the archaic lawless world of vengeance and demons is "transformed through Athena's agency into the new world of rational justice."[64]

At the heart of the issue of justice is the question concerning the nature and status of law, and why it ought to be obeyed by the citizens. The good man, the *agathos polites*, is the just man, the one who is himself *diskaios* and who is fortunate enough to live in a good city where the laws are just. Beyond that comprehension of justice the civic ethics does not reach. Everything else in it—both the virtues that pertain to the good man and the constitution of the good city—are derived from this conception of justice. Even at its most theoretically sophisticated, as in Plato's *Republic*, the civic ethics remains bound to these presuppositions.

We can study historically the various stages of the questioning of the law, which are also the stages in the transformation of the meaning of justice. To begin with, at the start of the polis culture, the law remains unquestioned.

For Tyrtaeus, who lived in seventh-century Sparta, the law as such is assumed to be just. As Adkins puts it, "*Eunomia* is used to commend a condition of good order in the state, *dusnomia* to decry civic disorder: the terms themselves do not imply that the laws themselves are good or bad."[65] Tyrtaeus—writing under the stress of the Messenian wars when Sparta was threatened by rebellion—is most intent on law and order as such, but Xenophanes in Colophon and Solon in Athens were more concerned with civil strife. Hence, they "wish to improve the organization of their respective states."[66] *Eunomia* for them stands for legislative reform: "*eunomia* will subdue *hubris*."[67] Theognis of Megara has an analogous conception of justice, and he goes on to give it an explicitly ethical meaning. He sums up the whole of the civic ethic in terms of it: "The whole of *arete* is summed up in *diskaiosune*; every man, Cyrnus, is *agathos* if he is *diskaios*."[68] Adkins comments that Theognis "is claiming that *anyone* who is *diskaios* is also *agothos*; and this smashes the whole framework of Homeric values."[69]

Homeric values and the whole heroic warrior ethos enshrined in the Homeric poems are themselves largely pre-ethical, as Adkins and other scholars have already amply demonstrated. Nevertheless, this is the ethos out of which the civic ethics derives and which it still continues, albeit in a transformed form. Thus, for example, the whole vocabulary of ethical terms in the civic ethics is already present in Homer, but in their later usage their meanings have subtly changed. We can illustrate this by examining the etymological origins of the key term *justice*, which to begin with had to do with stable order, not with ethics, as Sparshott shows:

> *Dikaiosuné*, "justice," is a noun derived from the adjective *dikaios*, "just," which means someone with a penchant for *"diké."* *Diké* means recompense for an offense against hierarchical and topographical order—in short, for the violation of boundaries. It also stands for the system that is thus violated. "Justice" as thus conceived becomes a word for the stable virtue of established societies, as opposed to the heroic virtue of individuals and chieftains.[70]

It is thus evident why it is this particular term that was so decisively taken over into the polis culture as the foundation of its ethical structure, one that became ever more removed from its pre-ethical Homeric origins. As Sparshott puts it in slightly different terms, "The exaltation of justice and the law was the mainstay of the 'bourgeois' morality that had replaced the status-values of archaic feudalism, and which Plato and Aristotle were, in effect, seeking to perfect by incorporating aristocratic ideals into it."[71]

The work of Adkins shows clearly how and how far the Homeric terms of commendation and blame had changed in the polis culture. These are words such as the "noun *arete*, with the adjective *agathos*, its synonyms *esthlos* and *chrestos*, the comparative *ameinon* and *beltion*, and the superlatives *aristos* and *beltistos* [which] are the most powerful words of commendation used of a man in Homer and in later Greek."[72] But in Homer "what is commended by these terms is firstly military prowess, and the skills which promote success in war, together with that success which is indistinguishable in Homer from the skills that contribute to it."[73] There is nothing ethical about any of this. Thus, "to say of an action 'it is *agathos* (*kakon*) to do X' is simply to say it is beneficial or harmful to do X, without passing any moral judgement on the rightness or wrongness of X."[74] It is not as yet very different for Tyrtaeus in the seventh century, for whom the highest virtues are competence and valor in war. However, once *agathos* is interpreted as *agathos polites*, the good citizen, as it became in later Athenian usage, then an ethical dimension began to emerge. For this usage "relates the *agathos* overtly to his city" and implicitly moves toward making *dikaiosune* a defining property of the *agathos*, "since most people would not consider 'the good citizen is just (law-abiding)' to be an analytic proposition and some might hold that it expressed an identity."[75]

This identity of the good citizen and the just man never became explicit till the later philosophers. What delayed it were two developments that weakened the Athenian sense of justice and law-abidingness: first, democratization and empire building revealed not only that the law was variable but that it could be changed at will to serve one's interests; second, the teachings of the Sophists, which opposed law (*nomos*) to nature (*phusis*), gave the law a purely utilitarian instrumental value. This led to a resurgence of what might be called Homeric values in late fifth-century Athens; in this situation "actions are evaluated primarily in terms of a system of values which raises only questions of success and failure."[76] The *agathos polites* is not seen in ethical terms as the just man, but rather as the man who "is expected to help his friends and harm his enemies within the city."[77] Thus, according to the so-called immoralists, such as Callicles and Thrasymachus, virtue is "skill devoted to securing personal prosperity, their own and their friends' success in politics, and the prosperity of their city in which, it is assumed, they and their friends will be dominant politically."[78]

However, in the longer term both these tendencies that seem so antithetical to ethical development, the cynicism of the Sophists and the political-realism of empire builders and statesmen, such as those portrayed in Thucydides, were crucial stages in the rise of the later philosophical ethics, with its more rationally developed conception of justice. This remains the key term throughout the whole history of Athenian debates on ethics, as these evolved from the earliest, barely ethical stages till the final intellectual expression of the civic ethic in the work of Plato and Aristotle, which is ethics in the philosophical sense.

The course of the debate and the disputes involved in it, with all their varying parties, can be followed in the works of the Athenian dramatists Aeschylus, Sophocles, and Euripides. In Aeschylus, the earliest, there is a clear and forceful, but as yet unquestioning, affirmation of the civic ethic as embodied in civic law as against a pre-ethical older ethos of blood-vengeance and blood-pollution. In the later Sophocles, difficulties begin to be perceived in an unrestrained civic law issuing from the arbitrary will of the civic authority, and refuge is sought in traditional religious restraints and checks that are presented as quasi-universal standards. In the latest, Euripides, the difficulties with the whole civic system of the polis are much more apparent and seemingly irresolvable; and civic ethics itself comes into question as Euripides' implicit critique of it reveals what such an ethic disregards and represses and why, therefore, it is liable to release irrational forces of ferocity that lead to tragic results. Thus the Athenian debate moved from the justice of simply obeying the laws to the justice of the laws themselves.

This set the stage for Socrates. For once the justice of the laws came into question, then the higher issue was raised, by what standards and criteria could the laws be judged? Furthermore, the question arose of how one could tell a just from an unjust city. It is true that the Sophists had already raised such matters, "they had raised and discussed questions like the source of authority of the laws and the nature of society," as Julia Annas states.[79] But they had asked such questions more in a theoretical skeptical spirit, not with the full existential intensity of Socrates, which made him the initiator of later ethical philosophy. It was Socrates who established ethical philosophy as a way of life—the questioning, searching, argumentative, dialectical life of the philosopher that, even though it took place in the marketplace alongside the ordinary citizen, went beyond that of the citizen to attain a higher sense of justice and virtue. Nevertheless, the basic conception of justice as obedience to the laws, inherent in the very nature of the civic ethic, was never abandoned by Socrates. Indeed, he proved himself a martyr to this conception, for by his voluntary submission to the law of Athens and its judicial verdict, even when this was patently unjust, he affirmed the primacy of the law above all other considerations.

Socrates' preoccupation with justice was definitive for both Plato and Aristotle. In the *Republic* Plato sets himself the primary task as defining the concept of "justice." Out of this attempt emerges the model of a just city and of the just men who live in it. This is to serve as an ideal standard for judging the justice of every existing city, including his native Athens. In this way his philosophy claims to have provided for the very first time a rational measure of justice. Using this as his criterion, he unequivocally condemns democratic Athens as the next most unjust city, barely above the very worst, that of tyranny. It seems, therefore, unlikely that he could recommend unqualified obedience to the laws of Athens, as his teacher Socrates had done. In affirming and demonstrating a higher law of justice, he implicitly allows that the existing law may be justifiably disobeyed, in something like the way Sophocles had shown in *Antigone*, but for rational rather than traditionally religious reasons.

Aristotle was not an Athenian, and he had no compunction in fleeing from the law of Athens when it seemed as if the Athenians were about "to sin for a second time." But his ethical theory is as much centered on justice as is that of his Athenian predecessors. This is perhaps not so obvious in his surviving works, which are largely edited lecture notes, and might have been more apparent in his earlier now lost books, which were explicitly on justice. But even though his main ethical work, the *Nicomachean Ethics*, does not begin with justice but with happiness, *eudaimonia*, and virtue, *arete*, it is justice that is of crucial concern and holds the central place even in that work, as will be presently apparent. The virtues are necessary for they make for good citizens, who in turn make just laws. But the virtues are only operative in the context of the legal-political system of the polis; that is, they cannot be considered on their own in isolation from the whole question of justice, which is much more than just another virtue. This is the reason that Aristotle's surviving ethical writings must be read together with his political ones; they do not make proper sense on their own.

This is how Sparshott reads Aristotle's main ethical work. He points to Aristotle's insistence "that a good human life cannot be lived outside a civic structure,"[80] for there can be "no real justice outside the very special context of a city ruled by law."[81] It "requires explicit law and the impersonal authority to enforce the law"; hence, "justice exists only among those who have an equal (or proportionate) share in ruling and being ruled." Thus for Aristotle, "justice proper has no reality outside the legal order, one cannot appeal against that order to some 'higher' justice."[82] In this respect Aristotle differs from Plato and later schools of ethical philosophy, especially the Stoics, and because of this he provides the most faithful theoretical account of the civic ethics as it actually existed, rather than seeking to change it in conformity with a higher philosophical ideal.

In Aristotle the whole content of the ethical life, "the ability to become good if one wants to, and perhaps even the project itself of leading a good life, largely depends on the sustained framework of the laws"—that is, on justice.[83] But since being a good man and leading a good life depend on an exercise of the virtues, it follows that all the virtues depend on justice. Without it and the framework of laws it presupposes, there would be no virtues. Hence, justice itself cannot be simply treated as one of the virtues, and it is, indeed, omitted from his list of virtues. But it clearly has a special role in relation to the virtues, for Aristotle designates it as "the whole of virtue in relation to others." Justice thus has an anomalous function in Aristotle's ethical system. His whole approach commits him to treating it as a virtue, yet it cannot take its place alongside the others. The only way it can be held to be a virtue at all is to give it an architectonic function as the virtue that governs the relationship between all the others in something like the way Plato set out in the *Republic*, where justice is the overall harmony of social functions and the virtues pertaining to them.

The relationship between justice and virtue is the critical problematic dimension in all the ethical philosophies that emerge out of the civic ethic. It governs the key relationships between law, politics, and ethics in this system—that is, between the good city and the good life. Since what is involved is an ethics of *civic* virtue, it is obvious that the concept of virtue invoked is one that requires law and political participation for its realization. As we previously stated, these civic virtues can only exist in the context of the polis and the laws that make it possible for men to live together—that is, to live a fully human life. Outside the polis, as Aristotle puts it, a man is either a beast or a god. The sense of virtue such as we find it in morality, where a virtuous life can be lived as a hermit in isolation or secluded in a monastery, is not in question.

The very word *virtue*—which derives from the Latin translation of the Greek *arete* and has the stem-word *vir*, "man"—connotes manly excellence. The term *arete* itself goes back prior to the civic ethics and has its etymological roots in the Homeric ethos of a heroic warrior society. In the vocabulary of commendation of that society, *arete* is what defines *agathos*; the excellences determine the good man. But none of these terms have as yet any ethical connotations, for, as Adkins insists, "what is commended by these terms is firstly military prowess, and the skills which promote success in war, together with that success which is indistinguishable in Homer for the skills that contribute to it."[84] Thus from the start, as in Homer, *arete* or virtue has to do with success and achievement, and with struggle and competition, *agon*, necessary to bring it about. As we shall show, this basic conception of *arete* would persist from the start to finish; but as the civic ethic arose and developed, so the kinds of things in which success and achievement were sought would change and gradually transform themselves into ethical virtues, but never completely so.

At the origin of the civic ethics in Sparta, the nature of *arete* had barely shifted from what it had been in Homer. Thus Tyrtaeus insists that "*agathos* must be *agathos* in war; this is *arete*."[85] That is to say, the good man is a warrior—by this stage a disciplined hoplite in a phalanx, no longer a Homeric hero, but his virtues are still military ones. However, this kind of *arete* is placed in the context of *eunomia*, the legal framework of the city, to whose defense it is dedicated. The sense of *arete* would persist for, as Adkins comments, "*arete* tends to have this predominant flavour even in fifth century Athens."[86]

However, this archaic stage of *arete* in the ethics of civil virtue was gradually transcended; that is, it was progressively more ethicized, which was done by linking it ever closer to law and justice. Thus according to Theognis of Megara, "the whole of *arete* is summed up in *diskaiosune*" (justice).[87] Also, *arete* began to subsume character qualities other than war-like prowess; intellectual abilities began to figure as well, as Xenophanes puts it, "far better than the strength of men and horses is my wisdom, *sophia*."[88] Thus step by step, as the process of ethicization proceeded, the *arete* of the Homeric *agathos* or his Spartan hoplite successor in the polis was transformed into that of the Athenian *agathos polites*, the good citizen. It is precisely in these terms that Pericles in his funeral oration contrasts the Spartan and Athenian conceptions of the *agathos*:

> There is great difference between us and our opponents. . . . There is a difference, too, in our education systems. The Spartans, from their earliest boyhood, are submitted to the most laborious training in courage; we pass our lives without all these restrictions, and yet are just as ready to face the same dangers as they are. . . .
>
> Our love of what is beautiful does not lead to extravagance; our love of the things of the mind does not make us soft. . . . We are unique in this. When we do kindnesses to others, we do not do them out of any calculation of profit or loss; we do them without afterthought, relying on our free liberality. Taking everything together then, I declare that our city is an education to Greece, and I declare that in my opinion each single one of our citizens, in all the manifold aspects of life, is able to show himself the rightful lord and owner of his own person, and do this, moreover, with exceptional grace and exceptional versatility.[89]

Yet Pericles' conception of *arete* is far from ethically consistent; it is still primarily oriented to competitive skills and success. Furthermore, Pericles supposed that all personal *arete*, the attainments of individual men, would be guided by their overriding love of the city, *politophilia*, and that their main concern would be the success and glory of their city. But this was an idealization that was far from the prevailing reality in Athens. In fact, the prevailing conception of the *agathos polites*, the good citizen, as Adkins sees it, was "inadequately civic": "the *agathos polites*, is expected to help his friends and harm his enemies within the city: thus his primary loyalties are to a group smaller than the state, in the last resort to his own family."[90] Even *dikaiosune*, justice, was on the personal level conceived merely as a means to this end; it was the well-ordered state of affairs both in the city and in the home that made for efficiency; it was linked to the *politike techne* or political skill that "entails skill in managing one's own household and in transacting affairs of state."[91] This was the sum total of *politike arete* required to be an *agathos polites* at this stage in Athens.

It was Socrates and his philosophical followers who took the ethicization process a stage further. In his various encounters with the Sophists, Socrates criticizes the older views then current that the *aretai*, the virtues or excellences, are skills, *techne*, leading to success and that the successful life is the good life. Implicitly or explicitly, as recorded in Plato's dialogues, he affirms the contrary valuations: that the good life is the happy life and that the virtues necessary for this are matters of knowledge, not of skill. His attention is mainly directed to the four canonical virtues that are ethical: wisdom, prudence, courage, and temperance.

In a slightly altered form, as wisdom, courage, temperance, and justice, these became the cardinal virtues in Plato's *Republic*. As we indicated before, the last of these, justice, is not really a virtue on par with the others; in Plato it stands for harmony of the whole city, where every caste fulfills its proper function and exercises the virtue specific to it. Unfortunately, Plato's treatment of the virtues in the *Republic* is overly schematic, for he is more intent on the overall system than on detailed analysis.[92] In the other dialogues he considers carefully specific virtues on their own but without bringing them together into a comprehensive whole.

It is to Aristotle that we must turn for both a detailed and systematic exposition of the virtues peculiar to the civic ethics. He provides an extremely comprehensive account, for as well as the canonic virtues he also discusses such other ancillary ones as friendship, liberality, and high-mindedness, which are equally ethically important. But he also includes ones that have nothing to do with ethics. As Julia Annas sees it, "Aristotle gives lists of virtues which range over the whole of social life and cover areas that we would not at all naturally take to be the domain of morality," that is, of ethics in our sense.[93] Thus "we seem forced to the absurd conclusion that not enjoying food is a moral vice, or that tasteful expenditure is a moral matter."[94] Seen in terms of ethics in the modern sense, that is, of course, an absurd conclusion, but it is not quite as unusual if seen in terms of the ethic of civic virtue, which is what Aristotle is concerned with, since he has no conception of any other kind. In the context of this ethic, the issue is what qualities of character are required to make for a good citizen, *agathos polites*, and in order to lead a good life in the polis. The issue is an all-inclusive one that concerns qualities that might be defined by us as ethical and others, no less necessary for this purpose, that are by contrast not ethical. Thus good birth and wealth or good fortune are essential conditions for happiness, though they would not be considered by us as ethical qualifications.

However, Aristotle is not interested in making such distinctions, since he does not have an exclusive concept of the ethical. It is true that Aristotle himself seems to have coined the word *éthiké*, which, as Sparshott explains, "is derived from *éthos*, which is used for the lairs of beasts, for the customs of societies and for the characteristics of individuals."[95] But this does not mean that he drew any firm distinction between the ethical and the non-ethical. No Greek thinker operated with any such clear-cut opposition. As Julia Annas notes, "Greek lacks a word or concept closely corresponding to moral" or to ethical in our sense, even though both of these words are used in translating Aristotles *éthiké*. And the plain and obvious reason for this is that the Greek civic ethic did not require such a distinction. It is the same as with the word and concept of "representation," which also does not exist in Greek for the simple reason that Greek politics did not have representative institutions or parliamentary arrangements. In fact, there is an analogy in the two domains, for just as Greek politics was averse to representation, so, too, was the Greek civic ethic averse to any firm delimitation of the ethical and its separation from the non-ethical. The civic ethic was concerned with regulating and evaluating life in a polis of citizen warriors, and this was an undifferentiated common way of life in which the aspects that we, from a modern standpoint, would distinguish as political, religious, economic, and ethical were all taken together. There was not even a clear separation between public and private. Hence, there could be no clear sense of the ethical as such, and virtuous of all kinds, both ethical and non-ethical from our standpoint, would be all lumped together, as they are even in Aristotle.

We should beware of reading the Greek philosophers with modern preconceptions of the ethical. All their philosophical writings refer solely to the civic ethic and to no other. Strictly speaking, they have no relevance to morality or the ethics of honor or duty. The sole exception is late-Stoicism, which, as we shall see, developed a conception of duty appropriate to the latter type of ethics. It is a historical fact, however, that in later ages these Greek writings were interpreted in the context of the other ethics without a proper awareness of the discrepancies involved. A striking instance of this is the application of Aristotle's ethics to the religiously sanctioned moralities of Islam, Judaism, and Christianity during the Middle Ages. It was a supreme instance of what might be called "creative misreading," for out of it arose the whole scholastic manner of ethical discourse. Such an accident of misinterpretation is not to be historically regretted, but it was liable to spawn misunderstandings, some of which persist to this day. For even now there are neo-Aristotelians who attempt to view the whole of ethics with the spectacles of the Aristotelian categories and end up seeing it as if through a glass darkly.

What such ethical philosophers fail to note, and which should give them pause, is the relative absence in Plato and Aristotle and the other Greek ethical thinkers of any major discussion of the key ethical emotions, shame and guilt. These emotions are crucial in other ethics, particularly guilt, which constitutes conscience in morality. But it is odd to note that in the civic ethic, guilt and shame play a relatively recessive role, though, of course, they are not absent since that would be impossible in any social ethos. The civic ethics does not depend on cultivating them; it does not value them and to a considerable extent even discourages them.

It is true that in the pre-ethical stages before the full development of the civic ethics, both shame and guilt were strongly stressed in the ethos. Shame, *aidos*, is in Homer a powerful motive for the actions of the heroes. As Dodds explains, "The strongest moral force that Homeric man knows is not the fear of the gods, but respect for public opinion, *aidos*."[96] In fact, Dodds refers to the Homeric ethos in general as a shame-culture, invoking a term popularized by the anthropologist Ruth Benedict. He sees the evolution of this ethos from Homeric society to that of the archaic age of the early polis as the transition from a shame to a guilt culture. He notes a "growing sense of guilt"[97] arising at this stage, which revealed itself in the religious beliefs of this period: a fear of demons and furies, a sense of blood-guilt and of *miasma*—that is, contagious pollution—that was also very prevalent. The story of Oedipus as dramatized by Sophocles is a clear instance of these archaic relgious beliefs, which survived well into the classical polis. Neither Homeric shame nor archaic religious guilt were ever completely eradicated in the polis ethos. They remained as constant psychic factors that had to be reckoned with throughout the history of the polis.

However, these relatively primitive emotions were never transformed into true ethical shame or guilt. The reason for this is that the polis civic ethics did not require them; they were not its main motivating factors. Thus, for example, the fear of *miasma*, the sense of guilt expressed as pollution, did not amount to a sense of ethical guilt. Adkins is emphatic on this point.

> But if "guilt" is taken in a moral sense, that is to say, if we expect the word to be used in a situation in which the society of the period held to be immoral, and for which the "polluted" person is in some sense responsible, and in no other sitution, then "pollution," *miasma*, is, as was shown with great eloquence by Rohde, far from being guilt. Yet this non-moral phenomenon is powerful, and its influence is felt strongly in certain moral contexts.[98]

Nothing in this statement would change if the word *moral* that Adkins uses was replaced by the word *ethical* and the comment applied to what we have called the civic ethics.

The civic ethic did not only not rely on ethical guilt and shame among its psychological resources, but, as it were, it was averse to these "natural" emotions and in many contexts sought to extirpate them. This is particularly evident in Sparta, where the prevailing *paideia* aimed at rendering the citizens to some extent bereft of shame and guilt. To inculcate bodily shamelessness, both youths and maidens exercised together in the nude. To render them impervious to feelings of guilt, young men, before their induction into the army and assembly as full citizens, were allowed a period of wild living marked by unethical lawlessness and were permitted and even expected to steal and to murder—in particular, to assassinate those helots who had shown themselves in any way insolent or capable of rebellion.

Hence, there is something correct in Nietzsche's view that the Greeks had no bad conscience:

> "foolishness," "stupidity," "a little mental disturbance," this much even the Greeks at the strongest, bravest period allowed themselves as a reason for much that was bad or calamitous—foolishness, not sin! you understand? But even this mental disturbance was a problem—"yes, how is this possible? Where can this have actually come from with minds like ours, we men of high lineage, happy, well-endowed, high-born, noble and virtuous?"—for centuries the noble Greek asked himself this in the face of any incomprehensible atrocity or crime with which one of his peers sullied himself. "A *god* must have confused him," he said to himself at last. . . . this is typical of the Greeks.[99]

As is usual with Nietzsche, the fulsome hyperbole to the Greeks in general is much exaggerated and lumps together features from early Homeric and later polis ethos. It also reflects aspects of Nietzsche's own imaginary master morality. Nevertheless, there is a kernel of truth in what he so forcefully asseverates—the Greeks of the classical period were not much concerned with shame or guilt in their ethics.

If we take sexual shame as an example, then it is obvious that it did not disappear from society but that it played only a minor role in the ethics of men. Women, to whom this male-oriented code did not apply and who led a very traditional life, especially so in Athens—as Pericles puts it, "the greatest glory of a woman is to be least talked about by men, whether they are praising you or criticizing you."[100]—women were still bound by all kinds of rigid shame conventions. But these did not figure in the civic ethics. For men, there was an extraordinary lowering of the barriers of sexual shame. If the illustrations on vases are anything to go by, then these reveal graphically with what openness and abandon all the possible variations of sex and sexual relations were practiced. This kind of polymorphous perversity was even a feature of Athenian *paedeia,* for it encouraged mature men to initiate youths into homoerotic relations.

If, then, neither shame nor guilt played a major motivating role in the civic ethics, if, as Nietzsche contends, the Greeks had no conscience as we understand it, what was it that made them adhere to ethical norms? If we ask what it is that made them obedient to the laws of their cities, the answer must be sought in a whole complex of motives both positive and negative. On the positive side there was all that which was involved in *philopolis,* love of one's city. What this amounted to in practice was an intense commitment to the city way of life and a strong desire to succeed in it, to prove oneself to one's peers according to the accepted standards and values. On the negative side, there was the fear of the consequences of breaking the law, which, in brief, was fear of failure and all that could result from that in the loss of esteem and position and, ultimately, exclusion. Given the almost total identification of self and city, this amounted to a loss of identity that was barely bearable.

In general we might say that the civic ethics was upheld by fear of failure and the ambition to succeed. Both of these motives were effective only as long as the citizen was under the watchful competitive eyes of his peers, as long as he was engaged in the *agon* of life in the arena of his polis. Failure under such circumstances resulted in humiliation and disgrace and could be more feared than death itself. On the other hand, success was more desired than life itself, for it brought one the *kudos* and *kleos* that carried one to the pinnacle of fame close to the heroes of mythology. What was failure and what was success was largely an intra-city matter, to be determined by the opinions and sometimes the moods of one's fellow citizens. There were also, of course, general standards in these matters, agreed definitions of what was *agathos*, applicable throughout the Greek world.

Such a fear of failure must not be taken as either shame or guilt in an ethical sense. The utmost humiliation of having failed could be evoked by the quite unmerited censure of one's fellow citizens, where there could be no question of having to be ashamed or guilty of anything in one's conduct. To take two perhaps extreme instances of this: the sole Spartan survivor of the battle at Thermopylae, who clearly had nothing to be ashamed of, was nevertheless so disapproved of by his fellow citizens, who felt that he should have died on the field of battle, that out of sheer chagrin he had himself killed in the next battle; Athenian generals who failed in some way, for which they were in no way to blame, were frequently humiliated, exiled, and even executed. However, once this fear of failure was lifted, once a citizen had nothing more to lose—if, for example, he was ostracized and sent into exile—then out of a desire for revenge he was capable of the worst treacheries aganst his own city. He was not inhibited by any inherent shame or guilt. And neither was this held against him by anybody, not even by his fellow citizens, for if it should later turn out that he was readmitted back into the city, he was not expected to atone for his misdeeds in any way. The case of Alcibiades is very revealing in all there respects. Before the Spartan assembly he declares without regret, "I claim also that none of you should think the worst of me, if, in spite of my previous reputation for loving my country, I now join in vigorously with the bitterest enemies in attacking her."[101]

Neither shame nor guilt feature in Greek ethical theory. There does not seem to have even been any extensive discussion of these emotions till very late. Socrates seems not to have been concerned with them. Plato in the *Republic* explicitly adopts a Spartan attitude with respect to shame, but he takes this even further; there was to be no inhibition or prudery; men and women should expose themselves to each other and engage in copulation with whomsoever the State designates as a suitable partner. Aristotle, too, had little regard for shame, "he remarks that dispositions such as a susceptibility to shame (*aidos*), a key concept in Greek popular morality, is not a virtue at all (a virtuous person has nothing to be ashamed of)," as Sparshott notes.[102] The ultimate step in this disregard of shame by the philosophers was taken by Diogenes the Cynic, another of the followers of Socrates, who argued that, since no natural act is vicious and no virtuous act is shameful, there is no reason not to copulate in public, and, as legend has it, proceeded to do so. In other words, in the Cynic ethical theory right and wrong, insofar as these are ethical matters, have nothing to do with shame; hence, avoiding shameful acts is an unnatural prejudice or convention that ought to be transgressed and done away with.

It is of a piece with this attitude to shame and guilt that the civic ethics is largely unconcerned with sexual matters or relations between the sexes in general. It has no explicit sexual ethic. Women have no major role in it, for as Pericles avers, they are best to remain largely invisible. Strictly speaking, the civic ethics is one for men only and exclusively for those who are citizens. In this respect it differs fundamentally from morality, especially in its Judeo-Christian expression, for there it is sex and the relation between the sexes that is at the heart of its inhibitions. The myth of Adam and Eve and the later doctrine of Original Sin, elaborated on its basis in Christianity, points to the crucial role of sexual transgression in generating a sense of sin, the guilty conscience that this morality requires and inculcates.

In all such major respects the civic ethics stands at the opposite pole to morality. As opposed to loving one's neighbor as oneself, including the stranger who lives within the gates, the civic ethics practices complete indifference in ethical matters to all those who are not like oneself—that is, male fellow citizens. Women, metics, slaves, and foreigners, particularly barbarians, are excluded from full participation in ethical life and are expected to meet only minimal traditional demands. The law protects them to a limited extent, which varies greatly from city to city. But that is all. Outside the city there are far fewer restraints. In times of war, almost none at all. These were dangerous tendencies in the civic ethics that led to extraordinary excesses throughout its history.

In these regards the civic ethics also contrasts markedly to the ethics of honor, whose cardinal requirements are regard for women, the protection of non-combatants, and coming to the aid of the weak and needy. The ethics of duty is also opposed in such fundamental respects to the civic ethics. Though it appears in the West in a setting of Greek cities, yet it derives from a quite different mentality; it is a product of the later Hellenistic and Roman empires, when the cities had lost their full political independence. It is the ethics of cosmopolitanism, of citizens of the world who were no longer exclusively bound to any single city. However, its initial appearance in history predates that of the West by many centuries, for it is first to be found in the East, in China and India. It is to these that we must turn before dealing with its Western manifestation.

Ethics of Duty

Ethics of duty have arisen frequently in history in many different civilizations, sometimes quite independently of each other. The three initial ones were certainly autonomous developments occurring in China, India, and Rome. These were Confucianism, Krishnaism, and late-Stoicism. To speak of them all as ethics of duty does not mean that they were all the same. As we shall see, there are crucial differences between them as well, but this should not preclude them from being taken together, for they also have basic features in common. Confucianism and Krishnaism are more definitive cases of ethics of duty; late-Stoicism is only partially so. Formally speaking, the difference lies in the manner of codification and exact prescription of the required performances. Where this is very precise and exacting, then it constitutes an ethic of duty, *proprement dit*, but where there is only a more general ascription of objectives and goals, then it would be more strictly correct to speak of an ethic of responsibility. In this sense, late-Stoicism is more of an ethic of responsibility compared to the others. Generally considered, Western ethics of this type tend toward responsibility and Eastern ones toward duty. However, there are exceptions to this rule, for some of the West European medieval ethical tendencies are more toward a fixed ethic of duty, as is in keeping with the hierarchical and almost caste-like nature of feudal society. In what follows we shall refer to all such ethics as ethics of duty, unless there is some special reason to emphasize responsibility instead.

All societies with a hierarchically fixed social order and a patrimonial system of authority have an ethos with carefully prescribed duties for all their members, from the highest to the lowest. Such societies are ubiquitous and are to be found at all times and places, from the earliest to the latest civilizations. However, only in rare cases, such as the three previously mentioned, have some of them developed true ethics of duty. For an ethic of duty calls for much more than an ethos of fixed social roles and their prescribed duties based on custom, tradition, and religious lore. It requires a transcendent or philosophical legitimation for an ethical system of duties that is rationally articulated. Typically, such a basis is the conception of a divine or natural order, an order to Heaven or Nature, or a *Tao* or *dharma* or some other such cosmic or "rational" principle. This calls for a social order with differentiated and prescribed roles from which duties can be derived, based on the assumption that the right way of life is one shaped in accordance with that order. Thus, for any given individual, the ethically proper life is one lived in obedience to the will of God or Heaven or in conformity to Nature and Reason, relative to a particular station in life.

An ethic of duty is typically the product of officials of one kind or another. They are usually functionaries serving a ruling power whose chief qualification is literacy. They tend to see themselves as scholars, philosophers, or office-holding priests or clerics whose role and status impose on them remarkable duties and responsibilities. The general run of ordinary people need follow only the more traditional customs and mores. This ethical conception they try to foist on the whole of their society, and it is usually accepted by everyone, including even the ruling strata to whom they are beholden. Thus even an emperor or king and his courtiers and soldiery can be drawn into the ethical system of duties expounded by the officials, who are otherwise in an inferior position. Often this imposition is unwillingly accepted and accompanied by considerable conflict. But if the officials are unswerving in their determination, then they can win out and make the ruling power as bound by their ethical norms as they are themselves. In this way they can actually come to dominate those whom they nominally serve.

Every ethics of duty spells out an ideal way of life and an ideal character model, one that can be roughly termed the gentleman scholar. This man of duty—and it must be emphasized that it is invariably a man, for women play little part in the ethical ideal—is someone who lives for duty and fulfills it for its own sake without thought of recompense or even consequences. Duties must be performed regardless of the results in any given situation. This brings with it a sense of disinterested performance of duty that is selfless and without regard to personal motives or feelings, which gives rise to a dispassionate, objective, matter-of-fact attitude both in work and human relations. The official following this ethic does his duty *sine ira, cum studio.* Ideally, he is conceived of as someone without any personal life and without any selfish wishes or desires or needs. Total impersonality and extinction of Self can be the most extreme manifestation of such an ethic. The official assumes a view of himself as completely instrumental and impassive—it is as if the fulfillment of duty takes place in him, without him actively doing anything himself to bring it about.

This, however, is merely the ideal image, for in reality the scholar official or today the expert bureaucrat is driven by very robust human, frequently human-all-too-human, motives and ambitions. His main psychological drive is the desire for success and the fear of failure within the terms of his status role. Though in the truly ethical types this can be sublimated and idealized so that an official out of office or even one in disgrace, when not due to any fault of his own, has a way of justifying himself and maintaining his dignity. Shame and guilt do not play a large part in the negative inhibitions of this ethic. Dereliction of duty and other wrongdoing associated with failure in office do not characteristically make the official cringe in shame or suffer pangs of bad conscience. Rather, they lead to humiliation and a loss of self-respect—that is, a loss of worth—and it is the fear of this that keeps him to his proper course.

The official is also motivated by the prevailing spirit of piety or respect for tradition. For this is the "spirit," in Montesquieu's sense, of an ethic of duty. It contrasts with Montesquieu's own conception of a spirit of honor, which, as we shall see, is characteristic of a different ethic. But the difference is not absolute; the one easily shades into the other. According to Weber, the socio-political basis for the distinction is that between patrimonialism and feudalism, which must also be treated as ideal-types that in historical reality can merge into each other.

> Feudalism rested on honor as the cardinal virtue, patrimonialism on piety. The reliability of the vassal's allegiance was based upon the former, the subordination of the lord's servant and official upon the latter. The difference is not a contrast but a shift of accent. The vassal of the Occident "commended" himself and, too, like the Japanese vassal, he had duties of piety. The free official also had a status honor which must be counted as a motive of conduct. This was identical in China and in the Occident.[103]

Thus piety and honor can easily be co-present in the one soul and guide conduct along similar paths. Though the ethics they entail can very generally be distinguished from each other as those of patrimonialism and feudalism, the two social systems must not be seen as exclusive of each other. Thus, for example, as we shall see, the Persian origins of the ethic of honor took place in a socio-political context that had features that were at once patrimonial and quasi-feudal. This would also repeat itself in the later incarnations of this ethic.

Piety took somewhat different forms in China, India, and the West. As Weber makes clear, in China, by contrast to India and the West, piety (*hsiao*) was not driven by any explicitly religious belief in a God or supreme spirit:

> In substance, the duties of a Chinese Confucian always consisted of piety towards concrete people whether living or dead, and towards those who were close to him through their position in life. The Confucian owed nothing to a supra-mundane God; therefore he was never bound to a sacred "cause" or an "idea." For Tao was neither; it was simply the embodiment of the binding, traditional ritual, and its command was not "action" but "emptiness."[104]

The point of contrast with Judaic and Christian types of piety is obvious, but the difference from Hindu modes of piety is also apparent. These differences express themselves in the various ethics of duty characteristic of these cultures. Thus, "Confucianism hallowed alone those human obligations of piety created by inter-human relations, such as prince and servant, higher and lower officials, father and son, brother and brother, teacher and pupil, friend and friend."[105] Within the context of the Judeo-Christian or Hindu religions, quite different forms of piety and duty obtained, as we shall presently show.

However, there are some similarities between the piety characteristic of China and that of late-imperial Rome, which made for close resemblances in their ethics of duty. Official piety in Rome also took a purely traditionalistic, ritual form, without any demands made on subjective belief in a higher deity, and was even compatible with certain types of atheism, such as that of the Epicureans. Cultic duties and the official forms of observance had to be kept to, for otherwise the order and functioning of state and society would be imperiled. The Stoics provided a philosophical rationale for all this, so theirs became the most publicly accepted philosophy to which many of the emperors subscribed, beginning with the aptly named Antoninus Pius, the predecessor of Marcus Aurelius, the most famous of the Stoic emperors. In their hands the Stoic ethics of responsibility assumed a semi-official status. But it could never achieve the supremacy or rigidity of the Confucian ethics of duty because it could not capture and systematize all the traditional forms, which varied widely through the different regions of the empire, and because it always had to contend with the competition of rival schools of philosophy, not to speak of the many kinds of religions that also circulated freely and widely within the empire.

Confucianism was the earliest of the ethics of duty. It was by no means laid down in this form by the historical Confucius himself but developed over many centuries at the hands of scholar officials—later known as mandarins and Weber calls them literati—who arose as a stratum of literary qualified contenders for administrative positions in princely states of the pre-imperial period, the so-called Chan-kuo era, and later during the empire itself. Confucius was himself merely one of these. It was they who "created the concept of 'office,' above all, the ethos of 'official duty' and of the 'public weal,' " as Weber states.[106] In their writings they "developed the rational system of social ethics" that we have called the ethics of duty.[107]

How much of this is owing to Confucius is now difficult to establish, for his teachings, as they might have been originally promulgated, are impossible to recover, as are the original teachings of the Buddha. What we now have is a much later amalgam of Confucius's work together with that of other philosophies, which were originally fundamentally opposed to his—above all, the contrary doctrines of the Legists and the Mohists. What is now known as Confucianism is a syncretist admixture of all of these, which first arose only in the Han imperial period.

What is characteristically Confucian in this ethics of duty, and very likely goes back to the founder, is the emphasis on "propriety" (*li*). As Weber sees it, "What gave this ethic its special stamp was that everything was to proceed within the confines of social propriety."[108] The proper Confucian "gentle-man," the "princely" man, "controls all his activities, physical gestures, and movements as well with politeness and with grace in accordance with the status mores and the commands of 'propriety.'"[109] In this spirit he will be duty-bound to perform all the old ceremonies and uphold the "prevailing customs." All duties assume something of a ceremonial aspect, such that "all duties bequeathed from feudal times, especially duties of charity" become "frozen into a symbolic ceremonial."[110] Even though the performance of du-ties becomes formalized and conventionalized, nevertheless, duties to others are always expressed in terms of personal ties and in gradations of subordina-tion. They are seen as matters of service: "to serve my father, as I would require my son to serve me . . . ; to serve my prince, as I would require my minister to serve me; to serve my elder brother, as I would require my younger brother to serve me . . . "[111] The notion of an impersonal duty or a duty to an abstraction or ideal cannot exist, since everything is personalized and placed in a hierarchy of superior and inferior positions.

As with every ethic of duty, the obligations of official duty in Confucian-ism have to be upheld in law. In this ethic there are two mutually comple-mentary conceptions of law: *li* and *fa*—that is, traditional law and positive law. The emphasis on *li*, translated in general as "propriety," derives from the specifically Confucian aspect of the ethic; the emphasis upon *fa* assumed priority under the rule of the Legists during the Ch'in dynasty when China was first unified. Despite the speedy overthrow of this draconian system, in the subsequent Han dynasty the basic principles of positive law were main-tained and remained in force throughout all of China's subsequent dynasties. This meant that all officials and agencies of state were primarily bound by a written and enacted law in the exercise of their duties and responsibilities. They had to rule according to law and were themselves bound by law in the fulfillment of their functions, on pain of severe punishment in case of any breach of the law. As Karl Bürger puts it, "Die Strenge Bindung der Beamten an das Gesetz war in China jedoch keine leere Phrase, sondern wurde gesich-ert durch Sanktionen gegen alle Mitglieder der Behörde, die in einer fal-schem Entscheidung mitgewirkt hatten."[112]

The Legist philosophy, from which this insistence on positive law origi-nated, may have been discredited due to its harshness and rigidity, but some of its basic teachings were incorporated into the ethics of duty. A representa-tive quotation from the *Hanfeizi*, a Legist compendium, brings this out:

Those who govern must take the majority into account not the minority. Hence their devotion not to virtue, but to law. . . . Order and strength result from law, weakness and rebellion result from bending law. If the ruler understands this, then he will be correct in his rewards and punishments without having to show humaness to his subjects.[113]

The anti-Confucian bent of this is unmistakable, especially the jibe at humaness (*jen*), the prime Confucian virtue. Nevertheless, despite this, the basic Legist prescription of the subjection of all men, including the officials themselves, to law was maintained in later Confucianism. As Heiner Roetz sees it, "The Legalist idea is that, in general, relations between men should be replaced by the orientation to the prescription of the specific role."[114] The policy adopted by rulers, the imperial authority, was one of the "strictly supervised delimitation of competence which keeps the scope of action of the subordinates as narrow and controllable as possible."[115] It is within this narrow space that duties were assigned.

However, if this were all to the Chinese ethics of duty, then it would be no more than what Weber calls a *Gesetzethik*, a purely professional ethos. But there was more to it than that, for the authoritarian prescriptivism of *fa* was moderated by *li*. *Li* could be made to serve as a corrective to *fa*, limiting it to traditionally sanctioned norms and values. *Li*, or the rules and rites of propriety, was embodied in the collections of writings from ancient times that the Confucians gathered over a period of many centuries, during and after the Han dynasty, in a process referred to as the Confucianization of law and sometimes misleadingly conceived of as a refeudalization of society. By a recourse to *li*, the officials or mandarins were able to stand up against the arbitrary exercise of imperial power in matters of law and justice, countermanding such impositions with precedent-setting examples that were recorded, collected, and handed down to posterity. Theirs was not the servile role of unquestioning obedience to authority, as it is now for so many of our bureaucrats, but an ethically conditioned fulfillment of properly authorized duties and responsibilities.

In the fulfillment of this ethically sanctioned role, the scholar official saw the ideal realization of his calling. As Peter Weber-Schäfer puts it:

Der Kaiser ist die von Himmel eingesetzte Spitze eines Beamtenstaats, in dem es die Aufgabe des konfuzianisch gebildeten Gentleman ist, die Aufgaben des Kaisers dadurch zu erfühlen, dass er diejenigen Regeln menschlichen Verhaltens peinlich genau beachtet, die ein Analogon der regelnden Kräfte kosmischen Gleichgewichts sind und durch deren Beachtung er zum Gentleman wird.[116]

However, this Chinese scholar gentleman, unlike his later European counterpart, the nobleman gentleman, never saw himself as an independent social being and autonomous actor relating primarily to his peers; rather he was socially located as either inferior or superior in a hierarchically organized series of status levels. His ethical duties were determined by his precise placement in this hierarchy. As Confucius declares, "Let the ruler be ruler, the subject be subject, the father be father, the son be son."[117] The two social poles of this hierarchy, as the quotation makes evident, were the family and the State, indicated by the ruler–subject and father–son relations. And though the former takes formal precedence over the latter, it is the latter— that is, one's family duties—that is more important, according to the teachings of Confucius. In cases of conflict, it is the duties owing to one's family that take priority over all others. Between the family and the state there are no other major foci of duty; in particular, city, religion, and nobility play little role.

As an ethic of duty, Confucianism contrasts sharply to morality, a contrast Weber never tires of emphasizing:

A true prophecy creates and systematically orients conduct toward one internal measure of value. In the face of this the "world" is viewed as material to be fashioned ethnically according to the norm. Confucianism in contrast meant adjustment to the outside, the conditions of the "world." A well-adjusted man, rationalizing his conduct only to the degree requisite to adjustment, does not constitute a systematic unity but rather a complex of useful and particular traits.[118]

The contrast implied here between Confucianism and Western morality is somewhat to the detriment of the former. Weber's ultimate aim is to explain the absence of capitalism or rational economic activity in China, despite the rational orientation of Confucianism to the affairs of the world. But unlike Puritanism in the West, Confucianism did not attempt to transform the world on a rational basis: "Confucian rationalism meant rational adjustment to the world; Puritan rationalism meant rational mastery of the world."[119] In the context of Weber's account, this seems to be a judgment against Confucianism. But unless one gives capitalism an absolute value, it does not necessarily follow that rational mastery of the world should be preferable to rational adjustment.

A contemporary exponent of Weber's approach, Wolfgang Schluchter, takes up the main tenor of this judgment against Confucianism and castigates it as a "ritualistischen Ethik" and a *Gesetzethik* rather than a *Gesinnungsethik:* "Der diesen Normensystem entschprechende 'Geist' ist, um mit Kant zu sprechen, nicht des der *Moralität*, sondern des der Legalität."[120] This is, indeed, as we have already indicated, partly correct; there are such opposed ethics and they differ in these respects. But it is mistaken in its implied adverse judgment, and Heiner Roetz is right in objecting against what he calls "the Hegelian-Weberian perspective," when it is taken to mean that this ethic of duty is somehow not as fully developed as is Western morality or that it lacks something, such as subjective inwardness or conscience, or that it is given to worldly compromise, and so on, for other such criticisms that are often voiced.

To argue like this is to impose requirements on an ethic of duty, which is what Confucianism is, that are not applicable to it. An ethic of duty is not a morality but a *sui generis* ethics of a quite different type. Its fundamental aims and values are quite other; the character type it propounds as an ideal is like no other. At his best, the Confucian gentleman was a man of extraordinary cultivation, well versed at once in the poetic and artistic accomplishments, the practical political and managerial skills, and the theoretical philosophical knowledge of his society. A more all-rounded human type is hardly to be found in any other ethos. Adaptation to the world in this case meant a comprehensive mastery of all that this particular world had to offer. For, as Peter Weber-Schäfer puts it, "Wenn es die Angabe des Menschen ist, sich der harmonischen Ordnung der Welt durch Erkenntnis und Charakterformung anzupassen, muss er imstande sein, ein praktisch unbegrenztes Ausmass an Erziehung zu emfangen und sich ihm anzupassen."[121] Adaptation to the world in this sense cannot be judged adversely as compared to any Christian stand, which typically requires rejection of the world. To judge the one as against the other is about as revealing as judging Chinese landscapes as against Byzantine mosaics. This does not preclude many useful kinds of comparative studies that do not require any invidious comparisons.

A much more obvious and appropriate comparison than that between Confucianism and Western morality is that between it and the other outstanding Eastern ethics of duty, which can be called Krishnaism; Weber calls this Bhagavata religiosity after its main text the *Bhagavad Gita*. Both of them invoke a cosmic principle of duty, the *Tao* in the one case and *dharma* in the other. Both terms signify a transcendent order that applies no less to human society than to the whole cosmos. The Indian *dharma* as an ethical concept derived from earlier ritual-bound beginnings, just like the *Tao* in China. Weber explains this derivation as follows: "Vedanta-teaching has always esteemed rites and 'work,' i.e. traditional social duties as valuable for salvation striving. . . . In the classical and later literature the concept of *dharma* came to the fore. For the single person this meant the binding 'path' of social-ethical behavior, 'duty.' "[122] However, the ultimate ethical nature of *dharma* was not established until the *Bhagavad Gita*, for only there did action in accordance with caste *dharma* assume holy value as the way of salvation. As Weber stresses, "This is what rendered the traditional performance of *dharma* or ritual and social duties into an ethic."[123]

The social basis of these two ethics of duty also has some analogies. The main carriers of both were a stratum of scholar officials, or intellectuals in modern terms, in service to a state ruling power. There is, of course, also a basic difference, in that the Chinese mandarins were a lay group that had no interest in personal salvation or an afterlife, whereas the Indian brahmans were scholar-priests who acted as ritual advisers and policy counselors to the *kshatriya* ruling elite of princes and warriors and were intent on salvation in the afterlife through a reincarnation in a higher caste status. The Indian ethic was inherently tied to a fixed caste hierarchy, whereas the Chinese had no need for such a rigid social order in a unified empire.

Krishnaism as an ethic begins a few centuries after Confucianism, under different historical circumstances and for quite different sociological causes. It is part of the process of the re-Hinduization of India after Buddhism, which culminated in the first century of our era with the final editing of the two epics the *Ramayana* and the *Mahabharata,* and, what is most crucial, the insertion into the latter of the *Bhagavad Gita*, the most definitive text for the ethic of Krishnaism. At about the same time there occurred the completion of the *Laws of Manu*, the most important Hindu law book. As with Confucianism, it is once more necessary to stress the proximity of ethics to law in the case of an ethics of duty. In Krishnaism, too, it would be impossible to specify precise duties owing without a legal code. The Hindu conception of law is that of *dharma*, which is a species of religious law approximating to the Roman *fas* in contradistinction to *jus*. *Dharma* is completely case-specific and cannot be established without identifying a person's caste position, which correlates with professional and work activities. Hence, *dharma* acts as a highly regulated professional ethic, much more so than anything to be found in any other society. There is a *dharma* for everyone, from the highest king to the lowliest beggar and prostitute.

As its most ideal, as in the *Bhagavad Gita*, Krishnaism presents itself as a completely depersonalized ethic of duty. All duties are to be performed for their own sake without regard to reward or to consequences. As Krishna himself states:

> You have the right to work, but for the work's sake only. You have no right to the fruits of work. Desire for fruits of work must never be your motive in working. Never give way to laziness either.[124]

All work is a matter of duty, but as such it cannot be freely chosen; it is fixed and predetermined for each person: "In the beginning the Lord of beings created all men, to *each* his *duty*."[125] What uniquely determines duty is social position or caste. For just as it is meritorious to perform the duties of one's own caste dispensations, so it is highly dangerous and harmful to do those of another:

> It is better to perform your own duty, however imperfectly, than to assume the duties of another person, however successfully. Prefer to die doing your own duty: the duty of another will bring you into great spiritual danger.[126]

Hence the work *per se* has no value; its worth lies solely as a caste-ordained duty relative to a given person. If people placed a value on work irrespective of its caste function and did what was not appropriate to them, then caste-mixture (*varnasankara*) would result and there is nothing worse than that. The labor of the whole cosmos is to ensure that this does not happen. As Krishna puts it, "Suppose I were to stop [working]? They [mankind] would all be lost. The result would be caste-mixture and universal destruction."[127]

It would appear from this that the whole point of Krishnaism is to maintain the caste system. The caste structure is certainly essential to it, for without it there would be no way of specifying duties, but if that was all that there was to it, then it would hardly be an ethics, rather merely a religious ethos, of duty. Yet there is much more to it than caste, which is the essential context in which the ethics operates but not its higher spiritual content, which is a kind of transcendence that combines at once inner-worldly conduct and world-indifference. This is the reason that Weber considers it "the crown of classical ethics of Indian intellectuals" and its inner-worldly ethics is "organismic in a sense hardly to be surpassed."[128] What he means by this is that Krishnaism recognizes the "equal and independent value of various spheres of life," but at the same time subjects them to "their equal devaluation as soon as the ultimate questions of salvation were at stake."[129]

What Weber is referring to is the paradoxical conjunction in the *Bhagavad Gita* of being committed to action in all worldly affairs as a matter of supreme duty but also of being supremely indifferent not only to the outcome of this action but also to its very nature as good or evil: "In the calm of self-surrender you can free yourself from the bondage of virtue and vice during this very life."[130] This is to be achieved through an extinction of self in dedication to Krishna—"Dedicate all your actions to me, then go forward and fight"[131]— and union with Brahman—"To unite the heart with Brahman and then to act: that is the secret of non-attached work."[132] For the "seers who renounce the fruits of their action, and so reach enlightenment" action and non-action are as one: "Action rightly renounced brings freedom: action rightly performed brings freedom."[133]

Behind this transcendent message of freedom and enlightenment in the Krishnaic ethics there are, of course, also more robust worldly interests at work, as is the case with every ethics. Freedom and enlightenment are defined in such a way as to counter Buddhistic notions and the Buddhist morality:

> He who does the task dictated by duty, caring nothing for fruit of the action, he is a yogi, a true sannyasin [monk]. But he who follows his vow to the letter by mere refraining: lighting no fire at the ritual offering, making excuses for avoidance of labour, he is no yogi, no true sannyasin.[134]

It is clear that Krishnaism would suit the upper-caste brahmins much better than would Buddhist morality. And this is also the case with their patrons, the kshatriya ruling nobility, to whom the Bhagavad Gita is addressed. It permits them to pursue their wars and affairs of state in a spirit of ruthless Realpolitik, indifferent to all moral considerations, justified in the belief that they are following the dharma of their caste. Furthermore, since all other castes were placed in a politically subordinate position to themselves, they were secure in the knowledge that none could be ethically legitimated in ever raising themselves against the kshatriya, who alone had the dharma to rule. This goes some way toward explaining why Buddhism lost out in India.

An ethics with the "organismic" consistency of Krishnaism never appeared in the West. There were moments when Western ethics made some approximations to it and extolled the principle of "my station in life and its duties," as F. H. Bradley phrased it, but that never came anywhere near to the Hindu system. During the Middle Ages, when European feudal society assumed an almost caste-like hierarchical structure, there were intellectual expressions of duty ethics along such lines. Thomistic ethics display some of these features. Later in Lutheran societies, especially those under patrimonial rule, there were also analogous ethical tendencies. They are to some extent even present in Kant. But in the West these ethics of duty always had to be made consonant with Christian morality. And their intellectual antecedent, whose influence was ever-present throughout Western history, was the typical Western form of the ethic of duty to be found in late-Stoicism.

An ethic of duty first appeared in the West in the Roman empire among imperial officials under the auspices if the then dominant philosophy, late-Stoicism. It was not as comprehensive or rigorous as such ethics were in the

East; it did not embrace the whole of society and did not prescribe rigid duties for everyone, which is the reason we have referred to it as an ethic of responsibility. Moreover, the group of officials it mainly affected did not constitute a caste but was socially very diverse, ranging literally from emperor to slave or, to be specific, from the emperor Marcus Aurelius to the freedman Epictetus, both notable Stoics. Epictetus had formerly been a slave owned by Epaphroditus, who had himself once been a member of the imperial service-slave household under Nero. Slave, freedman, publican, or patrician—the members of all the social orders who participated in officialdom and who came to espouse a late-Stoic philosophy subscribed to an ethics of duty.

The transition from republican to imperial Rome created an ever expanding circle of officials, a creeping process of quasi-bureaucratisation, which subverted the traditional Roman ethos and also had profound ethical consequences. The earlier Roman civic ethic, one of hidebound traditionalism as expounded by Cato the elder, gradually became more flexible and sophisticated under Greek philosophical influence. At first, this was Academic Skepticism, then Epicureanism, and finally the dominant role was assumed by Stoicism. But this was a two-way process of exchange, for under the influence of Roman patronage Stoicism began to transform so as to make itself suitable to Romans. It adapted itself to Roman traditions and law and through this process of adaptation it constituted itself as an ethic of duty. James Francis brings this out very clearly:

> A philosophical doctrine could hardly be found more congenial to the notoriously practical Romans. Indeed, the transplanting of Stoicism to aristocratic Roman soil resulted in the unquestioning acceptance of the customs of the upper class, customs that were, after all, the lot nature had accorded to them. Practices of social etiquette became subjects of moral precepts; the Romans made duties of their own conventions. The use of Stoic doctrines and the weight of the Latin term *officium* (duty as an ethical imperative) turned traditions and social and political functions into moral obligations, and so, traditional Roman veneration of the "ancestral ways" (*mores antiquai*) turned into foundations of philosophy.[135]

Indeed, as we shall see, this word *officium*, from which our terms *office* and *official* are derived, assumed currency in every subsequent revival of an ethic of duty in the West right down to Kant.

By the time late-Stoicism had assumed this form in the philosophy of Epictetus, it had already departed far from its original state in the philosophy of Zeno of Kitium. In its first version it had been an ethical philosophy closely related to Cynicism—Zeno had been a pupil of the Cynic Crates—

and it expounded similar socially radical doctrines of indifference to the world and to worldly conventions, especially those regarding the institutions of slavery, politics, sexual mores, and religion, namely, the very bases of social life in Hellenistic cities. However, with the founding of the so-called Middle Stoa under Panaetius the process of accommodation to the needs of Rome had begun. He was "the first Greek intellectual to offer a philosophical justification of the Roman empire," much against the whole drift of earlier Stoic doctrine according to which "empire was a form of slavery," as James Francis states.[136] Thereby, the "whole school began a drastic shift towards social respectability."[137] Under Panaetius "a new emphasis appears on *sophrosyne* (sobriety, discretion, self-control), which came to be identified with *decorum* in the Latin ethical vocabulary."[138] This step is already more than halfway toward an ethics of duty.

The process of revision toward further accommodation continued in the hands of Posidonius, a friend of Cicero. Cicero himself contributed considerably to the constitution of an ethics of duty with his classic work *De Officiis (On Duties)*, which remained one of the primary texts of ethical discourse in the West, one whose influence was particularly strong in the Middle Ages. The crucial step in the elaboration of an ethics of duty was initiated by the philosophical revision of Stoicism undertaken by Posidonius. As James Francis sees it:

> Posidonius abandoned the earlier explanation of human frailty and error as a weakness or defect of reason, which had been the sole attribute of the soul, and posited instead an active conflict between two elements within the soul: reason and passion. Given this conflict, no human action could ever be morally perfect. It therefore became the obligation of the individual not to aim at perfection, but to perform the duties nature set out before him to the best of his ability. For this reason, the good man will not change the rules of his life or society decreed by nature, but rather obey them the more strictly.[139]

A complete ethics of duty is here foreshadowed. From Posidonius it was then taken up by Musonius Rufus, who taught Epictetus, and who in turn passed it on to Marcus Aurelius.

For Epictetus, social duties are ethical imperatives. In a statement vaguely reminiscent of Confucius, he places the great emphasis in this respect on one's position in society and social role:

> Consider who you are . . . first as a human . . . next remember that you are a son. . . . next remember that you are a brother. . . . next remember, if you are a councellor of a city, that you are a councellor; that you are young, if you are young; old, if you

are old; a father, if you are a father. In every case each of these names, when it comes to be reflected on, suggests the actions that are appropriate.[140]

Thus, according to Epictetus, duties revolve around "citizenship, marriage, begetting of children, worshipping God, caring for parents, in sum, desire, aversion, choice, refusal, doing each of these things as they ought to be done, as we are born by nature to do them."[141] As Pierre Hadot puts it, "Duties are thus actions 'appropriate' to our rational nature, and they consist in placing ourselves in the service of human community, in the form of the city/state and of the family."[142] Thus by this circuitous philosophical route we arrive with Epictetus at an ethical position that displays strong analogues to Confucianism and Krishnaism.

However, what makes the Roman Stoic position so distinctive is its conception of Nature. This underlies the peculiar Stoic concept of law as Natural Law, which is unlike any other. Natural Law is simply the law of reason since Nature is identified with reason, so that "for Stoics natural law is simply correct moral reasoning, thought of as being prescriptive," as Julia Annas states.[41] Or putting it another way, since man is a rational creature by nature, nature is simply reason in man: what is rational is also natural and vice-versa. Thus the duties (*ta kathekonta,* in Stoicism) are "those actions which are appropriate to our nature" and which "can be considered as corresponding to that deeply embedded instinct which impels rational human nature to act for its own conservation," as Pierre Hadot puts it.[144] In this way, the duties—which in practice are determined by conventional social institutions and rules of law—can be justified as the outcome of a law of nature or ethical principle that subsumes them.

Once again, law in one form or another is as crucial to the late-Stoic form of the ethics of duty as it was to the others. At the very start of the Stoic school, Chrysippus, in his book *On Law* (now lost), had apostrophized it as follows:

> Law is king of all things, human and divine; it must preside over what is noble and what is base, and be their ruler and leader; and in accordance with this it must be the standard of what is just and unjust, and for creatures that are by nature social it must be prescriptive of what one should do and prohibitive of what one should not do.[145]

As early as Hellenistic times, this Stoic conception of Natural Law was turned to political ends in order to sacralize the law issuing from the ruling power, the Hellenistic monarchs. Louis Dumont states that "natural law, as 'unwritten,' or 'animate' (*empsychos*) law is incarnate in the ruler. It is clear in Philo, who wrote of 'incarnate and rational laws,' and in the Fathers . . ."[146] This Stoic conception of Natural Law was passed on from Greek officials to Roman officials and eventually inherited by the Christian clerical bureaucracy. It could readily be applied to Roman Law and used to validate its basic jurisprudential principles. Later in Christian times it could simply be referred to as God's Law, which the ruler as emperor or king was empowered by God himself to enforce.

Thus the late-Stoic conception of Natural Law was taken over by Christianity and became part of the whole Western ethical-legal heritage. Its vicissitudes throughout the medieval and modern periods are well known and have been extensively explored in the scholarly literature. In the medieval period it was continually reinvoked in clerical and philosophical writing, most notably in the work of Thomas Aquinas. In the modern period it was reinterpreted on a new rational and individualist basis by Grotius and Locke; as Natural Rights it became the mainstay of liberal theory. In this form it became enshrined in the American constitution and the French *Declaration of the Rights of Man* and many such documents subsequently. Today it plays a leading role in the United Nations declarations and American policy. All this is the abiding legacy of Stoic ethics.

However, what is of even greater historical interest in this context is how much more of the late-Stoic ethics of duty was directly taken over by Christian Europe. According to Stephen Jaeger, "Roman ideals of urbanity, linked to the ethic of state service, were kept alive in the Middle Ages through two channels."[147]

> One was the actual practice of these ideals in government and court life. Counsellors of the Merovingian kings were in part the direct heirs of the Roman statesmen (the old Roman senatorial nobility); in part they were the indirect inheritors of the ancient Roman traditions through the survival of the Roman system of education. . . . The second channel was ethical writings. The history of Cicero's influence on the Middle Ages is still to be written. His *De Officiis* survived and was an important school text. Along with Seneca, Cicero was the most influential of the Roman ethical writers. Their influence was felt in a variety of imitations and adaptations by Christian writers.[148]

Here we are not so much interested in the general ethos of urbanity, as more specifically in its counterpart "ethic of state service," which, of course, is the ethics of duty under discussion. As the names Cicero and Seneca make evident, this ethic is of late-Stoic derivation and, as we see, it continued well into the medieval period and beyond.

As is to be expected, its medieval form was characteristically embodied in a stratum of officials, the clerical administrators of Church and state. The very words *office* and *official* were reconceived and invoked in a Christian context, starting with Saint Ambrose's influential work *De officiis ministorum ecclesiae,* which was modeled on Cicero. The clerical bureaucracy of both Church and state was fully imbued with the ethics of duty through its educational grounding in such works. As Jaeger attests, "The language of ethics and the representation of men in public life were saturated with the ideas and terminology from these works."[149]

Jaeger focuses his study on a particular group of these clerical officials, the so-called courtier-bishops, who were particularly important in developing and spreading "a Christian-humanist ethic of worldly service."[150] As he shows, this arose mainly during the Ottonian era in Germany in the imperial chapels. The conditions were then particularly propitious for such a revival of Roman traditions. The Christian emperors cultivated a Roman imperial style and promoted an administrative apparatus whose model could only be Roman. "At the imperial courts there was fertile soil for a revival of the classics and of humanist notions of the dignity of man, but the narrower focus was state service."[151] This model of clerical service which originated in the chapel of the Ottonian-Salian dynasty spread throughout Europe, including the chapel of the Roman curia itself. It "shaped the values of clerical administrators generally."[152]

Jaeger's main case is that not only is "it visible wherever we encounter descriptions of clerics in court service . . . ," but that it also "appears in its most elegant medieval transmutation in the knight and lover of court romance."[153] In other words, he argues that the classical Roman tradition of an ethos of urbanity and ethics of duty is also the main source for the ethics of chivalry as well. Our disagreement with this view is largely based on the obvious historical and geographical disparity between what took place in imperial Germany starting in the tenth century and that which arose a century or more later in feudal Southern France. As we shall show, the content of the two ethics is also very different—though this is not to deny that the former might well have significantly influenced the latter. We shall continue this dispute in the next section.

The ethics of duty as it developed among medieval administrative clerics and particularly so among the courtier-bishops has obviously been influenced by many earlier sources. Its links to Christian morality are inextricable and, as Jaeger shows, it revives many forms of classicism. It is clearly an extremely mixed and eclectic type. It also shows considerable analogies with all three of the main types of ethics of duty: the Confucian, Krishnaic, and late-Stoic.

The last is easy to account for by direct influence through the inheritance of traditions. The other analogies are obviously not due to any kind of direct influence but arose out of a similarity of circumstances. Like the Confucian mandarin scholars, the medieval administrative clerics also expounded a uniform "philosophy," based on a canonic literature of texts that were similarly inculcated through an educational program of officially sanctioned schools. They also devoted themselves to state service, in obedience to the imperial or other monarchical ruling authorities. But, more like the Brahmin priests, they were also clerics bound to the doctrines of a religious orthodoxy and its moral teachings. This produced tensions that made it impossible for them to accommodate themselves completely to worldly concerns in the way that the Confucians were so easily able to do.

This brief comparative analysis, which will be later amplified, is indicative of the quite pronounced differences that exist in the three forms of the ethics of duty. These differences can be partly sociologically accounted for by the disparities between the three types of carriers of the ethics and the kinds of ruling authorities that they served. In general terms, each operated in the context of a patrimonial political and social system, but the Chinese, Indian, and Roman imperial state forms were very diverse. The Confucian literary scholars served a different master on quite different terms, compared to the religiously qualified Brahmin priests or the Roman imperial officials schooled in rhetoric and philosophy. The first of these were a professional status group, the second a ritually segregated caste, and the third a mixed social body comprising both those drawn from the highest senatorial nobility as well as *caesariani*, among whom were manumited freedmen and slaves. The three kinds of patrimonial rulers they served were also very different and could make quite different demands and have different expectations from their service officials. In all three cases they could expect the prime patrimonial virtue of piety, or reverence for authority and for the traditions and conventions of society, including the institutionalized religious rituals and beliefs. But the three types of piety were diverse: Chinese *hsiao*, Hindu *dharma*, and Roman *pietas* are not the same. Such differences underlie the three distinctive forms of the ethics of duty.

One can pose interesting historically counterfactual questions as to why any one of these cases did not happen to develop in some respect or other like another case. This is not mere idle musing about what might have been but a rigorous counterfactual way of testing what did happen and how it might have been otherwise if certain factors were different. Thus Weber considers the question why Roman officials did not develop into a fully professional bureaucratic stratum with total control of all administrative positions of power, like the Confucian mandarins in imperial China. His answer is that they could not claim for themselves complete and total ethical rectitude—that is, attain the kind of ethical monopoly in Rome that the Confucians had in China. They might have achieved this if "the Roman emperors of the second century had officially adopted the Stoic ethic as orthodox and had made the acceptance of the Stoic ethic prerequisite for delegation to state offices."[154] But this never happened, for it "was impossible in the Occident because no philosophical school claimed or could claim the legitimacy of absolute traditionalism."[155] In China, the Confucians made precisely this claim and, eventually, after many struggles, they succeeded in getting it accepted by the imperial power itself. In Rome, this could not happen for the previous reasons.

The administrative clerics of the Middle Ages, the courtier-bishops, would have had a much better chance of becoming as powerful as the mandarins in China, for they, too, could claim total ethical rectitude and exercise an ideological monopoly in the name of Christian doctrine. However, they found themselves in the middle of the conflict between Emperor and Pope, between secular state power and the Roman Church, that raged during the very centuries in which their formation and consolidation had taken place. In the ensuing Investiture Controversy they were placed "between the hammer and the anvil," as one contemporary expressed it.[156] The very heart of the controversy was precisely who should have the power to nominate and so to control these administrative officials and other clerical power holders. The secular rulers largely lost out in this controversy and could only play a limited role in the selection and installation of bishops. In the long run, however, both Emperor and Pope fought each other to a draw and canceled each other out, and both the Empire and the Papacy were weakened and discredited. Had the Emperor won and had the clerical administrators prevailed, then ethics in Europe might have become more like that in China.

Instead, what happened was that the conjoined temporary collapse of Empire and Papacy permitted other forces to gain the ascendency. The feudal system based on a division and decentralization of powers flourished. Local rulers and lords of all varieties prevailed. This created the social conditions for another type of ethic altogether to come to the fore, specifically the ethics of honor, to which we turn next.

Ethics of Honor

Our fourth and last ethical type is the ethics of honor. This is by far the least theorized or even historically studied of all the ethics. It has no philosophy worth speaking of, its main written expressions having been poetic and literary. It has not even received general recognition as an ethics. Its history remains to this day partly unknown; much of it can only be reconstituted with large gaps of uncertainty. Nevertheless, it must be acknowledged as an ethics of considerable importance since it prescribed an ideal way of life throughout the ages, at least for some kinds of aristocratic classes, through whom it also had a lesser effect on other ones. In the court circles where it flourished, it promoted extraordinary delicacies of refinement in behavior and comportment in general. Its catalogue of virtue is as pronounced and impressive as that of any other ethics. Among these were ideal standards that were as difficult to attain or even to approximate to as any other ethical ideals. Its model of the good man was the heroic figure of epic and romance literature that propagated these ideals. In the West this was the chivalrous knight, who later was transformed into the gentleman, a figure that persisted over the intervening centuries and survived practically till our time. And the same holds for his female counterpart, the lady.

In the East, among Persians, Arabs, and Turks an analogous ideal of the chivalrous warrior was current, possibly deriving from the same sources. Hence, this is by no means a coincidence, for clearly there is much historical evidence of commonality and mutual influence between the warring classes of East and West wherever they encountered each other, both in war and in peace. In fact, the ethics of honor is the only major instance of an ethic held in common both in the East and West, for early in the Middle Ages it circulated throughout the Muslim and Christian worlds, from the farthest reaches of Turkestan right through to the shores of the Baltic sea. Anyone traversing this huge Eurasian landmass would have encountered among the nobility of the various civilizations, Islamic, Greek, or Latin, a similar medieval courtly culture and a shared ethics of honor.

An ethos of warriors is extremely prevalent in history and is there in all civilizations. A specialized and usually more intense form of it is to be found among horse warriors or cavalry. But this in itself does not constitute an ethic—it is a large cultural jump to leap from cavalry to chivalry. As we shall see, chivalry is historically quite unique and only occurred under very specific conditions. Codes of honor among warriors and codes of war-making are quite common, ranging from the Aztec flower-warrior ethos of honor attained through captive taking for sacrifice through to the Bushido of Japanese samurai, but these do not as yet amount to ethics of chivalry. What is crucially at issue is the way the opponent is viewed. The aim of all war and battle is to defeat the enemy, but the way this is done and can be done appropriately varies enormously from one war-making code to another. In the chivalric code this can only be achieved honorably, for the courtly enemy, who is also an honorable man, must be treated as an equal worthy of respect. Hence, he cannot be mistreated in defeat, since defeat in itself is not dishonorable and is preferable to victory gained by underhanded ways. Only when the enemy is capable of fighting can he be even engaged, not when he is incapacitated, and those who are unable to fight or unworthly of fighting, such as women or peasants and commoners in general should never be engaged. Thus, one by one, all the elements of an ideal lifestyle devoted to fighting is constituted that far surpasses any mere warrior ethos.

When and where this first occurred is still only tentatively known. In order to arrive at the origins of the ethics of honor, we will need to work backward historically. We will start with the most recent case of the incarnation of the ethic and trace its most immediate sources, then the sources of these, and so on, till we arrive at what must be an original point of departure. The most recent case about which we know most happens to be the Western ethics of chivalry, which flourished from the early Middle Ages onward and is still alive in popular imagination. Our account will, therefore, begin with this and then seek to trace it back to a point of origin, which is the reverse of the procedure we adopted with the other ethics whose origins are indisputable.

In a somewhat old-fashioned way, one still marked by the gothic revival movement of the nineteenth century, Hearnshow writing in 1928 sees chivalry as clearly an ethics:

> For the strength and the permanent importance of chivalry lay in the fact that it was a complete way of life, moulding the character and determining the destiny of its subject from the cradle to the grave. As a type of training; as a code of honour; as a standard of good form; as a school of courtesy; as a norm of piety, ceremonious but not enthusiastic; in all these respects, chivalry made an enduring mark, not only upon the middle ages, but also upon all the subsequent centuries of Western civilization.[157]

Even though seen with moist romantic eyes, Hearnshow's perception of chivalry provides an accurate account of its ideals and virtues. The key norms he stresses are honor and truthfulness: "It held up a high standard of honour and required it to be maintained without any diminution. It insisted on a truthfulness, a truthworthiness and adhesion to plighted word, a fidelity of engagements, from which no allurements of advantage and no plea of necessity could cause any deviation."[158] Its ethical character is apparent from these norms and it is the reason that we have called it an ethics of honor but might equally well have named it an ethics of truthfulness. Honor and truth, as we shall show, are the essential features of the ethic from its very origins and have always persisted, despite all kinds of other additions, changes, and variations.

It is basically an ethic of an elite class of horse warriors, knights in medieval Europe, and all their predecessors in earlier cultures and civilizations. As Weber noted, such a class of noblemen and their royal leaders functions within a social system that is patrimonial and at least quasi-feudal; in Europe it was fully feudal. The functional role of chivalry within European feudalism is easy to determine: In a potentially anarchic society of warrior knights, it helped maintain a system of vassalage based on codes of allegience that provided a measure of predictability and stability in social relations. The Church encouraged it for these reasons and sought to control and to mold it to its own needs; it strove to impress upon it its own basic Christian norms and the minimal moral requirements that also served its interests. The whole ceremony of knightly consecration, with its vows of fidelity, reveals the influence of religion and the concessions it required; the knight undertook the following obligations:

> to refrain from the wanton giving of offence; to live for honour and glory, despising pecuniary reward; to fight for the general welfare of all; to obey those placed in authority; to guard the honour of the knightly order; to shun unfairness, meanness and deceit; to keep faith and speak the truth; to persevere to the end in all enterprises begun; to respect the honour of women; to refuse no challenge from an equal and never to turn the back upon a foe.[159]

Thus there is no denying that the Church had from the start a strong influence on the medieval ethics of chivalry. The scholarly work of Georges Duby, Maurice Keen, and Stephen Jaeger has brought out various facets of this influence and so revealed the specifically Christian elements in the code of chivalry.[160] Duby stresses the importance of the restraints on violence and war-making that the Church imposed through the Peace of God movement and the ideal of the *miles christianus*. Keen shows the relevance of monastic ideals to the crusading movement, which is also reflected in the rituals of chivalry and its romance literature. Jaeger goes back to an even earlier period before the Crusades and examines the role of worldly clerics in administrative capacities in the courts of the German emperors, starting with Otto the Great and later in the courts of other monarchs—such figures, as for example, Thomas á Becket, who was a typical clerical courtier before he became Archbishop of Canterbury.

Jaeger's case is the most challenging to the account presented here, for according to him courtliness is not an autonomous ethics and it owes nothing to non-Western influences, being wholly an indigenous Western form of classicism going back to and perpetuating Roman traditions of *urbanitas*: "Courtliness is medieval Europe's memory of the Roman statesman, of his humanity and urbane skillfulness in guiding the state and in facing the trials of public life."[161] According to Jaeger, "It is evident that the clergy were largely the bearers and transmitters of these ideals" of courtliness.[162] But as he makes clear, he does not mean the ordinary parish priests or the monks of the various orders but only "the worldly clergy, the high aristocracy in state service, members of the imperial church and those who strove for that position."[163] He points to what seems a significant fact, that most of the authors of the romances were clerics of this worldly kind, which is perhaps not so telling when the limited spread of literacy is taken into account. He insists that though these "chivalric narratives represent courtliness as a sublime ethical code," it is a code of mores that was already known in the West, at least from the time of Cicero's *De Officiis*, "Which acted as a key textbook of ethics from the early middle ages onwards."[164] In short, there is nothing unclassical or unchristian in the chivalric ethics of honor.

However, the two fundamental preoccupations of all the romances and the basis of their ethical code are knightly combat and erotic love. Both of these are unclassical and unchristian. For to elevate single knightly combat and individual prowess together with a romantic love that was frequently adulterous to the position of supreme accomplishments is from either perspective an impossibility. They go against any classical code of value in disciplined war-making and Christian chastity in love-making. From either side they must be accounted vices to be extirpated rather than virtues to be emulated. Jaeger himself admits to being somewhat baffled on the score of courtly love; he does not deny its reality as a literary sentiment, but as a social fact he finds "no trace of the exaltation of women, so prominent a feature of courtly literature," in the classical literature on which he has based his case.[165] He does not seem to realize just how far this goes against his case. For the ethics of romantic love and the role it endows to women must have had other sources besides the classical and Christian ones that Jaeger allows. What might these have been?

An unusual feature of this courtly love aspect of the ethics of honor is that it was largely created under the patronage of women; in this respect it was different from all the other ethics in which women played a lesser part and generally held an inferior role. Romantic love made its appearance in medieval Europe a little later than chivalry but in close association with it.

It first appeared in the great courts of Southern France, and its first literary expression is the love poetry of the troubadours, beginning with William IX of Aquitaine, the grandfather of Eleanor of Aquitaine, who together with her daughter Marie de Champagne were the leading patronesses of the style. The Plantagenet court of her second husband, Henry II, was also the literary circle in which the prose writing of lays and romances circulated in which the courtly art of love was expounded. Many of these dwelt on the Arthurian legends and other Celtic myths such as that of Tristan and Iseult.

This courtly *ars amoris* had many unusual features that distinguish it from any other kind of love. In most respects it is the opposite of Christian chaste love in marriage, being a highly erotic passion of a man for a superior married lady, where he is invariably the suitor and she the reluctant recipient of his advances, which must be restrained and are frequently frustrated. The relation was seen in feudal terms, "the lover becomes the vassal of the lady he loves, and this voluntary dependence allows him to attain the values of courtliness," as Christiane Marchello-Nixia puts it.[166] These values constitute the ethic as it was current in the West: "Love goes hand in hand with *courtoisie, prouess* (prowess), *largese* (largesse, generosity), and *oneur* (honor)."[167] Under the general designation of gallantry, this remained a constant feature of the Western ethics of honor.

This ethic was thus in constant conflict with Christian morality. For the "art of love" and subsequent codes of gallantry were from start to finish invariably adulterous. It is the only instance of an ethic that valorizes adultery on the part of wives. That it does so is certain. Hearnshow sees it as "a gigantic system of bigamy in which every lady was expected to have both a husband and a *paramour*; and every complete cavalier, besides the wife to whom for business reasons he was bound, a goddess, whose commands he unhesitatingly obeyed, and whose cause he upheld against all comers."[168]

This view has since been upheld by contemporary scholarship. Thus Joachim Bumke, writing about courtly love (*Minne* in German), insists that it not only allowed but required adultery, for such love is not possible within marriage:

> The disputed point—"whether true love could have a place between husband and wife"—was finally referred to the countess of Champagne, who announced her famous verdict in a letter dated May 1, 1174: "We declare and firmly establish that love cannot unfold its powers between married people." The countess justified her verdict with the argument that only lovers gave themselves freely to each other, whereas husbands and wives were bound by the law of mutual obligation. . . . There was also no jealousy among married couples.[169]

The last, somewhat surprising, comment, might have been true in the Middle Ages when love was not involved in marriage. Love had to be sought outside marriage, and as the cleric Andreas Capellanus, in his book *De Amore*, insists, "marriage is no real excuse for not loving."[170] The legends of Lancelot and Guinevere and Tristan and Iseult, even the real life story of Abelard and Heloise, reflect a similar attitude, one that is quite contrary to Christian morality. Lancelot shows himself fully aware of this when he states, in his reply to the holy hermit who reproaches him, in the romance *La Quête du Saint-Grael*, "It is true, I live in a state of mortal sin because of a woman I have loved all my life, Queen Guinevere, wife of King Arthur."[171]

This clash between Christian and courtly conceptions of love continued throughout the whole subsequent history of Western ethics. It is reflected in many of the literary masterpieces of European literature. As the works of Denis de Rougemont and other writers have shown, the whole subsequent European conception of romantic love was determined by this medieval code of courtly love or gallantry. And very frequently, this was an adulterous love or at least one outside the bounds of marriage. The great heroines of the novel, such as Madame Bovary and Anna Karenina, are adulterous wives, and though in the end they are punished, as morality demands, yet the value of their love is not denied.

It was not only in matters of love, but in respect of many other virtues as well, that the ethics of honor stood in opposition to Christian morality. Even in the medieval romances themselves some of the heroic knights evince a bad conscience in regard to their chivalrous exploits. Thus in *La Charroi de Nîmes*, the hero, Guillaume, reproaches King Louis himself:

> I have valiantly served you in arms
> And have often supported you in battle
> Thus killing many noble young men;
> The sin of this has pierced my heart.
> Whoever they were, God made them.
> May God save their soul, and forgive me.[172]

The Church authorities were always aware of these moral problems presented by the aristocratic ethics of honor, and as far as possible they sought to bring it to heel, at least to moderate if they could never completely extirpate it. This ethical battle went on throughout the centuries. Much of it took place in the education of adolescents, the crucial period in ethical development. Thus, for example, as late as the eighteenth century, "among Roman aristocrats born and raised in families teeming with cardinals and prelates, the code of ethics propounded by the high clergy was in a good position to combat the ancient code of chivalry. Thus adolescents were taught to avoid any cause for an 'engagement' [in love] or matter of honor."[173] How it is that the unchristian precepts of the old code of chivalry managed to survive and be transmitted to the youth of eighteenth-century Rome is a long and difficult story that need not concern us here. But passed on it was, not only in Catholic countries but Protestant ones as well. Affairs of honor and love affairs were its most lasting legacy, and these still survive even now in some countries.

In many of its precepts and valuations, the ethic of honor stood opposed to all other ethics. What is often considered a virtue in the former is a vice in the latter. This is particularly so with that sense of standing, dignity, and personal worth called pride. All the other ethics seek to repress it. The civic ethics is opposed to it, for it stands in the way of the discipline needed for citizenship, particularly for subjecting oneself to the yoke of the law and that of military obedience so essential for fighting as a unit in tight formations. Many are the stories of Roman fathers of the early period of the Republic who condemned their own sons to death because out of personal pride they broke ranks and accepted a challenge to single combat such as no medieval knight could have refused. Pride is also not a quality that any official could afford, for the ethics of duty is dedicated to service and the avoidance of self-assertion and self-display. Morality is no less averse to pride, as many of the stories in the Bible make clear. In Christian morality it was regarded as the deadliest of deadly sins, the sin of Satan no less—pride comes before the fall.

Yet it is precisely pride that is cultivated and valued in the ethics of honor. As Bumke notes.

> A person who met the requirements of hövescheit [courtliness] possessed *vreude* and *hôhen muot*. In religious thinking hôhen muot meant "pride" ("Wealth causes pride [hôhen muot] and arrogance and forgetfulness of God"). In the court context it stood for highmindedness and a knight's feeling of elation in social life. The term vreude ("joy") referred also to society.[174]

It is clear from this that all the moral valuations enjoined by the Church were subtly undermined and opposed in the courtly ethic. Thus, for example, whereas wordly renown or fame was frowned upon in clerical estimation, "fame is empty noise," the courtly poets, however, "summed up with the term êre [Ehre] everything that distinguished a knight in this world."[175] Some of the major poets in whose writings the ethic is affirmed are well aware of such difficulties and of the inevitability of clashes in basic valuations. Thus Walter von der Vogelweide asks despairingly:

How a man might gain three things at once and not one of them be ruined. Two are the honour and goods of life, which often damage each other. The third is God's grace, more precious than the other two. How I'd like to have all three in one casket. . . . Unfortunately, it can never be that in this world wealth and honour come together in one's heart with God's grace.[176]

Wealth, honor, and grace stand, of course, for the basic values of the three estates, the burghers, nobility, and clergy, and it is obvious that each of these reveals a different ethical bias. As far as possible, open ethical conflicts were avoided, and both theologians and poets played down clashes and sought hard to create reconciliations—perhaps no one more so than Dante, who was clearly aware of the numerous opposed ethical strains, as we shall show in the next chapter. According to Bumke, this was in time successful for "a new foundation for lay ethics was laid by the attempt of poets to integrate the social etiquette and worldly values of secular nobility into an idealized court image that also embraced the traditional ideas of virtue and took seriously the commands of the Christian religion."[177] This compound and complex lay ethic became the mainstay of European civility and a hallmark of its civilization. Its most ideal realization was in the figure of the gentleman, who evolved directly from that of the knight.

A key feature of the later lay ethic, one revealed very clearly in the role of the gentleman, was its emphasis on manners. This, too, derived directly from the knightly ethic of honor or chivalry, as Hearnshow puts it in his somewhat romanticised way:

[Chivalry] instilled a courtesy (courtoisie), a fine code of manners based on heartfelt consideration and genuine regard which immensely added to the delight of the intercourse of social life. Courtesy, especially in the relation of men towards women, although it had been anticipated in the Christian Church, was a new thing in the hard world. It differed in its grace and charm and geniality from the mere politeness, civility and urbanity (which, as the words themselves imply) were the forms of good manners evolved amidst the crowded and commercial populations of the towns.[178]

This is, indeed, a distinction that Jaeger fails to take into account. However, all these features of good manners and good form became a major preoccupation in the education of a gentleman and have remained key elements in the educational practices of some schools in European countries—above all, in the English public school system. "Manners maketh man," said William of Wykeham, the founder of Winchester, perhaps the oldest of all these schools. It is noteworthy that he did not say "morals maketh man." The reason for this is that within this conception of noble upbringing, no firm distinction was made between manners and morals. This view was to persist within the whole tradition of gentlemanly cultivation. Thus when in the later part of the eighteenth century Dr. Johnson accuses Lord Chesterfield of expounding in his letters to his son the "manners of a dancing master and the morals of a whore," it is not obviously apparent that the one is to be taken as any more heinous than the other; both are equally bad.

Manners and morals—or, to be more precise, rules of deportment and norms of conduct—are not clearly separated within chivalry or any other ethics of honor. They are taken together as the proper way of behaving or proper bearing, which, in all its aspects, is equally significant. Any breach of propriety in either is equally to be condemned; thus a gesture of intemperate disrespect toward a superior is just as bad as the murder in a quarrel of a lowly inferior. What matters is the scale of worth and the standing that people have within it, for that determines how they are to relate to each other. Improprieties become extremely significant when they constitute a challenge to the established status differences and the scale of worth based on it. Hence, minor breaches of decorum that can be taken as slights or insults loom very large in courtly consciousness. Among men, such differences must be settled by force of arms, the knightly challenge and later the duel. Only such a willingness to risk one's life for honor can restore honor and heal wounded pride. Not to be willing to stake one's life in such matters, often extremely trivial, leads to dishonor and irreparable shame.

The basic emotional charge behind the ethics of honor is shame, in all its varied and most refined nuances. Recounting an incident involving Edward II and Geoffroi de Charny, one of the most renowned knights of the Middle Ages and author of a book on chivalry, Richard Kaeuper and Elspeth Kennedy remark that "shame was the feeling or condition most to be feared by an honourable knight."[179] As this incident also reveals, such shame is felt most keenly in regard to one's superiors and peers; it is not aroused in matters where one's inferiors are concerned. The reason for this is that shame is indicative of a fear of degradation, that is, losing one's standing within the hierarchy of honor with which one's sense of selfhood is inextricably bound up. Not to feel the various manifestations of shame, ranging from slight embarrassment to the chargrin of deep humiliation, is not to be able to enter into the emotional sphere of an ethic of honor and, therefore, not to be able to take part in it. For it is this emotional sensitivity, and not conscience or reason or knowledge, that guides one in the intricacies of tact and refinement on which conduct reflecting good breeding depends.

Good breeding is an educative process of enculturation in which fine shades of difference and differentiation between people and, consequently, between actions and in how to behave toward others is continually being exercised. What degree of deference is owing to superiors, what kind of equanimity does one adopt toward peers, how much self-assertion is one to allow oneself toward various kinds of inferiors—all such questions are issues of tact and discretion that have to be learned through constant practice, which usually can only be done at court, the school of honor. Codified in the form of rules, such practices become *courtoisie,* or, literally, the ways of courtiers and court ladies. All our later practices of courtesy derive from this source. *Courtoisie* is also courtship and courting, the crucial aspect of good manners and morals in the relation between the sexes. In fact, all our surviving modern conceptions of courting derive from courtly conduct.

The origins of Western manners in court culture have been extensively studied in the work of Norbert Elias.[180] Elias shows in great detail how etiquette arose in relation to the most basic human functions, such as eating, defecating, sleeping, bathing, making love, and in acts of violence and aggression. He describes how all of these became surrounded with inhibitions against being displayed in public and were either completely consigned to a private sphere, removed from public gaze, or, if performed before others, then only in a ritualized way with due propriety. Thus, for example, eating in public could only be done with proper table manners, utilizing the special utensils invented for this purpose, such as spoons and forks, and adhering strictly to the convention of keeping one's own food separate from that of others in the process of consumption, such that bowls and plates were not to be shared. Invariably, the first and earliest forms of such good manners were to be found in good society, that is, in the practices of court circles in trendsetting countries such as France and Italy. Later they expanded to the aristocratic class as a whole; and later still they were taken up by the upper strata of the bourgeoisie, who were most intent on aping their social superiors; from there the process of diffusion downward into lower social strata was pushed forward by all kinds of social pressures; until eventually everyone, including the lowest groups, had to conform to some degree on pain of social exclusion.

Elias relates this spread of manners to psychological and emotional inhibitions and repressions—in particular, to a rise in the level of shame. All kinds of activities, which previously in medieval society had been freely and publicly performed, became surrounded with walls of shame, such that even the mere mention of them became embarrassing and pruderies of all kinds proliferated. As this shame threshold rose, so direct physical contacts in activities involving close proximity between people were rendered socially unacceptable. A sphere of bodily privacy was thus constituted around each person, and thereby the separateness of the person was enforced. Thus, for example, sleeping arrangements were so transformed that one could only sleep in one's own personal bed in a room set aside for this purpose, a bedroom, behind closed doors. To break these taboos on privacy was to incur shame to a degree that is hard for us now, when most of them have been broken, to imagine. According to Elias, this separation and isolation of people behind screens of shame set the stage psychologically for the rise of modern individualism.

Elias's work demonstrates that manners are not mere arbitrary social conventions that can be abandoned with impunity at little social cost. Rather, "manners maketh man," that is to say, manners shape personality and character formation by constituting a style of living by means of which people are socialized. Thus of late there has been a general relaxation of the standards of good manners, which have been reduced down to a bare minimum essential for the conduct of public life, and a consequent lowering of the threshold of shame to a level where almost anything can in certain circumstances be done in public—and if not done, then shown on television for public viewing. All this is bound to have profound psychological and ethical consequences. Elias was himself far too sanguine about such contemporary social decivilizing trends because he did not explore the interaction between manners and morals. He made no comprehensive historical study of the relation between ethics and etiquette, not even in the court culture of medieval Western Europe on which he concentrated.

This is obviously not the place for a general critique of Elias; however, a few objections of a purely historical kind must be voiced insofar as they bear on the history of ethics. Elias studies the origin of European manners in a way that is completely divorced from ethics, most crucially from the whole context of the ethics of honor in which they arose. Thus there is no reference to chivalry in Elias's work. In fact, the whole ethical and religious context of medieval society is discounted, and only the political developments of stronger monarchies, or what Elias calls monopolies of violence, are described in any detail and invoked to account for changes in manners. But between politics and manners there intervenes the whole of social culture, which in medieval society involved all the various ethics in complex relations to each other, and that Elias has omitted. His account is at best incomplete and at worst partial.

A fuller account of the origin of manners would need to place it back into its cultural matrix, the rise of the courtly ethics of honor in its Western chivalric form. All the various manifestations of Western etiquette receive their rationale in this ethical dimension and the cultural transformations that followed. Thus, to take but one obvious instance, the raising of the threshold of shame in regard to sex, or female delicacy and general increased prudery, was the result of the introduction of new ethical norms of courtship and courtesy, which came with gallantry and a complete revaluation of love and the role of women in the new cult of romance. Since Elias has nothing to say about that, he makes it appear as if the new standards of sexual shame simply arose as part of some general social repressive phenomenon of affect-control whose main causes were overall changes due to the increased levels of social interaction in economy and polity. But the changed attitude to women, noble ladies in the first place, and the whole refinement of sexual etiquette that it brought in its train, was initially and primarily a cultural matter that had more to do with the emergence of a new ethos than with anything else. How in this context there also arose a new ethic is not a question that Elias can pose, for his work does not lead him to see this as an issue. For us, however, it is the most crucial question of all.

From where did the Western ethics of honor originate? What were its immediate precursors? How far back can these be traced? What, if anything, was their original source? Namely, when did the ethics of honor first make its appearance in human history? With this last question we have arrived at the crux of our historical investigation of the ethics of honor. Given the historical strategy we previously proposed and following the lead of these questions, it would seem as if the only way to proceed is to move backward in time from the medieval period till we arrive at some initial destination. But in terms of exposition this would prove to be an extremely tedious process and would leave one constantly wondering where it was heading. So we shall take the opposite course of postulating a hypothetical point of origin, an initial form of the ethics of honor, then show that it is, indeed, the origin of the medieval ethical formation by demonstrating both that there are close similarities in content between the original and medieval manifestations and that there are plausible historical intermediate links through which the influence of the one was carried over time and space to the other. We shall proceed as if we were tunneling from both ends of history, forward and backward, hoping to meet in the middle.

The ethics of honor made its first appearance in the Persia of the Archaemenenian period—that is our initial assumption. If this can be shown to be true, then it would fit neatly our general supposition that all the ethics arose almost simultaneously during the Axial Age, respectively in Israel, India, Greece, China, and Persia. Persia developed its own ethical forms, which were quite different from any of the others. This was an ethic appropriate to the basic character of its society. The Persian empire was ruled by an aristocratic court society with many quasi-feudal features. Its political and cultural center was the court of the Great King, which was in turn imitated by the courts of the satraps, the King's deputies throughout the empire. A relation of vassalage based on personal fealty, trust, and mutual obligation obtained between the King and his satraps and in turn between the satraps and their warriors. Some of these warriors were already mailed lance-carrying horsemen, the first military version of later *cataphracts* and *clibanarii* and eventually of Western knights. Like the latter, the Persian warriors had to arm themselves and were provided with land holdings for this purpose. This warrior-aristocracy was highly hierarchically structured. At the top were the so-called friends of the King, those whose loyalty to the King was above all other ties, such as to family, clan, or country. Not all these were Persians by birth, for foreigners, too, could win a place within this service-aristocracy through the favor of the King. Thus many Greeks, exiled from their homeland, found a place and made their careers among the so-called great achievers (*eurgetai*) of the King.

All bonds between the various strata of the nobility were personally established and affirmed, as Reinhold Merkelbach puts it, "Diese Treueverhältnisse waren immer gegenseitig und sind durch Zeremonien besiegelt worden, durch Handschlag, Niederknien, Eid und gemeinsame Opfermahlzeit"[181] Through such bonding, mutual obligations were established for both parties, whereby in return for their loyalty the noble servants of the King were rewarded with his favor in the form of *polydoria* or royal gifts of titles, offices, possessions, wealth, and special privileges. Proximity to the King, precedence, and privilege became the all important matters of honor in the ethos of this court society. Special crests, insignia, and family escutcheons, which were established by royal prerogative, point to the importance of pride of place. Women played a crucial role in establishing and consolidating such personal bonding, for in this polygamous society the giving and taking of wives was a guarantee of the permanence of arrangements reached. In other respects women had considerable rights and independence. This then was the quasi-feudal ethos in which the first ethics of honor arose.

For such an ethic to emerge required extraordinary cultural changes that went way beyond the ethos itself and could only happen in the context of a new and spiritually revolutionary religious development—that of Zoroastrianism. The prophet Zarathustra, about whom little is known and everything is contentious, was undoubtedly a historical individual like Confucius and the Buddha. The original form of his religion can no longer be reconstructed from the surviving fragmentary evidence, which is even scantier than that of these other great religious founders. The first form in which the teachings of Zarathustra have come down to us might be gleaned from the Zoroastrianism of the Achaemenid period, for this became the religion of the later Persian kings, certainly so by the time of Artaxerxes (465–425 B.C.), who adopted the Zoroastrian calendar, but possibly as early as Darius, who worshiped Ahura Mazda (the good lord). This was no longer the pure religion of Zarathustra but a mixture of his doctrines together with elements of the earlier Iranian polytheism against which he had fought. It is said that never was a prophet so betrayed by his later followers as was Zarathustra.

The polytheistic features of Zoroastrianism that are of particular relevance to us here in accounting for the formation of an ethics of honor are those associated with the god Mithra. There is considerable dispute as to the role that Mithra played in Zoroastrianism; he is not mentioned by name in the early Zoroastrian texts, in the *Gathas,* in hymns from Zarathustra's own time, and in the *Yasna* from a few centuries later, but only in the younger *Avesta,* which was not recorded till Sassanian times. However, there is considerable extrinsic evidence that the cult of Mithra survived throughout the Achaemenenian and the later dynasties to resurface again during the Sassanian. Thus, for instance, two of the later Achaemenenians, Artaxerxes II Mnemon (404–359 B.C.) and Artaxerxes III Ochos (359–338 B.C.), refer explicitly to Mithra in their inscriptions.[182] It is also the case that the Greeks later mistakenly supposed Zarathustra to be the founder of the Mithra-mysteries, which suggests that the two strands of Persian religion had fused at some point and so became confused with each other to outside observers.[183] It is in this compound form of Zoroastrianism that the ethics of honor first revealed itself.

The cult of Mithra is particularly important in accounting for the feudal features, so to speak, of the ethic. Mithra was the keeper of oaths and promises, the guarantor of all agreements, pacts, and treaties. He was the intermediary god who maintained the integrity of human relations: "Diese persönliche Beziehung zwischen den Menschen—Vertrag (contract), Eid, Freundschaft—alles was in der Mitte zwischen ihnen steht und verbindet, war Mithra."[184] Mithra was initially and remained, through all his varied incarnations right down to the late Roman period, the god of personal loyalties. As such, he was particularly suited to warrior elites of rulers and their followers. Merkelbach calls him "der Gott der iranischen 'Feudalismus,' " but he also shows how this aspect made a version of his cult, known in the West as Mithraism, attractive to Roman legionaries and imperial administrators.[185]

In their original Persian setting, both Mithraism and Zoroastrianism could easily accommodate themselves to each other and fuse into what Zaehner calls "the capacious catholicity of the later Avesta."[186] Both of the respective major gods, Mithra and Ahura, "stand as guardians of Truth and Order, both were united against the Lie."[187] Thus the original puristic monotheism of the prophet Zarathustra, with its absolute moral dualism of *Asha* and *Druj* (Truth and Lie), became suffused with Mithra and all the other personages and powers of Iranian polytheistic mythology, such as the Fravashis, the Khware-nah, Ardri, Sura Ahita, Vaiju, and Verethragna, and these also made their subsidiary contributions to the ethics of honor that arose on this religious basis. Thus, for example, "the Khwarenah, that strange concept hitherto translated as 'Glory,' '*Glückglanz,*' etc., but more recently equated simply with *Fortuna,*"[188] survived not only in the Zoroastrian religious tradition, as Zaehner insists, but also in all the various later manifestations of an ethics of honor that no longer had anything explicitly to do with Zoroastrianism.

The basic Zoroastrian opposition of Truth and Lie or Righteousness and Unrighteousness also became constitutive of the ethics of honor. The insis-tence on absolute honesty, devoid of all subterfuge or deceit, was always a key characteristic of the ethic, one that is surely inherited from its Zoroastrian paternity. In this essential form the ethic goes back to the time of Darius, for Herodotus reports that the Persians taught their sons three things: to ride, to shoot a bow, and to tell the truth. This echoes the boast on Darius's grave inscription:

> Nach dem Willen Auramazdas bin ich so, dass ich das Recht liebe, das Unrecht hasse . . . was recht ist, daran habe ich Gefallen. Einem Lügenknecht bin nicht Freund . . . Kraftvoll bin ich mit Händen und Füssen. Als Reiter bin ich erprobt. Als Bogenschütze bin ich erprobt, zu Fuss wie zu Pferde.[189]

This might be regarded as the first public statement of an ethic of honor. In it, the ethical and physical virtues of the honorable warrior are, as yet, scarcely distinguished.

The ethical character of Zoroastrianism itself is highly pronounced. Apart from the initial opposition of Truth and Lie and the two spirits that preside over these, Spenta Mainyu and Angra Mainyu (Ahriman in Pahlavi), there is also the remarkable doctrine of the Bounteous Immortals, which also goes back to Zarathustra himself. These are the six personifications of ethical virtues and favorable qualities: *Asha* (Righteousness), *Vohu Manah* (Good Mind), *Khshathra* (Power), *Armaiti* (Suitable Disposition), *Haurvatat* (Health), and *Ameretat* (Immortality). Virtues and qualities of this kind were to become prominent features of subsequent ethics of honor. The basic Zoro-astrian dualism of a battle of Truth against Lie, Good against Evil, and Right against Wrong, in which men had to actively participate on the one side against the other seen as the enemy of mankind, clearly suited a warrior ethos and became constitutive of its ethics. Taken together with the Mithra principles of oath and promise keeping and loyalty to those to whom one is bound by pact, the Zoroastrian dualism and its ethical personifications of the Bounteous Immortals constitute a comprehensive ethical standpoint that cannot but have been an original ethics of honor.

There is considerable independent historical evidence that matters of honor and issues of status and standing, especially, in relation to the King, played a crucial role in Persian aristocratic behavior and bearing. Many decisive military moves seem to have been dictated by questions of honor, of which J. M. Cook gives the following examples:

> Xerxes was in honour bound to march against the Athenians whom his father had failed to punish. Megabyxos had to worst the King's generals in order to recover his self-respect. The stories of Pharnabozos and Tiribazos show that there was a limit beyond which personal honour could not be pressed; and in 334 BC Arsites insisted on fighting at the Graneikos rather than allow the King's land and his satrapy to be ravaged.[190]

In an analogous spirit, in personal matters "prestige was all important to a ranking Persian," and "status with the King took precedence over nearly all other motives."[191] Since lower strata of Persian nobility behaved in the same way in relation to their superiors, it is obvious that the whole of Persian aristocratic society was honor-bound by ties of loyalty and fealty in a quasi-feudal manner that had considerable ethical analogues with later feudalisms, those that are much more familiar to us and where an ethics of honor is unquestionably in existence.

The literature of other peoples who were in contact with the Persians at this time substantiates this picture of the Persian way of life. The Apocrypha of the Bible, particularly the book of Esther but also Ezra and Nehemiah, depicts a society where honor, precedent, and status in court ceremonials loom very large. These features of the ethos seem to have made a much stronger impression on the Jews than did Persian religious beliefs.[192] Something similar holds for the extensive references to the Persians in Greek writings; these, too, convey the general impression of an aristocratic honor-bound society that they saw in stark contrast to their own polis society. If one discounts the adverse judgments deriving from their own prejudices—such as those classical clichés concerning oriental tyranny, oriental luxury, the loss of hardiness resulting from this, and from the corrupting influence of women—it is clear that they saw Persia as an aristocratic society that they held in esteem and admiration and that in some respects they were inclined to imitate.

The recent work of Margaret Miller shows in great detail the influence that the Persian aristocratic ethos and the ethical values it embodied exerted on Greece at various stages of its development. In the earliest period of contact between the two peoples, at a time when "the traditional forms of honorific activity for the Greek elite in the archaic period . . . came to an end," there was considerable influence that led to "the accumulation of wealth and the material emulation of an Oriental elite which was at once more secure and more magnificent than any that could be found in Greece."[193] Later, during the period of democratization in Athens, "the Achaemenid world supplied models of behaviour and social distinction to the demos as well as to its elite . . . , it needed *Perserie* to create status-distinction and articulate its own world."[194] For by this stage, "state pay, once introduced, gave citizens the leisure to behave like an aristocracy, by being able to engage in public affairs."[195] The experience of those aristocratic Greeks who found refuge in the court of the King or his satraps, usually when ostracized and exiled from their native cities, also speaks for the honorific character of Persian society. They were invariably graciously received, even when they had been inveterate enemies, such is the case of Themistocles, or even when they had been captured in war, such is the case of Miltiades' son Metiochos. Many of them were given land-grants and found a place among the Persian elite. The style of life they led became endemic to aristocratic nobility throughout the ages, particularly so the addiction to hunting from horseback that the Persians practiced in specially constructed game parks called *paradeiso* (from which our word *paradise* derives and which gives one a clue as to what constitutes heaven on earth for such people).

Thus there is considerable evidence, both from external points of view and from internal remains of the culture, that the Persians of the Achaemenid period already had all the rudiments of an aristocratic ethics of honor. But the historical problem still remains of how this is to be linked to the later exemplifications of that ethic, in particular to the Western ethics of chivalry, given the breaks and discontinuities of Persian history and the enormous span both in time and space separating these societies. However, there were at least two periods in Persian history when these continuities were recovered and when an ethics of honor was once more reconstituted after a previous period of disruption. The first occurred with the onset of the Sassanian dynasty and the revival of an authentic Persian culture; the second, not long after the Arab conquest, when the Turkic peoples, such as the Seljuks, who had established sultanates in the Persian sphere, sought to recover something of the ethos and cultural trappings of the lost Sassanian glory. How from this distant place, but the same point in time, already within the medieval period, these influences eventually reached the Christian West is another story but one not too difficult to tell.

Despite the distance involved, that there was a connection between East and West is obvious when one compares the two epics that were the cynosures of the chivalric culture in the East and the West, the *Shahnahme* and the *Song of Roland*. The latter, composed by Turald around 1100, embodies the chivalric ideals of the Franks in this period, which it projects back three centuries to the time of Charlemagne and his campaigns in Moslem Spain. The influence of the Moslem chivalric ethos is unmistakeable, as it is also in such later epic traditions as that of El Cid. The Moslem warriors are depicted as worthy opponents and partners in knightly combat with their Christian antagonists, and both are shown to share the same predisposition to an ethics of honor. Just how this ethics was conveyed from East to West—for it is most certain that the course of transmission went mainly in that direction—we shall explore further after we have first examined its Eastern epic expression in Firdousi's work.

Firdousi composed his book in Samarkand around 1000 A.D.—that is, at least a century before the *Song of Roland*—at the behest of Mahmud of Ghazni, who conquered territories embracing Iran, Iraq, and parts of India and thus constituted the first of many Turkic empires in this region. The Turks infiltrated into the Moslem sphere, first as soldier-slaves and eventually as de-facto rulers and frontier warriors against the heathens and the Christians, those of Byzantium and the crusader states. Their role in relation to the Moslem world was analogous to that of the Franks to the Christian world, who were at the other end of the Eurasian landmass but with whom they entered into frequent contacts as a result of the Crusades. Between their two distant territories there lay all the varied Arab domains of the Islamic *eucumene*, and these, too, acted as a continuous transmission belt of cultural influence. Thus it is not implausible to suppose that something of the chivalric code could have passed from the *Shahname* to the *Song of Roland* through a chain of contacts extending from Samarkand to Cordoba and from there across the Pyrenees to France.

We know it as a fact that this was precisely the route taken by the intellectual current of Aristotelianism, which went from Ibn Sina ('Avicena) in Samarkand to Ibn Rushd (Averroes) in Cordoba and from there to Abelard and others in Paris. The work of Aristotle had survived in Persia, when it was largely forgotten in the West, due to the closing of the pagan schools of philosophy in Athens by Justinian in 529. Many of these philosophers fled to Sassanian Persia, where they were warmly received. A few centuries after the Arab conquest of Persia, there occurred a philosophical revival that centered on Aristotle. This then became the basis of all medieval scholasticism, Moslem, Judaic, and Christian in roughly that order.

Knowing this trajectory of medieval philosophy makes it all the more certain that other cultural influences were conveyed along the same route. As we shall show, literary influences in numerous forms, ranging from lyric poetry to epic and romance, were undoubtedly passed on. A whole aristocratic ethos of activities, pastimes, games, and ways of bearing and feeling went with this. In this context it is highly likely that the chivalric code took the same road from the *Shahname* to the *Song of Roland*.

When Firdousi completed the *Shahname*, continuing the work begun by an earlier poet in Samarkand, Daqiqi, he was consciously and deliberately seeking to forge an expression of legitimacy through a renewed Iranian tradition for his warrior patron, Mahmud of Ghazni. Once forged, it spread among Turkish warriors throughout and was taken over by later Turkish rulers, such as the Seljuk sultans Alp Arslan and Kilidish Arslan, the conquerors of Anatolia. They imbibed the heroic legends of Firdousi and accepted his work as their chivalric bible, so to speak, next to the Koran. In this way they harked back to historically forgotten and almost lost Persian traditional lore from the Sassanian period, before the Arab conquest. This lore and the literary ethos that it fostered suited their interests as conquering warriors from outside the Arab world much better than anything they could find in Arab culture, for it was much closer to their own steppe traditions. Even though they no longer knew the names of the Sassanian kings and anything from before that period had become the stuff of myth, so that even Alexander was a legendary figure for them, yet they were drawn to the heroic deeds and chivalric exploits of the characters of the traditional Persian stories to which Firdousi had given renewed literary embodiment.

These stories had crystalized from the oral narrations of the Parthian bards, the *gosans*, from the Arsacid period before the Sassanian. Such, for example, was the story of Vis and Ramin, a tale of love and adventure, which became a model for *Tristan and Iseult* of European medieval romance. Many such stories, constituting an Iranian national epos of heroic lore, were retold, completed, and compiled during the decidedly chauvinistic Sassanian revival of Iranian national consciousness. By the close of the reign of Chosroe II (590–628), a compilation entitled the *Chvadaz-namaz* (the *Book of Kings*) was in existence. This was a mixture of heroic sagas and *beau gestes*, together with wise sayings, debates, and dialogues concerning religious, philosophical, and ethical matters and royal testaments and proclamations whose main focus was always questions of justice, religious observance, and the idealized depiction of a noble lifestyle. As Joseph Wiesenhöfer notes, the *Book of Kings* was not only an official history but also a text of social instruction conveying the moral and political ideals and virtues that the Sassanian monarchs wished to impress on their nobles and through which they sought their legitimacy.[196] "Gehorsam, gutes Benehmen, Bildung, Spiel und Jagd wurden verlangt und geübt."[197] Thus it is clear that during the Sassanian period something very close to the later versions of an ethics of honor was already in existence.

This Sassanian period and its culture act as the historical bridge between the early Achaemenid period of the Persian national tradition and its later post-Moslem forms, such as are to be found in the work of Firdousi and among his Turkic patrons and readers, the new sultans who arose out of the collapse of the Abbasid caliphate. The Sassanians self-consciously went back to and modeled themselves on the Achaemenids and, in particular, they strenuously revived the old Persian religion, Zoroastrianism, which had in the meantime, during the long Parthian period of the Arsacids and the previous shorter period of the Seleucids, more or less been lost sight of and it had largely gone underground. How Zoroastrianism survived during this long non-Persian interregnum is still something of a historical mystery, but survive it did, for it came back with a vengeance during the Sassanian period. It was preached and imposed with a particular intolerant exclusivity, driving out all the other religions that had in the meantime established themselves, such as Greek polytheism, Christianity, and Manichaeism, the latter a distinctly Persian religion, founded by the prophet Mani during the reign of Shapur, which also played a crucial role at various times in Western history.

For the Sassanians royalty and religion were well nigh identified: "Religion is royalty, and royalty is the Religion,"[198] as Zaehner puts it. Ardashir, the founder of the dynasty, is quoted as saying, "Religion and kingship are two brothers, and neither can dispense with the other. For whatever lacks a foundation must perish and whatever lacks a protector disappears."[199] Thus "once the royal power is firmly based on the Good Religion, and the Religion is protected by the King, a just society will arise."[200] Among the sayings attributed to Chosroe, the ideal king, in the *Denkart,* a later tenth-century collection of Zoroastrian writings, is one to the effect that when religion and royalty support each other, "the Empire will prosper, the common people will be freed from fear and enjoy a good life, science will advance, culture will be looked after, good manners will be further refined, and men will be generous, just, and grateful; many a virtue will they practice and perfect will their goodness be."[201] It is clear from this that the unification of religion and royalty is in effect the linking of Zoroastrianism to a court culture, with its distinctive aristocratic ethos and ethics of honor.

Aspects of this Persian ethics of honor were conveyed through the work of Firdousi, first to the whole Moslem cultural world and then to the Frankish Christians. The key points of transmission from East to West were the frontier regions where the two conflicting religions confronted each other, both in war and peace. Primarily, these were Spain and the adjacent regions of southern France, southern Italy and Sicily, the crusading regions of Palestine, Syria and Egypt, and the Anatolian routes that crusaders took. Just how this transmission was effected is too historically detailed to be conveyed here. Frequently, there were personal meetings and encounters between prominent Moslem and Christian rulers involved, particularly so during the Crusades. There is the well-known story of the relationship between Richard Lionheart and Saladin, who was a Kurd from the Persian region. The work of Rudolf Fahner is particularly rich in many other such illustrative examples concerning meetings between the German emperors on crusade and Turkish Seljuk rulers through whose territories they had to pass, such as that between Henry the Lion and Kilidish Arslan II in 1170–1 and Philipp von Schwaben and Keyhusrev in 1192–6.[202] The emperor Frederick II was especially close to the Moslem cultural sphere, both through his Sicilian possessions and through his crusading activities. Stories from the literature of both cultures testify to the common chivalric codes and values that had come to prevail. Thus Fahner quotes from the touching story of Sharkan and Abriza in the *1001 Nights* collection and from Wolfram von Eschenbach's romance epic *Willehalm*. He also mentions that some of the German Minnesänger, such as Friedrich von Hausen, perhaps the first of them all, accompanied their lords on crusade and brought back with them something of the Moslem lore of chivalry and gallantry.

Gallantry is the other aspect of the ethics of honor that we have already mentioned and that can be also shown to have Persian roots. It is the crucial feminine component of the ethics that governs relations between the sexes, initially noble lords and ladies. Its cult of love received literary expression in the West in the poetry of the troubadours of Southern France, trouvères of Northern France, and Minnesänger in German lands. From the medieval period onward, as romantic love and courtship, it remained permanently in European culture and its ethics.[203] Debased versions of it are still to be found even now in popular literature and films.

The Persian sources for this poetry and the associated cult of love are unmistakable. Its most immediate influence came from the Arabic poetry of southern Spain, where Al Hatham's collection, *The Dove's Necklace*, was already available in 1020, about a century before William of Aquitaine, the first of the troubadours. The convention of love poems addressed to a cruel mistress had begun long before among the Arab Andalusians, being current at least since 820. This had clearly Persian sources going back to the pre-Islamic past. The work of Julie Scott Meisami on Persian court poetry shows that the "courtly ethic that informs this poetry had its roots in antiquity."[204] This ethic, as she goes on to say, "influenced not only the Persian literature that developed in the Islamic period, but the Arabic tradition as well (through which it may even have extended its influence to medieval Europe)."[205] Her cautious scholarly formulation need not be taken as doubt, in the light of the evidence Meisami herself adduces.

According to the earlier work of Denis de Rougemont, other Persian-derived influences also played a vital role in the origins of the poetry of courtly love—above all, the Persian-developed religion of Manicheaism. He writes, "that as early as the ninth century there occurred an equally 'unlikely' fusion of Iranian Manichaeism, Neo-Platonism and Mohammedanism in Arabia, and the fusion was reflected in religious poetry employing erotic metaphors that are strikingly akin to those of courtly rhetoric."[206] We cannot go into all the detail that de Rougemont adduces to prove his case, but there is enough to show that there are close parallels between what he calls the "erotico-religious language of Arab mystic poetry" and later Christian courtly and mystical poetry as well. The influence of Persian Manichaeism is often prevalent, as in the work of Suchrawardi of Aleppo, who mixed neo-Platonic teaching with Zoroastrian ideas, "indeed his neo-Platonism displays marked Persian mythical features."[207]

As is well known, de Rougemont's main case is that the new troubadour poetry derives much of its inspiration from Catharism, the heretical Mani-chean religion of the south of France that flourished simultaneously with the troubadours until it was destroyed in the Albigensian crusade. There is much evidence for this contention, particularly so as often the very same people, generally noble ladies, patronized both the religion and the poetry at once. But there is also evidence against it. We cannot buy into this debate here. However, if we provisionally accept his conclusion, then it would follow that Persia exercised a most remarkable double-pronged influence on Europe, for "there occurred during the twelfth century in Languedoc and in the Limou-sin one of the most extraordinary spiritual confluences in history,"[208] as de Rougemont puts its. On the one hand, Persian Manichaeism spread through the Byzantine empire and eventually reached Italy and Southern France as Catharism, where it came together with another movement also emanating from Persia, which traveled by way of Turkic and Arab courts and through

Sufi mystical sects of Iraq and elsewhere till it reached Andalusia, from where it went to Southern France. If de Rougemont is right, which is not altogether certain, then, as he puts it, "courtly lyric was the offspring of that encounter" of the two streams of influence emanating originally from Persia. This is a bold historical hypothesis that obviously suits the case developed here, but one that can still be maintained in a more muted form even if de Rougemont's grand theory is insupportable.

Comparative Studies

As we have seen from the preceding accounts, there have been throughout history quite different types of ethical systems. Ethics has taken many diverse forms deriving from quite different origins, and these have been most frequently in opposition and conflict with each other. For in their content, in terms of what each enjoins and forbids or praises and blames, the four types have almost nothing in common with each other. It is true that there is a basic vocabulary of terms applied in ethical matters that is common to many languages, words such as *good* and *bad* or *evil*, *right* and *wrong*, *proper–improper*, *just–unjust*, *virtuous–vicious*, and so on. But that does not attest to any common content, for these terms can also be applied in non-ethical contexts, and when used in ethics their meaning shifts, depending on the ethics in question. It is a commonplace to note that what is good in one is bad in another, what is just in one is unjust in another, that the virtues of one become the vices of another, and so on. However, as we shall show, this observation does not lead to complete ethical relativism, for content is not all that counts in ethics.

Nevertheless, to begin with, it is necessary to stress the oppositions and, indeed, contradictions between the ethics, for that best brings out their characteristic peculiarities. In their pure and original form they are irreconcilable. However, as we shall also show, this has not prevented attempts at mediation between them that have constantly been taking place throughout history and that have frequently been highly successful, leading to the creation of the syncretist unifications that are the ethics known to us now. Most of the ethics now practiced throughout the world are the outcomes of such successful historical reconciliations and consolidations. Hence, the oppositions between the ethics can be overcome but only at the cost of departing from their original principled purity. What this means we shall see in the more detailed historical investigations of ethical developments in the universal cultures that follow. But before we can come to that, we must first examine with greater specificity in which ways the fundamental types differ from each other.

We might begin to distinguish the four basic ethics according to differences in what Weber calls the "external and internal guarantees," on which every ethic relies for its efficacy. As Weber puts it, "an 'externally' guaranteed order may also be guaranteed 'internally.' ";[209] indeed, in ethics it must be so guaranteed. It is true that "external guarantees will be usually lacking where the violation of the standard does not appreciatively affect the interest of others," but only if this is understood in the sense of "legal guarantees through police or the means of criminal or private law"; for Weber himself grants that "possibly they may also be guaranteed conventionally (in our sense of the term), i.e. through disapproval or boycott." Weber goes on to note that "ethics, which is valid in the sociological sense, usually is guaranteed by convention, i.e. by the probability of its violation meeting with disapproval," and that is also a kind of external guarantee. But, as Weber also notes, the "ethical standard, which is one that applies to human conduct that specific kind of evaluating faith which claims to determine what is 'ethically good,' " is also "frequently guaranteed religiously," that is, "innerly" guaranteed. Or as he puts it elsewhere with specific reference to the Protestant ethic, "we are interested rather in the influence of those psychological sanctions which, originating in religious belief and the practice of religion, gave direction to practical conduct and held the individual to it."[210] As we shall see in what follows, not all such psychological sanctions originate in religion. Those that do hold a special importance in the history of ethics and these we have designated as conscience. However, there are also psychological sanctions of various other kinds that we shall study presently.

Every ethic has to rely on both internal and external guarantees, for otherwise it is ineffective—though in exceptional circumstances the one or the other can be reduced to a minimum. Usually, however, an ethic will utilize various kinds of sanctions of a social and psychological nature at once. The external guarantees are usually publicly enforceable rules, laws, and norms that are imposed either by conventional means of disapproval and commendation or by more stringent formal ones of punishment and reward. The internal guarantees are self-enforcing psychological dispositions, such as emotional complexes, attitudes, beliefs, and qualities of character. In these ways every ethic molds people to suit its own unique requirements and ensures that they will be innerly directed as well as externally guided; able to decide what to do in any predicament requiring an ethical response, guided both by what is required of them by their community and by what they themselves judge through deliberation and proper feeling (we shall deal with these two aspects more fully in chapter 4).

Feeling has to be particularly emphasized in any study of ethics that wishes to get beyond the aridities of philosophical theorizing. Feelings, which comprise a whole gamut of ethical emotions, are the most powerful of the inner guarantees. Such feelings are not naturally given but must be acquired through refinement and cultivation. To be brought up ethically means to undergo an education of the emotions, for which different types of personality have more or less aptitude. Emotional differences between people are just as marked as intellectual ones, though, of course, the two are not to be dissociated in the classical style of reason versus the passions, for there is such a thing as emotional intelligence and it is this that is crucially involved in ethics. It is impossible to conduct oneself ethically by simply going by rules and prescriptions; those who do so become legalistically hidebound and unable to respond where the law does not spell out precisely what they are to do. Such people are barely ethical beings; unfortunately, today they constitute the overwhelming majority. To be an ethical person leading an ethical life, in which all kinds of contingencies must constantly be encountered on which the ethical law is silent or wrong-headed, calls for qualities of character in which refinements of feeling and delicacies of tact are necessary to determine what is the proper course to pursue. Those who have failed or been unable to develop such qualities cannot know or do what is right.

Ethical emotions are neither natural nor universal; every system of ethics cultivates those that are peculiar to itself. What it has to work with are very basic human feelings, some of which are common to all of mankind, such as shame and guilt, which are a necessary part of any socialization, whatever form it takes. But such basic and primitive feelings are far from being ethical emotions, which are motivational, attitudinal, and ideational complexes that are the products of a long-sustained ethical education. Through such an education ethical feelings become a second nature, one that inheres in a person as character qualities. Such feelings are involved in judgments of aversion or approval that can often follow what seem like instinctive reactions, ones that do not call for explicit deliberation or even thought. Often such judgments of feeling can be surer and sounder than long-deliberated decisions. In ethics, as in aesthetics, the initial reaction can often be the most critically just one; it is in this sense that intuition plays such a crucial role in both fields. Such intuitions need, of course, to be justified in a more rationally discursive fashion, usually after the act, but without them the process of judging could not even begin in most cases.

Every ethic has as its inner guarantee two poles, positive and negative, of complexes of feeling. At the one polarity are those positive feelings that incite people to desire the good, to value what is worthy, to believe in what is right, and to motivate them to act in the right way. At the other polarity are the negative feelings that serve the opposite function, to make people averse to what is bad, to despise what is unworthy, to discredit what is wrong and not to do it. As with all complexes of feeling, there are the inevitable ambivalences, such as those of love-hate and the desire for forbidden fruit, but we shall for the moment disregard these and consider the ethical emotions as if they were quite independent of each other, which in reality is often not the case.

Thus, as our previous study has shown, the religious ethics we have called moralities have as their inner guarantees the positive emotion of love and the negative one of guilt. But, as we pointed out, it is a special kind of ethical love that is involved, such as the Judaic love of neighbor or the Christian *caritas*. This love is defined in contradistinction to all other kinds of love, typically *agape* is contrasted to *eros* and even to *philia*. To be capable of *agape* is to be brought up as a Christian or to achieve this through conversion, and it is only on the basis of this capacity that a Christian moral life can be led. "Love, and then do what you like" is St. Augustine's somewhat extreme expression of this standpoint. He was also keenly aware of the negative pole of morality: the special feeling of guilt called conscience, which on the Christian view follows from Original Sin. Psychologically seen, this is, of course, not an inborn but an inculcated propensity to experience the guilt of sin and culpability. It can be explained as a process of internalization that constitutes a super-ego censor whose breach leads to self-torment, which is graphically conveyed in the Middle English phrase "agenbite of inwit." Its contemporary critics view it as moral masochism. However, without it there can be no morality, even if other forms of guilt are manifest. Radcliffe-Brown's view that "what is called conscience is . . . the reflex in the individual of the sanctions of society" is not only historically incorrect, since not every society produces people of conscience, but is also psychologically shallow in its understanding of what it takes to induce this specifically moral form of guilt.[211]

We can find analogous polarities of feeling that act as inner guarantees, in Weber's sense, in the ethics of honor. They are highly specific cultivated forms of pride and shame, which are refined versions of the ordinary emotions that are universally prevalent. The pride of a sense of honor is not just any ordinary feeling of status and superiority; it is the sense of being a certain kind of noble man, the aristocrat or gentleman who is by "nature" obliged to act ethically—"noblesse oblige" is its watchword. If he were to betray this nature inherent in his good "breeding," then he would suffer the shame of dishonor: the extraordinary shame of degradation and derogation, a sense of losing his worth and not being himself, which he would experience even if nobody else was aware of his dereliction. He feels ashamed of himself before his own eyes and not necessarily those of another. Hence, this is different from the ordinary shame all people feel at being disgraced or humiliated in the eyes of others, which the Chinese call "loss of face." Every ethos utilizes this ordinary kind of shame but allows it to be redressed by simple acts of evasion or compensation for the shameful deed. However, the shame of dishonor can only be expiated by a whole life course dedicated to righting the wrong and winning back one's own self-respect—that is, regaining one's honor.

As we previously noted, the ethic of civic virtue does not depend to any extent on either deep shame or deep guilt; it works with other emotional means for its inner guarantees. Its positive motivating emotions are a complex of feelings to do with *philopolis,* love of one's city or patriotism, and the desire for achievement and glory, *kleos* and *kudos.* Its contrasting negative feelings that guarantee adhesion to the city and its laws are a complex of fears, ranging from the simple fear of punishment to all the other anxieties and apprehensions of failure, disgrace, and rejection by one's fellow citizens. Both the positive and negative complexes are "other-directed" feelings, ones that are invoked in the context of fellowship with others, in the public life shared with fellow citizens, and that are consequently weak when this commonality no longer obtains. Hence the tendency of those in exile to turn against their city. They are not deeply internalized emotions that become constitutive of the whole inner soul or personality. Thus patriots and nationalists will sacrifice themselves and everything else, typically their families, for their country while they are bound to it, but if circumstances change and they feel rejected, they are also liable to turn against it. It is quite different with the more deeply internalized emotions of morality and the ethics of honor, to which changed circumstances make little difference.

The internalization of emotions in the ethic of duty lies somewhere between these extremes. To be a man of duty is more binding than being a good citizen but not quite as compelling as being a man of honor or a man of conscience. The official can maintain his sense of duty with utmost dedication and devotion so long as he holds office, but once out of office it becomes much more difficult for him to maintain his dutiful bearing. This was the typical perplexity of the Chinese mandarin once dismissed, frequently unjustly so—how should such a "gentleman" accept his fate? It is a typical ethical problem reflected in Chinese poetry and painting. It is possible to maintain a sense of oneself as a man of duty even if one has been cashiered or demoted; such a person will console himself by saying, "I did what I had to do even though I suffer for it." The positive feelings motivating such a man are the complex emotions of piety and propriety, a sense of reverence and decorum, respect for authority and abiding by traditions, and these can be maintained even in adversity. The negative feelings are fear of disgrace, humiliation, and other consequences of failure, and these are more difficult to bear in adversity. Hence, a man of duty is more dependent on external circumstances, above all on the will and favor of those in authority, than is the moral man or man of honor, but not as much as the man of civic virtue.

We can see from the preceding that the kinds of emotions typically invoked in the various ethics differ in their coloring from each other. Those of the ethics of duty tend to the cool pastel range of the muted emotional palette; those of the civic ethic to the strong contrasts of calm blue and red-blooded hot and passionate hues; morality is more like an emotional chiaroscuro black and white of perdition and innocence; and the ethics of honor shines with the gold and glory glitter of the noble sentiments. As the ethics differ emotionally from each other, so they also differ in the kinds of character and personality types that each promotes. The image of the good man or woman in each is very different. They are opposed in the way of life each enjoins and in the virtues and vices this involves. It is impossible to live by more than one type of ethic at any one time if this is taken in its pure form. Though obviously, as we shall see in the next chapter, all kinds of mixed hybrid or syncretist forms of ethics are also available. These also bring with them mixed feelings or modulated emotions and variegated character types.

The various types of pure ethics can also to some extent be distinguished according to the external guarantees that they rely on to ensure social conformity. As Weber has shown, there are three basic kinds of external guarantees: those sanctioning laws, conventions, and norms. Laws are sanctioned through external coercive means involving physical or "spiritual" punishments. Physical punishments are typically imposed by a legally instituted apparatus for the dispensing of violence and "spiritual" ones by instituted processes of rejection or exclusion, such as excommunication or ostracism or some other denial of fellowship. Conventions, which include a wide variety of practices of the mores and manners kind, are sanctioned quite differently, through largely informal means. According to Weber, a convention "shall be said to exist wherever a certain conduct is sought to be induced without, however, any coercion, physical or psychological, and, at least under normal circumstances, without any direct reaction other than the expression of approval or disapproval on the part of the persons who constitute the environment of the actor."[212] There are various types of convention that are enforced in this general way but with significant social differences.

Norms are quite different again from laws or conventions; consequently, they are socially sanctioned in a different way to either. A norm is not a simple prescription for conduct that can be stated in the form of a rule, but only as a general directive whose fulfillment or breach is always a matter of judgment, which can be contested and so needs to be justified, for it is not immediately apparent. Thus the rule "never utter deliberately what is not true" is a simple social prescription that needs to be taught to small children but that would be utterly debilitating if practiced in adult life. Whereas "never tell a lie" is an ethical norm that relates only tangentially to the previous prescription because whether a specific untruth is or is not a lie is a matter for judgment that must take all kinds of other factors into account besides the simple fact that what one has said knowingly is not true. It is similarly so with the act of killing and the crime of committing murder or taking property and stealing. Hence, whether or not one breaches a norm is always a complex and contested matter of deliberative judgment. There are also norms that do not take an either-or, guilty or innocent, form, but that as Agnes Heller puts it, "are prescriptions which one neither completely fulfills nor completely infringes but to which one lives up to varying degrees."[213] The fulfillment or infringement of such a norm cannot, therefore, be expediently and expeditiously rewarded or punished either by the coercive means of law or the social sanctions of conventional approval or disapproval. Rather, it reflects itself in one's general standing or reputation within an ethical community, that is, in one's good or bad name, which is earned and deserved not merely for any specific acts but for conduct extending over a period of time sometimes lasting as long as a lifetime. Thus someone who earns a reputation for honesty, for not telling lies or deceiving, does so on account of a permanent disposition to act in truthful ways in many and varied circumstances. The threat of losing that reputation then acts as a powerful disincentive against telling a lie on any one specific occasion. This is much more weighty than conventional current disapproval of a single bad deed or the threat of legal sanctions.

Ethics differ from each other to the extent to which they rely on these different types of external guarantees, the various modes of social sanction associated with laws, conventions, and norms. Of course, all ethics utilize all three, but they do so to varying degrees and with different emphases. This is partly a function of the general ethos in which each ethic is culturally embedded and so it can change as this ethos changes. Hence, an ethic might begin by relying largely on laws and over a time shift to relying on conventions, or vice versa; or it might begin with the main emphasis on norms and end up with laws, or vice versa. Numerous such variations are known to us from the history of ethics.

The civic ethics, which began in the ethos of the polis culture, relied mainly on law for its external guarantees. Thus Ion greets Medea, in the play by Euripides of that name, with the words, "The land of Greece is now your home, you have learned justice and to live according to the law," which shows that law enforcement was initially of crucial importance to this ethic. However, conventions and norms, such as justice that was not enforced in any legal way, were also present. According to Agnes Heller, Aristotle explicitly recognized this and "in his theory of *mesotes* discussed virtue norms in exactly this way"—that is, "offering greater personal spare for deliberation, judgement and choice."[214] In time, however, when much of the civic ethics lost its legal basis, it became purely a conventional matter of social approval and condemnation. Eventually, in later European history, it ceased even to be conventional and became a choice of general humanistic norms that were part of the classical cultural heritage maintained by scholars, intellectuals, and patriots who were classically minded.

It was the reverse of this process in the case of the history of the moralities. These generally began with generalized norms, such as that enjoining charity, which stemmed from prophetic enunciation. Only gradually did these norms become conventionalized in common social practices and eventually legalized explicitly in the form of religious laws of various types. Due to this process, the moralities changed fundamentally, moving from being primarily what Weber calls a *Gesinnungsethik* to a *Gesetzethik*. We can see this transformation taking place in the history of Judaism, from the morality of the prophetic books to that of the rabbinic form inscribed in the Talmud, where eventually all the moral norms were systematized into 613 commandments, the *mitzvot*. An analogous process of codification took place within Christianity, where the general norms of the early Christian communities were eventually, by the early Middle Ages, enforced through the explicit injunctions of Church Canon law. Within the Christian churches of contemporary times an opposite process seems to be taking place, as the enforceable laws of Christian discipline are once more returning to their initial state of advocated norms for those who wish to live a fully Christian life.

The ethics of honor began neither with norms nor with laws but primarily with conventions in the form of good manners. Codes of etiquette for knights and ladies were elaborated as guides to proper action and enforced through the pressure of class conformity, such as the obligatory aristocratic ceremonial of court society. They were imposed much in the same way as fashions, any breach of which threatens to make one a laughingstock and exclude one from the social circles that count. Attempts were made during late medieval times to translate these codes of manners into ritual laws and enforced ceremonial procedures, which resulted in the punctillio of the late medieval courts of Burgundy, Spain, and eventually France, especially under Louis XIV. The contrary course ensued in Protestant countries, such as England, where the chivalric codes became norms of gentlemanly and ladylike comportment. Through this shift from convention and law to norm, the knight gradually turned into the gentleman.

The ethics of duty has always relied for its external guarantees on a complex admixture of law, convention, and norm. The official is bound by the regulations governing the exercise of his office, by the conventions of propriety of what he can and cannot do outside his explicit competences, and by the general norms of conduct governing how he shall bear himself as a man of duty. However, there has historically been enormous variation in the kind of law applicable, in how conventions are imparted, and in what ways norms are exercised. Thus the law by which an official is bound might be sacred law, as in India; enacted positive law, as in China or Rome; Canon law, as in the medieval church; or legislated statutes, as in modern bureaucracies. These different kinds of law lead to quite different conceptions of duty and how it is to be carried out. Once again, we find continuous transitions taking place from one form of law to another. At present, the ethics of officialdom is diluted and threatens to dissolve altogether by the steady encroachment of statute law and administrative regulation that erodes customary convention, the proper forms, as well as the norms of duty. To realize what this means, one need only consider the transitions in German officialdom from the Prussian civil servant of the nineteenth century to the bureaucrat of the Nazi state in the twentieth. The current "privatization" of official functions through short-term contract outsourcing, which threatens to destroy an independent civil service altogether, is also bound to have dangerous ethical consequences.

Ethical transformations become even more complex when changes in the inner and external guarantees take place in conjunction with each other or, as sometimes happens, when one of these changes but the other fails to keep pace. In the latter case all kinds of ethical anomalies and even contradictions can arise. Thus, for example, when morality comes to be enforced as law and purely externally guaranteed through coercion, then the psychological states, the emotions, and character qualities, on which it depends for its internal guarantees, will tend to be eroded. An anomalous state ensues of both enjoining yet frustrating the ethical norms and their purpose. Such incoherencies are to be encountered in the history of all the ethics. In every one, situations arise where what society officially requires and what people feel and desire privately can move out of phase with each other. Usually, what happens is that new currents of feeling and thought, new inner guarantees, arise in some groups to which the society in general, especially acting through its political authorities, cannot as yet adjust or accept and insists on maintaining and enforcing the old external sanctions. Or it can happen the other way around, that a society through its political bodies seeks to impose by means of external sanctions what cannot as yet be innerly guaranteed for people are not ready for it psychologically. In due course, societies stabilize and do attain a state of ethical equilibrium when a particular kind of ethic does consolidate itself, and then both kinds of guarantees harmonize with each other. The more traditional an ethic, the more this ensues. Eventually, a state of inertia supervenes and further change becomes more difficult, if not impossible.

All such changes in ethics must be considered not just in the context of each of the four fundamental types taken on its own, but even more so in the context of conflicts between them, which can often result in eventual mergers. When this happens, then the internal and external guarantees of two or more ethics enter into opposition with each other, which leads to enormous tensions, for such a turbulent situation can last for many centuries before some kind of fusion is attained. This struggle can be waged both externally and internally, both socially and psychologically, and not only as between groups or individuals but within them; it can take place in families or in the psyche of the one individual torn between different tendencies. Some of these complexities will be exemplified in the next chapter when we consider the actual historical interactions of the various "pure" types of ethics with each other.

However, before we begin the discussion of the actual histories of the ethics in relation and opposition to each other, especially as this occurred in the West from the early Christian period onward, it is necessary to clarify some very general issues about ethical history. There are many ways of approaching this history, which differ depending on the presuppositions adopted as to the nature of historical change in general. Frequently, such presuppositions were derived from other areas of study and applied to the history of ethics without a proper regard for its peculiarities. Here we cannot outline and refute every one of many such theoretical assumptions; we will only mention a few in passing. As opposed to these, we shall specify on a few crucial points how our own approach differs. We begin with a general consideration of what are origins in ethics and what role they play in subsequent history.

Every one of the four fundamental types of ethics as we previously examined them existed in a particularly "pure" and clear state close to its origins. This runs counter to the common evolutionary and progressivist assumption that the further back we go in the history of ethics, the more we encounter ethics that are crude and simple versions of their own later states. Weber, however, insists that this is not the case: "The argument has been advanced that the 'simple' must have stood at the beginning of 'evolution'; that does not always hold in this field."[215] Thus the origin should not be conceived of as the state of inchoate abstractness that later dialectical development must unfold, according to Hegelian theory. Nor is it the *fons et origo* of traditional theology, according to which everything is already given in the beginning so that even the end is prefigured in it. In their original state the ethics are already fully formed, both whole and complete in themselves. But this does not mean that all subsequent developments are already contained in them. Such developments are frequently complications that depart from the original "purity," but they are not for that reason degenerations. The origin must not be conceived in either of these teleological ways, as containing fully formed all that came later or as being merely the germ that tends toward a predetermined development.

By insisting on the completeness and purity of the ethics in their original states, we are not taking sides with those reformers known as purists or Puritans in the West and now called fundamentalists throughout the world, who advocate a return to origins as the solution to current problems. Such there have been throughout the ages. Invariably, what they advocate is a reversion back to the fundamentals that they suppose were once and for all time laid down in the beginning, demanding a return back to first principles, back to the intentions of the founders and the sacred texts, back to the original community, back to everything that once was and is no longer. For every departure from these sacred origins they see as an inevitable corruption. Such demands can, of course, never be realized in reality; there can be no such thing as literally a move back to origins, since the past is not repeatable. In fact, as we shall also see, such puristic attempts to recall the origin are frequently not even traditional but highly innovative and revolutionary in their effects. Many new ethical movements began in this way. Whether any of the present fundamentalist movements will also be innovatory is doubtful, for they seem to be merely traditionalistic.

These views of the traditionalists that purity and integrity are to be found in the origin stand opposed to secular historicist assumptions that there is ethical progress, whether this is seen as a steady and continuous social evolution or a dialectical revolution through contradictions leading from lower to higher stages. Progress or regress, evolution or devolution—which of these characterizations fits the facts of ethical history? The one is a mirror image of the other and simply reverses the patterns of the other. Modern theories of ethical progress or development upturn and invert the more traditional assumptions of degeneration and corruption. The latter see the departure from origins as an ever greater diminution and loss of vigor or purity; the former see the origin as only the starting point of a journey from the inchoate and indefinite to the more fully realized, and, therefore, as a gain in that energy and actuality whereby something becomes what it was not before. The battle of the ancients and the moderns on the ground of ethical history is still to this day being fought out in these terms. The contemporary exponents of ethical modernism, such as the philosopher Habermas or the psychologist Kohlberg, are only the most current expounders of historicist theories going back through Dewey and Hobhouse to Hegel, St-Simon, Condorcet, Kant, and other progressivist thinkers of the Enlightenment. The ancients, too, have their contemporary representatives in such traditionalist thinkers as Voegelin, Strauss, Arendt, and their teacher, Heidegger, who believed in the primacy of origins as constitutive of all later developments, a view he undoubtedly derived from traditional theological sources.[216] Both sides presuppose à priori philosophical schemes without any detailed studies of ethical history.

The history of ethics is much more complicated and differentiated than either of these simple patterns can allow. It reveals no unambiguous linear progress or regress. In fact, it is not the one history, but four different historical trajectories that take off from quite distinct origins, which later meet and interpenetrate in a bewildering variety of ways, producing all kinds of ethical complexes and compounds. The ethics that are still current today are but the latest surviving forms, themselves of very many different kinds, of these historical confrontations that have been taking place in various places in the world since the Axial Age, the period of the inception of the four basic types. Such is the tangled story of ethics that we have to tell, but it is a truer history than the simpler semi-mythological accounts put forward by contemporary ancients or moderns.

The history of ethics is largely one of oppositions and conflicts. As we have already shown, even at the very start, each of the ethics had to contend against the prior pre-ethical ethos, and the ensuing cultural battles internal to a civilization could go on for a very long time. But they pale into insignificance when compared to the clash of two divergent ethics. These were the most world-shattering and world-shaping events of cultural history. Their outcome was always unpredictable and led to varying results in the different civilizations where they occurred. In our historical account we shall mainly deal with what took place within the Roman empire when Judeo-Christian morality encountered the civic ethics of Hellenistic classicism, out of which eventually emerged the hybrid ethics of medieval Christian Europe. But there are many other examples of such historical confrontations, which had very different outcomes. The almost parallel meeting of Buddhist morality with the Confucian ethics of duty in imperial China during the same period resulted in a quite other settlement of differences, one that produced the typical separate paths of traditional Chinese culture. Somewhat later there occurred an analogous encounter between the conquering Moslem morality of the Koran with the Zoroastrian-based courtly codes of Sassanian chivalry, which resulted in the peculiar Shiite forms of courtly Persian ethics and culture. When this ethics of chivalry made its appearance in Western Europe it, too, clashed with the prevailing Christian-classical ethics, and the outcomes of the resultant medieval tensions were the Renaissance and Reformation ethics, which were a prelude to modernity. In none of these cases can one speak of progress or regress in any obvious sense. There is no logic that can account for them. What happens in ethics follows the main lines of human history and is as meaningful or meaningless as that is.

However, some discernable patterns tend to recur in the history of ethics. One can recognize two very general propensities: there is a principle of conservation and a principle of adaptation at work. On the one hand, every ethics seeks to assert itself and exclude every other, hence the clashes between them. But, on the other hand, every ethics tries to adapt itself to reality, and that also can mean having to accommodate itself to another ethics that is present in its cultural environment. These are, of course, only the most general formulations for all kinds of processes at work in the history of ethics, which we shall study in greater detail in the next chapter.

In their original and relatively "pure" forms, so to speak, all the ethics tend to repel and stand in fundamental contradiction to each other. Hence, the conflict between them is severest on their first encounters. In their initial confrontations they cannot even understand each other. The concepts they employ are glaringly different. And even where linguistically the terms are the same or close approximations in translation, yet their meaning can be utterly diverse. We can exemplify this with a term like *justice*, which is widely current in most ethics and has close analogues in many of their languages. But what it means to be just in one ethics is not what it means in another.

In one, it is always just to harm one's enemy; in a second, it is never just to do so; in a third, it is just to kill one's enemy when he has the same opportunities (as in a duel); in a fourth, justice must attend on the formal procedures of law, which alone can sanction execution of one's enemy; or the law may forbid this but leave it open to private vengeance; and so on. Justice toward enemies is very variable, depending on the ethics in question.

However, this does not mean that the relativist's case, succinctly summed up in Hamlet's words "there is nothing right or wrong but thinking makes it so," is correct. It is true that what is right or wrong depends on the ethic. Hence the absolutist or universalist case, that there is but one standard of right or wrong for all time, cannot be sustained. But the converse relativist view, that anything can be as right or as wrong as one chooses to consider it, does not follow. Every ethics has its own integrity, such that it can admit some things but not others, for otherwise it would negate itself or lead to self-contradictory confusions. Something akin to a coherence theory of truth works best for ethics: something is right or wrong depending on how it fits into the whole ethical complex. This is an objective and not subjective matter—thinking does not make it so. Thus, in relation to an ethical tradition, ethical norms can in this sense be objectively founded. And such a tradition itself is not freely chosen or established by arbitrary fiat; it is historically given. It is the expression of a particular ethos and underlies a whole way of life and the forms of knowledge that go with it. In this way, too, it is objective in a social sense.

But, as between themselves the ethics differ fundamentally, particularly so in their original or "pure" forms; in later versions there has often occurred a degree of adjustment to each other and, therefore, there is far more similarity of outlook. Still, the fundamental differences persist and we can bring these out by examining their various responses to the three most crucial activities of human life that are universal constants in all societies: killing or violence, sex or reproduction, and exchange or commerce in general. Making war, making love, and making money are the three most highly fraught aspects of all ethics. How an ethic regulates these determines its essential character to a large degree. And, as we can show, the ethics differ radically in how they treat the three necessities of life on which the success or failure of an individual so crucially depends. For prowess, erotic love, and wealth are the three basic criteria of well-being in almost all societies, and, therefore, they are quasi-universal conditions of human happiness.

Ethical rulings on killing are extremely varied. Thou shalt not kill is a norm in all moralities, though it takes more or less of an absolute form in each of them. In the other ethics not only is it allowed to kill, but in some it is highly laudable to do so in the appropriate circumstances. In the civic ethic there is nothing more praiseworthy than killing in combat the enemies of one's city, nation, or state. In the honor ethic, one is obliged to give battle and never turn one's back in war; any injury or slight to personal honor has to be requited with death, and not to respond to a challenge to mortal combat is the highest dishonor. In the ethic of duty, the official is bound to oppose with arms and execute all traitors, rebels, and heinous criminals. Thus most ethics do not have any great difficulties with killing, but with morality this becomes an issue of greatest consequence. Some moralities absolutely prohibit killing not only human beings but creatures of any kind. Such is the morality of the Jains in India, and the Buddhists, too, follow it to some degree, absolutely so in as far as it applies to monks. No Western morality ever went that far in prohibiting killing. Some, such as Christianity, began with a complete ban on killing human beings, for it enjoined one to love even one's enemies. But in time this absolute prohibition had to be weakened and modified as soldiers were admitted to full participation in the communion of the Church. Killing first came to be generally allowed in pursuance of a proper military vocation, then in defense of the faith in wars against heretics and heathens, and eventually in all wars with just causes. The Muslim morality also sought to restrict killing to holy wars and made it a sin to kill fellow believers; in this it was almost from the start unsuccessful, as battles for the succession to the caliphate arose that were settled by violence.

In the next chapter we will take further the history of the Christian accommodation to the taking of human life, which is a key example of the process of adaptation to the necessities of the world. This adaptation to reality Christianity had to undergo if it was to suceed as an established church and eventually as the compulsory religion in the Roman empire. But it entailed a startling reversal in its original moral premises. In this, it was no more paradoxical than Buddhist morality, which also had to reverse itself on the absoluteness of its norms and accommodate itself to the necessities of success in war. The theological contortions that this entailed were extremely intricate, as Weber explains:

> The bodhisattva appears, like Krishna, ever anew on earth and can— corresponding to the *trikaya* doctrine—according to the ethical needs of the world, appear in any form and profession according to demand. . . . Hence, he appears also, above all, as a warrior. According to his nature he would fight only just and good wars. But when he does fight he will be unhesitatingly free of scruples. This theory, in practice, represents the most extensive adaptation to the needs of the world.[217]

The point of Weber's closing remark is apparent if one recalls the Buddha's original teachings. But is the disparity any greater than that between Christ's original gospel and what Christian morality came to permit later under the pressure of worldly needs? Yet throughout Christian history there were those, always a small minority, who sought to return to the purity of the original pacifist morality. If they did not perish through attrition or were exterminated as heretics, such peace-loving groups could at best survive only as small sects, such as the Quakers at present.

The methods of adjustment and strategies of accommodation whereby such changes occur are many and varied and call for the inventive faculties of all kinds of interpreters. Intellectuals of various types are very active in these endeavors. They are required to undertake all kinds of conceptual activities: distinctions need to be established, terms need to be strictly defined, categories delimited, and principles restricted. By these means, all kinds of excuses are elaborated for mitigating or completely evading the original norms. The norms are said to apply to some people but not to others, on most occasions but not to some where escape clauses operated, in respect of certain classes of things but not to all, and so on. Casuistry of this kind becomes a regular occupation in all moralities. Those who fulfill it best are usually philosophers, theologians, legal scholars, and textual interpreters.

Much of the same kind of account that we have presented concerning violence can also be given with respect of sex and family or reproductive matters in general. Once again the four basic types of ethics differ totally in their attitudes and rulings on these issues. The civic ethic is extremely libertarian and permits not only all kinds of heterosexual arrangements of marriage, concubinage, and prostitution, but also homosexual relations, which are sometimes valued above all others. In this ethic the erotic is the sphere of free and uninhibited expression, provided only that it is done in moderation. But this applies only to men, not to women, who are far more restricted. At the opposite extreme are the ascetic moralities, in which all sex is sin and best avoided altogether. But if it cannot be abstained from, it is best contained within chaste monogamous marriage, to be undertaken solely for the purpose of conceiving children and no other; for if it is indulged in for pleasure or even enjoyed, then this is equally sinful. Perfect chastity is virginity, which, if possible, should be upheld for life. But if this is not possible, then it were "better to marry than to burn," as Augustine puts it.

The other ethics fall somewhere between these two extremes in regard to sex. The ethics of duty, as one would expect from its traditionalist orientation, takes a more matter of fact approach to love and marriage. Sex is held to be of no great importance, neither the root of sinfulness nor erotic gratification, but to be practiced in a regulated and proper manner according to established customs. One marries and has children because that is what fulfilling one's responsibilities according to one's position in society requires. Otherwise, one avoids love affairs or extramarital relations or any other sexual escapades, for that would only interfere with more important matters. By contrast, for the ethic of honor it is precisely in such adventures of the heart that the highest purpose of life is sought. Nothing is more important than love practiced according to the code of gallantry. According to some versions of this code, such love is impossible except in adulterous relations. This is the only ethic that not only permits but enjoins female adultery.

Once again, it is morality that has the greatest difficulties with sex. Morality originates from ascetic religions, so it can never accept sex simply as a fact of life. Buddhism was highly ascetic from the start; the Judaic moralities only became so gradually, till eventually among the Essenes and the early Christians sexual asceticism became the norm. But invariably, accommodations had to be made. Christianity had to adjust to the accepted standards of its lay adherents. It could only impose much stricter requirements on its monks and nuns, and at first only on some of its clerics. The rule of complete clerical celibacy took many centuries to establish itself in Western Christianity. However, it did succeed in proscribing a long list of supposedly "deviant" sexual activities, among them homosexuality and polygamy. Hence, the adjustments that took place did not completely surrender its basic principles.

The tension between adaptation and conservation plays itself out ever anew on all kinds of grounds and under various conditions, as we shall see in the next chapter. It is particularly prominent in commercial activity, as we know from the work of Weber. Of all the varied economic undertakings, it is the sphere of commerce or money making that is ethically most highly fraught, especially where it involves money lending on interest. The mercantile occupation as such elicits quite different responses in the various ethics. In its original form, the civic ethics was most averse to it, as befits a stratum of citizen warriors. The good citizen can acquire wealth and utilize it in all kinds of ways for his own benefit, but he cannot actively seek it in trade, except perhaps by proxy through his slaves, for to do so directly would be demeaning. It is even more humiliating for any aristocratic exponent of the ethic of honor to engage in trade, though acquiring wealth in every other way, through marriage or booty in war, for example, is highly desirable. Money, as opposed to inheritable property in land, is not to be kept or saved but spent easily, for on that depends one's reputation for liberality and magnanimity so essential to one's status worth. Saving is not a virtue but a sign of miserliness.

The ethic of duty takes the opposite approach. Commerce is an activity like any other, traditionally sanctioned for those born into it, whose duty it is to follow it, but permitted for all others as occasion requires. There is nothing wrong for the official to strive to be wealthy and to save, putting his money to good use by lending it out on interest. Moralities take a more circumspect and cautious attitude to trade, wealth, and money. At their most extreme, they shun wealth and property altogether and adopt a mendicant lifestyle, as in Buddhism, or extol the virtues of poverty, as in early Christianity. This attitude is expressed in the gospel sayings of Jesus: "If thou wilt be perfect go and sell what thou hast and give it to the poor and thou shall have treasure in heaven. . . . It is easier for a camel to through the eye of a needle, than for a rich man to enter into the kingdom of God" (Matthew 19:21–24). But this was never taken literally, and later only monks were expected to live without personal property. For all others, even private or public bodies, including the institutions of the Church, such as monasteries, property and wealth were acceptable. Trade, too, was sanctioned as lawful work. But there was strong objection to gain without work, such as that achieved through interest on money lending or usury. All the moralities were averse to usury, especially where this involved lending to brothers in the faith. The whole fate of capitalism, especially in the development of a capital banking system and financial market, was historically dependent on the resolution of this conflict with morality. Invariably, sooner or later, all the moralities have had to adapt to the economic exigencies of money, so that now capitalism functions on a global scale with almost no moral restraints whatever, except from a few fundamentalists in some religions. Gradually, piece by piece, all the aversions of all the other ethics were also overcome. It became no longer shameful to engage in trade and to make as much money as possible by lawful means, which became increasingly more elastic. It is now considered almost folly not to do so and everyone invests in the share market directly or indirectly.

It is clear from the previous brief survey that moralities have been in sharpest tension with the worldly realities of violence, sex, and commerce. They have had the greatest difficulties adjusting to the needs of military prowess, erotic love, and monetary wealth, the basic conditions of worldly success. The other ethics have also militated against one or another of these, but never against all of them at once. In this sense morality is the most unworldly of all ethics and in it the disparity between what "ought to be" and what "is" is most keenly felt. However, no ethic is so completely adjusted to the conditions of worldly success that no such tension can ever arise. In all of them, principled ethical behavior can, and regularly does, result in worldly failure. The righteous do not necessarily prosper. That is part of the ethical irrationality of the world, as Weber puts it.

Only in contemporary times has adjustment to worldly realities proceeded so far and success in worldly matters been so keenly sought that almost no tension is allowed to arise between ethics and the world as it is now constituted. This has had the profoundest impact on morality, but other aspects of ethics have also been corrupted by it. It is reflected in the so-called "conformism" of contemporary society and the "idolatry" implicit in the fact that most people are said to worship the "bitch goddess" of success. There are now few if any inhibitions, apart from legal sanctions, on the pursuit of success in worldly affairs. On a state and national level even these restraints have disappeared. Total war is one of the inventions of our time, the sexual revolution is another, and global capitalism is now pursued under the slogan of "greed is good." To see how this condition was reached, we must turn to historical explanations and proceed with historical studies, which we shall do in the next chapter.

CHAPTER 2

⌒

Processes of Transformation and Development

Adaptation, Conservation, and Syncretism

A full history of all the four forms of ethics from their origins till now is far too long, too intricate and involved, to be undertaken here. However, this history reveals characteristic recurring processes of change and persistence that can be briefly expounded and illustrated. These are patterns of transformation and development, such as the one that we have already touched on before, that of adaptation to reality—that is, the compromise with the basic needs of all human life, primarily those involved in violence, sex, and commerce, without which no ethic could survive. Such adaptations are operative in all ethics at all times, for an ethic that refuses to adapt perishes, as can be instanced by some highly puritanical moralities that refused to sanction sexual intercourse and so died out literally for an inability to reproduce themselves. Adaptations must also take place to social and cultural conditions that fall short of being basic human needs but that constitute the historical context in which an ethic operates. Certainly, the chances of success of an ethic, if not necessarily of its simple survival, depend on these latter kinds of adaptations. An ethic that is unable to adjust to changing historical conditions can survive in small sects, but it cannot spread beyond that limited extent.

Adaptation is but one such characteristic process or pattern of development current throughout the history of ethics, and there are many others that we shall study in what follows. These can be seen as strategies of survival or success that are not necessarily deliberately planned by their protagonists but result as unintended consequences from the decisions that they do deliberately make. There are many ways in which this can happen that are more or less consciously willed by individuals or groups. The transition from subjective action to historical process is extremely varied but in itself not difficult to understand or explain. There always is such a transition involved since what happens to an ethic depends on what its protagonists do or fail to do. Ethics are not autonomous historical actors following ends of their own; as we previously stated, any such teleological approaches to ethics, either of the theological or progressivist variety, are here shunned. Any indications to the contrary are to be seen and excused merely as a *façon de parler*, which is sometimes unavoidable for the sake of conciseness but which must not be taken literally.

We shall begin with the process of adaptation to socio-cultural conditions and then go on to consider the opposite process of conservation or resistance to change, which takes all kinds of traditionalist and conservative forms. The latter is an essential counterbalancing tendency, for if an ethic were so plastic as to alter itself in response to every demand made of it, then it would soon lose its identity and cease having any continuity. Preserving an essential core intact is, therefore, a necessary process and, as we shall see, most ethics are highly traditionalistic and conserve all kind of features of their earlier stages. However, ethics can change drastically and perhaps at no time more so than when they enter into syncretic fusion with each other. When different ethics confront each other within the one society, the outcome can vary from total hostility and mutual exclusion to complete reconciliation and eventual fusion. The latter outcome is an extremely important process of change, for it gives rise to new ethical systems. The impulse to renovation can also take the opposite course, a refusal to compromise or be reconciled with others and an affirmation of essential identity by a return to first principles or origins. Such is the process of purism or puritanism, which can also transform an ethic beyond recognition, for any such call to return to origins rarely succeeds in reinstating an earlier state but is much more likely to produce something quite different and never before encountered.

The history of all ethics is subject to the previous processes of change. But there are others that are much more typical of Western ethics and generally only to be encountered within its history. Such is the process of secularization—namely, the detachment of ethics from religion and the sacred in any of its forms. This has been particularly prominent in Western history since the Enlightenment of the eighteenth century. It is closely associated with another universal process that has assumed increasing prominence in the West: that of rationalization. The rational systematization and ordering of an ethic can take place on the basis of any one of a number of principles of rationality, which can roughly be distinguished as formal and substantive in the way first formulated by Max Weber. Weber's theory of rationalization as a general process in history is also applicable to ethics, as, indeed, he had himself shown in his various studies of world religions, particularly so of ancient Judaism and Protestantism. For Weber, these were the main exemplars of the key stages of the process of ethical rationalization. It is noteworthy that he did not place a similar emphasis on Greek philosophies of ethics, which tells us much about what is meant by rationality in this context.

Finally, we shall touch on a process that is largely to be found only in this latest stage of Western history, when it has merged into and become world history: that of de-ethicization with particular regard to demoralization. This is a subject that has only recently begun to be raised, for it is a process that has only recently become visible in the course of contemporary events. It is a peculiarly paradoxical process, for it does not involve a change from one ethics to another but rather a turning against ethics altogether.[1] It is a pattern of dissolution, fragmentation, and reduction taking place within ethics that is leading to its potential displacement and substitution by other ways of regulating conduct. For, of course, the failure of ethics does not result in anarchy, as some traditional minds imagine; the absence of ethics gives way to other kinds of regulation, in some cases the much more sterner ones of "law and order." Whether this will completely supplant the need for ethics and to what extent it is already doing so is the subject of this book, for it concerns the current phase in the history of ethics.

Viewing the whole history of ethics in terms of such processes or patterns of transformation and development upholds neither a progressivist nor a traditionalist view of ethics. Those who from Hegel onward have believed in ethical stages of progress or evolution can take little comfort from a history in which all these types of processes have been taking place in no foreseeable or logical sequence, often at cross purposes to each other, and producing different results in the societies of the West and of the East. The forces that have propelled these trends and their outcomes need not have anything in themselves to do with ethics and can be highly contingent. But this is not to say that ethics is merely an ideological epiphenomenon of other more basic levels of society, as Marxist theory maintains. The way an ethic will change in response to outside changing conditions is variable and unpredictable, as is the very future of the whole ethical enterprise itself, for it has no pre-ordained goal. Ethics is not bound to reach its end, in any of the senses of that equivocal word; neither *telos* nor *finis* need necessarily await it.

This is no consolation to the traditionalists either, for their belief in essential principles laid down in a primordial origin that nothing in the vicissitudes of historical change can alter is also not upheld by an account in terms of interacting processes of change. It is undeniable that ethics has an historical origin, or better put, as we have already shown, it has numerous points of origination, none of which can be deemed truer or more authentic than any other. Hence, there can be no one perennial ethical tradition or truth. Starting from their original states, all the ethics have undergone changes according to the various processes we have outlined. Indeed, the puristic call for a return back to the origin is itself merely one of the tactics of change, which does not bring back the truth of first principles but creates its own temporary solution to current problems.

The sheer variety of the processes at work is also the reason that both traditionalists and progressivists can point to history in support of their case, for some of the patterns of transformation and development seem to uphold traditionalism and others progressivism. Clearly, the processes of conservation and of purism favor traditionalist readings, whereas those of adaptation and rationalization seem to vindicate progressivist ones. If one focuses unduly only on the process of de-ethicization or demoralization, which looms so large at present, one is bound to adopt a highly pessimistic view of the whole of ethical history as leading to inevitable collapse, such as taken by Heidegger and many of the more recent prophets of doom. Though the situation of ethics at present is, indeed, grim, yet there is no more justification for that doctrine of despair than for any of the other partial and biased perspectives that look to history for vindication.

The process of adaptation to changing social and cultural conditions affects all ethics at all times in so many different ways that any listing of such examples would be an endless task. It takes place particularly as an ethic departs from its original founders and carriers, who will invariably only be a small group, and broadens out to embrace other groups, other classes, other nations and peoples, and eventually even other cultures in distant civilizations. Every such transition calls for immense adaptations. A morality originally designed for monks, for example, when it is taken over by warriors has to make all kinds of requisite internal adjustments, as happened when Buddhism became the state religion in India under Ashoka or when the ascetic Christianity of the monastic orders became that of the knightly ones during the Crusades. In moving from a Roman to a tribal Germanic ethos, Christian morality had already made considerable accommodations to its new cultural environment, such that even Christ had to be conceived of as a heroic warrior. Thus much of the earlier emphasis on meekness and humility had to be modified. At present a similar process is taking place among the newly converted Christians in Africa and other non-European parts of the world.

There are many ways in which such adjustments are elaborated and recognized. New kinds of exceptions are made so that what holds for one class of people need not hold for another; for example, killing is forbidden except for those whose profession it is, such as soldiers and knights. New kinds of excuses are allowed; thus one may kill in just causes, such as in defense of the faith or in holy wars, or simply in the pursuit of a military vocation. Dispensations are granted for specific purposes; for example, one may kill tyrants or heretical rulers. Such and many others are the techniques for coming to terms with necessities. This can be done by deliberate rulings issuing from authorities such as councils or synods or learned thinkers or saints, but it may also take place imperceptibly as the gradual acceptance of alternatives to the accepted norms. Sometimes what comes to be so accepted does so in the face of authoritative condemnations and denials that it is taking place.

Many of these features of adaptation can be seen in Weber's studies of how the various moralities accommodated themselves to the necessities of commerce, particularly to finance and banking associated with capitalism. All moralities reject usury, for that goes against the basic moral principle of loving one's neighbor and helping him in need—the appeal to brotherliness without which no morality is worth its name. Yet every morality had to devise ways of accommodating itself to the needs and interests of merchants. This was particularly difficult with respect to the charging of interest on loans. Yet from the early Middle Ages onward, when the growth of cities and trade made this imperative, ways had to be found to permit banking transactions to take place. At first, purely casuistic arguments were used to excuse certain kinds of loans and returns, such as the medieval *commenda* partnerships, but in general what we would now consider a market price on money could not be charged. This changed drastically with the Reformation, when the Calvinist preachers argued explicitly that interest taking is lawful. However, the Catholic Church resisted this *de jure* till well into the nineteenth century, though *de facto* this had no effect, and now even such formal restraints have been tacitly forgotten and all participation in banking activities can be engaged in with a clear conscience. Moslem morality has still not reached this stage of accommodation to finance capitalism, and for devout believers subterfuges are still necessary when banking.

As this and other examples make evident, adaptations in morality or the other ethics are reached in the interest of necessities that cannot be realistically opposed or defeated. Interest in general plays a vital role in such measures. But this is not to argue that morality or any other ethic is merely an ideology that is a disguised way for a class or group to pursue its own interests. For frequently, moralities act against their own worldly interests in defense of their own integrity. Thus, for example, the sexual morality banning abortion and even contraception is probably against the interests of the Catholic Church as a political organization; nevertheless, it is still enforced with great severity, at least in official pronouncements. Though it is likely that in time an accommodation will be reached with the need to hold world population increase in check, what form this will take is not now apparent. Moralities are not weathervanes, turning with every passing wind of change; they maintain their own fixed directions, for otherwise they would soon lose their bearings.

Hence, there is always an opposed process to that of adaptation operative, that of conservation or conservatism, which keeps an ethic on its course and ensures that it remain true to itself. Normally, ethics tend to be highly conservative systems that adapt only incrementally and rarely change in any drastically radical way. The ethics of the fathers are usually passed on to become the ethics of the sons, and so on, from generation to generation. This means that they preserve earlier features—above all, those of their initial foundations. The first principles of an ethic generally remain with it, even though they might take a different form in later versions. Subsequent changes and accretions are also frequently conserved by tradition and maintained for long periods, even when they are no longer historically relevant. To take an extreme example, the morality of rabbinic Judaism elaborated in the Talmud, the so-called Ethics of the Fathers, *Pirkei Avot,* has been maintained to this day among orthodox Jews, despite all the turmoils of two thousand years of Jewish history. Few adaptations are officially approved of or even recognized by rabbinic authorities, though undoubtedly many have in fact taken place. Christian morality has obviously changed much more over this period, but it, too, conserves the basic features of the moral teachings of Christ, as well as those of the early apostles and Church Fathers of the primitive church, still hiding in the catacombes. And in this early foundation, much of Prophetic and something of Pharisaic morality was preserved. Hence the church's refusal to abandon the Old Testament and its condemnation as heretics of all those who advocated a complete break with Judaism.

This process of conservation is evident from the very origin of each of the major ethical types. They all preserve features of the very pre-ethical ethos out of which they first arose, and they maintain these throughout the later stages through which they pass. Some of these features are quite archaic; some are even primitive taboos; others come from the ancient civilities of the early civilizations. What it is that each of the ethics has inherited in this way from its preceding ethos is in many cases still uncertain, for so little is known about their earliest periods. What do we now know about the cultures and societies in which the prophets of Israel, Zoroaster, Confucius, or the Buddha lived? Not all that much.

The civic ethic of Greece allows us perhaps some better insight into its own origins, for we have a unique text, the works of Homer, which is set in and reflects the heroic ethos immediately preceding this ethic. Here we can study in some detail what was conserved from the ethos and passed into the ethic to be maintained in its later traditions. It is these features of conservation that give the impression of antiquity to Greek ethical history and make it appear, quite misleadingly, that there is already an ethic of civic virtue in the Homeric epics. Indeed, there is some warrant for such scholarly errors, for the terms are often the same. Thus, for example, *themis* and *dike* occur both in Homer and in the later ethical discourses. However, their meaning is no longer the same; in Homer they refer to customs and accepted social conventions, not to any transcendent notion of justice as *nomos,* as in the later civic ethic. There are even incipient ethical notions in Homer that were never developed in later Greek history, such as the rudimentary sense of honor with which Hector answers the entreaties of his wife, Andromache, not to go out to fight. But this does not mean that there was an ethic of honor among the nobles of Homer's time in any way comparable to that which developed among the Persians somewhat later. These Homeric pre-ethical or incipiently ethical notions have mostly to do with the family and warrior proprieties of an oikos society, such as leader-follower and master-servant relations, and are not to be confused with the ethics of the polis as this developed later. Generally, these are to be located more in the *Odyssey* than the *Iliad,* which is the reason that Aristotle considered the former to be more "ethical."[2]

The later Greeks themselves believed that their civic ethics was already there in Homer. Thus the qualities of an Achilles or Hector continued to be lauded and referred to as confirmations of current conduct among the hoplite citizenry of the polis, who were no longer warrior heroes. And, indeed, there was good reason for them to do so, for much of the Homeric ethos was conserved in the civic ethic. Thus a term like *arete,* "excellence," which referred indifferently to those traits of body, spirit, and personality that were essential in the competition for *kudos* and *kleos,* continued to be used close to the Homeric sense. Hence, ethical virtues could never be fully separated from other qualities of character or personality that had no ethical value in themselves. This ambiguity continued throughout the history of the civil ethic, for when *arete* was translated into Latin as *virtus*, it carried all the old Homeric connotations of manly warrior virtues. Thus these features of the Homeric ethos were preserved till well into the modern period. For example, when Machiavelli sought, in vain, to revive a classical civic ethic in Renaissance Florence, he also laid great stress on *virtu* in something like its original sense and sought to counterpose it to Christian moral virtue, which, used in amoral context, gave the term a quite different meaning. Similarly, the patriotic re-evocation of civic virtue by the French revolutionary Jacobins also sought to make use of the original meanings of virtue, which had been conserved in a continuous tradition since Homer.

Each of the major ethics conserved in this same way features of the pre-ethical ethos in which it first arose. A study of those parts of the Old Testament that pre-date the Torah morality of the Levites and the prophets could reveal such vestiges of earlier stages in our Western moral traditions. The same holds for Confucian ethics, which valued and preserved the preceding ethos contained in the traditional odes and ceremonies. Analogously so, there is much in Buddhism of the older Hindu religious ethos, mostly associated with the doctrines of rebirth and *karma*. All these survivals attest to the strong conservatism of ethical traditions. They frequently maintain principles whose point has been forgotten and practices whose purpose has been lost. But without such a mooring in the past, ethics would drift aimlessly in later currents.

Nevertheless, all ethics are subject to change, sometimes dramatically so. The situations that are most conducive to change are those when one ethics confronts another within the confines of the same society. The outcome of such a confrontation can vary from a hostile stand-off in opposition to a mutual fusing in an eclectic synthesis that produces a new hybrid. In the former case, both ethics maintain their own undisturbed identity and even tend to assert their separate distinctiveness by exaggerating those of their characteristics that stand in direct contradiction to those of the opponent seen as the enemy. This outcome can easily give way to puritanical fanaticism and result in open conflict or repression of the weaker by the stronger. In the latter case, a peaceful reconciliation ensues, as both ethics are submerged within the larger whole of the syncretist outcome.

Historical examples of both these outcomes, as well as many others that fall somewhere in between these extremes, can be found in the histories of all ethics. The history of Islamic morality, which originated as a narrower and more puritanical version of Judaism and Christianity, evinces many instances of a self-assertive stand-off, a rigid self-affirmation against the ethics it encountered in its numerous conquests and penetrations right around the low latitudes of the globe. Any desultory attempts to produce syntheses out of the diverse ethics of their subjects by such rulers as Mehmed, the conqueror of Constantinople, or Akhbar, the great Mughal of Delhi, almost always failed, defeated by strong puritanical reactions from the shariah. Thus Moslems and Byzantine Christians stood opposed throughout the history of the Ottoman empire, and Moslems and Hindus were locked in bitter conflict in India that has lasted till this day. It was only in Java, where Mohammedanism was brought by peaceful traders, not carried on the points of their swords by holy warriors, that a kind of *de facto* fusion occurred between Islam, Hinduism, Buddhism, and the native pagan cults. Another example within the Muslim world of at least a partial synthesis occurred in Persia, where the Shiite form of Islam absorbed some elements from the previous Zoroastrian culture and where, as we saw previously, many features of a chivalric ethic survived the conquest to reappear later in a new guise.

The most outstanding and most complete examples of the process of syncretist fusion occurred during the history of Christian ethics. By origin a Judaic morality, Christianity confronted numerous contrary ethical currents within the Roman empire. Some of these it opposed from the start, such as the specifically pagan elements of the Roman civic ethic; others it accepted, such as Roman civic duties, on the doctrinal formula of "render unto Caesar what is Caesar's, and to God what is God's." Later in its history it confronted ethical movements emanating from Persian dualism, Mithraism, and Manicheaism, and those, too, it opposed but partially absorbed. It was much more predisposed to accept the late Roman Stoic ethic of duty, which was made all the easier when, after Constantine's conversion, it became the official state religion, and, therefore, the religion of the already Stoicly indoctrinated imperial officials. Thus the Roman who became a Christian by this time generally found that there was little he had to abandon of his classical ethical heritage. Christian morality had blended with the Greco-Roman ethic of civic virtue, the Stoic ethic of duty, and other philosophical as well as religious ethical trends, such as neo-Platonism, current in the Roman empire.

On the whole, as historical evidence reveals, the early Christian emperors changed very little in the ordinary affairs of daily life and the laws, conventions, and norms binding on Roman citizens. The enforcement of Roman Law played a significant role in maintaining continuity. Christian Church Fathers and theologians found ways of ethically validating every kind of work that the state and society required, with the exception of a few, such as prostitution, circus and theater performance, and usury taking, which they condemned outright. Every other line of work and professional occupation was considered ethically legitimate, provided it followed its own traditionally prescribed rules and regulations, in a kind of Christian version of the ethic of duty. Thus, according to Maximus of Turin, the Gospel prescribes for every Christian of whatever status, occupation, or age the requisite duties of his station in life.[3] This was obviously meant to include the military profession as well, provided it was carried out in a disciplined way, without resort to pillage. In the *Constitutiones Apostolicae*, it is expressly stated that soldiers are to be admitted to communion if they take no more than their due pay. John Chrysostom and St. Augustine both confirm this verdict and teach the acceptance of fighting as an unavoidable obligation in the fallen condition of human existence.[4] According to St. Ambrose, all officials should observe the proper laws of their professions and otherwise carry themselves as good Christians. In this way, step by step, much of the civic ethic, which was crucially concerned with military and civic service, was absorbed within the Christian ethic.

This does not mean that Christians abandoned the demands of their morality or forgot the basic teachings of the Gospels. Thus the moral imperative to love one's neighbor was interpreted to obligate a whole range of charitable activities for the poor, the sick, widows and orphans, and so on. The giving away of one's wealth for these purposes became a highly laudable act of moral virtue. Personal service in ministering to the needs of the poor and suffering was considered meritorious for all Christians, including the most highly placed, in contradistinction to what had previously obtained among highborn Romans. Every kind of labor was now considered worthy, if undertaken in the traditionally proper manner or in a good cause. In time the whole notion of work, which Greeks and Romans had considered degrading, became positively viewed. This merged with the Christian moral emphasis on humility.

However, none of this moralizing revaluation of ordinary life activities meant that all Christians had to live up to the full rigor of the moral demands of the Gospels—that is, to lead the apostolic life in all its purity. The demand by some that the morality of the Gospels should be binding on all had led to the Donatist heresy in North Africa. The dominant Church took a different view; it enjoined a kind of double ethic, one for ordinary Christians and another for those following a holy vocation. Churchmen, clerics, and monks were expected to live closer to the Gospel morality, and for them all kinds of worldly activities were forbidden. Ordinary lay folk were, by contrast, only required to live up to a much modified and weakened version of such requirements. It was meritorious to do more but not obligatory. Those who wished fully to give themselves over to the moral law had to withdraw from all worldly concerns and escape as hermits to the desert or later as monks to the monastery. Thus in this way a graduated ethic arose for different kinds of Christians, with eventually an ever-sharper separation between holy and lay vocations.

Christianity had learned to make such separations from its Judaic antecedents. In the synagogues through the Roman world, in which Christianity had its beginnings, there was a graduated series of distinctions between Jews and God-fearing gentiles—namely, those who were fellow-travelers of the religion. The full rigor of the Mosaic law was demanded from the former, but upon the latter, prior to circumcision and full conversion, only the most basic moral norms were imposed. Also, what was permitted in relation to fellow believers was marked off from what was permitted in relation to nonbelievers.

There are numerous such strategies of maintaining a double or diversified ethic of graduated expectations, and their purpose is to mediate the tensions between one ethic and another, particularly so within a syncretist ethical system. Christianity is a particularly rich field of such devices, which permit diverse ethics to coexist, though not without inner tensions. By these means Christianity has been able to absorb a number of quite diverse ethics that originally might have been quite contrary to it. Thus later, during early medieval times, it was able to successfully absorb the ethic of honor, in its Western form as chivalry and courtliness, and so to Christianize this potentially dangerous development in the ethos of the aristocratic knightly strata. The extraordinary success of Christianity as an ethical system might be ascribed to its syncretist capacities to absorb within itself even that which is most hostile to it. This has produced continual difficult tensions and inner oppositions within it, which constantly call for extraordinary creative endeavors to contain and reconcile. Much of the vitality of the history of Christian ethics reflects itself in such efforts, which have been going on unceasingly since its origins. A religion that began as an abomination to Jews and stumbling block to Greeks had to develop a rich store of strategies to overcome ethical incompatibilities.

The other great missionary world religion, Buddhism, developed in a quite different way. It also formulated a double ethics for monks and lay adherents, and it also came to co-exist with various other opposed ethics. But it never undertook extensive syncretist activities, being usually content to operate besides or even above other ethics, not to attempt to absorb them within itself. This can be seen particularly clearly exemplified in the role Mahayana Buddhism had assumed in China, where, like Christianity in Rome, it also had the opportunity to establish itself as the dominant ethic of a large empire. It failed to do so. Instead it came to co-exist with the other major ethics of China, Confucianism and Taoism. It was not exclusive in the way of the Judaic religions. It frowned ironically on the alternative beliefs and practices of its lay adherents but did not censure these as evil or idolatrous. Only the monks were required to subscribe fully to all that Buddhist morality demanded. All others could turn to any other ethics as circumstances dictated or as their needs called for. Thus a typical lay person could follow a Confucian ethic in the affairs of state and public dealings but revert to Buddhist morality in personal religious contexts or in retirement after his official career had ended.

The three processes of adaptation, conservation, and syncretist fusion were so successfully carried out by Christian morality in the late Roman empire that the resultant composite system that arose established itself as the basic ethical foundation for the whole of the subsequent history of the West. It set the groundwork for the two later developments in that history, the rise of medieval ethics during the twelfth and thirteenth centuries and of modern ethics in the period from the seventeenth to the nineteenth centuries. These, too, involved processes of adaptation, conservation, and syncretism. However, modernity also brought into play processes of puritanism, rationalization, and secularization, so we shall consider it in the next section. Both medieval and modern ethics constituted momentous transformations in the ethos of Western Europe, with enormous eventual consequences for the whole world.

As in all such historical transformations in ethics, a crucial role was played by the ancillary spheres of philosophy, law, and literature. These intervened decisively at the very start of the Western civic ethics in Greece and continued to be important right throughout the ethical history of the West. It was somewhat analogous with the ethics of China, where philosophy, law, and literature were also involved in its ethical origins and continued to be so throughout its history. This was much less so the case in the other ethical traditions, particularly with respect to philosophy in Judaic morality. A full examination of their influence in all the ethical traditions is beyond the scope of our present study, but details of it will emerge throughout this work. Their present lack of relevance to ethics and the consequences of this will be discussed in part II.

During the two major periods of Christian syncretism in ethics, in the late Roman empire and at the start of the Middle Ages during the so-called twelfth-century renaissance, the influence of philosophy, law, and literature was particularly marked and of great importance in effecting these two crucial transitions. During both periods, Christianity maintained or revived basically pagan classical forms of philosophy, law, and literature. This remained the perennial tradition of classicism in the West, which has had such profound ethical effects. Without it and the syncretic processes it encouraged, Judeo-Christian morality would have molded Western ethics in a very different way.

We have already seen something of the effect of philosophy on the development of the civic ethics through our study of Plato and Aristotle's ethical writings, which continued to exert an influence on Christian ethics. We examined the role of philosophy in ethics in our account of the influence of late-Stoicism in enabling the development of a Western form of the ethics of duty. But this influence was by no means exhausted with the rise to dominance of Christianity in the late Roman empire; it continued in other forms and, in fact, it has persisted ever since. However, even prior to this Christian version of late-Stoicism, another philosophy had a decisive effect on the new ethics, and that was neo-Platonism.

Neo-Platonism, which arose in Alexandria, was from the start close to Christianity. Thus, for example, both Plotinus and Origen were pupils of the pagan philosopher Ammonius Saccas. Through these contacts, the whole Alexandrian school of theologians was imbued with neo-Platonic modes of thought and by this means they made the most important contributions to Christian theology and some crucial ones to Christian ethics as well. As Charles Cochrane explains:

> It has, for instance, been noted that Clement put forward a theory of Christian gnosis which is hardly to be distinguished from that professed by contemporary pagan mystics, whereby the *logos* serves to guide the neophyte through successive stages of illumination. At the same time he advocates a scheme of Christian propaedeutics which is obviously based on Neopythagorean-Platonic practice. With Origen the admission of pagan ideology is hardly less apparent. He has been convicted of a wholesale adoption of Aristotelian terminology and definitions. And, in his great work On First Principles (*peri archon*), he envisages his problem in terms of pagan science.[5]

Much the same holds for Athanasius, perhaps the most influential of the Alexandrian theologians, after whom the eponymous creed is named. Thus Timothy Barnes asserts that "Athanasius appropriates the language and ideas of Greek philosophy without embarrassment, and he expresses his position easily in the prevailing terminology of Middle Platonism."[6] The chronic disputes on Christology, in particular that between Athanasius and Arius, are scarcely conceivable outside this philosophical matrix.

The second major theme that preoccupied Athanasius also arose from Coptic sources in Egypt; that was the contemporaneous rise of monasticism. Athanasius was directly involved in that movement, eventually writing a hagiography of Saint Anthony, the desert anchorite, which was the first of its kind and the model for all others. During his long periods of exile in the West, at Trier and elsewhere, he was undoubtedly influential in spreading the idea and practice of monasticism throughout the Christian churches in the Latin regions. Monasticism marked a new stage in the practice of Christian morality, that of ascetic withdrawal from the world. This was a departure from the original moral premises of love of neighbor and a move toward unworldly service of God for the sake of the salvation of one's soul—a much more Buddhistic emphasis. Though this path was only fully open to the religious virtuoso, the monk, yet it had profound consequences for the whole of Christian morality and so for all others in the Church.

Athanasius' two major preoccupations—intellectualist theology based on philosophy and monasticism based on ascetic practice—came together in the Church as a whole in a way that was decisive for at least the next thousand years. This conjunction had a profound effect on Christian ethical syncretism. The formulation of theology, or religious intellectualism following neo-Platonic principles, reinforced the emphasis in Christianity on faith; it made mandatory the ritual requirement of assent to a creed—that is, the adhesion to dogmatic belief that made for orthodoxy. The rise of monasticism was a parallel development with the opposite emphasis on practice, for it encouraged an ascetic flight from the world. But this was only possible and only was expected to be undertaken by the few religious elect who had a calling to serve God. The life of ordinary Christian laiety was only indirectly affected by it. Provided the ordinary Christian assented to the articles of faith, not much more was ethically required from him or her by the Church than to follow a traditional form of life, with its conventionally prescribed duties. The intellectual and ascetic virtuosi—"athletes of God," who were mainly theologians and monks—were the exceptions. Thus a pattern of graded statuses of ethical being was established that persisted in Christianity at least till the Reformation.

The absorption of neo-Platonism into Christianity reinforced this conception of grades and stages of ethical perfection. If the most perfect being was the saint—who was no longer the martyr once Christianity had become the state religion, but increasingly became the ascetic or monk—then the next grades were occupied by other religiously dedicated specialists; below them was the middle-ranking of ordinary good lay people; and below that, it was all the way down through the various kinds of sinners to those who were pagans, heretics, or simply wicked. The life-course of the individual as it proceeded from infancy to adulthood to old age and death was also conceived of in terms of such grades of perfection as an upward progress from the natural fallen state, through all the trials and tribulations sent to test one during a lifetime, to the ultimate crown of sanctity. Augustine's *Confessions* is already cast in this mold. This basic schema of grades of perfection was of a piece with the neo-Platonic conception of a Golden Chain of Being stretching from the inchoate darkness of mere matter to the ultimate light of the pure One, with a continuous band of grades of beings connecting the two—like Jacob's ladder that stretched from earth upward to heaven.

What followed from this in ordinary ethical practice was that most people could continue leading their quotidian lives more or less as they had under paganism, with perhaps a little leavening of Christian morality. Their previous classical ethos did not have to be abandoned but merely enriched morally. Provided they did nothing untoward against the faith, not much more was expected of them ethically. Though increasingly newer theological requirements were made, these had no ethical consequences; all that was asked for was ritual assent to this or that extra piece of Christological doctrine or whatever other articles of faith became doctrinally elaborated by the various church councils. It was different for the religious virtuosi or those who sought a vocation in the service of the Church; on them fell the full burden of Christian morality, for they alone were seen to be walking in the footsteps of the apostles.

For those who took up a vocation in the Church and filled one or other of the religious offices, another philosophy became important, late-Stoicism. This was the philosophy that some of the Western Fathers of the Church, such as Ambrose and Augustine, particularly favored. They used it to define a Christian version of the ethics of duty, one appropriate for clerical officials within the Church. Thus, as we previously noted, Ambrose elaborated a Christian version of Cicero's *De Officiis*, his *De Officiis ministorum ecclesiae*. The ethics of Christian duty formulated in this manner was, of course, of great practical importance in the establishment of a clerical bureaucracy. As this chaplainocracy, as Weber terms it, grew, a moralized version of the ethics of late-Stoicism was completely absorbed into the Christian syncretist amalgam.

Another aspect of Stoicism, the doctrine of Natural Law, also played a leading role in Christian ethical thinking, as is evident from Augustine onward. He made the initial interpretative move of identifying the Stoic teaching on law with the biblical teaching, so that the Natural Law of Reason emerged as identical to the moral law of Relevation—God's will was Nature's law. Thus the basic moral commandments of the *Decalogue* became laws of reason that all human beings had engraven in their hearts and inscribed in their consciences. The eternal law of God (*lege Dei aeterna*) is simply the voice of Nature in Man, which all human beings can discover for themselves. These laws are, therefore, valid for all men and they existed even in the natural state before the Fall. Thus the Golden Rule in its negative form, "do not do unto others what you would not have others do unto you," becomes nothing but a principle of moral reason. Kant's categorical imperative is but a more fully rationalized and secularized application of this idea, for Kant, too, was indirectly reliant on late-Stoicism. Its invocation by Augustine serves as a perfect example of the process of syncretism at work.

Even before Christianity, the Stoic teaching of Natural Law had exerted an influence on Roman Law and in this form, too, it was passed on to the later tradition. Roman Law remained more or less unchanged in the new Christian religious regime of the late Roman empire. This continuity of Roman Law—assiduously maintained by all the Christian emperors from Constantine onward—also had a profound impact on the formation of Christian syncretism in ethics. It was the later Christian emperors, Theodosius and Justinian, who carried through the decisive codifications of this law. Clearly, it was of great political benefit for them to maintain Roman Law and to permit it to remain largely unchanged.

The changes that were undertaken in Roman Law to make it conform with the requirements of Christian morality were, so to speak, largely cosmetic and superficial. Constantine, who styled himself *pontifex maximus* in the old pagan tradition, did not even legislate the abolition of pagan practices of worship. It was only much later, under Theodosius in 391, that pagan temples were closed, offerings to the gods forbidden, and all state offices denied to apostates. Only in a few restricted respects, mainly to do with the Christian calendar, were there changes made to the law. Attempts at more significant alterations to bring the law into line with Christian morality at first failed completely. Thus, Constantine's legislation to abolish the exposure of newborn infants and to ban the sale of children was ineffective, and these laws had to be rescinded. What seem like legislative reforms in conformity with Christian principles were often inspired by a general changing sense of justice common to the ethical teachings of the schools of philosophy.[7] A serious attempt to Christianize the law only came much later, in Byzantium under Leo III, the Syrian, in 740 and in the West soon after under Charlemagne. Both of these projects proved failures; Emperor Basil I of the Macedonian dynasty made a determined move to bring back genuine Roman

Law so as to strengthen imperial power; and the same thing happened a little later in the West.

The attraction of Roman Law for nearly all the Christian emperors is easy to understand. It enabled the civil power and civil administration to function unimpaired, despite the new religion and its demanding morality. Under the early Christian emperors, this meant that both Christians and pagans could share the basic political and legal forms that enabled the classical civil ethos to continue as a common civic life. Christian moral principles were fitted in as a supplementary adjunct and not as a replacement for this classical ethical culture. In time, as Christianity became the sole and exclusive religion, it established new social institutions on the basis of its moral teachings. Above all, there were provisions for charity to care for the needy, the sick, widows and waifs, and so on. Also the most offensive features of the previous pagan culture were proscribed, mainly those to do with the circus, the theater, and various forms of legalized prostitution, such that the gladiator, the actor, and the prostitute were no longer acceptable professions. These were all the legal changes required to conform with the new moral dispensation.

It was not only the continuity of Roman Law that facilitated this syncretism of Christian ethics in the late Roman empire; so, too, did all the other continuities of classical culture—above all, that of classical literature. Under Christianity, the basic mode of classical education was carried on, and this mainly involved literary and humanistic studies. For this purpose, almost the whole corpus of works of the Greek and Latin authors was retained. Only a select few books were found to be so offensive as to need censorship. The influence of this literature on the whole mentality of Christianity, and its role in enabling an ethical syncretism to take place, was decisive and was perhaps more important than anything else in this process.

Surprising as it might seem to us now, the early Christians in the empire made no attempt to found schools of their own; they simply accepted the established Hellenistic-Roman regimen of teaching and educated their children in exactly the same way, together with the pagans. This meant that they received a basic grounding in the classical ethical dispositions then current in the empire, in the older traditions of civic virtue, and in the new ideals of the ethics of duty, which became more or less fused and were no longer clearly distinguished. This is summed up by Pierre Riché as follows:

> The classical education in the West was uniquely literary. It sought to give the young Roman the means to take his place in the society that judged a man essentially on his qualities as an orator. It likewise permitted him to become a citizen capable of serving the State by directing the numerous offices upon which the organization of the empire depended.[8]

The educational ideal was that of the orator as citizen and official, and it was one to which Christians subscribed as fully as pagans. As Riché sees it, "State control of the school should have disturbed the Church whose mission was to teach Christian truth [and] moreover, the moral principles of the Gospels were far removed from the humanist ideal fashioned by centuries of paganism"; but, by and large, it did not, for the syncretist tendencies of those who had already been brought up in this way proved stronger than their opposed impulses to separate themselves from the pagans on moral grounds. The diametrically opposite course was taken by the Jews in the empire and reveals itself in the totally different development of rabbinic morality; the same was later true for Moslems as well.

It is undeniable that this wholesale acceptance of the classical schools and of the classical humanism that went with it was not achieved without continual spiritual disquietude and inward torment. No one was more torn by it than Tertullian, who was, on the one hand, keenly aware of the idolatry and immorality of the classical authors but, on the other hand, realized that without a classical education a Christian could not read or interpret the scriptures and holy books. Hence he arrived at the somewhat illogical conclusion that Christian children should study in the schools, but adults should never teach there. This advice was not heeded; Christians became teachers from early on, and only ceased temporarily when the pagan emperor Julian sought to purge them. Jerome, too, was inwardly riven by the conflict between Christian morality and classical virtue, a struggle that he enacted as a battle of the books. As he wrote in a letter of 384, ". . . even as I was on my way to Jerusalem to fight the good fight, I could not bring myself to forego the library which with great care and labour I had got together in Rome."[9] The urge to read the classical authors was an ever-present temptation to him that he tried to resist by fasting and the perhaps equally ascetic torment for a literate Roman, learning Hebrew: "Thus, after having studied the pointed style of Quintilian, the fluency of Cicero, the weightiness of Fronto, and the gentleness of Pliny, I now began to learn the alphabet again and practise the harsh and gutteral words."[10] Once in Jerusalem he was unable to resist the temptation to read from Plautus, whereupon he had a self-accusatory dream in which he stood before Divine Judgment and was condemned with the words: "Liar, you are no Christian, you are a Ciceronian."[11] On waking from this nightmare, he resolved never to read secular books again.

But as against such puritans as Tertullian and Jerome there stood a whole galaxy of Fathers of the Church, both Eastern and Western, who took delight in the Greek and Latin authors and advocated classical education. As might be expected, the Alexandrian Fathers, for whom knowledge was all important as the way to spiritual enlightenment, sought to propound a view of education that would reconcile the teachings of faith with the classical tradition and thus develop a complete educational course, *enkyklios paideia*, for the Christian way of life. Both Clement and Origen wrote books in this vein. The Cappadocian Fathers, Basil of Caesarea, Gregory of Nysa, and Gregory Nazianus, were also intent on making classical learning acceptable to Christians. In the West a more lukewarm advocate of secular learning of some types was Augustine, who wrote a number of books on the issue. James Bowen sums up his views on education as follows:

> Utilitarian skills connected with the pursuit of daily life were of obvious value, but those whose aim was completely aesthetic, chiefly music and the arts, were to be avoided. Along with Augustine's views on learning emerged also his idea of the teacher. He should be versed in the skills of the liberal arts, since logic, rhetoric and grammar give him that ability to order materials and the necessary eloquence to elicit answers from his students, while the study of mathematics provides personal insight into the divinely ordered nature of the universe.[12]

But in the last resort, however, "the principle of *askesis* remained central to Augustine's teaching: his views were essentially idealistic and eschatological, man's vocation being the attainment of complete union with god, the achievement known as beatitude."[13]

It was more or less in this Augustinian spirit that Western ethics entered into the Dark Ages, following the collapse of the Roman empire. The *askesis* of monasticism became prevalent, and an education based on monastic schools, mainly oriented to Christian doctrine and its eschatological premises, began to take over from classical schooling. However, not everything of the Christian-Hellenistic syncretism was lost. One of the last of the Roman Christians, Cassiodorus, who was a contemporary of Boethius and Benedict of Nursia, initiated a new course of monastic education dedicated to what he called *civilitas*, in which many of the classical traditions were preserved. This became the basis of monastic culture for over five centuries, till the great revival of education in the so-called twelfth-century renaissance. Thus something of the Christian-Hellenistic ethical synthesis was also preserved. As Henri Marrou puts it in his study of education in the West:

> Hence arose one of the characteristic features of medieval Christianity, of the whole of Western civilization in fact: however original its first inspiration may have been, however much opposed to the spirit of the old humanism, it was not fundamentally different from it. It was not an absolutely new beginning, a fresh start. From the beginning and throughout its subsequent history it drew so much

from the old classical sources that it seems to appear as a continual Renaissance. Despite the barbarian interlude there was a certain continuity of matter, if not of form, that made Western man the heir of the old Classicism.[14]

In other words, the initial ethical syncretism was decisive for the whole of Western ethical history. This is born out by the second great phase of Christian syncretism, which occurred during the Middle Ages.

This began with the so-called twelfth-century renaissance, which was precisely a renaissance of the philosophy, law, and literature of the first syncretist phase in the late Roman empire. But as well as that, it was also a further development of the Christian tendencies that had only started then; above all, the two we previously referred to as jointly associated with Athanasius—namely, theology and monasticism. These Christian revivalist movements climaxed in the twelfth century and at their most intense were embodied in the figure of St. Bernard and the whole monastic order that he represented. His great antagonist—or, should one say, victim—was Abelard, the first of the Western neo-Aristotelians who represented the renaissance in philosophy and the foundation of the new educational institution of the university. This had already begun previously in Bologna as a school for the study of Roman Law. Together with all of these more or less orthodox tendencies, there emerged in this same century numerous heretical ones, above all that associated with the Cathars. This fed into the new literature of the troubadour poets, which was associated with the knightly stratum and which, due to the Crusades and the *Reconquista* in Spain, was also subject to numerous influences from the Muslim East. All these developments and movements had different ethical predispositions that came together and clashed in this pivotal period for Western Europe.

At this time all kinds of opposed ethical tendencies asserted themselves and strove for supremacy. Each was driven by its own social forces, released during this period of intense social ferment and conflict. In the religious realm of the Church, the resurgent monasticism begun by the Cluniacs and carried further by the Cistercians—which had the support of the Papacy they more or less controlled—strove for a renewed Christian life that featured the rigid, strict, and intense practices of ascetic morality. This had a profound influence on lay society, especially in the economically burgeoning cities, when a little later through the newly established orders of friars, the Franciscans and Dominicans, movements of lay reform were launched. At the same time these same cities had already moved to establish their own independence from Church political control and the rule of their bishop-princes. Particularly among the cities of Italy, this led to a renewal of a lay humanist civic ethics and made them very responsive to a revival of Roman Law. Roman Law was also favored by the courtier-bishops of the chancellery of the imperial power in Germany and later by all the other monarchical rulers with territorial state ambitions. The ethics of duty in its late-Stoic form also reappeared among the officials in these courts. But at the same time the noble courtiers and knights and their ladies were predisposed to a chivalric version of the ethic of honor whose cults of erotic gallantry were directly contrary to Christian morality. Thus in the very same society monks, office-holding clerics, courtiers, lords, ladies, and burghers pursued their diverse and often contradictory ethical trends. Such a degree of ethical diversity had never before been found in any one society.

In this respect medieval ethics was as diverse and variegated as medieval law and medieval politics, which also functioned in numerous distinct forms. Different varieties of law and trial procedures co-existed in the same medieval societies. There were numerous kinds of Church law, common or customary law, feudal law, urban law, royal equity law, statute law, and Roman Law on top of all that. There were many different kinds of courts and ways of proceeding that involved trial by ordeal, by peers, by jury, by learned judges, and before the king himself. In an analogous way there were numerous medieval forms of authority. This Marx calls "the motley pattern of conflicting medieval plenary powers [which were later transformed] into the regulated plan of a State authority."[15] As we shall see, something analogous happened in law and ethics as well.

During the Middle Ages, all these various ethical strata did not simply co-exist in indifference to each other in separate spheres, as might have been the case had this occurred in China. In Western Europe they entered into interactions with each other, involving fusions but also intense inner tensions and sometimes even conflicts. Christianity, for one, could not rest indifferent to the presence of other opposed ethics; it had to confront them, and if it could not extirpate them, then it had to absorb them as best it could. Ideally, it aimed to achieve some kind of grand synthesis; and this is how its intellectuals, especially the schoolmen philosophers, tried to present it. In practice, what resulted was the peculiar medieval syncretism summed up later in the formula of *coincidentia oppositorum* (Cusanus).

This formula expressed the unity in diversity that was so typical of medieval cultures in general. It is clearly reflected in the medieval arts. The new art of musical counterpoint simultaneously brought together different melodies with utterly divergent words—perhaps a hymn to the Virgin and a lover's plaint to his mistress at once—united solely by the tempo and the musical harmony. The visual arts featured seemingly incongruous juxtapositions of the sacred and profane within the same frame or on the very same page. Collections of stories, such as those of Boccaccio or Chaucer, place next to each other tales that convey utterly divergent morals in the literary sense, perhaps one in praise of absolute chastity and another taking delight in utterly uninhibited sensuality. No conformity of viewpoint or unity of perspective was expected or required; that only came later with the Reformation and Enlightenment in modernity. The medieval mind could accept diversity without requiring consistency. Even in the strictly rational intellectual sphere of philosophy, it extolled dialectics and the contention of contradictory positions in the formalized debate of thesis and antithesis.

Medieval ethics is somewhat analogous to all this; there, too, a kind of *coincidentia oppositorum* came to prevail. All the then available ethical viewpoints were accepted and embraced in a syncretism where not too much weight was placed on consistency. At best, what was striven for was a kind of "organismic" order, in Weber's sense of the term, where different ethical requirements or duties were placed on the different groups of society. A knight could behave in ways that were forbidden to a cleric, a cleric to a merchant, a merchant to a peasant, and so on; and in general men had different standards to women. What tended to be condemned was not difference, which was acknowledged as unavoidable, but excessive difference or the exceeding of due measure.

Excess was seen as the basic cause of vice and moderation of virtue. Thus, for example, the seven deadly sins, a typical medieval conception of vice, are all sins of either too much or too little: lust (*luxuria*) is too much or the wrong kind of sex, gluttony (*gula*) is too much eating and drinking, avarice (*avaritia*) is too great desire for money or power, sloth (*acedia*) is too little activity, wrath (*ira*) is too great anger, envy (*invidia*) is excess spite and resentment, and pride (*superbia*) is excessive self-assertion. If not taken to excess, none need be evil in itself; but beyond due measure they all become vices. Hence, much to our surprise, too much eating and drinking becomes a deadly sin fit to be punished in the afterlife, rather than the indulgence, whose consequences are at worst fatness, which we take it to be. No lesser a medieval mind than that of Dante sees it more or less in these terms and conceives of the seven deadly sins as things that are loved too much or too little. He structures nearly the whole of the *Purgatorio* on this scheme.

The *Inferno* is also structured on the conception of an excessive or defective love of things. The tragedy of those who are damned, and the most impressive among them are indeed tragic figures, is not that what they stand for and embody is in itself evil but that it is pursued to excess and to the detriment of other values that are no less essential. The love of Paolo and

Francesca is not in itself wrong, but it leads them to the transgression of physical union instead of an ideal sublimation. Farinata is not condemned for his patriotic devotion to his party and its cause of winning back Florence, but only for ruing its failure more than the damnation of his soul—for which Machiavelli was later to praise him. Brunetto Latini's devotion to humanist classicism was shared by Dante, his pupil; it became culpable only when it led him to disregard Christian teaching.

As Dante's epic poem reveals, nearly all the ethical contradictions of medieval Europe came together in the turbulent city of Florence. Florence saw the first stirrings of renaissance classical humanism in all its forms, particularly so politically as civic republicanism and artistically in the new literature of Dante, Boccaccio, and Petrarch and in the new representational style of Giotto and the movement of classical realism that he launched in painting. Roman Law was renewed, after the example of nearby Bologna, in a never completely extinguished notary tradition stretching back to the ancient world. The courtly ethos and the poetry of love were cultivated among the merchant princes of the city patriciate, such as the Medici, who were continuing earlier noble traditions. The Medici were also the patrons of a revival of neo-Platonic philosophies of love. But at the same time the Church had a strong and unshakable grip on the city through its institutions, particularly the monastic orders—above all, those of the Franciscan and Dominican friars. Florence was also crucially involved in the medieval political struggle of the Imperial and Papal parties, the Ghibellines and Guelfs. Dante was caught up in all these ethical conflicts and remained all his life immersed in them. His epic poem is a record of how he tried to reconcile it all in a literary manner, a way of dealing with it that few of his contemporaries could appreciate.

Other medieval minds, such as philosophers, theologians, and jurists, also sought to express and accommodate the immense turmoil of medieval ethics contained in the unfolding syncretism of the age. For the philosophers, Aristotle proved most useful for this purpose for his doctrine of the mean—that virtue lies in the avoidance of the excess of too much or too little—permitted the acknowledgment of a large variety of discrete virtues, each of which could be presented as tending to moderation. The problem that these virtues would sooner or later clash with each other, regardless of how moderate they were in themselves, for they derived from opposed ethical traditions, could be elided and not confronted openly since it was assumed that they could be made coherent by means of ordering within a hierarchical system of virtues. All medieval schoolmen were engaged in this activity and none performed it more successfully than Thomas Aquinas, whose work has remained as the paradigm of ethical thinking for the Catholic Church ever since.

Aquinas's work is typical of the philosophic way of dealing with ethical diversity and its problems of contradiction and conflict. The philosopher seeks to transcend the actual differences that arise in practical ethical life by constructing an ideal system of general categories and over-arching principles where oppositions are mediated and resolved. It is a kind of intellectual sublimation to a theoretical level, where practicalities do not need to intrude. Aristotle's philosophy lends itself particularly well to such an activity. His general categories of modes of being and acting, his propensity toward establishing hierarchies of ends, and his emphasis on distinctive virtues can be applied to any ethics whatever, even such as are far removed from the civic ethics for which it was originally intended. This goes partly toward explaining why all theorizing attempts in Islam, Judaism, and Christianity first turned to Aristotle.

The juristic way of dealing with ethical diversity is the opposite of the philosophic. It emphasizes practicalities and the need to resolve concrete problems. Hence, its tendency is toward casuistry, which is at the opposite pole to theoretical system building. The casuistic method of case studies features prominently in all the three major traditions of sacred law: the Judaic, Muslim, and Christian. In the last of these it took the form of Canon law, which was much more formalistically rational than any other type of sacred law. Furthermore, as Weber points out, "from the very beginning its relations to the secular law was one of relatively clear dualism, with respective jurisdictions fairly definitely marked in a manner not to be found elsewhere."[16] This dualism of sacred and secular law meant that the moral injunctions of Christian teaching did not unduly interfere with ordinary practical secular matters; they could be made inapplicable by general rulings in a way that was impossible in Islam and Judaism, which were reliant on a uniform casuistic response adjudication of cases, or what Weber calls khadi justice. By contrast, under the rule of Canon law the Church could issue "general decrees by which economically burdensome and impractical prescriptions, for instance, the prohibition of usury, could be treated as permanently or temporarily absolved."[17]

Also, Canon law had to recognize the superior claims of Roman Law, which the Church acknowledged from the very beginning; as Weber puts it, "the ancient Church had regarded the Roman Empire and its laws as definitive and eternal."[18] Thus the effects of Christian morality on ordinary life conduct, which was governed by Roman Law, were on the whole minimal, as we have already seen. The upshot was that Roman Law continued effectively to exclude Canon law and the claims of Christian morality. Hence, "the theoretical claim to an all-embracing substantive regulation of the entire conduct of life, which Canon law shared with all other systems of theocratic law, had in the Occident relatively harmless effects upon legal techniques."[19]

Thus the revival of Roman Law during the twelfth-century renaissance and repeatedly at later times served to resist the inroads of Christian morality through Canon law and helped, therefore, to perpetuate the ethical diversity of medieval Europe. "And where the Canon law tried to extend its dominion it met with the vigorous and successful opposition of the economic interests of the bourgeoisie, including that of the Italian cities, with which the Papacy had to ally itself."[20] These were precisely those cities most active in the propagation of Roman Law. The revival of Roman Law was also promoted by the anti-Papal powers for interests of their own—above all, by the imperial chancelleries of the German emperors and later of the other major monarchical rulers. They were intent on affirming the "sovereign position of the monarch as it appears in Justinian's codification."[21] The effect of the eventual triumph of Roman Law or of the other systems of legal codification modeled on it was to suppress the demands of Christian moral absolutism, above all, or of any other kind of ethical exclusivity and thereby to ensure a much more fluid and diversified ethical regime than that to be found in any other culture.

Literature has a different way again of dealing with ethical diversity. It neither theorizes differences away, like philosophy, nor reduces differences to adjudicable practicalities, like law; it confronts them by representing them in real situations. When literature takes a dramatic form, then opposed values and standards are embodied in specific characters or points of view between whom a dramatic conflict ensues. Such a struggle can be presented under a tragic or comic aspect. It is handled tragically when the conflict is exacerbated to the point of mutual destruction. The salutary purpose of this is to act as a warning that differences must not be taken to their extreme and that reconciliation is to be sought before the point where tragedy will inevitably ensue. To handle a conflict comically is to show that reconciliation can be achieved through what is common that unites all of those who are in the same society, through an appeal to higher or more basic values or through the universal mechanisms of human union such as marriage. In such ways literature both realizes and resolves ethical diversity and conflict by depicting it in concrete real-life situations and dealing with it as an ongoing condition that has to be faced ever anew in the predicaments in which people are embroiled.

Many of the medieval conflicts and tensions of ethical diversity are thus rendered in the works of Chaucer. Mostly, they have a comic treatment and resolution, though tragedy in the medieval sense of a fall from fortune is also sometimes employed. The stories and characters in the *Canterbury Tales* are comic almost throughout. They embody all kinds of medieval values, from the sacred to the sacrilegious, from the exalted noble to the vulgar common, from the idealistic to the realistic in all the possible shades of these opposites. The whole of medieval society is presented in the full scope of its orders and degrees of status and rank. And though they are embraced by the framing device of the story that is given in the religiously conventional terms of a pilgrimage to Canterbury, the Church, and the shrine of the martyred saint Thomas á Becket, this is by no means the sole goal of each individual pilgrim in his or her own life. They do not all aspire to sainthood, though they all recognize this as the highest state of Christian life, for each has also a standard more apt and becoming to his or her specific station in life. An "organismic" solution to ethical diversity is implicitly affirmed by Chaucer.

At the conclusion of the Middle Ages, on the threshold of modernity, the full scope for tragedy in ethical diversity is realized in the plays of Shakespeare. Hamlet's ethical tragedy is largely expressed in one of his most self-doubting lines, "thus conscience doth make cowards of us all." This expresses the clash between the call of conscience that insists on moral standards of action and the cowardice that this appears to be from the point of view of a cruder ethic of honor that requires revenge and requital by any means available. Hamlet enacts in himself the contradictory ethical demands placed upon the multifaceted Renaissance individual, and his thoughts and acts, driven in different directions by these ideals, veer from one extreme to another. He is in an ethical whirl as he tries to sustain the numerous roles, each with its own ethical standards, of the courtier, scholar, soldier, lover, and actor—the last perhaps typifies him best, for he is a player of all these roles. But as well as all these roles and the diverse ethics they entail, he is also prey to the rigors of a post-Reformation Puritan conscience that threatens to make a coward of him. This conscience, with all its self-torments and propensities to self-deception, is perhaps the main focus of Shakespeare's ethical concern for he dramatizes it in a number of his plays. However, his interest also embraces other Western ethical traditions, going right back to the Romans and Greeks. This is what makes him unparalleled as an ethical thinker in literature.

But Shakespeare was no historical prophet and he could not foresee what would come of Puritanism and that the irreconcilable ethical conflicts it engendered in England would eventually issue in civil war. Its role in the rise of capitalism was also, of course, hidden from him. We now know that this inaugurated the transformation to ethical modernity, which we shall discuss in the next section. In this transition to modernity in ethics, philosophy, law, and literature played crucial roles. But unlike in the Middle Ages, these were no longer the classical forms. A new kind of modern philosophy associated largely with the rise of science was to develop. A new kind of law issuing from the modern Sovereign State was to be enacted. And a new literature based on such new forms as the novel would also emerge. To discuss what role each of these played in modern ethics is beyond the scope of our present inquiry. We can do no more than to advert to it every now and again. In part 2 we shall also have something to say about the distancing from ethics of much of contemporary philosophy, law, and literature. The now current largely Positivist philosophies and positivistic doctrines of law have forfeited any influence on ethics; and modernistic literary writing, in pursuit of an aesthetics of *art pour l'art* and formalist experimentation, has also removed itself from ethical concerns.

Puritanism, Rationalization, and Secularization

Puritanism, or purism in general, was the initial generative process in the transition to ethical modernity. It was accompanied by the process of rationalization and followed by that of secularization, which together brought about the next phase of ethical modernity, that of the Enlightenment. The fact that these three processes came together in interaction with each other was peculiar to modernity; it had not taken place before. Singly by themselves, each of these processes had occurred before at various times in all kinds of ethical traditions, both in the West and East. As we shall show, there is nothing inherently new or modern about purism or rationalization or secularization; each is ubiquitous, but their conjunction in modernity was unprecedented and of far-reaching consequence.

Purism in the post-Reformation period largely took the form of Calvinist Puritanism. And as we know from the work of Weber, this initiated a process of rationalization in many spheres of social life, above all in the economy, where it promoted the rise of capitalism; in politics, where it was conducive to liberalism; and in science and philosophy, where it encouraged the new modern methodologies of the Scientific Revolution. Ethical rationalization was a part of all these developments. Puritanism initiated two rationalizing trends: one is what Weber calls "disenchantment," that is, the elimination of all magical or propitiatory procedures; and the other is what he calls "methodism," that is, the pursuit of a rigorous and consistent way of life. Both these features of modern ethics remained in place even when it lost its religious bearing and became secularized under the impact of such worldly forces as capitalist wealth and intellectual enlightenment. It is easy to see this taking place in Scotland, England, and New England as the Presbyterians, Methodists, and Congregationalists of one generation become the Utilitarians and Transcendentalists of the next. Perhaps not so clearly evident, but still traceable, are similar secularizing sequences in other countries, as, for example, in Germany, where the Pietists of one generation become the Kantians and Hegelians of the next.

However, purism, rationalization, and secularization must not be simply seen in generational terms. They are general social processes that are constantly at work. Ever newer puristic movements arise and eventually give way to secularizing trends. This is particularly evident in America even now. Nor is it always the case that these processes follow each other. As we previously stated, each can occur by itself on its own. Hence, to properly understand them, we need first to study them separately.

Purism, or Puritanism, as it is generally known in the West, is a widespread process occurring in all ethical traditions at all times. It is the opposite tendency to syncretism or reconciliation with other ethics. Often it occurs as a rejection of syncretist efforts and reaction against any diluting of an ethic. It is the self-affirmation of an ethic in the face of others, the insistence on its own essential identity. This takes the form of a call to return back to the purity of origins, back to roots, back to first principles and away from all compromise seen as adulteration. Such puristic movements as are taking place even now, especially so in Islamic societies, are known as fundamentalism. They have been a recurrent feature of the whole history of Islam. But they are also present in all other religious and ethical traditions.

Puristic or puritanical processes are not merely traditionalistic and opposed to any change. Often they can be highly innovatory. For under the slogan of a return to origins, something radically new can be introduced. Since the origin is frequently not precisely known, and even if known it is unrepeatable, the revivalists and reformers who seek to return to it invariably achieve something else and frequently initiate a new beginning. This might not be their conscious intention and it might happen quite contrary to what they think they are doing. It is one of the ironies of history that frequently they produce the opposite of what they intend.

Such paradoxes of purism are particularly evident in the two kinds of puristic revivals that are a feature of Western traditions: the classical and the moralistic. Throughout the history of the West there have been movements calling for a return to classical origins and usually opposed ones calling for a return to moral origins. The former are generically known as renaissances and they advocate a revival of some aspects of Greco-Roman antiquity, usually under the slogan of back to the natural or rational or humanistic, which invariably brings in something of the ancient civic ethics or the late-Stoic ethics of duty. The latter are known as reformations and advocate a return to Judeo-Christian morality, to the purity of Gospel teaching and the apostolic way of life. The Great Renaissance and Reformation of the sixteenth century were merely the most spectacular and climactic of these revivals, and each of them was led up to and followed by many others of a smaller scale that were less successful. We shall examine both of these puristic traditions separately in turn.

Classical renaissances have recurred throughout Western history. In Roman times they took the form of Attic revivals, the attempt to recover the purity of some favored period of Athenian culture, usually the age of Pericles. Such was the Attic revival movement that took place under the emperor Nero. These were not merely aesthetic movements but ethical ones as well, for usually they involved a demand to return to the classical civic virtues or some adapted variant of these. The aesthetic and ethical propensities were closely related in the classical tradition of purism. This was always evident in the later renaissances in Western history. In the medieval renaissances—beginning with the Carolingian literary revival and continuing throughout the rule of the Ottonian emperors and, above all, during the climactic twelfth century—it was Rome that was seen as the cradle of virtues. The tradition of republican virtue or civic humanism was particularly prominent, as we have already seen, in medieval Florence. Here once again aesthetics and ethics came together. The pride of the city commune was expressed in its civic institutions and the classical republican spirit that enthused its citizens, as well as in the pioneering achievements of its writers and painters. Brunetto Latini—whom we have already encountered in Dante's hell, ostensibly for his homosexual practices, nearly always a sure indicator of classicising tendencies—was one of the earliest of the exponents of the republican civic humanism that remained a prominent feature of Florentine thought, one perpetually at odds with its Christian morality. One of its last and greatest spokemen was Machiavelli, who had the presumption to extol these republican patriots, such as Farinata (also placed by Dante in hell), who held the greatness of their city above the salvation of their soul. It is understandable that in the same city at the same time the Dominican monk Savonarola should have launched a reformation designed to reverse that emphasis by burning classical vanities and reinstilling the fear of hell for the sake of the salvation of the soul. In Florence both renaissance and reformation revivals met in a headlong clash and neither decisively won out, for an uneasy compromise was reached eventually under the Medici dukes.

Once established in Florence and broadcast abroad, the tradition of republican civic virtue and its humanist attachments had a pervasive and long-lasting influence throughout Europe and later in America. From the hands of Machiavelli, Guicciardini, and other Italian thinkers it was passed on to Bacon, Harrington, and even, to some extent, Milton in England. It inspired the outstanding ethical-political thinkers of the next few centuries—above all, Hobbes, the first theorist of the modern state, who lived through the Civil War in England; Spinoza, the first secularizing thinker of Europe, who wrote at a turning point of the Dutch Republic; and Rousseau, the author of model constitutions, who was influential both on the new American and French republics. In America Thomas Jefferson was the leading exponent of the ethic of civic virtue, and his strong neo-classical predispositions were exemplified both in his political and building activities; the ethical and aesthetic here, too, joined hands, as was to be expected in this tradition. The republican spirit of the United States was marked by both these features throughout its history.

In Europe the French Revolution purveyed the republican spirit of civic virtue through all countries. In the hands of the Jacobins and their successors it became particularly fanatical and promoted a narrow sense of patriotism. In other countries it transmogrified into nationalism. This was particularly evident in Germany, where Winckelmann's revived neo-Atticism in the eighteenth century became the official state-sponsored classicism in the nineteenth, particularly so in Prussia where it was invoked to uphold an authoritarian ethic of bureaucratic officialdom. But it also promoted the classical literature of Goethe and the other *Dichter* and *Denker*, as well as the humanistic spirit in which Wilhelm von Humboldt reformed the universities. Through the mouth of Fichte, however, it merged with the call to nationalistic self-assertion and German unification. This was the benign prelude to the eventual German national catastrophe, when under the Nazis the neo-classical aesthetic and ethic were revived as subterfuges for the worship of the state and its Führer by classicizing writers and thinkers such as Jünger and Heidegger. Something similar occurred in Italy under Mussolini. However, in England the outcome was very different, for in the context of constitutional monarchy the classical spirit infused itself into the movement for liberal democracy with its conception of active citizenship as public service.

Classical puristic revivals still occur even now both in aesthetics and ethics, but they have receded in importance and are of trifling proportions.

Thus, for example, under the general guise of postmodernism, the classical orders of architecture have made a belated reappearance, but, unfortunately, only as decorative embellishments without any real stylistic meaning. Much the same has been the effect of the demands for a reintroduction of the classics into higher education. It is not that this is of no educational value in itself, but that it is of no public consequence; it will not address the failures of civic ethic in our societies. What these are we will examine in part 2.

Moral purism or Puritanism, the process of change that resulted in numerous reformations, is the complementary and frequently opposed process to that of classical purism, which produced renaissances. In the history of Christian morality one of the earliest instances of such a development was the Donatist heresy, which arose in North Africa starting in 311 A.D. over an internal Church controversy about re-admitting lapsed Christians back into the fold. The Donatists, under their bishop Donatius, were intent on "preserving the original purity of the faith."[22] They lost out to the more latitudinarian Catholic clergy of the early Church. Whether such a puristic moral reformation is declared heretical or absorbed within the Church is a matter of historical circumstances and the extant configuration of parties and forces. A particularly salient instance of this occurred during the medieval Franciscan puristic reformation. Francis of Assisi sought to recall Christians back to the moral purities and simplicities of the apostles at the origin of the faith. It was touch and go whether the Papacy would anathematize him as a heretic or promote him as a saint. During his lifetime, the call to reform was conditionally upheld. But after his death, the order he established split into two parties, the more puristic of which, the so-called Spirituals, was declared heretical and sternly persecuted. The other, more conformist, group under St. Bonaventura was officially accepted and as Franciscans had a powerful influence on subsequent Christian morality.

The greatest puristic reform movement of European moral history was, of course, the Reformation. The impact of this on the whole ethical history of the West was unprecedented, for it was the essential prelude to the onset of modernity. But it began as a backward-looking call for a return to origins, to the initial teachings of the Gospels, to the apostles—above all, Paul—and even further back to the prophets of the Old Testament. The great reformers, Luther, Calvin, Zwingli, and others, were intent on moral purity through the elimination of all accommodations and compromises that they considered the Church to have made in the long course of its worldly career. The philosophically sanctioned scholastic formulae of Canon law were particularly abhorent to them, especially those made in the name of the pagan philosopher Aristotle. Other classical tendencies were also hateful to them, perhaps more so to the former monk Luther than the humanistically educated Calvin. But all insisted that Christian morality be stripped of its pagan ethical excrescences and brought back to what they thought was its original state.

As we now know, what actually resulted was quite other. Instead of the historical impossibility of returning to the early Church, what they gave rise to were new churches and new ethics, now collectively known as the Protestant Ethic after the studies of Troelsch, Weber, and others. Following Weber, we shall concentrate only on one type of this ethic, that developed by Calvin, which in English-speaking countries assumed the common name of Puritanism.

The Puritan Ethic was a most rigorous and coherent amalgamy of many of the traditional Western ethical types. At base it was extremely moralistic, for, as Weber sees it, "a more intense form of the religious valuation of moral action than that to which Calvinism led its adherents has perhaps never existed."[23] But its moralistic nisus was directed to the fulfillment of duty—not to love in the world, but to work in the world—for "the valuation of the fulfilment of duty in worldly affairs is the highest form which the moral activity of the individual can assume."[24] As Weber's studies show, this resulted in the channeling of the full thrust of Christian moral motivation into inner-worldly activities that served as the driving force to implement the new developments of the modern world, particularly to capitalism, but also to science and technology, liberal politics, and many other features of modernity.

Thus, starting off as a fervent Christian morality, Calvinism also became an ethic of duty, mandating work in a calling. The idea of vocation, a notion that Catholicism had developed solely for monks or those entering holy orders, the Calvinists generalized to all Christians regardless of their profession. As long as the work was morally sanctioned, or at least traditionally not reproved, it had to be undertaken with complete commitment for its own sake and not because it constituted the charitable endeavor or "good works" of the Catholic dispensation. The duty was to the work itself, irrespective of its results or its outcome for others. One's duties were whatever the legitimate work of one's vocation required. But unlike the older ethics of duty, such as Confucianism, Krishnaism, or Roman late-Stoicism, inheritance or tradition was not allowed completely to prescribe what one's work or station in life was to be, for one was also duty bound to improve oneself—to reap the rewards of God's providential bounty and one's own good husbandry—so that one could change one's status in society and acquire new callings and responsibilities. The Protestant Ethic of Calvinism made it otiose to prescribe traditional lists of virtues for people in different stations in life and occupations. Devotion to the work itself prescribes its own virtuous conduct and mode of sober and serious bearing—a mode of living that its opponents were to castigate as ageless joylessness.

The Protestant Ethic of Calvinism achieved a most rational and consistent resolution of all the ethical tensions of the Western tradition. According to Weber, unlike the other Christian ethics, "the God of Calvinism required of his believers not single good works, but a life of good works combined into a unified system. . . . The moral conduct of the average man was thus deprived of its planless and unsystematic character and subjected to a consistent method for conduct as a whole. It is no accident that the name of Methodists stuck to the participants of the last great revival of puritan ideas in the eighteenth century."[25] As Weber points out, this has some analogues to rabbinic Judaism, for, as the Talmud insists, the fulfillment of the duties commanded by Law *(mitzvot)* is ethically more important than mere moral beneficence.[26] But Calvinism went much further in rationalizing conduct: "Puritanism objectified everything and transformed it into rational enterprise, dissolved everything into pure business relations, and substituted rational law and agreement for tradition."[27] Once again, we see here the devaluation of tradition and its substitution by rational norms, which was so characteristic of Calvinism as an ethic of duty and made it so distinctive when compared with all previous such ethics.

It is this basic conception that decisively shaped modern ethical culture. As Weber puts it, "rational conduct on the basis of the idea of the calling was born . . . from the spirit of Christian asceticism. . . . For when asceticism was carried out of monastic cells into everyday life, and began to dominate worldly morality, it did its part in building the tremendous cosmos of the modern economic order."[28] What Weber calls "ascetic rationalism" not only had a decisive influence on "the content of practical social ethics, and thus for the types of organization and the functions of social groups from the conventicle to the State," it also had a "relation to humanistic rationalism, its ideals of life and cultural influence."[29] Out of the "idea of duty in one's calling, [which] prowls around our lives like the ghost of dead religious beliefs,"[30] has emerged the practice of rational conduct and the belief in a rational ethics governing such conduct.

Thus rationalization is the second crucial process of change giving rise to a modern ethics, as it is also in modern law and much else in modern culture, particularly that kind that is given to formalism and individualism. As is well known, the concept of rationalization plays the key role in Weber's whole conception of history, from the primitive to the modern age. It is, therefore, a universal process that in principle can apply to everything. Anything can be rationalized in all kinds of different ways. This holds for ethics as well. In fact, the rationalization of ethics proceeds in conjunction with all the other rationalizations of social activities, both intellectual as well as practical, ideal as well as real. For the more it takes place in one sphere of social life, the more we can also expect it in the others. Ethical rationalization is both a resultant of rationalizations in other spheres, as well as the cause of such developments elsewhere, as we have already seen with respect of the Puritan ethic in its relation to capitalism, liberal politics, and science.

Rationalization is a very variegated process and can mean many different things. Weber distinguishes a number of different forms of rationality, and we have done so elsewhere as well.[31] Briefly put, it can take a more ideal or more instrumental form:

> It means one thing if we think of the kind of rationalization the systematic thinker performs on the image of the world: an increasing theoretical mastery of reality by means of increasingly precise and abstract concepts. Rationalism means another thing if we think of the methodical attainment of a definitively given and practical end by means of an increasingly precise calculation.[32]

The origin of ethics itself is both the product of such diverse processes of rationalization, which, as we saw, took place during the so-called Axial Age in a select few societies, and, at the same time, it provides the impetus to a further increase in rationalization throughout the social fabric, affecting many other types of activities. The rationalization of worldviews in the direction of a transcendent Reality, such as took place in the universal religions and philosophies, was crucial for the emergence of ethics. But this was also dependent on the rise of more pragmatic means-ends rationalities in the articulation of social practices and techniques, particularly so in legal procedure. Subsequently ethics itself had a profound impact on both worldviews and social practices of all kinds.

Rationality in ethics also takes the form of what Weber calls "systematic arrangement": "all kinds of practical ethics that are systematically and unambiguously oriented to fixed goals of salvation are 'rational,' partly in the same sense as formal method is rational, partly in the sense that they distinguish between 'valid' norms and what is empirically given."[33] Ethics oriented to salvation are primarily those we have called moralities; their two initially most important exemplifications are Judaic monotheism and Buddhistic soteriology. Both of these were historically decisive developments in the historical process of ethical rationalization. The crucial role of rationality within moralities was promoted by two further factors: the emergence of redeemers or prophetic figures of salvation, and the urgent moral need to elaborate a theodicy of suffering to account for what Weber calls "the ethical irrationality of the world." As Weber puts it:

> A rational conception of the world is contained in germ within the myth of the redeemer. A rational theodicy of misfortune has, therefore, as a rule, been a development of this conception of the world. At the same time, this rational view of the world has often furnished suffering as such with a "plus" sign, which was originally foreign to it.[34]

Weber's extensive studies of the world religions are primarily concerned with examining the effects on ethics of the various theodices of suffering, such as the Indian doctrine of *karma*, the Zoroastrian teaching of a good and evil god, and the Calvinist concept of predestination. The effect of the latter on the emergence of the peculiar Puritan variant of the Protestant ethic is a subject to which Weber devotes considerable attention. As he shows, in general the rationalization of morality and the problems of theodicy are particularly closely connected.

But ethics can also be rationalized in quite other ways. Thus Confucianism developed a rational ethics of duty quite uninfluenced by any of the factors that touched morality and affected Calvinism; indeed, in a certain sense, apart from religion altogether, as Weber explains:

> Confucianism is rationalist to such a far-going extent that it stands at the extreme boundary of what one might possibly call a "religious" ethic. At the same time, Confucianism is more rationalist and sober, in the sense of the absence and the rejection of all non-utilitarian yardsticks, than any other ethical system, with the possible exception of J. Bentham's.[35]

But, as Weber also makes clear, in every other respect Confucianism is far less rational than the two decisive ethics of the West: that of prophetic Torah Judaism and that of Calvinist Puritanism.

According to Weber, the rationalism of Confucianism is still wholly traditionalist; it does not possess the rationalizing potential of Puritanism. Though both are comparable as ethics of duty, yet they are also fundamentally opposed. As his decisive pronouncement has it: "Confucian rationalism meant rational adjustment to the world; Puritan rationalism meant rational mastery of the world."[36] For Weber the difference is absolutely crucial. It entails two quite different orientations to the world: either that of an ethic that makes rational ethical demands on a recalcitrant world and so finds itself in inevitable tension with worldly life, or that of an ethic that rationally adjusts itself to the demands that the world makes of it and so finds itself in harmony with worldly life. "Confucianism was (in intent) a rational ethic which reduced tension with the world to an absolute minimum. . . . the world was the best of all possible worlds; human nature was disposed to be ethically good," and so on. But for Weber this was not a critical form of ethical rationality, because "every religion which opposes the world with rational ethical imperatives finds itself at some point in a state of tension with the ethical irrationalities of the world."[37] Only Puritanism confronts the world from that critical position: "in contrast to the naive stand of Confucianism toward things of this world, Puritan ethics construed them as tremendous and grandiose tension toward the 'world.' "[38] In other words, the things of the world are not to be accepted as given but opposed in the name of ethical imperatives and, as far as possible, transformed through work and other kinds of striving. The Puritans "alone 'had striven for God and his justice';"[39] for the Confucians, by contrast, "there had never been an ethical prophecy of a supermundane God who raised ethical demands."[40]

Weber's contrast between the ethical rationalism of Confucianism and Puritanism could be extended to other ethics as well. However, the opposition between no two Christian ethics could ever be as sharp as this, since no Christian morality could adapt itself to worldly realities to the extent that Confucianism did:

> Outwardly some patriarchal aspects of a Thomist and Lutheran ethic might appear to resemble Confucianism, but this is merely an external impression. The Confucian system of radical world-optimism succeeded in removing the basic pessimistic tension between the world and the supra-mundane destination of the individual. But no Christian ethic, however entangled in mundane compromises could attain this.[41]

Yet the ethical rationality of Puritanism, its "methodism," so to speak, was of a greater severity than that of any other Christian morality. Catholicism and Lutheranism remained "entangled in mundane compromises" of all kinds; that is, they had learned to adapt, whereas Puritanism kept to its puristic reforming rigor much more tenaciously for much longer. This is one reason why it, much more so than any other ethic, became the precursor of rational modernity.

What, then, does rationality amount to in ethics? As Weber's studies make clear, it is not a mere matter of providing rationalizations for one's ethical precepts by means of discursive arguments and justifications. Every

ethic that is tied to a philosophy or some other system for providing rationales can do this. Classical ethics, as expounded by the Greek philosophers,
could do this to very great extent at a very high level of rationality. Medieval
scholasticism could also elaborate highly involved philosophical proofs for
whatever it was it wanted to prove. Even talmudic Judaism operates with
highly refined casuistic modes of argumentation; and Muslim scholarship
does the same. Rationality in this sense is quite common and is not the
sense in which Weber singled out prophetic Judaism and later Puritanism for
particular attention.

Weber bases his primary notion of rationalization on two criteria, which
in the first place he applies to religion but which have also a ready reference
to ethics:

> To judge the level of rationalization a religion represents we may use two primary
> yardsticks which are in many ways interrelated. One is the degree to which the
> religion has divested itself of magic; the other is the degree to which it has system-
> atically unified the relation between God and the world and therewith its own
> ethical relation to the world.[42]

In respect of ethics, the elimination of magic means that no extraneous and
arbitrary stipulations are applicable in ethical matters. Thus, for example, in
a rational ethic it is not possible to grant or procure indulgences from binding norms or make any other such arbitrary exceptions. Nor can one set up
as norms or principles purely ritualistic requirements, ones that make no real
ethical demands on people, such that their fulfillment is solely a matter of
opportunities and means. Thus, for example, it is not possible to pronounce
ethical judgments based on ordeals or trials of chance. Nor can one judge
actions purely as performances, without taking the subjective motivation of
the actors into account. These and many other such stipulations are involved
in the "disenchantment" of ethics, which is part of its rationalization. The
other aspect of rationalization in ethics is the constitution of an ethical
system, its unity as a network of norms covering all of life's potential happen-
ings, at least in principle, so that nothing can escape from ethical consideration or judgment where this is relevant. At the same time the norms
themselves are systematically unified under higher principles and more general maxims and values. In theory, ethics can be thus completely rationalized, but in practice, in the actuality of historical cultures and their ethos,
this is far from the case, for there always remain tensions, oppositions, and
disparities that cannot be resolved. The rationalization of ethics is like that
of law: formally speaking, it looks feasible, but in the messiness of life's diver-

sities it breaks down. Schemes to this effect that look theoretically plausible, such as Utilitarianism, are soon found to be unworkable.

However, attempts to rationalize ethics, even where this is only partially successful, have enormous consequences. They lead to the segregation of a sphere of ethical exclusivity where the ethical "ought" is sharply delimited from every other value and where the ethical imperative loses all relation to anything outside their domain, to practicality, utility, society, economy, politics, or law. And in turn, these other spheres become dissociated from ethics. Thus, for example, legal validity is assessed according to formal criteria that make no reference to morality or any other ethical norm. Even if ethics still claims priority in principle over all other valuations and judgments—such that where these clash, it is the ethical verdict that, from the ethical point of view, ought to take precedent over every other—it can no longer substantiate or enforce this claim. Thus a rationalized ethics might seek to set itself up as the ruling valuation in life, but by the same token this becomes a contested position, since every other sphere affirms its own priority and is equally intent on preserving its autonomy to the exclusion of ethics. For example, the whole development of a rationalized politics of *raison d'état* means the elimination of ethics where issues of state power and interest are concerned. And the same is true of every other major sphere. Thus there arises the characteristic war of values, the battle of every value sphere against every other that Weber likens to the warring gods of ancient mythology.[43] Hence, the ultimate upshot of rationalization is polytheism in this sense.

These paradoxes of rationalization make it impossible to view increased rationality as any kind of unambiguous progress. It is true that a more rationalized ethics is more sophisticated, more discriminating, and in that sense more advanced than a less rationalized one, for it makes more distinctions and is far better ordered and articulated. But that in itself does not mean that it is superior in its primary functions of regulating conduct. A less rationalized ethic might suit the overall ethos of a society far better than one that is over formalized and too structured. Ethics is analogous to art in this respect, for often a simpler and purer style is aesthetically greater than one that is over-refined and over-elaborate. Rationalization also gives rise to problems of the dissociation of spheres of value such as we spelled out previously. We shall presently see how this was particularly the case in late modernity, when the rationalization of ethics was also accompanied by its secularization.

Secularization is also a recurrent and ubiquitous process in the history of ethics. It is closely related to disenchantment, for what it means is that an ethic is detached from any religious grounding and also in this sense removed from any metaphysical or supernatural or magical influences. Once secularized, an ethic is no longer subject to any religious sanctions or explanations and its norms no longer religiously justified or seen as soteriological requirements. The ethics abandons any transcendent validation, such as, typically in Christianity, that which invokes the will of God or eschatologies of heaven and hell. A secular ethic is practiced as a social activity without any sacred awe or aura.

There have been phases of secularization throughout the history of ethics, but these have usually been fitful and brief, for no ethic could maintain itself independently of religion in traditional societies. Even Confucianism, the most secularly inclined of the traditional ethics, an ethic of religiously sober officials, had to attach itself to ancestral cults and transform itself into a quasi-religion of traditional pieties if it was to succeed in the patrimonial society of China. In the West there have occurred episodes of quasi-secularization, usually associated with Greek philosophy, in periods of intellectual enlightenment. The first such enlightenment took place early in the history of philosophy and was carried through by the Sophists, who undertook to expound and teach the civic ethics quite apart from the civic religion. The reaction against this secularizing trend by the religious conservatives in Athens led to the expulsion of the Sophists as a danger to the civic cults and eventually also to the trial of Socrates on similar charges of corrupting the young. Another such secularizing tendency ensued in the last phase of the Roman Republic under the instigation of Epicurean philosophers, who expounded the doctrine of the indifference of the gods to human affairs, including ethical behavior. This brief secularizing enlightenment, as expressed in Lucretius' famous poem *De Rerum Natura,* was soon brought to an end by conservative trends associated with the establishment of the empire by Augustus, when the more religiously minded Stoic philosophy came to predominate. But a secularizing mentality could not be completely erased for the two approaches in philosophy that promoted it, that of the Epicureans and the Skeptics; both remained as accepted and state-sanctioned schools. Lucian of Samosata is one exponent of such a semi-secular skepticism in later imperial times. With the onset of Christianity as the state religion, secular sentiments regarding ethics could no longer be freely expressed and this more or less remained the situation till the modern period of secular Enlightenment.

The Enlightenment was a historically unique process of secularization, in that it succeeded, for the very first time, in secularizing morality, the specifically religious ethics. Morality was detached from its Christian moorings and set adrift on a sea of natural sentiments or rational interests, free to develop itself according to its own inherent principles. Historically considered, this was one of the unintended consequences of the Reformation and the Protestant Ethic. With the "disenchantment" of religion and its separation from magic and sacred awe, ethics, too, was brought closer to a secular state. Since, according to puritanical Calvinism, ethical endeavor was totally bound up with the ordinary course of one's vocational life, including its very ordinary successes and failures, it became easier to lose sight of the transcendent sanctions for ethical conduct in the other world. Also, in promoting a rational and, in time, scientific approach to everything, Calvinism encouraged such an attitude to ethics itself. In economics this produced the mentality of the "spirit of capitalism," in science the uninhibited pursuit of a rational and objective truth, and in ethics it encouraged either a utilitarian approach to valuations of good and bad or a deontological approach to judgments of right and wrong. What made this secularization even easier is that Calvinism placed the whole burden of ethics on the individual and his autonomous conscience. Once that conscience detached itself from religious belief, a secular mentality in ethics ensued as well—though not without the scrupulousness that had previously characterized it. Secular puritanism was a prominent feature of nineteenth-century English moral thinking, such as that of George Eliot.

The Enlightenment secularization of ethics took place everywhere throughout Europe, for sooner or later by degrees it occurred in all the major Christian faiths. By the late eighteenth century, as a delayed reaction, it also affected Jewish ethics in a movement known as the *Haskalah*. Eventually, in the twentieth century, it even reached Islam and all the other religious ethics of the world. The effect was that in Christianity the exclusiveness of morality was abrogated; the "one thing needful" for the salvation of the soul was no longer deemed necessary. In other religions the effects were analogous; the rigidity of moral sanctions was loosened. It was made to seem as if life could be led more freely with a greater variety of ethical norms from which to choose one's ethical course. The political liberalism that accompanied ethical secularization provided a protected sphere of private life where one could realize oneself ethically and pursue ones own happiness without regard to traditional sanctions.

The main effect of secularization on society in public life was to free the various spheres of public activity from religiously sanctioned ethical controls. Thus business, politics, law, art, and knowledge, to mention but the most important spheres, were freed from many of the restrictions that Christian ethics had traditionally placed on them. Of course, this was not altogether a new development, as we have already seen in relation to rationalization; it had been going on in a partial and limited way since the great upheavals of the sixteenth century. But the Enlightenment and what followed from it gave the process a huge thrust forward, and from that point on it has been proceeding ever faster. Each of the major spheres of activity then began those developments that we now associate with their modernity, and the removal of ethical inhibitions was a major factor in this.

In each of the major spheres of social life, autonomous values and standards began to be followed, ones that had nothing to do with ethics. Thus in business, profitability became the sole criterion of success and all the older purposes and ends of a commercial life were abandoned. In politics, a new realism of power in policy decision making ousted all earlier political goals. In law, formalism of procedure and codification became all important, above all other issues of substantive justice. In the sciences, a new ideal of objective truth to be attained through unfettered research, regardless of consequences, was followed. In the arts, self-expression and the cult of genius took over from the previous aesthetics of order and representation. So, one by one, all the major social preoccupations removed themselves from ethical controls and influences under the guise of freeing themselves to develop their own autonomous potentials.

As a result of this segregation of value spheres, the whole course of social life became compartmentalized. The most basic separation was that between public and private life. The former was that of the public occupational spheres, where the major work activities were carried on; the latter was that of the intimate spheres of personal life, which increasingly tended to take on an individualist turn of family and friendship. The relocation of work into offices and factories, away from home and dwelling, furthered the processes of a dissociation of value spheres. The home became a haven in a heartless world, as we see it so often in the novels of Charles Dickens—for example, Mr. Wemmick's "castle" in *Great Expectations*. Public life, on the other hand, was the arena of economic and social competition, but also of social intercourse and civic affairs, where public duties were carried out and public opinion was expressed.

The effect of this compartmentalization of life was that morality was increasingly pushed into the private sphere and detached from the public one, where different values obtained. Moral questions became matters of private conscience, which generally concerned issues of religion or the decencies of personal behaviour. It is in this sense that parliamentarians still speak of a vote of conscience where they are not bound by Party discipline. For women, who were mostly excluded from public life, morality was even more narrowly interpreted, so much so that feminine moral virtue became almost identified with sexual prudery and for a woman to be called immoral could only mean one thing. For men, the range of moral conscience also narrowed, yet was still much wider, for unconscionable behavior in a man could concern many more kinds of things, mostly private but to some extent public as well.

To foreshadow what is to come later, it might be noted that the separation between public and private life has now almost completely collapsed because both public and private spheres are fast eroding and becoming vestigial. The formation of public opinion is now tightly controlled by the media conglomerates, and public debate on most issues can only be conducted by the grace of the media proprietors in the full glare of media publicity. A vigorous social civic life in a city environment has been largely replaced by publicity shows and mass entertainment, as city and suburbs become separated from each other. Political life is conducted through the electronic media, and public meetings have been rendered into so-called photo opportunities. Some authors now speak of the "end of public culture" altogether and of a failure of civility, which is perhaps an exaggeration.[44] Yet the erosion of the public sphere is so severe that people retreat to the intimacies of private life. But they only find cold comfort there. All the influences of an overpowering publicity follow them into their homes. Through television, the video, and the Internet, all the doings of the media have invaded the privacy of the home as well and are daily enacted in the living room. Modern methods of communication and surveillance have enabled the workplace to invade the home, as people have to make themselves constantly available to their bosses and supervisors and can be called upon at any time to comply with work requirements. As a result of all these pressures and strains, the family is collapsing, with all the consequences this has for relations between spouses and between parents and children. Intimacy becomes more and more of a beckoning mirage, to be sought but never found. The ethical consequence of a collapse of public and private life is a process of de-ethicization of which the most salient aspect is demoralization in all the varied senses of the term, which we shall study in the next section.

But before we come to that, we must first examine the role and place of ethics in the preceding era of so-called bourgeois society, largely during the extended nineteenth century from the French Revolution down to the First World War. This was the period in which the processes of rationalization and secularization, which had merely begun in the previous period of Enlightenment, finally came into their own and assumed massive social dimensions. However, Puritanism was still very active and all the other religious moralities, particularly a revived Catholicism, were forces to be reckoned with in all European societies. As all these processes confronted each other, fierce ethical clashes arose. The forces of revolution and reaction were at each other's throats in a struggle to the death in the political arena; the forces of reform and conservatism were less fiercely engaged and more willing to settle their differences by liberal democratic means.

We begin by outlining the effects that the forces of revolution and reform had on ethics; the reason that this was so strenuously resisted by the forces of reaction and conservatism will be obvious. It is not, of course, our purpose here to take sides in these battles of the past, nor does it make any historical sense to wage them anew now when so much has intervened and when conditions and the problems they create are so utterly different to what they were even a century ago. We have already outlined some of these differences in the introduction and will go on to consider them further in part II.

Beginning with the French Revolution, secularized ethics, freed from its religious moorings, was set adrift on a liberated course and took on a mostly liberal character. It focused increasingly on legal reform carried out by political means and the legislative activities of the new state power, one that arose out of the previous revolutionary transformations. The growth of the state was matched by the growth of reform movements that demanded state intervention to right the wrongs of society. These demands were expressed in terms of the new liberal legal conceptions of "rights" and "freedoms." We can see this first politically articulated in the declarations concerning human rights in the constitutions that accompanied the rise of the new revolutionary states in America and France. Such demands for rights and freedoms remain key features of all reformist and revolutionary movements down to this day; they are now inscribed in numerous United Nations declarations, and nearly all states now pay at least lip service to them. Hence, this constitutes a radical new departure in the civic ethics of the modern period, one that cannot now be curtailed without risking extremely dangerous consequences. But it must also be recognized that it is liable to lead to a juridification of ethics that also has deleterious results in the long run, as we shall go on to show.

The new civic ethics that arose in the context of an enlarged and more dominant state power was not restricted to propounding liberal principles of social reform; it was also directed to inculcating new civic virtues, particularly such as were conducive to the new version that patriotism took in becoming nationalism. These civic virtues governed the changed relation between the individual and the state; the individual, who had been a mere subject of royal authority under the *Ancien Régime,* now became a citizen participating in a republican polity. This brought with it new rights but also new obligations. The rights of participation in the new, increasingly democratic forms of representation were matched by obligations to render services to the state. What this amounted to in practice was mainly compulsory taxation and conscription for war. Through these impositions, generally accepted as ethical duties by the citizens themselves, the state was able to enlist the new virtues for its own purposes. Ultimately, it meant that it was able to call upon its citizens to sacrifice their means and their lives on its behalf in a civic ethic vaguely reminiscent of the ancient polis. But actually, as the two World Wars were to prove, it led to the betrayal of ethics.

This outcome, promoted by the state and by the social forces upholding it, was made possible and facilitated by a new form of secularized belief generally known as ideology, which is a peculiar amalgam of religion, ethics, and politics. Initially, this arose out of the revolutionary movements, both radical and reactionary, that developed during the French Revolution and the political turmoils surrounding it. The major ideologies were founded in that period. These grew throughout the nineteenth century and assumed the ominous aspect of secularized religions and crusading movements that could command fanatical devotion. The radical ideologies, such as Socialism, Communism, and Anarchism, gave rise to new revolutionary movements attacking the then current monarchical and bourgeois state regimes. The reactionary ideologies, such as Nationalism, Conservatism, and the beginnings of what would later become Fascism, tended to defend the state regimes that were in their hands. All such idealogies incorporated diverse values and ideals but removed them from the ambit of ethical practice by shifting them into that of politics with religious dogmatic aspirations. For to achieve perfect justice on earth or to defend order against anarchy, any means were deemed permissible, even those requiring extreme violence and terror. Thus those who sowed the seeds of total ethical goals in the nineteenth century would reap the bitter harvest of totalitarianism in the twentieth.

These ideological sowers generally came from a new class that first rose to prominence in the nineteenth century: the intellectuals. They were prominent in all European societies in both revolutionary, reactionary, and liberal manifestations. Their attitude and relation to ethics is, therefore, of particular importance. In general, the intellectualization of ethics is itself a process that had very pronounced features in this period. In itself, intellectualization is one extreme form of rationalization, traditionally carried through on a philosophical basis. In the nineteenth century, however, it assumed a new scientific guise in line with the burgeoning growth of the new sciences and the spread of university studies. The idea of a scientific ethics was one of its products. This conception of an ethics based on science was to prove extremely fateful and fatal when it was linked to ideology. Many of the worst ethical crimes of the twentieth century derived their justification from it and were committed in its name. And there were always intellectuals behind all these developments.

Many of the theories propounded by intellectuals, even where they were scientifically valid, tended to have a dubious effect on ethics. Thus, for example, the theory of evolution by natural selection as developed by Charles Darwin—himself a very moral English country gentleman—led to the social movement known as Social Darwinism, which from its first inception by Herbert Spencer to its ultimate invocation by Adolf Hitler, can only be seen as harmful to ethics. Marxism, which also has its scientific merits, in the hands of Lenin and Stalin—themselves intellectuals of no mean standing— was utilized to justify some of the worst crimes of mankind. Nietzscheanism fed directly into Fascism and Nazism with well-known results. Even Freudianism, a seemingly harmless practice of private therapy, was not without its insidious consequences for ethics when it was used for the exorcism of shame and guilt. However, the full effects of all these theories were not evident till well into the twentieth century.

The intellectual was not like the older-style gentleman. He did not represent a complete and coherent ethical way of life; he lacked integrity in the traditional sense. The intellectual was generally an enthusiast who pursued a narrower goal with passionate intensity. There were many different kinds of intellectuals in the nineteenth century, devoted to many types of ideal causes. Political intellectuals expounded ideologies. Philosophical intellectuals, such as the Utilitarians in England and the Positivists in France, were driven by utopian theories of various kinds. Scientific intellectuals sought practical social amelioration. Artistic intellectuals, such as many of the romantic poets, painters, and composers, saw art as the salvation of society. All of them despised and attacked the older ideal of the gentleman and regarded themselves as superior to it. Yet in many respects they did not measure up to it.

The gentleman remained the stalwart of the established nineteenth-century ethics now known derisively as Victorian morality. Despite all the separations of spheres of value and compartmentalizations of life activities that began, this was still a fairly integrated ethics compared to what was to come later. One might go so far as considering it the last of the coherent ethics of the West. It retained most of the Western ethical traditions, included many surviving elements of an ethic of honor. Some of the more restrained of these were inherent in the English conception of the gentleman, who was much more sober and civil than most of his continental counterparts—*the*

honêt homme, the *cavaliere*, the *Herr*—who were still given to exacting satisfaction and affairs of honor.

Such a general gentlemanly bearing was by no means confined to the
aristocracy but also extended to the middle classes, especially to the new
groups of university-trained professionals. These also developed on this basis
a new conception of duty or responsibility. Most of the current professional
ethics, especially those for the then key professions of medicine and law, owe
their basic form to the standards of responsibility and accountability that
were introduced during the Victorian era. The ethics of civil service—which
is now being so drastically undermined by the current privatization of bureaucracy—was also first instituted at that time. All these professionals and
others who aspired to the status of gentlemen sought to carry themselves
accordingly in all public respects.

The nineteenth-century English novel is almost wholly an ethical explo-
ration of the figure of the gentleman and his female counterpart, the lady.
From Jane Austen to Joseph Conrad, all the authors of Dr. Leavis's so-called
Great Tradition were preoccupied with the question of what it means to be
a gentleman or lady in the ethical sense. Perhaps nobody was more concerned with this question than Charles Dickens, who in novel after novel
explored the issue of who was a real gentleman and how it was possible to
become one if one was not one to begin with.

In all the literatures of this period in which the novel flourished, a figure
appears who is more or less the equivalent of the Victorian gentleman in
England. The latter was the cynosure of gentlemanly standards of conduct
throughout Europe, just as he set the dominant styles of dress and bearing.
The gentleman descended historically from the knights of the Middle Ages
and the courtiers and squires of later periods. He inherited from these ances-
tors an extremely refined sense of honor and a cultivated manner. The English gentleman was less inclined to affairs of the heart or the sword than his
more hot-blooded continental peers, but he was nevertheless susceptible to
romantic love. Even when no longer a believing Christian, he was a man of
conscience whose morality frequently bore traces of a Puritan sense of duty.
This would often take the form of public service, especially when it was
buttressed by a public school and university classical education extolling
Roman models of virtue. All in all, the gentleman was the final coherent
expression of the Western ethical ideal before it broke down and broke up.

The gentleman died on the battlefields of the First World War. "Dulce et
decorum est pro patria mori" could no longer be maintained as an ideal in
the trenches after the glorious cavalry charge became obsolete. The other
gentlemanly ideals also became less and less supportable in the postwar cli-

mate of economic malaise, egalitarianism, democratization, and in many countries also revolution. The aristocratic way of living could no longer be sustained for all these political and economic reasons. But it was also ethically discredited since it relied on subservience and exploitation, especially in rural areas. A class that depended on status hierarchy and inherited landed wealth could no longer maintain its privileges in good conscience. But with its decline and fall a whole ethical era had also come to an end.

Demoralization

The Western ethical system remained more or less intact till the First World War, despite all the attacks against tradition and its institutions and the privileged class-society launched by revolutionaries and intellectuals from the French Revolution onward. It was only following the unprecedented carnage of that war and the disruptions wrought by this in many European societies that the whole ethical tradition also began to be seriously discredited in a grave way. The Second World War, with its unparalleled bestialities and other inhumanities, promoted this process further. Since then, despite the prevalent peace and prosperity in all Western societies, there has been no ethical recovery, for the Cold War that ensued was not conducive to any revival of ethical life. Ideological warfare promotes feelings of self-righteousness that are the converse of ethical sincerity.

In this postwar period of prosperity and self-indulgence in the shadow of nuclear annihilation, social life took a form that was contrary to the seriousness of ethical life. Economic affluence gave rise to a consumer market ethos that eroded ethical ties and commitments. Communal solidarities were lost as people retreated from the cities to the dormitory suburbs of home and hearth, away from any public life. Eventually, the nuclear family also began to break up under the stress of outside pressures of work and schooling and inwardly from the contradictory demands made on it. The state and its legal apparatus began to play an ever more dominant role in social life when under the pretense of ameliorating everything, it ended up by regulating everything. We have already mentioned something of this in the introduction and we will go on to study it further in part II.

Thus, from the time of the First World War, the Western ethical system, built up over the preceding two millennia, began to fragment and dissolve. A process started that had few previous historical parallels, one that we shall call de-ethicization—an ugly but unavoidable term for an insidious development. It is the process of discrediting, dissolving, reducing, and winding down of ethical ways of regulating conduct and shaping personal character in favor of others that in this period have been mainly political, legal, and institutional. As ethics comes to be spurned and its values debased, what ensues is a general attitude of cynicism regarding right conduct and virtue outside the ambit of the law.

This process is particularly pronounced in respect of morality, the ethics that stems from religion, for as religious belief falters, so the ethical forms that are associated with it also become discredited. Hence, demoralization is the salient form of de-ethicization. Brief demoralizing periods have occurred previously in Western history, usually in times of crisis when people were driven to abandon their primary values and beliefs. But these have never lasted very long. Demoralization had never before been a consciously pursued aim to be undertaken by intellectual and practical means, leading to the debasement of morality, and so it could never become a permanent condition. Now it is conducted with deliberate intent, but unforeseen effect, and this could end up with the complete disappearance of morality. A demoralized society would then ensue, which would also have catastrophic consequences for the whole of ethical life. This would in turn be bound to transform the whole ethos and produce a new kind of paradoxical civility never before encountered in any previous civilization.

However, the actual situation as it confronts us now is still some way from this potential outcome. The trends toward demoralization have also been offset by other positive ethical developments, though these have been mostly of a legal nature. Morality itself is still in a very parlous state, with no evident signs of any forthcoming recovery. The inroads of demoralization are very difficult to undo, for they are not responsive to any legislative endeavors or any planned projects of social reform. What is called for is a transformation in people's mentality and that can only be achieved by a long and intensive course of upbringing and re-education of the kind that is counter to most current practices. Yet the effort to effect a character change must be made to whatever degree this is still tolerated by contemporary society.

The state of morality is largely bound up with the fate of the individual, the person of conscience and autonomy. Without such individuals, morality in any serious sense cannot survive. But most of the dominant social trends have been against this kind of individual being and in favor of mass society and its conformist tendencies. All such mass movements have had a de-individualizing propensity and so have acted against morality, even when they were launched for ostensively moral causes.

Morality has suffered most from the inroads of ideologies and the political mass movements to which these have given rise. Most ideologies current in the twentieth century arose in the previous nineteenth as movement of secularized belief that preached ideal moral causes in a political guise. Thus socialism, in the name of social justice and equality, advanced a highly moralistic program of social reconstruction, above all to eliminate economic exploitation. In its most revolutionary form, as communism, it assumed the dimensions of a crusading Party dedicated to transforming the whole of social life according to the moral ideals of brotherhood, solidarity, and perfect equality. This soon assumed the aura of a pseudo-religious faith; especially so when as Bolshevism it came to power in Russia. The Party became a surrogate church that in theory was considered infallible. Intellectuals, such as the philosopher George Lukacs, took on the role of pseudo-theologians in elaborating the dogmatic doctrines of this new religion. Thus the ground was set for the greatest debacle that morality has ever suffered. Once more we are reminded of George Eliot's prophetic warning: "There is no general doctrine that is not capable of eating out morality if unchecked by the deep-seated habit of direct fellow-feeling for individual fellow men."[45] And this was precisely what the Bolsheviks, from Lenin down, lacked. They tended to disguise this lack by denouncing writers such as George Eliot, in the name of Marx, as bourgeois moralists to whom no heed need be given by those who loved humanity and stood for the higher socialist ethics of the proletariat.

The story is well known and needs no reminding here of what ensued as Bolshevism became a totalitarian regime that arrogated to itself the right of moral judgment on all matters. First Lenin, then Stalin became the keepers of conscience of all true-believing communists all over the world. No demand that either made could ever be considered wrong by their followers. And so all the crimes of mass murder were in good conscience carried out by functionaries on orders from above emanating ultimately from the will of the Supreme Leader. The demoralizing consequences for those who survived, even those who were innocent of any overt immoral deeds, are apparent in the present state of Russian society. Traditional religion become the only refuge for those who wished to hold on to any moral sense. The great Russian authors in this period—above all, Pasternak and Solzhenitsyn—advocated the Russian Orthodox faith as the only possible counter to the debasements of morality that were suffered under the Soviet regime.

Right-wing ideologies, Fascism and Nazism, carried through analogous processes of demoralization. The leaders of these totalitarian movement, Mussolini and Hitler, were also designated as the keepers of conscience by their followers. Intellectuals of the Right were only too ready to provide rationales for this moral surrender. Thus the Italian philosopher of Fascism, Giovanni Gentile, argued that conscience was the voice of society within the individual, and the Leader, il Duce, as the supreme representative of the collective will, was therefore entitled to dictate his will to all.[46] Heidegger, the Nazi philosopher, provided a similar justification for total moral submission to the will of the *Führer*, Adolf Hitler: "Do not seek the rules of your being in dogmas and ideas, it is the Führer himself, and he alone, who is the German reality of today and tomorrow," he declared in his November 3, 1933, *Appeal to Students*. Official ideologues, such as Hermann Göring, put it more simply: "I have no conscience! My conscience is named Adolf Hitler."

This abrogation of morality produced the most gruesome moral crime in history, the Holocaust. The morally insidious nature of this crime is that it was not just perpetrated by ideologically convinced Nazis, who believed that Jews were the very incarnation of evil, but required the active participation, collaboration, or at least non-interference from the many who held no such beliefs and yet were drawn into the process of acting as if they did. Thus many millions of Christians and their church leaders either took part or stood by while it all happened. The demoralizing consequences were devastating. In those terrible years Christian morality was in the hands of isolated individuals, not in those of church dignitaries. In one's most pessimistic moods, one cannot help wondering whether this will eventually be the fate of morality in general.

The reason that the ideologies were so successful in distorting people's consciences was that they had a perverted pseudo-ethical basis. Thus, for example, Nazism contained elements drawn from all the Western ethical traditions, but amalgamated in such a way as to elicit total obedience to the regime and the Führer's will. The civil ethic was revived in a travesty of its original polis form to demand total sacrifice to the state. The ethic of honor was enlisted to elicit total fidelity—"loyalty is my honor" was the motto of Himmler's SS troops who modeled themselves on the Teutonic knights of the Middle Ages. The ethics of duty was invoked to command total subservience from functionaries and bureaucrats—"I was only doing my duty according to Kant's categorical imperative," said Eichmann in self-exculpation.

What this example reveals is that the greatest dangers to ethics do not lie in straight-out denials of it—that is, in outright immoralism—but in its perversions for ideological ends. At present, because of the decline of the main political ideologies, such dangers seem to have receded. If there is a threat of this kind, then it is to be feared as coming from those religious fundamentalisms that have taken an ideological turn and are pursued with political aims. But these are only prevalent in Third World countries, where they lead to theocratic forms of totalitarianism. However, apart from such isolated cases, this does not appear to be a problem on a world scale.

The threat, especially in the so-called advanced Western societies, is not anything as obvious as that but rather a kind of creeping obsolescence of ethics, the gradually growing irrelevance of ethical considerations in most spheres of contemporary social life. This has affected morality perhaps more than any other aspect of ethics, so it presents itself as the ever more insidious specter of demoralization. But all kinds of other modes of de-ethicization are also appearing. "What is honour?" asks Falstaff and answers, "a word"—what was once comic repartee is now much closer to prosaic reality. Duty is also now often no more than a mere word, one most often confused with obedience, so that the ethic of duty is invoked whenever one has to do what one is told to do. Not much is left of the civic ethic either, except for the formalities of citizenship and the formal requirements of democratic participation.

There is, of course, nothing against leading an ethical life, especially in liberal democratic societies where in one's private capacity one can live as one chooses. So, provided it does not interfere with one's public role or the law, one can choose whatever ethics one happens to fancy. But there seems less and less reason to do so. "What is the point of being ethical?" is often an unspoken question on people's lips. "Why should I be moral?" is implicitly asked whenever it is in one's interest not to be so. Many people are already acting as if they knew the answers to these questions; they have already twigged to the cynical truth that ethics is a lie that only deceives fools. Perhaps a venerable lie, perhaps a noble lie, but a lie nonetheless that anyone with any up-to-date intelligence need not be taken in by.

There is little, if anything, in current thought about ethics to gainsay such a realization. Contemporary philosophies, which present ethics as a matter of preference or choice or commitment, implicitly back it up. If one is free to choose ethics, then one is also free to refuse it, and the contemporary tenor of life makes choosing to be ethical a rather stupid-seeming choice. Ways of presenting, explaining, and justifying ethics must be found that show it to have a worth that cannot be gained otherwise, that it enables one to give one's life a meaning that cannot be attained in any other way. We shall return to this issue which is outside the purely historical account we are presenting here, at the conclusion of our work.

Thus far in our account of the development of ethics in the contemporary period since the First World War, we have concentrated solely on the negative trends of de-ethicization. But it would be a one-sided picture to leave it at that, for there were during this period also positive ones, leading to greater ethicization in key social respects. This is the great ethical paradox of our time, whose elucidation will concern us as we proceed. How is it possible that the retreat of ethics in demoralization should be matched by contrary ethical advances in other ways?

It is undeniable that some aspects of ethics have advanced, mainly through the agency of law. Many are the ethical principles and values that were never given legal sanction before in any previous society but that are now firmly inscribed in law and enforced by the state power. And this is not merely an institutional matter, one that has little to do with the will of people, for behind these legal measures are social forces of a political reformist type that agitated for the legislations before they were passed and can still be called upon to maintain them. It would not be advisable now to abolish any of the major rights, freedoms, or entitlements that were frequently achieved through personal valor and heroism in the face of entrenched opposition during the course of the last turbulent century.

But this was not always so. Indeed, it is one of the great ironies of history that many ethical achievements were due to the wars, revolutions, and even totalitarian regimes that otherwise caused so much ethical damage. Thus, for example, some social welfare provisions were sometimes first pioneered in the totalitarian states and only later introduced in the democratic ones. The wars, too, contributed to such ethical trends. The emancipation of women owes much to the war-time requirements of mobilizing women in industry. The establishment of international organizations, such as the League of Nations and the United Nations, was a direct result of the two World Wars; this promoted many positive steps in the international recognition and validation of basic ethical principles in many areas of life. The fundamental precepts of Natural Law are now affirmed in many such international charters and declarations and most states have officially bound themselves to enforce them in civil law. At present almost all states subscribe to most of the basic human rights, and those that do not are subject to the condemnation of world opinion and pressures from other states, above all from the United States, which has taken on itself the role of the guardian of international ethics. Right from the end of the First World War, America has taken the leading part in these developments and is still doing so now.

America was also in the forefront of political developments toward greater freedom and democracy. It was due to Woodrow Wilson's fourteen points declaration that the principles of national self-determination and individual democratic participation first received international recognition Much of this became a dead letter in the period of totalitarianism between the two wars and later was cynically misused during the Cold War by both sides. Nevertheless, these principles survived to become the basis of the present world political order. Every state, as a participant in the United Nations and the world system of states, is formally committed to fundamental human rights and freedoms and the rule of law. It is true, of course, that some states honor this more in the breach, yet the expectation is there that it should be fulfilled. The rule of law—based on the premises of equality before the law, due process, *habeas corpus*, and so on—is now considered an inherent part of any civil ethos, so much so that any society that departs from it is unequivocally condemned.

The development of the Welfare State also occurred mainly in this period, though its roots go back into the nineteenth century. This brought into effect a network of laws and institutions to provide for people in all kinds of situations of need. It replaced much of the reliance on personal charity and that of church and parochial organizations. It seemed ethically superior, for it gave people as a right that which they had to solicit before as a favor. However, as we previously noted in the introduction, there are ambiguities in all this that makes it somewhat dubious when looked at in terms of its overall effects on ethics.

Such ambiguities hold for many of the state's ethical measures and their legal institutionalization. Nevertheless, much was achieved without which life in modern societies would have been intolerable, as it is still in those where the modernizing trends have already advanced so far as to destroy traditional protections, but as yet little if anything has been developed by the state in compensation for what has been lost. Hence, under present conditions there can be no question of giving them up, and where these provision are under attack—as they have been of late as a result of the new free-market economic rationalist policies—they ought to be defended on ethical grounds. It can never be ethically right to leave people destitute.

The realization of ethics in law through the legislative activities of the state has achieved much in correcting or compensating for many of the inequalities that traditional societies condoned, accepting them as part of the inevitable nature of things. Above all, the most fundamental inequality of all, that between the sexes, has been gradually corrected by a whole sequence of laws, beginning with rights of property and rights of suffrage and now extending to such things as gender discrimination and sexual harassment. Though in such matters a law of diminishing returns, ethically speaking, begins to be felt, so that it becomes dubious whether much more can be accomplished by legislation alone, which is not to gainsay what was achieved so far. Analogously so, laws to protect minorities of all kinds, including ethnically distinct racial groups, have also greatly contributed to the ethics of civil society.

One of the greatest ethical achievements of the modern period, especially so following the Second World War, was the discrediting and outlawing of racism. None of the traditional ethics could do much about racism. It was more or less tolerated by all religions. Thus Christian morality could do little to counter the colonial rapacity of the European powers, from the Spanish *conquistadores* through to the British and French imperialists and colonialists, who were conquering and all but enslaving the native people in all the continents outside Europe. Traditional morality proved itself impotent to counter these crimes, which extended for so many centuries. Ideological racism, which culminated in Nazism, was also proof against any moral censure, and for the most part it was implicitly condoned. Yet in the long run the counter trends against racism eventually won out. These began with the campaign to abolish slavery early in the nineteenth century and the gradual acceptance in the twentieth century of the equality of all people, irrespective of race. But it was only when de-colonialization was undertaken in earnest and new states representing all the races on earth took their seats in the United Nations that racism finally lost its validity and its hold on most people's minds. It has, of course, not completely vanished; it is doubtful if it ever will as long as racial differences remain, but it can no longer be ethically countenanced anywhere on earth. Further laws to counter racial bias are also now bringing diminishing returns. So to reduce it further, other methods of a more educational kind will have to be employed.

With these positive considerations, which will be further amplified later, we conclude our historical account of ethics in the twentieth century. As we have already noted, it presents a curiously ambivalent picture, for we have traced both de-ethicizing trends and ethicizing ones at once. On the one hand, there are all the demoralizing predispositions that promote cynicism regarding ethics as such, but, on the other, there are movements for ethical reform in many social spheres. What is most curious about this situation is that these opposed trends are not in conflict but in collusion with each other. It is not as in past societies, where different ethics clashed so that one movement fought against another. Now there are no such conflicts between these different developments. On the contrary, they are mutually supportive: the more the personal side of ethics declines, the more the institutional side predominates; the more people lose in character, the more they gain in rights; the more they abandon trust in each other, the more they can look to the law for security; and so on. Hence, there is a logic to the opposed trends, which brings them together as aspects of a more-embracing global development. The one generally promotes the other in a cycle of mutual causation. For the more people turn to the law, the less personal regard they have for other people, and vice versa. The whole process proceeds seemingly inexorably. Where it will end, we do not as yet know. Yet we do know that we must proceed to act against it. But how much of it we can deflect is also beyond our present ken. But try we must, if we are to remain ethical beings.

This concludes our brief historical survey of ethics in the twentieth century. The reason for this hasty brevity is that in order to say more on the subject, we must shift from simple history to sociology and proceed with a more detailed social analysis of the current ethical condition. We shall, of course, be intent not merely on interpreting the present situation but on changing it as well. With this in view, our main constructive program is to develop an ethics suitable for the social conditions that we will confront in the twenty-first century.

PART II

THE PRESENT

Preamble

Where does ethics stand today in our contemporary global civilization? It stands where the historical process has brought it. The last century has seen the constant disruption of ethical traditions in all societies all over the globe, both in Western and Eastern cultures. Demoralization and the other forms of ethical destruction have inevitably left their marks on the contemporary condition of ethics. The weakening of all ethical inhibitions has been repeatedly demonstrated in the crimes and despoliations accompanying the wars, revolutions, and upheavals of the twentieth century.

Is all this merely a matter of disruptions, of longer or shorter duration, or is it indicative of a more fundamental change in the nature and function of ethics in society? Are these ethical buffetings manifestations of a permanent cultural transformation, like the storms and unseasonal weather patterns that are symptomatic of a climatic change? Can we try to reverse or at least to delay what seems like winding down of ethics, just as we try to slow down the warming of the planet that is the cause of the weather changes? What social forces can we look to in trying to effect such a conserving operation?

Such questions do not have merely a general social relevance but translate themselves into personal existential concerns as well. Thus, it is, for example, of some interest to parents whether their children are to be brought up with an ethical character and imbued with the typical ethical emotions of guilt, shame, respect, pride, and piety or whether it were better for their fortunes in a future managerial world not to burden them with the emotional ballast of a superseded past. These questions are not mere matters of intellectual curiosity, for they are being implicitly asked and answered in practice not only by concerned parents but also by all others who deal with the upbringing of children, such as teachers, social workers, psychologists, and various kinds of child minders. The purely personal decisions that parents and others involved in child care make about such matters convert themselves over time into general practices of social behavior that ultimately determine what role ethics is to play in our society. What kinds of educative procedures in regard to ethics we institute is thus of great interest to anyone who cares about the survival of ethics in our culture. And so, too, with many other social practices that have an impact on ethics.

In this part II of our work we shall be dealing with the problem of the survival of ethics from these different aspects. First, in the next chapter, we shall be examining it sociologically in terms of the social forces and other impersonal agencies that work against ethics. It is important to know this so as to find ways of counteracting them. Second, in the following chapter we shall shift from the purely social to a cultural perspective and study the way in which ethics functions as a practical cultural institution. Here the analogy between ethics and art as cultural forms will be invoked to elucidate the various roles or functions of all those who are involved in the ethical enterprise. Finally, in the last chapter, we shall arrive at the personal or existential level of the individual and begin considering those vital questions on whose answer depends whether and how one is to lead an ethical life. "Why be ethical?" is the very first of these; and if one has opted for an ethical life, then the next is "How to be ethical?"

The three aspects mentioned, the social, cultural, and existential, will be dealt with separately in the various chapters, but they are not to be taken as distinct, for they are no more than different levels of analysis of ultimately the same thing. Thus the separate chapters are conjoined parts of the one investigation. In studying the field of ethics as a whole, one must be aware of how its various levels interact. Thus any account of the social forces impacting on ethics must be mindful of how these are shaped by cultural practices and their institutionalization. A description of these must in turn show how they relate to the daily decisions that people make in doing or forbearing to do that shapes the pattern of their lives. But this must also be seen the other way round, for the choices that are available for an individual to make or whether they are made easy or hard depends on the practices current in a given culture, and these ultimately are upheld by or have to struggle against the dominant social forces prevalent in that society. The intertwined nature of these levels, of society, culture, and individual lives, means that what happens at the one will have its inevitable repercussions in what takes place at the others. Hence we must attend to all of them at once if we wish to understand ethics and to know something about it.

The main aim of this work is to provide ethical knowledge. Hence its purpose is educative, to teach people what is involved in an ethical life. This might be of some use to them in leading their own lives or in bringing up their children. But beyond the purely individual concern, it might also indicate what is called for in safeguarding ethics as a cultural form and social institution. A sense of the difficulties in doing so will inevitably emerge, but this need not be so overwhelming as to paralyze one into immobility and inaction. A realistic appreciation of the grave condition in which ethics now finds itself is the necessary prelude to doing anything about it. Ultimately, the whole point is not merely to know the ethical but to do it.

CHAPTER 3

~

Ethics and Society

Ethics and the State

In every developed society there are always forces that uphold and sustain the ethical functions and forms, those that are indifferent to them, and those that run counter to them. As we shall see, in the societies of a global technological civilization it is the latter two that are dominant and the former that has weakened and become recessive. It is our intent to explore the effect this has had on ethical life in its various manifestations.

Historically considered, the social forces that brought the various ethics into being and enabled them to maintain themselves for a period of two and a half millennia were the dominant groupings and institutions of what we can now consider to be largely superseded traditional societies. It was the universal religions, specifically Judaic monotheism and Budhistic soteriology, that established morality, and the later successor religions to these, especially Western Christianity, that maintained it and extended it. It was another kind of religion, Persian Zoroastrianism, that helped bring to birth an aristocratic ethic of honor, and later court societies and nobilities both of East and West propagated it, in the West during the Middle Ages as the ethic of chivalry and later as gentility. It was the Greek polis that first practiced an ethic of civic virtue and this ideal was passed on throughout the whole history of subsequent Western political life wherever it was based on autonomous cities and, later on, states of other types. And, finally, an ethic of duty was first elaborated by state officials, such as the mandarins of China, the politically engaged brahmins of India, and the imperial officials in Rome—above all, the caesariani of the emperor's entourage. All these ethics, in their various more or less pure or hybrid forms, were always maintained and developed by these social forces and their successors, by religious associations based on a temple or church, by aristocratic bodies based on a court, by citizens in autonomous cities or other such polities, and by officials in some kind of state bureaucracy.

What has happened to these social forces and their groupings in contemporary societies? What ethical role do they play? What is their influence on the rest of society? The answers we give to these questions will determine how much of the traditional ethics has still survived in our ethos. Of course, only a diehard conservative would hold that this also decides the issue of the state of ethics in our time in general, for it is well possible that new social forces have arisen that uphold ethical standards either of a traditional kind or new ones altogether. We must not rule out any such alternative possibilities. However, it is obvious that the old traditional cultural carriers of ethics no longer sustain it, at least not in the way they once did, for their present role and significance in society is very different to what it once was.

Modern society no longer places much weight on the traditional social forces that were supportive of ethics. Instead new social forces have emerged that are indifferent to it. Perhaps the most important among these has been the rise of the modern state, now a gigantic organizational framework that dominates all aspects of social living. Together with the state, in parallel stages of historical development, there has grown a capitalist economic system of production whose market culture has ramified throughout all the branches of civil society. At present this capitalist system has become global and extends beyond the reaches of any single state. But both states and the big business conglomerates usually work hand in hand in a harmony of mutual interests. Ethics is hardly one of these. In effect, the outcome of these social forces on ethics has been little short of catastrophic, as we shall proceed to show in this chapter.

Due to such developments, the numerous cadres of officials constitute the one social grouping that seems to have immeasurably increased its power and importance as compared to all previous societies. It is a sociological commonplace that we now live in highly bureaucratized societies and that state and other bureaucracies, such as those of the big multinational corporations, manage all social affairs. Up to a third of all working people are now employed by the state alone. This would seem to suggest that an ethic of duty is now the widespread and predominant ethic of our societies. But this is far from being the case.

For many complex reasons that will need to be carefully unraveled, contemporary bureaucrats are not motivated by ethical conceptions of individual devotion to duties and responsibilities. They do not possess an ideal conception of their role, a sense of the dignity of their status, and what it means to gain life satisfaction and fulfillment in it. Instead, they are mostly driven by cruder ambitions of career and success, by a greed for promotion that makes them servile and obedient instruments in the hands of their masters and superiors. Obeying orders from above has been utterly confused with doing one's duty, so much so that carrying out ethically dubious or even immoral orders is sometimes justified on the grounds of duty. The behavior of bureaucrats during the totalitarian era in Germany and Russia is still green in the personal memory of those who lived through those times and it reminds us of what officials are capable, so much so that in current parlance the words *bureaucrat* and *ethical* are almost taken as contradictions in terms. And yet, historically considered, officials have almost universally played an extremely important ethical role.

One of the main reasons that they no longer do so lies in the changed nature of education and the place that ethics has in this. The forms of education that traditionally produced qualified officials were through and through geared to ethical concerns. By and large, it was a literary and philosophical educational curriculum that held ethics to be of paramount importance. For example, in China it was based on the Confucian and other literary texts; in Europe it was the *litterae et mores*, based on the works of Latin and later humanistic authors; in both cases poetry played a significant part. Such an educational background gave the officials a common, well-understood ethical set of standards, an ideal conception of themselves and their role, an *esprit de corps* and, what was most important for each one as an ethical individual, the incentive not to betray his calling and the consolation and self-justification if it so happened that unjust punishment or failure ensued. The educational qualifications of officials and bureaucrats at present are almost the very opposite of this traditional course. Theirs is a specialized training in expert disciplines, such as a specific natural or social science, particularly economics or studies in management or law. None of these, not even law as currently taught, has much to do with ethics. The consequences of this on the ethical bearing of the individual and of the group as a whole are such as we have already indicated.

The prevalence of bureaucracy in all public affairs is itself symptomatic of the decline of the civic ethics. Any such ethic of civic virtue has invariably been sustained by a vigorous ethos of civic life focused on the city and on politics in general. From its origins this was always the ethics of citizens, whether of the Greek polis, of the Roman civis, of medieval communes, or later of the republican state. The emergence of the latter, largely during the course of the nineteenth century following the American and French Revolutions, introduced a new conception of citizenship and with it another variant of the civic ethics. Citizenship involved political participation and civic responsibilities in the context of civil society. All kinds of political and cultural developments came together in this dual conception of the *citoyen-bourgeois*; politically, there were continual moves in the direction of liberalism, democracy, and republicanism; culturally, there was the steady growth of individualism. The state and the citizen entered into a kind of ethical symbiosis with each other, as both assumed reciprocal rights and obligations over each other. The key rights of the citizen were to take part in political affairs at a local and national level and the key obligations were to pay taxes and render military service.

This balance in the relation between the state and the citizen has now largely broken down, as most of the affairs of state have been taken over by professional bureaucracies and as citizens withdraw more and more from political participation into a kind of limbo of consumer privacy. As a result of these trends, civic ethics has largely disappeared. The symptoms of this are everywhere evident in a multitude of different respects. For the vast majority of citizens any kind of participation in public life, not to speak of devotion to public service, is no longer in question. In some democracies, such as the United States, hardly half the citizens bother to vote even in the most important elections. As far as local civic affairs are concerned, cities have lost any autonomy or common civic life; they have become vast metropolises whose administrative arrangements, mainly having to do with physical facilities, have passed into the hands of bureaucrats and cliques of large property owners. Citizenship has been largely reduced to the formalities of holding a passport and paying taxes. Patriotism and national pride still play a small part in the minds of some citizens, and it can be amplified by the jingoistic propaganda of the media during wars, but even this is receding as globalization ensues and as war becomes the business of professional soldiers, which does not touch ordinary citizens.

The civic ethics has largely succumbed to these changes both in the nature of the state and in the character of citizenship. The state no longer needs citizens to engage themselves in its affairs, and citizens see no virtue in doing so and prefer to withdraw to the privacy of their own personal concerns. A transformation in the whole conception of the individual has promoted the tendency of withdrawal from public affairs. Bourgeois individualism—which was still strongly correlative with the conception of an active, participatory citizenship—has evolved into an atomized and privatized consumer individualism. A self-absorbed preoccupation with work, leisure time, and family, where this is still viable, become the main concerns. As Jean Leca puts it, "Each person is a conscious and intelligent owner of his own abilities and desires in a game where the impersonal 'system' is more and more important (whether one plays the game or 'cheats,' from evading tax to pinching things in the supermarket), and the political community more and more suspect and thus exposed."[1] For such people, any commitment to public service is time and effort lost to one's own chances of success. Such matters are best left to the professionals, who approach them as a job to be done as expeditiously and efficiently as possible, without any ethical predilections.

Public service is no longer a vocational choice, in the ethical sense of a calling. Families among whom public service is considered a duty are now rare exceptions. As aristocracies lost political power, and frequently wealth as well, they ceased to cultivate their status ethics. The surviving aristocratic circles in different parts of the world no longer see themselves as the custodians of a distinct ethical way of life, but at most of certain traditions of manners and mores, such as fox hunting in England. Their previous adherence to Good Society, with its elevated ethical and aesthetic standards, has been displaced by the glamor of High Society, where together with the media stars and jet-setting billionaires they indulge in the mindless escapades that provide media entertainment for the masses. Even royalty has been swept up in this bustle, as the sad life of Princess Diana demonstrates. Of pride, dignity, self-respect, *noblesse oblige*, or any of the other old virtues of nobility, there is hardly a shred left among such people.

The aristocratic ethics of honor is no more. There are still some men who consider themselves gentlemen and even a few who demand satisfaction when slighted, and there are women who wish to be treated as ladies. But increasingly, this has now an antedeluvian air about it, and it cannot be taken too seriously. Chivalrous conduct or gallantry with regard to women is now almost a complete joke. However, of greater seriousness and some importance are the surviving codes of good manners and public courtesy. In highly simplified and reduced forms these still function as the accepted rules of conduct in interpersonal relations, especially among strangers in public venues. They are like the simplified forms of traditional Western dress that everyone all over the world is now obliged to wear in international business or other cross-cultural affairs, resorting to native dress only for special ceremonies or to make a political point. Manners are still taught in schools to some degree, but only in the English-style schools are there some attempts made to link this to a wider ethic of gentlemanly behavior in the form that the nineteenth century public school developed this, stressing group loyalty and solidarity rather than aristocratic individualism. Something of it also survives in countries that have long lost their aristocracies among military officers and in schools inculcating military traditions. In these, considerable emphasis is still placed on character and on an instinctive sense of right and wrong conduct.

Aristocratic ethics of honor have always stressed a spontaneous and intuitive sense of how to act, considering the *beau geste* as basic to character and as expressive of an innate nobility of soul. Careful deliberation about what to do or knowing and philosophizing about ethics were not valued in this tradition, and the ethical prophet was extolled only when he could provide a cause and leadership. Obviously, this is not an approach to ethics that can be advocated in this day and age, despite the fervent advocacy of some thinkers, such as Nietzsche and his followers, who see what is best in ethics very much in these terms. Nevertheless, we must recognize that something vital has been lost to ethics when the spontaneous impulse to ethical action is no longer cultivated. For it is this more than anything else that enables people to act in the heat of the moment in situations of emergency or of great personal danger, when ethical courage and resilience has to be demonstrated without hesitation.

Finally, in this assessment of the social forces that make for ethics, we come to religion, which, as our previous historical studies have shown, was the unique source and carrier of morality for most of its history. Indeed, it cannot be denied that even now the churches and the institutions of the other major religions are still very active as social forces advocating morality—that is, preaching and teaching a moral message. But how effective are they, that is the question. Whether they are even fully serious about it is also questionable. Their behavior in some ethically critical situations during the last century, in which religious bodies should have played a decisive part, makes it extremely doubtful whether they practice what they preach. The failure of the churches to oppose the Holocaust is only the most obvious of these situations. And even now the tendency of so many religions toward fundamentalism and political ideology makes their moral message ever so much more dubious.

Nevertheless, religion was and remains a crucial social force with a lasting impact on ethics. The great moral revolutions and reforms of the past have come from religious prophecy. And it is these religions, whose rituals have provided the context of daily practice for the masses of people, on whom the social institution of morality depends. Scrupulous moral judgment, in particular, has developed from religious practices. The scrupulous examination of conscience, the weighing up of actions done or left undone, the probing of motives, the calling to account, all this is most pronounced when it is an issue of sin and the salvation of the soul is at stake. The practice of confession, which is found in some religions, is also conducive to self-examination and the self-critical faculties of ethics, as well as the cultivation of moral judgment. It is clear that the state of religious ethics, that is, morality in a given ethos will be indicative of its critical acuity in general, for the religious forms of conscience and scrupulous probing of intent once established in the social psyche extend to other forms of ethics as well, even to highly secularized ones.

Though its origins are always religious, morality can also exist in secular forms. The fear of God might be the beginning of wisdom, but it need not be its end. Moral beliefs and practices do not need to be based on a conception of divine retribution; humanist values can also sustain them. And yet, the kind of moral conscience that is constantly preoccupied with judging itself and others is scarcely conceivable outside a religious context. Those who have it invariably inherit it from their religious background, even when they are no longer believers themselves. For how many generations such a judgmental conscience can maintain itself without renewed religious support is an open question. Those who are religious will argue that it cannot do so indefinitely; that once it is gone, then the whole function of judgment also recedes and critical awareness in morality in general loses its hold. However, this case has not as yet been conclusively demonstrated. Though many attempts to found a lasting secular morality have failed, there is nothing in principle to preclude such a thing from succeeding.

At present in nearly all societies, religion remains a major social force and in a few traditional ones it is still dominant. But discounting the latter, it is apparent that religion, though prevalent as measured by such sociological indicators as church attendance, is not any more a major moral influence. Religious worship is practiced as a social convention, and religious authorities are becoming more indifferent to the moral life of their adherents or conceive of it so narrowly, in terms of a select few dogmatically defined issues, as to amount to an indifference to all others. This is particularly evident in periods of social upheaval or times of war, for then the religious organizations have tended to look to their own interests and those of their faithful or only to uphold those causes that are directly in line with their main theological preoccupations. The needs that most major religions have in maintaining a large following, frequently spread all over the globe among different cultures and nations, prevent them from being too exacting in most moral matters. Various kinds of recent religious revivals and the spread of new sects, some of which make efforts at moral renewal, have not really helped, for many of these tend to a morally limited, and sometimes fanatical, fundamentalism and others to irrational superstition.

The present Christian fundamentalist sects of Western societies are a case in point. It is undeniable that they have had a morally ameliorating effect on their members, reestablishing simple norms of decency and probity, particularly in private life. However, their general social effect has been far less salutary. They have attempted to resort to political means to impose the straitjacket of their limited doctrinal morality on everyone. As their persecution of President Clinton in 1998 revealed, they are oblivious to any wider ethical consequences of their own moral self-righteousness. It is true that Clinton's behavior reflected some of the amoralities of the so-called Baby Boom generation in personal conduct. But to turn such peccadilloes into a political crusade of such overwhelming importance as to discount everything else is to take the old Roman adage "fiat justicia, pereat mundus" with deadly literal seriousness. This is all the more dangerous since "pereat mundus" is no longer a rhetorical literary flourish, but a real possibility.

As this example goes to show, religious morality is no longer a coherent part of an integrated social ethics but has assumed narrow and sometimes extremely moralistic manifestations. Of the other ethical traditions, only fragments still survive. Their hold and sway is not what it used to be, since the social influence of the traditional forces sustaining them is now so much reduced. Nor do they work together to constitute any longer a comprehensive ethical culture. Despite the inner tensions, oppositions, and even contradictions of traditional ethical ethos, there was, nevertheless, a basic cultural integrity there. Now there are displaced and disjointed fragments of ethics, most of which derive from very different ethical traditions, which are not in any inherent relation to each other. At the level of global society there is complete ethical confusion, as what is left of the various divergent ethical cultures enter into merely superficial relations with each other, for there is no possibility of any deeper coalescence being worked out between them. The functional separations between different spheres of life, between private and public, work and leisure, family and business, religious and secular conduct, and the different kinds of cultures that each person inhabits in a global society prevent any ethical integration.

All in all, we can conclude that the main social currents in contemporary times are not conducive to ethical life. Of the traditional forces that promoted ethics in the past, only the state is still a source of dominant influence. The others, such as city, court, and church, do not figure as they did in the past. As we have shown, the city is now more of a demographic rather than socio-political entity and citizenship is a legal status rather than an ethical prerogative. Court society has either disappeared or become vestigial and the aristocratic class, or what is left of it in some countries, is not intent on affirming its nobility in any ethical sense. Religion is still very prevalent, but its moral teachings are no longer definitive as a way of life, except for small minority groups. That only leaves the state as a potential social force for promoting ethics in society. Insofar as the state does this, it does so primarily through law. Hence, it is on law that we must concentrate next.

The relation between ethics and law is historically a highly variable one; it changes as the conceptions of what is ethics and what is law alter. On the whole, the more traditional a society, the more there tends to be an identification between ethics and law and the more modern a society, the more there is a separation. In some traditional societies the identification between them is of such an extent that the possibility that something lawful can be unethical is scarcely conceivable. Modern societies have gone almost to the opposite extreme and postulate a functional segregation between ethics and law. Positivistic legal philosophies completely divorce the two such that the issue of what is legally valid and what is ethically right cease to have anything to do with each other. However, of late Legal Positivism, which was pre-eminent till the Second World War, has gone into decline. The Nazi Nüremberg Laws and other such seemingly valid legal enactments in other totalitarian regimes since then have convinced many legal philosophers and juristic scholars that a total separation between validity and right lends itself to misuse, and some have tended to retreat from such an extreme position. But any better-worked-out conception of law in its relation to ethics is still lacking.

Legal Positivism might be wrong as philosophy, but it is correct as social science. It reflects an ever-widening separation between the social spheres of law and ethics that has been proceeding since the rise of the modern state. The more law became subject to the legislative decision of a sovereign—a monarch or a parliament—the more it distanced itself from ethical restraints. At the start of this process, in the political theory of Hobbes, law was simply the sovereign's will; and since the sovereign could do no wrong; whatever was so decided was law, and what was lawful was right; there was to be no other source of right to challenge it; in particular, conscience had no claims to preeminence. The later theory of Natural Rights expounded by Locke did set limits to this potentially tyrannical sway of state power, and these quasi-ethical limitations on the scope of law-making have since been incorporated into all the major liberal constitutions, starting with that of the newly founded United States of America.

But the Natural Rights doctrine has only limited the sovereign sway of law, preventing it from exercising tyrannical abuse in its application to individuals; it has not restrained its continuous extension. The steady creep of legislative enactment has gone on apace in direct proportion to the growing power of the state. The great historic milestones in the expansion of the state have also been stages in the proliferation of law and its intrusion into social life. Thus the states that arose out of the French Revolution and its Napoleonic aftermath, the Bismarckian German Reich, the welfare states of the twentieth century, all these produced legislative reforms that widened the scope of law. By now there is hardly a social practice that is not subject to detailed legal regulation. All the previous ways of regulating conduct in the ethos have been translated into law, so that what formerly were distinguished as morals and manners, ethics and customs, traditions and taboos, and so on, now appear indifferently as laws. Like money in the economy, which produces a uniform measure of value, so law in society gives rise to a uniform standard of adjudication; on any matter whatever it seems that all we need ask is whether it is legal or illegal. In that blanket judgment, all finer distinctions and differences tend to disappear. Thus the whole ethos has been uniformly juridified.

This has by no means been a wholly negative phenomenon, as we already established previously in relation to numerous ethical matters. Those ethical norms and principles that found their way into the legal code and were given legal backing have been much more thoroughly enforced than ever before. Thus, for example, the exploitation of workers or abuse of wives and children is now less possible than in previous patriarchal periods. And this holds for many other ethical norms that previously the very powerful or rich were able to suborn. Now such are only rare and exceptional cases, at least in advanced Western societies, for on the whole the law there is applied effectively and without overt bias. However, such a process of juridification—that is, the translation of ethics into law—is by no means the panacea that some legal scholars, such as Richard Dworkin, imagine it to be.

Treated as law, ethics is only as good as those who interpret and enforce it. All laws can be perverted to unethical uses if those in power choose to do so. We are startlingly reminded that even the very best of laws, such as the American Bill of Rights, have been put to unethical ends through legally proper interpretations, as John Ralston Saul notes: "It was the Bill of Rights itself, as interpreted by the Supreme Court, which made slavery legal . . . ," that is, in the United States before the Civil War.[2] He goes on to add that "our confidence in the courts, when coolly examined, turns out to be confidence in the judge."[3] the confidence we have in judges depends, of course, on the political and social pressures that they work under and that are obliquely exerted on them. When these tend to unethical ends, then the whole judicial system will follow suit, as happened repeatedly in the twentieth century in many countries.

But there are also other and deeper problems arising out of the juridification of ethics. Ethics is an extremely variegated and differentiated system, with many subtle gradations of value that distinguish levels of seriousness, significance, and predominance. In every ethical system, clashes are bound to occur; one is constantly mediating between conflicting values and principles, always trying to choose the greater good or lesser evil, according to circumstances and the precise specification of the case in relations to oneself. In a legal system most of this scrupulous discrimination becomes impossible. The distinctions between types of law are crude by comparison; such oppositions as that between criminal and civil law or crimes and torts do not go very far. Rendered in the standard form of law and adjudicated in the same formal way, ethical subtleties are lost. Ordinary people find it almost impossible to tell those laws that serve an ethical purpose from others that are mere social utilities, conventions of society, or even political requirements of their particular regime. If their ethical sense is not firmly grounded and sure of itself, they will tend to confuse these types of laws and obey them indiscriminately, especially if they labor under the authoritarian misapprehension that all laws have to be obeyed as a matter of duty.

But even if one tries hard to untangle the intricate strands of law into their various ethical components, it is sometimes impossible to do so. The tax laws are a case in point, for those usually satisfy many evaluative standards at once in an undifferentiated way. Hence it is impossible to determine to what extent one pays tax because it is one's ethical civic duty, to what extent one does so because it is the law and it is socially customary to obey it, and to what extent one is simply paying tribute, if not protection money, to the state. Those people who perceive their tax-return declaration solely in the light of the last of these consideration, in many countries the great majority, will tend to calculate the gain from understating their income as against the potential loss of being found out. On the other hand, those who scrupulously disclose every penny gained and every benefit acquired, no matter where and how, as if it were a supreme ethical duty to report on everything on which one can potentially be taxed, can be rightly considered somewhat naive in such matters. In a decent society most people will fall somewhere between these two extremes and pay their taxes for implicit ethical, customary, and prudential reasons. But the law itself does not spell this out; it contains no indication as to how it should be taken; its status, ethically considered, is not clear. And the same holds for many other types of laws where it is not at all apparent what, ethically considered, breaking them involves. In this way the law obfuscates the difference between the ethical and the merely legal.

But not only does the law confuse people as to its ethical status, so that they are never sure how seriously to take it, it also tends to confuse them as to whether they have committed a transgression or not. This happens increasingly as the law branches out into innumerable detailed regulations and rules of enforcement. There are now so many laws on the statute books that it is highly unlikely that one has not broken one or another of these. Morgan and Reynolds point out that "it has been estimated that more than 300,000 regulations at the federal level [in the USA] are criminally enforceable," and "that when state criminal laws are considered, there is more truth than humor in the observation that we have achieved 'the criminalization of nearly everything.' "[4] In one way or another, everyone breaks the law and is, formally speaking, a criminal, even when judged according to "twenty-five rather common crimes (petty larceny, illegal drugs, drinking in public and so forth)."[5] According to a *Wall Street Journal* survey, even decent people confessed to numerous crimes; "an Episcopalian priest confessed to twelve crimes."[6] The only reason that everyone is not in jail, apart from the logical absurdity of it, is that public prosecutors and the police have the sense to know whom to charge and whom to leave alone—the vast majority, as it happens. In other words, they exercise ethical discretion in applying the law. If they were to lose that sense of relevance or if they deliberately forfeit it for ulterior motives, then judicial malpractices result and anyone can be had up on trumped up charges and convicted according to the law.

The confusions of ethics and law have of late become worse confounded because of the ill-conceived attempts to enforce ethical proprieties by means of criminal law. This juridification of ethics and the damage it creates we have already explored in the introduction so we will only deal with it briefly here. Morgan and Reynolds show how the whole spate of post-Watergate ethical legislation in the United States has led to all kinds of legal and ethical pathologies. Ethics has been harmed because "by so expanding the universe of federal crimes, we have dissipated one of the most precious resources for moral instruction."[7] What they mean by this is that where everyone is potentially a criminal, susceptible to prosecution for some breach of law or other, the real criminals, even when convicted, are no longer considered the heinous exceptions they used to be. They are no longer looked on with ethical disdain but lumped together with others convicted according to the technicalities of the law, sometimes for purely political motives. Where there are too many crimes and too many types of criminal proceedings, a process of inflation occurs, devaluing the severity of criminality.

In the highly juridified societies that we now inhabit, all such attempts to criminalize breaches of morality only succeed in substituting law for ethics, but law cannot adequately replace ethics for it cannot perform the same social function. There is a world of difference between professional ethics and the legal liability of the professional enforced through the courts. The doctor, lawyer, engineer, or other professional who acts on a truly internalized sense of responsibility and ethics of duty toward his or her clients will behave very differently than one who wishes to avoid legal liability and merely do that which the law requires. In many respects these ways of acting are the opposite of each other. Thus all the attempts to enforce professional ethics by legal means have largely resulted in its destruction. The over-regulation of professional practice and the ever-present threat of legal suits for malpractice results in a self-protective attitude among professionals, whose main concern becomes to follow the proper legal formalities and cover themselves against the risk of charges than to do that which really serves the best interests of their clients. Legislating ethical proprieties is always a dangerous measure. Sometimes there is no choice but to do so, where there has been a serious decline in ethical standards. But it should only be done as a last resort; if there is any other way of repairing the ethical damage, that should be tried first.

A people whose ethics is highly juridified is also rendered unfit to exercise its ethical discretion and discrimination. Individuals look for judgment to the formal processes of law and not to their own judging capacities. But ethical judgment is very different from legal judgment. Ethical judgment allows for differences of view and encourages debate in which one can maintain one's opinion against all others, for ultimately no one is authorized to pass judgment for anyone else; in that sense there are no ethical experts. By contrast, legal judgment emanates from legal experts, principally judges and lawyers, sometimes with the aid of juries, who issue one binding final decision, the verdict, in every case. Hence, a society that relies excessively on the law produces people who tend to look to authority and the judgment of others for their decisions; they remain immature and in a state of ethical tutelage. They go by the law or other such prescriptions and rules, rather than making an assessment of the full complexity of the ethical predicament. They become always intent on acting in such a way as to look good by legal criteria. Thus an appearance-ethic, such as Morgan and Reynolds castigate, tends to predominate, as people, especially those in official positions, become intent on avoiding the appearance of impropriety rather than doing their ethical duties.[8]

The transformation of ethics into law is not a new phenomenon; it has often occurred in the past in highly regulated societies. What is unprecedented about its present incidence is the scale on which it is taking place, resulting from the comprehensive formal rationality exercised through the modern state and its bureaucratic legal apparatus. But any large society with organized political authority will necessarily require extensive law as well as ethics for its regulation. Ethics completely without the backing of law has rarely prevailed beyond short periods in small sects. There has always been the necessity to uphold ethics by law, which has always also produced tensions between them. Some equitable balance has had to be attained, but this has been precarious. In the established religions the historical tendency has been to multiply laws, which is invariably to the detriment of ethics and has resulted in them becoming more rigid and doctrinaire as they became more established. Antinomian counter-movements have also invariably arisen, calling for an adherence to the spirit rather than the letter of the law—that is, to re-emphasize ethics at the expense of law. A similar sort of tug-of-war between ethics and law occurs in secular contexts as well.

The degree of juridification undertaken by the modern state has by far surpassed anything achieved by any political or religious organization in history. This is what Weber referred to as "the iron cage of bureaucracy," and the bars of this cage are made of iron laws. This comprehensive regimentation is not a tyrannical imposition, in which case it could be fought by political means, but is the outcome of requirements of the very bureaucratic organization of modern society, which is what makes people helpless in the face of it. The state was frequently compelled to legislate in new areas, sometimes even against the will of the politicians, by popular demands and even revolts that called for new institutions entailing far more laws and regulations. Thus, for example, the labor movement of trade unions and Socialist parties has enforced through the state a whole new code of laws and regulations governing the employment and treatment of workers in minute detail and particularity. There is no denying that in most respects this was an ethical improvement on past unregulated practices and resulted in a much more just way of treating workers. But at the same time it made all relations between employees and employers purely impersonal, a matter of market forces and legal entitlements governing the behavior of both parties to each other. Personal relations and ethical obligations were annulled and ceased to matter. Thus the very attempt to achieve social justice has also had the paradoxical unintended consequence of rendering ethical justice otiose.

Legal uniformity of regulation is both a symptom and cause of the uniformity of society. Standard ways of acting and standard relations of people to each other are characteristic of a society where everything is standardized. The regulated sameness of ordinary life bespeaks a well-ordered bee-hive society governed by innumerable laws and by-laws that is in many respects the opposite of an ethical society. The fact that people are not called upon to relate to each other in an ethical way means that they do not need to exercise those powers of personal discretion that always make for individual differences. For no ethical relation and no ethical act or judgment is ever quite the same as any other, in the same way that no work of art is identical with any other. And, as in art where there can be stylistic forms in common, so in ethics there are common norms and standards, but such similarities do not amount to the blanket sameness that the law requires. Contemporary life can so easily be regulated by law and requires so little ethics precisely because it is pervaded by so much uniformity.

It may be thought that such a uniform social condition cannot persist for very long, that sooner or later a crisis is bound to eventuate that will call into question the authority of the state and the legitimacy of the law that issues from it. It may be contended that law without ethical backing will undermine and destroy itself. For law to be accepted as valid it must derive from legitimate authority—in the case of the modern state, from a democratically elected representative assembly or parliament. But the law itself cannot endow legitimacy to authority, for that calls for beliefs and values that have a basis in ethics. Without an ethical underpinning and the ideals and even sometimes ideologies that pertain to it, the legitimacy of the law can scarcely be maintained. And law that is not believed to be legitimate, but only imposed by a dominant ruling power, cannot be enforced in the long run. Force and violence do not suffice to maintain it permanently, as has historically been shown time and time again, most recently in relation to the communist regimes.

Such an argument has close affinities to Habermas's conception of a legitimation crisis.[9] Unfortunately, it suffers from the same defects as Habermas's argument. A legitimation crisis can be almost indefinitely averted by all kinds of stop-gap measures, and it has been easily avoided in the quarter of a century since Habermas first propounded his theory. In this respect it is like Marx's prognostication of the inevitable collapse of capitalism, which has also not eventuated. And the same might be true for any analogous crisis of legal legitimacy. Like capitalism, which continues to grow without any evident sign of an end, so, too, the legal system might continue to expand. Eventually, it will become global and embrace the whole world in one more or less uniform network of laws, in which only a few local peculiarities distinguish one country from another. The traffic laws are almost the same everywhere, except that in some countries people drive on the left and in some on the right, and the reason for that is that cars and highways are the same everywhere. In a similar way, since the basic conditions of life are everywhere tending to a uniform pattern, so the legal systems become more alike. There are also other pressures working to produce this outcome. Multinational corporations need a stable, predictable, worldwide legal environment; international organizations seek to establish universal conditions; and the movement of tourists all over the earth creates expectations of the same basic legal standards.

Once again, it needs to be remembered that within this seemingly inevitable trend to comprehensive global legality there are some ethically salutary and very positive developments. The acknowledgment of fundamental human rights as an indispensable minimum of every legal code continues on a world level the earlier European liberal doctrines of Natural Rights. It is an essential move in bringing backward, wayward and still not democratic countries into a world community of states. Analogously so, the worldwide extension of labor, refugee, and poverty relief laws creates minimum standards of humanity for the protection of potentially every human being on earth. General environmental laws for the preservation of nature are also necessary and desirable. In all such respects legal universalism is unavoidable. But must it necessarily be achieved at the expense of all local particularities in ethos, as well as other ways of regulating behavior, above all, ethics?

Neither must it be forgotten that there are still many places on earth, perhaps the majority, where legality has not yet been achieved. The endemic corruptions of Third World countries and others are inimical to the rule of law, especially where the laws are in place but not properly enforced. Lawlessness is increasing everywhere among poor people in the ghettos and barrios of the slums of the large cities all over the world. The incidence of crime is rising even in the so-called advanced societies, due to such factors as family break-up, unemployment, drug abuse, and other demoralizing trends. All this leads to the cynicism of the so-called slum culture that for many remains a permanent condition passed on from generation to generation. The law is then seen simply as the rule of the policeman, which in some respects seems worse than the rule of the criminal.

But even if legality were to be achieved and the rule of law instituted all over the world, this would still not deal with the ethical problems. The state by itself, even if it were a veritable *Rechtstaat*, cannot raise the ethical quality of its people. In fact, too much law would still constitute a danger to ethics, for a people habituated to obeying the law unquestioningly, without occasional protest and even the threat of insurrection, become unfit as individuals to stand ethically on their own. Civil disobedience as an antidote to too much conformism must be upheld, even if it sometimes takes irrational forms and seems like sheer perversity. Individuals must be allowed to resist some of the legal impositions placed on them in acts of civil defiance.

"One law for the lion and the ox is oppression," said William Blake, but the Bible also tells us that the law makes us free. These contradictory statements point to the complex and ambivalent relation between law and ethics. Without law and basic social order, as the grounding for ethical life, ethics would not survive, but with too much law individual discretion is removed and the freedom necessary for ethics is lost. Somehow we must learn to do justice to both side of this dilemma.

Ethics and Civil Society

Thus far in this chapter our main concern has been to study the effects on our ethical ethos of the social forces and agencies that are involved in the workings of the state—above all of law, citizenship, bureaucracy, and politics in general. We turn next to those forces involved in what is traditionally termed civil society—above all, the market, work, professional life, education, science, technology, and the media. But any such clear cut separation between state and civil society no longer applies in our time, for both sets of forces and the activities they engage in are closely bound up with one another. Thus the market or the capitalist system as a whole works hand in hand with the bureaucratic agencies of the state; education is largely a state-financed and controlled matter; science is also directed by the state through funding of research establishments; and even the media are deeply implicated in the political process, as the media magnates manipulate political influences to their advantage. Hence, any sharp separation between state and civil society or between public and private is now purely formal and is belied by the actual intertwined connections between them.

However, the power balance between the institutions of state and civil society is a fluctuating one; in some countries the state is more powerful, as is still the case in socialist societies, so-called, and in some periods even in capitalist societies the state was far more dominant than it has now become. Since the ending of the Cold War, the state has generally been in retreat and has been giving way to the market forces of global capitalism. Deregulation and privatization are some of the manifestations of the winding down of state controls and welfare state provisions. The nation state has also been losing power to international and regional agencies and, of course, to large multinational corporations. All these changes have consequences for the ethos in general and for the condition of ethical life in particular. Ethics now has to contend with a free-wheeling global capitalist economy with its own mobile task force of corporation personnel, sometimes without fixed domicile, who serve it. These are the most successful and prominent people. Most others live more and more in fear of their jobs and failure, of being suddenly unemployed or declared redundant or dismissed when their part-time contract expires. In such a situation of market uncertainty, people are simply intent on securing themselves and have no time or thought for any-thing except what the market requires of them. They are completely at the mercy of their employers and have become more obedient and conformist than ever before. The training in subservience now begins with the educa-tional program very early in life; it continues throughout young adulthood in the desperation to find a suitable job and lasts almost without cease during working life till death in old age. In the process ethics is often dispensed with as an unaffordable personal indulgence.

In our time, perhaps more than ever before, it is market forces that domi-nate and determine people's lives. Belief in the market is almost unques-tioned. The market and the capitalist system that is behind it have proved themselves extraordinarily economically successful till very recently, en-abling nearly all people in some societies and a minority in most societies to attain ever rising levels of material affluence, and it promises to provide the same boon for many others. Of late it has began to falter, but that has not discredited it, for there seems to be no alternative to it. It has become the preferred economic system almost throughout the world, having easily swept aside the rival system of socialism and even that of moderate state planning. And everywhere where it has succeeded, it has brought with it a competitive work ethos and a consumerist lifestyle, usually accompanied by all the trap-pings of American mass culture. Those societies that are attempting to resist this flood of modernist materialism, usually by resorting to religious funda-mentalism, as, for example, in some Islamic countries, tend to become the economic losers and to be left completely behind in all the key indicators of a modern society. So it is doubtful whether they can keep up their recalci-trant resistance for long. Soon we can foresee a world of market uniformity.

The ethical costs of this market success have been enormous. At first, when global capitalism began its worldwide advance, it seemed as if it would have very beneficial ethical consequences. The wealth created by the capital-ist enterprises—taxed through a progressive scale to finance welfare state provisions of every imaginable variety—seemed to have solved many of the old ethical problems, such as those of poverty, exploitation, injustice, and ignorance, which traditional societies had grappled with by means of ethics but never successfully overcome. Hence, it seemed as if ethics itself was no longer necessary, for it had been superseded by these economic and political measures. As we have already noted in the introduction, many of the old moral virtues seemed about to become obsolete.

The success of capitalism and the market was not conducive to ethical life for many other reasons as well. The prevailing ethos of capitalism leads to the autonomy of the economic process free of any ethical inhibitions, except for those stipulated by law, which have to be kept to a minimum if business is to thrive. For in any capitalist enterprise the overriding goal is profitability, and anything else, including ethical considerations, is necessarily peripheral, for otherwise failure ensues in the competitive struggle of the market. People adjust to these requirements in their own lives. In owning or managing a business, they simply look to financial returns and nothing else; whether what they do is socially useful or harmful is literally none of their business. Trading on the share-market makes it almost impossible to think otherwise. The popular sayings "business is business" and "business is not charity" sum up this pragmatic attitude to things. In private life, too, the main emphasis falls on success as determined by market values. In seeking employment or a career, the main criteria are salary, promotion prospects, pension provisions, perks, and so on. In doing one's work, the main concern is to employ the most efficient means, those that are most cost effective, for the task in hand. Anything else is economically irrational and spells ruin.

The cynic, who, according to Oscar Wilde, knows the price of everything and the value of nothing, is only the economically rational individual or *homo economicus*. In the life of such an individual everything is in the last resort evaluated in terms of gain and loss, usually calculated in exact monetary prices. It is not merely the pathological misers who think like this; in a capitalist society everyone has to some extent to adjust to this mentality, for in such a society most things have their price and can be bought. Even those things that are not commodities, that cannot be bought outright, are only available to those who can afford them. Thus political office, though not itself procurable, is nevertheless expensive for it can only be contested by those with sources of finance—in the United States by those who are themselves millionaires or have the backing of others. Academic degrees, though they cannot be bought outright, nevertheless require wealth, for courses of study are expensive in most societies, now that free education has almost ceased. This accounting could go on to many other endeavors and show that without money one cannot do very much or hope for many worthwhile things.

The obverse facet of this mentality of economic profitability is that anything that can be obtained for nothing is usually worth nothing. This means that anything that cannot be sold or somehow converted into market value is worthless. Since ethics almost by definition has no market value it, too, becomes devalued and is not worth much. Hence it profits no one to be virtuous or to do the right thing. On the contrary, by acting in this foolish way, one only ensures that one ends up a market failure. The soft-hearted casualty of the market has become a figure of fun; terms like "sucker" in America and "freier" in Israel mock such a person, and "do-gooder" has everywhere acquired dismissive connotations. All this is symptomatic of the destruction of ethics and of every other non-commercial value in the global capitalist society.

The dangers of global capitalism and the mentality of economic rationalism that goes with it are now amply apparent and cannot be dismissed as temporary difficulties. Even a highly successful financial speculator, George Soros, sees the problem as follows:

> The functions that cannot and should not be governed purely by market forces include many of the most important things in human life, ranging from moral values to family relationships, to aesthetic and intellectual achievements. Yet market fundamentalism is constantly attempting to extend its sway into these regions, in a form of ideological imperialism. According to market fundamentalism all social activities and human interactions should be looked at as transactional contract-based relationships and valued in terms of a single common denominator: money. Activities should be regulated, as far as possible, by nothing more intrusive than the invisible hand of profit-maximizing competition. The intrusion of market ideology into fields far outside business and economics are having destructive and demoralising social effects. But market fundamentalism has become so powerful that any political forces that dare resist it are branded as sentimental, illogical and naive.[10]

These "destructive and demoralizing social effects" we have already noted and examined in many other contexts apart from the market, but at present it is the market that is the most intrusive and dominant of the forces governing the lives of ordinary people.

Soros is but one of many authors who write of the cultural depredations of global capitalism. Jean Chesneaux puts it in very similar terms: "Profit, now that it extends beyond the specific sphere of production and invades the entire social arena, profoundly transforms the political scene. . . . Every person's life is tightly controlled in all directions. . . ."[11] The spread of global capitalism is not only outward from society to society all over the earth, but also inward from one sphere to another of the social complex. As "the economy spreads throughout the whole society, it dematerializes as it preys on diversity, it operate in a kind of unreal hyper-space which will eventually dissolve the social foundations on which capitalism was built."[12] But before capitalism will dissolve, the society it needs for its own perpetuation, it will already have destroyed the ethics that enabled that society to be established in the first place. As other authors have already amply demonstrated, the very predatory virtues of capitalist entrepreneurs that made capitalism thrive are now falling prey to the accountant's mentality of the managers, who are the ones who control the system at present. As John Ralston Saul writes, the managers, who constitute the elite of our society, "may utterly betray it while singing the sweetest lullaby to the contrary. While singing their heart out for capitalism, competition and hard-won success, they may devote themselves to the employee's life, well-paid and self-indulgent."[13]

All these developments inimical to the ethical life recorded by Soros, Chesneaux, Saul, and other contemporary authors are but the latest manifestations of the development of capitalism in its global, high-technology phase. However, even earlier phases of modern capitalism were in tension with ethics. Much of the work of Max Weber is devoted to exploring these oppositions. According to Weber, both economics and ethics have undergone large-scale historical processes of rationalization that were in principle contrary to each other. Modern capitalism, the most developed form of a rational economy, must stand opposed to all ethical considerations, for "the material development of an economy on the basis of social associations flowing from market relationships generally follows its own objective rules, disobedience of which entails economic failure and, in the long run, economic ruin."[14] This is the reasons that "there is no possibility, in practice or even in principle, of any caritative regulation of relationships arising between the holder of a savings and loan bank mortgage and the mortgagee who has obtained a loan from the bank, or between a holder of a federal bond and a citizen taxpayer . . ." and so on for many other such economic relationships. This explains why "it is above all the impersonal and economically rationalized (but for this very reason ethically irrational) character of purely commercial relationships that evokes the suspicion, never clearly expressed but all the more strongly felt, of ethical religions."[15] Weber sets out the clash between morality and capitalism as follows:

> For every purely personal relationship of man to man, of whatever sort and even including complete enslavement, may be subject to ethical requirements and be ethically regulated. This is true because the structures of these relationships depend upon the individual wills of the participants, leaving room in such relationships

for manifestations of the virtue of charity. But this is not the situation in the realm of economically rationalized relationships, where personal control is exercised in inverse ratio to the degree of rational differentiation of the economic structure.[16]

In the contemporary social order, not only in the economy but throughout the whole social structure, fewer and fewer relations depend any more on the "individual wills of the participants," leaving less and less room for the manifestations of charity or any other ethical virtue whatsoever. Ethics simply becomes irrelevant, and the exercise of any ethical virtue or norm is counterproductive to the success of one's enterprise, whatever it may be. And the more ethical considerations are excluded, the more the unfettered drive for the worldly values of success, achievement, efficiency, and the other sought-after goals of contemporary society can be given free expression.

All the ethics of the past have taken account of such ethically counterproductive relations and have in a multitude of ways sought to restrict the unfettered pursuit of worldly values. This has particularly been so with economic success or the pursuit of money. As we have already shown previously, in most ethics, though by no means in all, the engaging in commercial activity was either completely shunned or surrounded with all kinds of limitations and restrictions. The citizens of a Greek polis could not directly engage in trade, and those in Rome of the patrician order only indirectly through slave surrogates. Similar inhibitions applied to aristocratic classes at other times and places. The attitude to commerce among the various religious ethics, the moralities in our terms, varied enormously, as Weber's extensive work on this subject reveals. At times it was as severe as the Christian saying "cupiditas est radix malorum" shows it to have been, but at other times it could also be relatively lax. Nevertheless, the ban on usury was very prevalent. In Christianity it was only lifted—in a very special way for very special reasons—among the Calvinist Protestants, which permitted the expansion of finance capitalism in those countries where they predominated, such as Holland and England.

As the work of Weber, Karl Polanyi, and many other economic historians shows, it took many radical and extraordinary transformations in Western society to undo the effects of ethical restraints and allow capitalism to attain its full potential. This had the effect of changing people's whole attitude to ethics in general. It took some centuries for this to manifest itself in all social relations. Now the process is being magnified on a global level, as all societies fall under the sway of the forces of global capitalism.

The effects of this are visible in the daily lives of all people everywhere.

In general, economic values displace ethical ones. For where price is the key criterion of value, any other standard recedes to the point of inconsequentiality. The more expensive a thing or activity or even person, the better it is held to be; in this way not only items of use but everything else in our consumerist society tends to be evaluated, whether it be a work of art, the services of a professional, an education, a project of scientific research, or whatever. Consumerism, which is the way of life of most people, simply means the pursuit of expensive commodities irrespective of other values. As a result, such people's capacity to acknowledge values other than monetary ones becomes limited and such values are marginalized in society.

Personal life in a consumerist society becomes an unceasing striving for success after success without cease till death intervenes. Success is in the first place defined in monetary terms; it is that activity of work or career that earns the highest and most secure rewards. But money is not the only measure of social success; other worldly values, such as power, prestige, status, and even personal satisfaction, can also feature to a greater or lesser degree. There are some people who will choose these other kinds of values over money where a choice has to be made. But there are very few who will prefer ethical attainment over worldly success.

The key to success is work, but that, too, has changed its ethical meaning. Once when only some people worked, mainly men in the middle and lower classes, it was an indication of a steady and sober life and a reliable character. Now that it is the fate of everyone, women as well as men, it no longer has any ethical significance. There are no longer any leisured classes; sooner or later everyone works, usually at a more or less specialized activity colloquially known as a job, the choice of which is determined by educational certification and salary scales. There is some degree of freedom in the preparatory stages for work when embarking on an educational course to qualify for the job; there is not much after that. Once in a job, one's activities are governed by the work routine and the functional rules of competence that specify what one can and cannot do. Ethical norms play only a very restricted part in such work specifications. There are ethics of professional conduct for the traditional occupations, such as medicine and law, but the newer ones tend to lack even these.

It was perhaps the most important ethical discovery of modernity that work *per se*, no matter of what kind, is ethically valuable. In no previous ethical tradition was work as such seen as meritorious; in most it was shunned as unworthy of the noble or good man. Only in a few cases, such as early rabbinic Judaism where learning a trade was considered meritorious and in

the Christian monastic precepts of *ora et labora*, were there premonitions of
the modern revaluation of work. It was not until Calvinism that the work
ethic of modernity arose; work in one's vocation was mandatory for everyone
as the fulfillment of a divine purpose. This was given a secularized rendering
during the Enlightenment, as is already evident in Diderot's *Encyclopédie*,
where the arts and crafts are depicted with the dignity due to every kind of
work. Thus work eventually became the ethical basis of most of the secular
reform movements of the nineteenth century, especially so of socialism and
its ideological derivatives, where the figure of the workman or proletarian
assumed heroic proportions.

In the twentieth century the worthiness of work and the viciousness of
idleness were almost unquestioned. Robert Lane's magisterial tome *The Market Experience* is an extended demonstration of this attitude to work. As he
puts it, "One of the main themes of this book is that most work is not
degrading; rather, under certain circumstances, it is a major source of both
happiness and human development."[17] On this view, work in itself, apart
from any consideration of remuneration, is a beneficial experience. Work is
not the penalty for gaining a reward, a disutility in the jargon of the economists, but itself a major utility. It brings self-esteem and dignity, it is conducive to learning and rationality, and it develops a stable, disciplined
character capable of self-control and delayed gratification. Lane shows that
this can be so even for modern factory labor, which is not mere routine
drudgery. Even in such conditions he finds "the work ethic strong, though
transformed, in the modern market economy."[18]

In a more recent publication Richard Sennett more or less begins where
Lane leaves off.[19] He implicitly agrees—though, unfortunately, he does not
mention Lane—that the older, now being rapidly superseded, capitalist market economy did generate forms of work that gave rise to stable and secure
jobs and careers, which more or less fits Lane's account of the work experience. Even a lowly janitor, whom Sennett interviewed, could look forward
to permanent employment with small incremental improvements and predictable attainments. But now, so argues Sennett, under the impact of the
new capitalism of a computerized global economy, all this is changing and
work is becoming a more erratic, transient, and risky experience. The job is
assuming its oldest etymological meaning of an isolated piece of work. A
series of such jobs does not constitute a career, especially so as the new work
regimen is one of increasingly more frequent part-time work, particularly for
women and minors, continually changing places of employment and occupational shifts, working in teams, flexible time, and even work at home.

Far from benefiting workers, all these presumed liberations from drudgery only lead to a "corrosion of character" and negate the ethical value of work. "The conditions of the new economy feed instead on experience which drifts in time, from place to place, from job to job. . . . short-term capitalism threatens to corrode character, particularly those qualities of character, which bind human beings to one another and furnishes each with a sense of sustainable self."[20] This in turn has a profound effect on the work ethic, which is "the area where the depth of experience is most challenged today."[21] The reason for this is the way work is now organized in teams and "modern forms of teamwork are in many ways the opposites of the work ethic as Max Weber conceived it."[22] This is because "the power relations contained in teamwork, power exercised without claim to authority, is far distant from the ethic of self-responsibility which marked the old work ethic with its deadly serious, worldly asceticism."[23] Furthermore, a sense of insecurity and failure is endemic for most people in the workforce at all levels because of the ever-present threat of downsizing and reengineering, and what makes this worse for them than for previous generations is that they lack the inner moral resources to cope with adversity. Hence, loss of morale is now prevalent in all forms of work, in all occupations and professions, and the work ethic is losing its validity. This loss of morale leads sooner or later to the demoralization Sennett calls "the corrosion of character."

But even when the work-ethic was still effective, it had a most unfortunate ethical consequence that is another of the peculiar paradoxes of modern ethics. It was soon found that motivated by the work ethic, by the desire to work even when this is not an economic necessity, most people will continue doing their job no matter what the ethical results of this might be. That is to say, they take no ethical responsibility for the outcome of what they are doing and are in that sense ethically irresponsible. These results have been born out most startlingly and even horrifyingly by the behavior of people under totalitarianism. The Holocaust is the prime example about which perhaps more is known than any other. For it to have been carried out so smoothly and efficiently, without the least social disruptions, required the coordinated activities of millions of people, only a fraction of whom— though a much larger one than was previously supposed, as the recent researches of Daniel Goldhagen have revealed—were directly engaged in the killing operations; as for the others, all that was required of them was that they continue pursuing their normal work routine and ask no questions. This they did almost without exception. The "banality of evil," that much misused phrase of Hannah Arendt, has some relevance in regard to such people. It is not necessary to detail here how bureaucrats prepared plans for evacuation, how policemen herded groups of helpless victims, how railway men drove the trains, how scientists produced the poison gases and designed crematoria, how doctors made selections, and so on, and so on, for all the specialized functions of this industry of death. A similar story could also be told for the Gulag in Russia and has been told by Solzenitsyn and others. What made all these mass crimes possible is that people in general did not take themselves to be ethically responsible for the results of the work they were doing.

This is no less true of people living under conditions of freedom in liberal democratic societies, where the rule of law obtains and there are constitutional guarantees preventing ethical crimes from being perpetrated. Yet the swiftness with which Hitler was able to reverse such provisions in the Weimar Republic must give one pause even now in feeling complacent. Nevertheless, where there are no unjust laws or illegalities, ethical breaches cannot be of that magnitude. Yet they do occur at other levels of wrongdoing because people are no more inclined to assume ethical responsibility for the consequences of what they are doing in the normal course of work or professional activity.

This can be illustrated with countless examples; we shall restrict ourselves to a few drawn from business life. To take a topical case to which we have already adverted, all those who engage in financial transactions, such as bankers, hedge fund managers, arbitrageurs, stockbrokers, and so on, take no ethical responsibility for the effect of their investment decisions and money transfers. Thus, as recent events have shown, hundreds of millions of people can be rendered destitute, many reduced to malnutrition and even starvation, by these movements in the so-called global money market. And yet nobody feels ethically responsible for the harm and hurt. It is the same in all realms of business. Factory managers who decommission whole industries in given regions, rendering masses of workers unemployed and frequently without the capacity to earn a livelihood, are not obliged to take any ethical cognizance of the their policies. On the contrary, the more efficiently and, as a consequence, ruthlessly they do it, the more they are rewarded and praised. A man renowned for this activity, Al Dunlap, has become an international celebrity. When reproached, such people tend to justify themselves by replying that what they are doing is economically beneficial in the long run, that more people will eventually benefit from efficiently run business. Strictly speaking, economically considered, in the long run this might be true, but in the long run we are all dead, as Keynes put it; in the meantime many of us suffer and the ethical damage is done.

A similar logic applies to all the major areas of modern society; in each of which there has occurred an efficiency-driven process that leads to an irremediable dissociation from ethics. Thus it is an inherent part of the bureaucratic ethos that no bureaucrat is responsible for the ethical consequences that result from a proper exercise of his professional competence. Indeed, the bureaucrat as an individual might disagree with the policy he is bound to carry out and even be appalled by it on ethical grounds. Yet if bureaucrats did not impersonally and dispassionately administer that which personally they disapproved of, there could be no efficient, rationally functioning bureaucracy. Indeed, it is part of the professional ethic of officialdom that one is duty bound to carry out that which one disapproves of personally. According to the ethic of this profession, it is derelict not to do so to the best of one's ability. Yet the moral consequences of doing so might be horrendous, for in some situations this leads to Auschwitz. It is true that in normal circumstances the bureaucrat has the option of resigning. But that is an extremely limited recourse that usually assuages one person's conscience but makes no difference otherwise, because for every principled bureaucrat who resigns on a matter of conscience, there are always a hundred quite willing to go through with it. Hence, policies are carried out by the bureaucratic machine regardless. Administration—whether public or private, state or business, or that of any other institution—is driven by the very logic of the work involved to take no account of ethics.

It is true that government bureaucrats can always pass on responsibility for the policies they are required to administer to the politicians who determine these policies. Politicians, in turn, pass responsibility on to the people who elect them and so, formally at least, give them a mandate to put their political platform into effect. The people hold the politicians responsible for the consequences of carrying out policies, for they do not vote for every specific item in the election platform nor do they vote on how it is to be implemented; frequently, they are not even told clearly in advance what is to be implemented, for often there is a hidden agenda and, mostly, the political leaders themselves do not know what their policies will be once they are in power. Thus the form that representative democracy takes in modern states means that nobody is clearly responsible for the outcomes of political decisions. If an electorate is moved by ethical issues, then it can, in theory, affirm these through the democratic process by electing representatives with such mandates. In practice, however, ethics plays a minor part in political elections or in governmental policies. Usually, economics, such as the provision of jobs, taxation, and social services, or foreign policy, or the personal standing of leaders are far more important electioneering considerations. Of course, there is a professional ethic binding on the behavior of politicians as individuals—they must not be seen to lie or cheat or falsify election results or the sources of their income; in some countries they are even expected to lead innocuous sexual lives. But this is marginal to the main business of politics, which is mostly free of ethical concerns, and necessarily so if a modern state is to be maintained.

It is the same in science and, with some minor specific qualifications, in the whole world of learning. Scientists, scholars, and engineers are, of course, bound by the specific ethics of their professions. They have to strive for the truth and must not falsify results or rig experiments and in most institutions, apart from the military ones, they are obliged to publish their findings and so make them available to everyone. However, they do not take any ethical responsibility for the uses to which their discoveries and inventions are put; namely, they are not answerable for the consequences of their work. If pressed about this, they will abjure responsibility in the familiar exculpatory pattern of shifting blame on to others, to those who put discoveries to practical effect, to those who use the final products, or ultimately to those who determine policies, who will invariably be the politicians elected by the people. We have already seen what passing the buck in this way amounts to. But the subterfuge is effective, for few scientists or engineers have been dissuaded from producing the most horrendous weapons of mass destruction. Thus poison gas, chemical and bacteriological weapons, and, most dauntingly, nuclear bombs have been produced by eminent theorists and technologists under all regimes, both democratic and totalitarian, without any evident compunction. Rarely have individuals opted out on ethical grounds from such activities and almost never have they kept their findings secret for fear of the potential uses that will be made of them. In any case, given the nature of modern science and technology, it is in principle impossible to tell in advance how a particular general finding might be applied. Hence, no discovery or invention in any field can now be considered inherently "innocent"; all might have some potential application to war-making or some other ethically dubious purpose. Hence, the very nature of scientific and technological work means that it cannot in principle be restricted to ethically good ends. If it is to be pursued at all, this must be done without regard to ethics.

The nature of work in modern society is such that all fields of endeavor are autonomous spheres functionally segregated from each other and, above all, what is here so important, removed from ethical controls and ends, apart from the minor restraints of professional ethics. This is the consequence of work specialization. And specialization in all fields is unavoidable if these activities are to be pursued according to their own inherent goals—in other words, if they are to be carried on in a functionally rational way. The whole trend of modern "progress" tends to this functional rationalization of all spheres of activity, to what Weber called formal rationality and the Frankfurt school thinkers, Adorno and Horkheimer, dubbed instrumental rationality. Without this development, most of these activities as they are now practised are inconceivable. And what it inevitably entails is the marginalization of ethics.

This even holds for those jobs whose very *raison d'être* is ethical and designed to help and succor people, the traditional professions such as medicine and education and the host of new helping professions, such as the social services, counseling of all kinds, and ministering to the poor and needy. Invariably, there occurs a process of functional specialization and bureaucratization whereby the ethical ends of the work are compromised or abandoned altogether. Thus social workers become more intent on keeping their clientele, rather than freeing those who temporarily need them from permanent dependency. Educators, whose work is now organized and unionized, become less concerned with whether their students learn anything and more with easing the burdens of their work and maintaining the conditions and perquisites of their jobs. Doctors have gradually transformed their traditional independent professional practices—with their clear sense of individual ethical responsibility—into medical businesses, multi-partner clinics, and hospitals with a division of labor that feeds into the whole specialization of what can now only be called a medical industry of testing laboratories and research institutes. Who is responsible for the fate of the patient is no longer clear. It might be argued that this is inevitable, for the efficiency and level of care now provided for patients are technically superior to the previous more personal relationship. Yet many ailments are not susceptible to purely technical treatment, and a more preventative approach also calls for a more personal relationship between doctor and patient.

Besides all this, there are many new professions whose present goals are, to say the least, ethically dubious and other more traditional ones that have undergone a process of corruption in a similar direction. Those to do with advertising and the media fall into the first category. The main function of advertising, which is to inform the public of the commodities available and to persuade people of the superior qualities of the products advertised is, of course, ethically innocuous; it is simply part of any market culture. But modern advertising techniques have also assumed other functions, which are ethically far more questionable. Advertising campaigns are designed to sell not just a product but a whole lifestyle, and often what is thereby being extolled is a life of indulgent pleasure-seeking and selfishness that is quite inimical to any ethical education. Typically, these campaigns are directed at adolescent youth and even young children at the most critical point of upbringing. It is said that one such advertising promotion can undo years of effort at school and in the family. The media are guilty on similar counts of ethical irresponsibility. Though the effects on character formation of constant exposure to violence in cinema and television shows are hard to quantify experimentally, they certainly cannot be but ethically damaging, as recent outrages have revealed. Even journalism has fallen into analogous ethical problems. Under the influence of the complete commercialization of the press, now mostly in the hands of multinational media moguls, news has become just another commercial product to be edited, distorted, and dispensed according to its salable value as the entertainment of the masses. The role of the journalists has been reduced from its previous independent professional status to that of paid hacks who follow editorial orders in the interests of the owners. Only very rarely can a journalist keep any kind of independent voice and retain an ethical role in writing the truth with a full sense of responsibility.

It might be thought that all these diminutions of ethics have only taken place in work and public affairs and that in private life and personal dealings ethics is still definitive. This is as much as to say that ethics might not count for much during the working week, but that it does on Sundays. Such might have been the situation a century ago, when Christian morality had already lost much of its hold on secular professional activities, especially those to do with business, but it was still dominant in church, family, and social roles. Then the segregation of business from private life was still intact and women were the minders of the moral hearth and the guardians of the ethical home, the keepers and teachers of the proper ways of behaving for their children in the households of all classes except for the most destitute. Charity begins at home was as true of learning as of practising.

But private life has now lost its separateness and independence, and so also its ethical exclusiveness. Where both partners, who might no longer even be formally husband and wife, work, there the home is but an extension of their job, the place for respite and recuperation, and not much more than that. Leisure-type activities generally take the form of play and indulgence dictated by current fashions; sport watching as a spectator amusement assumes a frequently preponderant role; alcohol, drugs, and rock music provide the social lubricants for entertaining at all age levels, except for the very youngest and oldest. People pursue their own personal satisfactions or what they call having fun. They tend to marry, have children, and divorce without much regard for the consequences on their partners or their children, and women do this as much as, if not more so, than men. Hence, family ethics is breaking down and the ethics of friendship is in an even more parlous state—if you want a friend, get a dog, said Al Dunlap.

Such ethical dislocations and the changed status of ethics in Western societies reflect profound transformations in everyday life and of personal being. What we have called consumerist individualism, which is linked to various forms of egoism, is becoming the norm that defines the kind of being one is—that is, one's basic personal identity. This is displacing the earlier norms of ethical individualism. Every kind of ethics cultivated a form of personality through its ideal definition of what it is to be a good man. In the later traditions of Western ethics, at least since the Reformation, such ethical models of the good man became increasingly more individualistic. The Protestant emphasis on individual conscience made the crucial difference in this respect. Following the Enlightenment, more secularized types of ethics propounded ever more individualist conceptions of character and personal identity. But these ethics were overwhelmed as the social forces of the marketplace became more powerful and irresistible, and so the whole nature of individualism took a consumerist form. Personal identity has now become more a matter of what one can buy and consume, rather than of how one behaves and bears oneself. For the consumerist individual, ethical character is of no great consequence; what matters is the lifestyle one can afford.

In a consumerist society, driven by the competitive struggle for success, everything assumes a quite different cast to what it once had in more traditional societies. In general, ethical values are displaced by others that are more efficient—that is, more conducive to success. Thus basic forms of living, such as the bringing up of children, are changing to accord better with these requirements of the marketplace. As both men and women are driven to work in the pursuit of careers, there is less time, care, or concern for family matters, particularly for the bringing up of children. Ethical upbringing, character formation, and moral education, which have their initial source in the intimate setting of the family or some such locus of personal influence, are no longer of prime concern. Instead, the nurturing of children becomes geared more to bodily health, primarily through games and sport, and to the development of clever skills useful in later striving for success. A good example of the latter is the emphasis now placed on computer skills, misnamed computer literacy, which usually comes at the expense of real literacy. Most rearing and teaching is now undertaken by professionals away from the family home in specialized venues and schools and usually comprises a training regimen and organized activities. Little attention is paid to ethics.

Ethics has receded from education in general. As the curriculum in schools and universities takes on an increasingly more technical aspect, in preparing young people for professional careers, so it sheds all those subjects that were informed by ethical concerns and so conducive to ethical education. A mere vestige of religious instruction still remains in some schools, which nobody takes seriously because it has nothing to do with the passing of examinations, which is necessary for scholastic success. In schools run by churches and other religious bodies, a greater effort is put into moral instruction as part of teaching the religion, but the effect of that in a secular society geared to the drive for success is likely to be limited in most cases. For there is nothing to compensate for the absence of a cultivated form of literacy at all levels, which in the past was the main vehicle of ethical education. In the West the Bible and the Latin classics played that role; in the East there were analogous texts. Surrounding these basic works, there was usually a literary culture of other kinds of works, typically in the West made up of poetry, plays, and novels in the vernacular, which also had an ethical import. All of this, which was inherent in being an educated person, made people understand that ethics mattered.

Now most of that literary education has disappeared and been displaced by scientific and technical subjects that cannot make people feel that ethics matters to anything like the same extent. These are much more limited in their ethically educative effect. There is no denying that a scientific or technical training does inculcate some ethical norms and values, but these are very specialized and narrow. Truth in the pursuit of knowledge, truthfulness in its reporting, objectivity in assessment, matter of factness, and impartiality, such are the general intellectual virtues realized in scientific research and acquired as part of the tacit knowledge on which this research depends for its veracity. But such virtues tend not to translate into other areas of life and do not form an overall personality type. Many are the instances of scientists who observed the highest standards of truth in their research, yet in political, practical, or personal life were susceptible to all kinds of mendacities. Being a truthful scientist does not make one an honest person. Science does not constitute an overall approach to life; there is no such thing as a scientifically ethical way of life. Science itself arose and was made possible by the secularized ethical ethos of the Enlightenment, which did not come from science and originally had nothing to do with it. Frequently, it derived from a Puritan religious conscience. Throughout its subsequent history, science has tacitly relied on such ethical traditions. Now that these traditions are weakening and being eroded, science is beginning to falter and all kinds of ethical abuses or pathologies are starting to appear in scientific work, as the numerous scientific scandals testify.[24]

What is even more dangerous is that there is nothing inherent in scientific research itself that specifies the purpose for which it is being carried out. Science does not have its ends inscribed in itself, for these mainly come from outside and are specified by other interests, generally those that provide the necessary funding.[25] This is the reason that science lends itself so easily to the most abhorrent uses. There is nothing in the narrowly delimited range of ethical norms necessary to carry out research to prevent this from happening. This is something we have witnessed repeatedly in this troubled century, that scientists of all types, who themselves were decent people given to the most stringent standards of truth and objectivity in their work, have nevertheless lent themselves and their work to every imaginable purpose. No totalitarian dictator ever had the least problem recruiting the scientific manpower for every one of his projects, including those that led to the most horrific crimes of history. It is true that in democratic societies there were always a few exceptional cases of scientists who refused to engage in certain kinds of ethically dangerous research, but that research went ahead nevertheless, for there were always a great many others prepared to step into their shoes and carry on.

The lack of any intrinsic relation between science and ethics highlights the very problematic nature of the ever-growing preponderance and increasing numbers of scientifically and technically trained experts in contemporary life. There is usually nothing in their education to give them any understanding of ethics or frequently even of the narrow professional ethics they ought to know to do their work with even a limited sense of responsibility. When firm ethical standards are lacking in private and public life in general, this makes the work of experts even more dangerous because it is ethically uncontrolled. As long as experts were placed in professions where a traditional professional ethic obtained and as long as they were still motivated by a sense of vocation, no serious ethical problems or corruptions appeared. But now when new categories of work and technical competence are continually emerging, and these have no traditions of professional ethic, and when the key motives of those entering them are careerism and money, for any sense of vocational calling has disappeared, only now are we beginning to experience the full effects of an absence of ethics.

Such ethical problems are starting to appear even in the old established professions, as these proliferated into numerous narrow technical specialities. Thus as medicine has become a medical industry, financed by state agencies or private insurance companies that determine the conditions of treatment, it becomes less evident what it means for the various specialized technicians to be devoted to healing. On the peripheries of medicine all kinds of other specialities have arisen, whose notions of disease and treatment and whose professional ethics are even more dubious. The psychiatric professions in particular are now beset by ethical problems arising from a failure to clearly specify what it is that requires treatment. A clear symptom of this is the ever-growing number of hitherto considered slightly unusual or even eccentric types of behavior that are now officially defined as "illnesses," requiring the services of professionals and most frequently the products of drug companies. The official guidebook to mental health, *The Diagnostic and Statistical Manual of Mental Disorders*, listed a mere 60 illnesses in 1952; this grew to 145 in 1968 and in 1994 stood at 410, with strong potential for further growth. Particularly badly affected by this constantly creeping diagnostic expansion have been children, whose least oddity or not quite normal (frequently confused with average) quirk is now assigned to some syndrome or other and treated with behavior therapy and drugs. The ethics of all this is rarely called into question.

The ravages perpetrated on childhood by various kinds of professionals are among the most serious ethical problems in education of our time. The teaching of children is now consigned to the least qualified and able of all the professionals, those unable to obtain better jobs elsewhere. Without a vocational commitment to teaching, such as most teachers would have had to some degree until recently, without any dedication to their work, without even any liking for children, such people can often not accomplish even the most basic goals of elementary education. Of any ethical education, there can be no question. Such problems are not confined to the elementary levels; they proliferate on the secondary and tertiary levels as well, including university studies. Professors, too, have generally lost any sense of vocational ethics and are more devoted to their promotions and career prospects than to their students.

The recent introduction of a spate of courses on ethics in higher education is more symptomatic of the problem than indicative of a solution. Such courses have appeared in response to an evident need for ethical education but one that they are by themselves unlikely to meet. To be taught the basic principles of business ethics, medical ethics, or legal ethics in a short course that is adjunct to a long professional training on the way to a career is not likely to give students much ethical knowledge or the incentive to practice it. At the very best it will make them aware of a few specialized norms in a narrow range of problems and issues. Ethics is not a technical subject that can be taught piecemeal, like some branches of law or like accounting procedures that can be succinctly expounded by lecturers, memorized by students, and tested in examinations. Ethical education does not lend itself to such teaching. Ethical knowledge had to be gradually inculcated in different contexts and various areas of application. It calls for extensive discussion and argumentation in a dialectical spirit, concerning general principles as well as concrete cases. It requires an understanding of whole ethical traditions and extensive background cultural knowledge. We shall return to the issue of ethical education in what follows and consider in particular what form it should take in university studies. What passes at present for courses in ethics bears little relation to such an idea of ethical education.

In the process of the persistent elimination of any ethical component in education—which seems to be happening in direct proportion to the ever-increasing average years of schooling and the rise in the degrees of qualification—an ever-growing "educative" role is being taken over by the media. It is through their exposure to the media, especially television and its electronic adjuncts, that children acquire much of their extracurricula ethical sense of what is right and wrong, as judged by the implicit values and standards that the media generated messages convey. Mostly, this takes place through identification with the media promoted "stars," the celebrities drawn from films, entertainment, sport, or politics, who become the role models for young people in their sense of how to behave, what to aspire to, and what to value. Hence, as one group of "stars" gives way to another—sometimes swiftly in a matter of a few years, for their rate of obsolescence is rapid—so the whole sensibility of the new "generation" of the young, also a short-lived cohort, changes. Peer-group pressure to adjust ensures that few young people can resist such switches in fashion that are heralded as "revolutions" in lifestyle. There is, of course, an obvious economic rationale for this process, which is controlled by the big media companies.

The ultimate upshot of these lifestyle changes is that fashions have displaced the older traditional ways of regulating conduct. The older customs, mores, and manners were also subject to alteration but in a much more graduated way, so that succeeding generations could more easily adjust to changes and absorb them into their lives. Now fashion changes in ways of living are much more superficial and alter repeatedly over the course of a lifetime, so that they cannot be properly internalized. Fashions in life-styles—in what is *in* and what is *out* in regard to behavior and relations—can now be manipulated as easily and as quickly as fashions in clothes or in pop music. The trend setters of the latter are also the *arbiter elegantiarum* of the former. And they act at the behest of powerful market interests, such as the record companies, design houses, and of late even pharmaceutical firms producing the latest "designer" drugs. Frequently, these are part of integrated cartels with large media companies, the very ones who through their programing and advertising practices purvey the lifestyle changes that their commercial interests require. It is in these ways that what is now known euphemistically as the rock-generation, but which was really a series of brief-lived youth cohorts, was induced to follow the trends that are the contemporary equivalent of manners.

In the more traditional societies manners stood next to morals. "Manners maketh man" is the Wykehamist motto that became the foundation of the English public-school system of education. It derives from and still partly reflects a medieval ethic of honor that helped produce the English gentleman. In itself, it is a restricted view of ethics, but as the educational preparation for a later more mature ethical life it, or something like it, is indispensable. It is the basic *Sittlichkeit* that as *Üblichkeiten* serve to inculcate an ethical predisposition. There is much more to morals than mere manners, but the latter is still as good a preparation for the former as any. Now the role of schools in inculcating manners is being taken over by media-promoted fashions with all too predictable results. Anyway, most schools have already given up the attempt to teach manners, for that calls for personal effort and commitment on the part of teachers that few are willing to make.

The media purvey what the Culture Industry produces: cultural commodities for a mass market designed to give as many people as possible what they can be made to believe they want. Such "shows" are intended to captivate and titivate, and if they set out to instruct, then it is by arousing the most trite of sentimentalities. The ethical content of these "literary" productions rarely rises above the level of the fairy-tale, especially in programs designed for young people. Frequently, such programs in fact promote immoral attitudes by implication. When the difference between good and evil characters is that the former have the law on their side but otherwise behave just as badly, then a creeping cynicism begins to appear. An even worse form of cynicism is when the good are shown as losers and the evil as canny opportunists who deserve to win.

Of late, a tendency has developed in the media not to discriminate between fact and fiction—that is, journalistically speaking, between news and entertainment—which has the effect of weakening people's capacities to distinguish the real from the illusory and to tell truth from lies. What is considered newsworthy is invariably an indigestible farrago of the trivial and momentous, in which one is hard put to tell what matters. Thus in the plethora of mostly pointless information about celebrities, local crime, and sport routinely published in most newspapers, an important matter of fact can be hidden from view and lost to the mass of readers. We now recall with horror that during the Second World War the truth concerning the Holocaust was published as it was happening, but its presentation was so surrounded with such obfuscating material that few readers could realize what was going on and respond to it with any active outrage. At present this is the situation with the famine in North Korea, which the media is barely reporting. Analogous phenomena of what might be dubbed information blindness are very common. All this makes it difficult to treat the affairs of the world with ethical seriousness and weakens one's sense of responsibility.

There are analogous phenomena of the obfuscation of truth even in scholarly and scientific publications. What is and what is not published often reflect status and position in the academic hierarchy. But even if it does appear in print, the work of lesser-placed individuals tends to be lost from sight in the mass of published materials. If it is important, then this will only be discovered later, perhaps too late to do any good. The fate of Gregor Mendel is by no means a unique case; on a lesser scale similar incidents occur all the time. In scholarly publication any idea or issue that does not command authoritative support will not be seriously debated; it will be off the agenda for discussion. The ethics of all this hardly needs to be spelled out. What is called for are the scholarly equivalents of "whistleblowers" to arouse attention to what is being denied or neglected. But for that to happen, an ethical motivation is required that is now generally lacking.

The whole ethos of contemporary civilization, even where it is not hostile to ethics, is indifferent to it. Ethics has been marginalized, and morality, in particular, excluded. Max Horkheimer already saw this happening half a century ago when he wrote that "morality is disappearing. It was the autonomous version of faith and is now being replaced by the increasing scope of social and governmental directives."[26] Such directives of all kinds, enforced in all kinds of ways, are conducive to an ethos of conformity, to going along with the flow of things as they are. It is always personally easier and costs less in self-interested terms to do what one is required to do, to conform with the "system" of rules and regulations rather than to act against it, even if what it obliges one to do is scarcely ethical or of dubious morality. The very systematicity of modern life is conducive to such conformity, even if it does not coercively require it.

All the main social forces associated with what is called "modernization," such as systematization, organization, technification, and rationalization, in general, though not in themselves unethical, are destructive of ethics. The effect of their introduction and institutionalization is to displace ethics with directives—that is, with regulation and juridification. For the more personal relations are rendered impersonal, the less they are subject to ethical discretion and the more they are bound to be governed by an objective order of regulations. People no longer relate to each other with all the complexities of human variability and fallibility—with determination and a feeling of engagement, as well as with the corruptions of status and power differentials—rather, they relate impersonally in their roles as agents of corporate bodies. Response and responsibility, sense and sensitivity, spontaneity and accountability no longer come into it. All that matters are roles and functional competencies and the rules governing these, and the consequences of dereliction in transgressing them. Ethics ceases to matter. So much so, that even activities that are intrinsically ethical, such as charitable undertakings, have to be conducted in an organized business-like way to be effective and they, too, begin to lose their distinctive ethical feel and character. The big charitable foundations operate like any other enterprises even though their purpose is quite other.

This is but one example of the way in which whole areas of public and private life become organized and fall into corporate hands. Institutions, departments, firms, agencies, and other organizations now handle most social activities, so people have fewer and fewer dealings with each other in a purely personal capacity. They confront each other as members of organizations: as employees, functionaries, agents, and other representatives. In such official capacities they can only treat each other in terms of their functional competence and according to the prescribed regulations and directions. Once such a process of corporatization begins in a society, it tends to be self-reinforcing, for the best way of confronting corporate bodies and organizations is by means of others of like ilk; otherwise, the individual is at an impossible disadvantage.

The ultimate upshot of this process of corporatization is that even private individuals have to incorporate themselves as if they were small firms or organizations with a single member. Frequently, this is forced on them by taxation laws that favor corporations and trusts rather than people and that demand strict accounting procedures even for personal activities. Gradually, leading a private life becomes akin to running a small business. The pressures toward this also come from the necessity of utilizing professional representatives in transacting one's private affairs, for one is constantly having recourse to lawyers, accountants, agents, consultants, and advisers of various kinds, including such contemporary "father confessor" figures as psychoanalysts, gurus, and, for some, even astrologers. The mentality that permeates all these transactions is that of business, of interests calculated in terms of profit and loss, of what benefits accrue from any initiative and what needs to be paid for it by the expenditure of time, energy, money, or any of the other investments from which one expects to gain a return. Ethics ceases to be a factor in the calculations. An exchange relationship comes to the fore in all personal affairs: "What do I need to outlay and what can I get out of it?" becomes the uppermost question. Anyone who still invokes ethical considerations is looked upon as a naive idiot who deserves to be taken advantage of, even if only to teach him a lesson for his own good.

All these trends are accelerated by mechanization, the introduction of machines and technological systems into the ordinary activities of daily life. The more machines are utilized, especially those of high technology, the more those activities in which they operate must be systematically organized and regulated. And the more this happens, the more ethical considerations are driven out and eventually eliminated. Taken in themselves, machines and instruments are ethically neutral, but organized as a system this is no longer so, for a technical apparatus of interconnected machines renders an activity impersonal and makes ethics redundant.

This can be illustrated by a simple and obvious example in comparing the conduct of people as pedestrians and as drivers in motorized traffic. People who encounter each other on foot are usually still bound by the older ethos of manners, politeness, and tact; those in motor cars, only by the rules of the road. On the street, who has right of way or precedence in effecting an entrance through a passage or doorway is decided by all kinds of imponderables that are a factor of age, gender, fitness, beauty, status, urgency of need, and dozens of other considerations of all kinds, depending on context that might make one give way to another person, judging this almost instantaneously in a momentary glance. Where there are doubts, smiling looks of mutual understanding are exchanged; nods of appreciation are expressed from one to another; glances of anger are directed at anyone who is a tactless boor or ill-mannered hooligan. Even ethics plays a part among pedestrians, for one is obliged to come to the assistance of those in need of help, even if only in crossing the road, and certainly to intervene where someone is being attacked, for not to do so is irresponsible and heartless. Few if any of these considerations arise when one is traveling in a motor car, especially at high speed on a motorway. Issues of right of way or any other such matters of precedence call for no discretion or judgment, for they are determined automatically by traffic lights and by the traffic laws that govern how one is to react to fixed indicators, such as lines and signs. These laws are assiduously enforced by the police; to break them is a crime. Human relations that obligate manners, politeness, and tact are not involved, having been displaced by mechanical systems and directives.

Something along these lines takes place wherever mechanization is introduced and an organized system is in force. A preordained routine, which generally cannot be altered or stopped, is operative and people have to fit in on pain of failure or punishment. To go against the system is to be a danger to oneself and others, like going against the flow of motorized traffic. So the speed and rhythm of the system determines how human beings are to proceed even where it is against their inclinations. People become prisoners of the machines, as has so wittily been satirized in Charles Chaplin's film *Modern Times*. This happens whenever a technified process holds sway, not only in factories but also in hospitals, in offices, in educational institutions, in prisons, and in research laboratories. And everywhere that such rationalization takes place, ethics is displaced by directives that generally have the force of law and a human ethos gives way to a systematic process.

We can see this taking place in the most recent developments of technology, such as in the so-called Information Revolution. The technification of communication through the introduction of computers and automatic processes in all kinds of activities, which were previously transacted by people, means that human relations are displaced and, with that, ethical issues disappear. Increasingly, one finds oneself dealing with a computer and its inflexible routine rather than an understanding human being. "Our computer does not allow this" has become an oft-heard excuse when one finally does get through to a person.

It might be imagined that to compensate for this inflexibility of automation brought about by the Information Revolution, there is the flexibility of communication achieved through the Internet and e-mail. But the human and specifically ethical costs of these are great and continually increasing. The Internet is fast becoming a rumor-mongering mill with no restraint and no accountability; lies, calumnies, deceits, propaganda of every imaginable type, obscenities beyond compare, incitements to immorality and crime, in short, anything that a perverted or cynically calculating mind can dream up comes on the Net and circulates freely to everyone. Impressionable young minds have access to effusions of this kind with no way of discriminating among them. The traditional ethics of communication—what one can and cannot say and to whom and about whom, and any other such cautions and restraints—have completely disappeared. Even such a seemingly harmless technical advance as e-mail exacts an ethical cost. The old proprieties of letter writing and answering are no longer observed; now one pleases oneself with which e-mail messages, among the plethora that arrive, one replies to and which messages one discounts as trash. Even telephone-answering machines serve as a similar filtering device. In this way people make themselves inaccessible and the promised democratizing effects of the new devices, which supposedly allow anyone to communicate with anyone else, in effect have the opposite result; they reinforce unaccountability, in not requiring anyone to answer to anything.

All the factors that we have previously outlined have decisively altered personal dealings and encounters. The whole ethos of civility and the ethics governing it have been reduced to the bare essentials and no more. In this lies a large part of the cause of the cynicism that is the prevailing temper of our time. Cynicism is the corrosive emotional acid that eats away at all human relations. Ethical cynicism is particularly pronounced. Much of the humor and many of the jokes of our time express an attitude of ethical nihilism, an awareness that ethics is a sham, that nobody is ethically better than anyone else, that everyone is ultimately out for what he can get. Such a cynical view of things is also frequently to be found in hard-boiled popular literature, such as romance novels that convey the prostitute's view of love, crime fictions that uphold the criminal's view of justice, murder mysteries in which murderers bear no guilt, political thrillers in which the spy's view of the legitimacy of spying is unchallenged and the conspirator's view of politics uncriticized.

Higher and more sophisticated versions of cynicism have taken root in contemporary intellectual culture. This is the cynicism of unmasking, exposure, demystification, and so-called ideology critique. Generally deriving from such now-classic sources as Marx, Nietzsche, and Freud, as well as from many contemporary thinkers, whose theories are taken as a license for cynicism, the whole thrust of these critiques is turned against ethical culture. Thus morality is stigmatized as bourgeois morality, slave morality, or repressive morality, and there seems nothing better than to be free of it. And if one cannot destroy it, one might as well laugh at it. The derisive scorn of an Althusser, Foucault, or Lacan now resounds throughout the halls of academia, echoed by countless professors. Peter Sloterdijk has made a lengthy compendium of such intellectual attitudes that are conducive to cynicism in a book whose main thesis is that "discontent in our culture appears today as universal, diffuse cynicism."[27]

Cynicism, both popular and learned, is the symptom of the diseased state of ethics in our culture. It arises from the processes of de-ethicization that we discussed historically in the previous chapter and of the corruptions of ethics that we have catalogued in this chapter. The most prominent and perhaps most destructive of these processes is demoralization, the dissolution of morality, the ethical tradition inherited in the West from Judeo-Christian religion and based on a notion of conscience that bears guilt. This kind of moral conscience is being gradually eroded through the abjuring of guilt promoted by all kinds of therapies, the decrying of any notion of culpability, and the suspension of judgment. Ethical shame, which is the basis of a sense of personal self-respect or honor, is suffering a similar erosion through unabashed self-exposure and self-advertising, the shrinking space of personal privacy, and the media intrusions into private life. Respect for any kind of authority, whether institutional or educational, is almost nonexistent. The breakdown of personal relations, whether within the family or among friends or associates, has accelerated all such emotional dessications, and this affects ethics even more than changes in beliefs and values. The outcome is an absence of trust and commitment, whose main symptom is a resort to contracts and lawyers to secure oneself against the likelihood of betrayal. Even marriage contracts are now in vogue.

Obviously, not everyone is equally touched by these general demoralizing conditions. Many people retain something of their ethical traditions and some even make valiant attempts to go against the current and to lead an ethical way of life. But in the changed social circumstances, this becomes ever less possible because it ceases to have any social relevance. Those who are still given to take life seriously in this way appear to others as eccentrics. As Gernot Böhme puts it, "Diese Situation is von Moral entlastet . . . der Entwurf einer eigenen Lebensform gerät durch den Mangel einer öffentlicher Relevanz zum Hobby."[28] In the absence of social supports and with an "anything goes" attitude, which reveals itself in an arbitrary choice of lifestyles, it is no longer possible, even with the best will in the world, to maintain any kind of coherence in one's ethical life or, indeed, to achieve personal integrity. At best, one can only select and save ethical fragments, like the resalvaged pieces of old handicraft that one tries to fit into the decor of a modernist ambience. But as Gernot Böhme also insists, "Die moralische Existenz bezieht sich aber nicht bloss auf Kompetenzen und einzelne Akte, sondern auf die Lebensform im ganzen."[29] Ethics as a "Lebensform im ganzen" does not exist anymore. None of the basic ethical functions can any longer be carried out in a coherent way in relation to each other. Consequently, one cannot be true to oneself in this ethical sense either. This is not to deny that some people still try their utmost to perform good deeds; they try to reflect ethically about themselves and others and to provide some kind of ethical education for their children, but most frequently these activities are disjointed and without bearing on each other.

But even this might be considered a luxury of affluent societies. For the masses of people in Third World countries, there are other problems to those encountered in Western societies. Such people are frequently still in touch with their ethical traditions and often not as demoralized as the rich in their own societies. However, they tend to suffer from a lack of the basic standards of civility that are taken for granted by well-off people in more modern countries. What they need is impartial law enforcement, uncorrupt courts, policing without brutality, not to be dominated by criminal cliques or street gangs, not to have to resort to drugs or prostitution for a living, to have access to the basic amenities of health, schooling, and services, and so on, for the most basic features of civilized living. For all such people civilization itself is in doubt. It has yet to be proven that a global society can attain the minimum levels of civility for a great majority of its people. If this is not achieved, then it is possible that global civilization will collapse, since it is difficult to envisage civilized islands of a wealthy elite surviving in a sea of destitution and disorder without being sooner or later swamped by the waves of desperation and despair. What would ensue in such an eventuality is beyond speculation at present.

There are those in many countries who have already decided that global civilization and its ancillary forms of modernization are the main problem. They see as the only solution to this a return to the traditional ethos, such as obtained before modernity made its inroads in the West and before the West asserted itself over all the other civilizations. Such people are now colloquially known as fundamentalists; they are present in all religions and countries, but nowhere in such large numbers and with as much social influence as in the Islamic ones.

But as recent events have demonstrated, a resort to fundamentalism solves nothing, for it cannot really cope with the problems of modernity. It only seeks to escape from them by wishing them away. It can do nothing for poverty nor can it re-establish civility, even of a traditional kind. If anything, it is likely to destroy civil peace by exacerbating conflicts of all kinds, religious, ethnic, social, and national, and so render worse the very problems it sets itself to overcome. The wish to return to a now nonexistent and impossible-to-achieve traditional society is illusory. However, this does not mean that an intelligent traditionalism, a genuine conservatism that is fully aware of what it is up against, might not be helpful in stemming the worst forms of degeneration in society. Where fundamentalism is already entrenched, everything should be done to encourage it to transform itself in this direction.

It is undoubtedly the case that the still surviving traditional social forces have something to contribute to a possible regeneration of ethics. How they might do so will depend on historical exigencies and on the general social configuration that is impossible to predict in advance. As Jean Chesneaux states, "It remains to be seen what historical crisis, what social forces, will be capable of promoting a political society worthy of that name, i.e. a society concerned first of all about humanity's common interests."[30] Such a political society would also, of course, be an ethical society. But what kind of historical crisis might it be to galvanize masses of people and so to invigorate those social forces that might lead to such a positive outcome? At present we cannot say, for nothing like this is in the offing.

CHAPTER 4

~

Ethics and Culture

Ethics and Aesthetics

Ethics is a cultural formation not unlike some of the other major activities of society, such as law, politics, religion, science, or art. Like these it, too, is a highly diversified set of practices involving many distinct functions and specialized activities frequently carried out separately by different kinds of people. It is a cultural network of many types of overlapping roles and dispositions. To elucidate the structural framework of the culture of ethics, we shall take art as our main focus of comparison. Ethics can also be usefully compared to law, politics, religion, and science and we have already had something to say about these connections, but to take this any further would far exceed our present scope. However, in this context art does suggest itself as the most apt parallel and this also fits in with the traditional coupling of ethics and aesthetics. There is little further need to spell out in detail the differences between ethics and art or any other of the major cultural activities. Briefly put, as we have already indicated in chapter 1, ethics is almost entirely a matter of ethos, the sphere of conduct, feeling, and value, whereas art is mostly a matter of the production, perception, and appreciation of artistic objects and performances in respect of their form, content, and media.[1]

The other main reason for choosing art as the comparative focus is because ethics and art are in a very similar predicament in contemporary society; both are, in a sense, endangered cultural species, the ones most at risk. Both have been diminished by processes of reduction and fragmentation, such as the process of demoralization that we previously studied in ethics, and there are similar anaesthetic processes at work in the arts. Though we cannot yet speak of the extinction of either, nevertheless, both have been subject to destructive attacks resulting in such mutilation and diminution that their most complex and culturally refined forms have almost disappeared. The state of art and ethics throughout the world is such as to make it barely possible to recognize in these present remnants the full stature of these forms as they were even a mere century ago. Then they assumed many diversified modes and played crucial cultural functions at all social levels. Now they have been reduced to a few residual roles of lesser importance, compared to other activities. For mass involvement, sport outdoes them. As foci of interest and topics of discourse the news-media fare absorbs much more attention. As learning experiences for the young, computer information and even computer games are fast taking over from works of literature or books of ethical import.

Nowhere today is there a coherent aesthetic culture in evidence, that is, an artistic way of life being pursued that is productive of a range of works of art marked by stylistic unity and integrity of value such as was more or less the normal aesthetic state in most past societies. Instead, we now have a predominance of commercial arts, mostly pop-art products of the Culture Industry, set over against what is preserved of the traditional arts, mainly moribund museum masterpieces stored in galleries, libraries, theaters, and concert halls. The former are produced for a mass market in specialized formuli adjusted to the various age cohorts from tiny tots to so-called "golden oldies," and they are marked and marred by a plethora of stylistic features drawn from every conceivable source and subject to rapid rates of obsolescence. The latter are unaging monuments of former glory, repeatedly displayed or performed on semi-ritual occasions. The people who attend concerts and theaters or visit museums and galleries are like those who still go to church and listen to sermons; it plays a certain residual traditional role in their habits but is not decisive for their lives. This is more or less like traditional ethics, fragments of which still survive but also in a largely moribund state. They are overlaid and frequently overpowered by the constantly changing lifestyle innovations that are closely linked to the changing cycles of fashions promoted by the major media companies in their frenetic bid to sell new products.

There are some exceptions to this established dispensation in ethics and the arts. There are small groups of traditionalists or sectarians who seek to lead a wholly antiquated and now superseded lifestyle and to cultivate the old folk ways. Diametrically opposed to these are the revolutionaries and avant-gardists, those at the other extreme, who experiment in new ways of living and dabble in new art forms. Neither extreme, the traditionalist or the modernist, can produce a viable ethics or art. Often they cancel each other out. Some of the student revolutionaries of the 1960s and 1970s ended up as fundamentalists later, but in neither role did they have any sustained social effect. The predominant mass ethos of the market prevailed. Now in ethics, as in art, all coherence is gone; all is supply and relation.

Both ethics and aesthetics face analogous difficulties. The impediments to leading an ethical life are not unlike those of maintaining some minimal standards of taste in art. For just as people become indifferent to their surroundings and the objects of daily use, so, too, they grow insensitive in their personal relations; inured to crudity, they become coarse and sometimes even callous. Amid the clatter of mechanical noise, enveloped in the contrived ugliness of an almost wholly man-made environment full of high-rise buildings and traffic, exposed to a constant stream of electronic imagery, much of it brutal or pornographic, most people become vacant and dull, unable to respond to anything subtle or more muted. For analogous reasons, when people are blasted with a constant stream of fact and fiction, news and shows, the one frequently only barely distinguishable from the other and both mostly compounded of crimes and follies, they lose their emotional and ethical sensitivities and can no longer distinguish anything but the grossest contrasts of right and wrong, good and bad.

For such people ethics is reduced to law or, practically considered, to what the police choose to enforce and the judges to punish. In other areas of life the policing and judging roles are served by supervisors and disciplinary committees, who are there to establish and maintain the limits of the permissible. And in all these affairs there are lawyers involved, representing clients who can no longer act for themselves in almost any public matter at all; and they are invariably preoccupied with manipulating the technicalities of the law and of court procedures for the benefit of those who pay them the most. The really famous and rich can have their trials publicized and even televized; their high-earning lawyers feature in a kind of theater for the masses where law-dramas are enacted that show how the privileged can be helped to evade just punishment. In our societies these ritualized performances are like the trials of ordeal and public exorcisms of more primitive societies; in them ethics and aesthetics fuse together into a kind of ceremonial show.

Ethics in such difficult times has to be learned and lived quite differently than it was ever before, as holds for art as well. Even at best, both are now minority interests of small groups, each of which is preoccupied with one kind of ethical or aesthetic matter in isolation from any other. Sometimes the main responsibility falls on single individuals. This is so in ethics with the so-called "whistleblowers," those who stand up to and call powerful interests to account and sometimes tend to be punished rather than rewarded for it. We have not yet reached the cynical nadir, where, as the popular saying goes, no good deed shall go unpunished, but often it has to be its own reward for there is no other.

What can be done in such a situation? How can it be repaired? The question applies equally to ethics and aesthetics. In both spheres the immediate outlook for any dramatic improvements is bleak. But the possibility of individual action is not hopeless. Much can still be done by anyone mindful of doing something. And if only enough people were similarly minded, then incrementally, step by painful step, society might gradually change as well. But to change the world, it is first necessary to interpret it, and to improve one's ethical condition, it is also necessary to understand it. To achieve such a better grasp of the workings of ethics we shall develop further the analogy with art.

Of the many close parallels between ethics and aesthetics that could be brought out and discussed, two stand out as of crucial importance. First, both art and ethics are not solitary pastimes but social practices that require very special communities: in art, that of artists and the art-lovers who are their primary public, the patrons and connoisseurs in aesthetic matters; in ethics, that of the often self-chosen primary practitioners of a code, the upholders of righteous conduct, the keepers of conscience, and the cultivators of a given ethical way of life. But, second, set over against this commonality of group practice, there is the single creative act or right action or good deed that frequently issues from the single individual who is held responsible for it. In art we create alone and appreciate together; in ethics we deliberate together and act alone. To say this is not to deny that there are group artistic performances, just as in ethics there are joint actions and cooperative ventures; but even in these, those involved must take individual responsibility and often it is one individual who plays a leading role in initiating the project and in guiding it as it proceeds. Hence, it is possible to distinguish a communal and individual aspect in the practice of both art and ethics.

These features are by no means unique to ethics and art; they are also to be found in other cultural activities. Thus in the world of learning there is a community of scholars but individual contributions, and in science there is also a scientific community but findings or theories are mostly ascribed to individuals or shared by just a few cooperating together. Scientific communities and their operations have been extensively studied in the sociology of science, artistic communities have been explored to a lesser extent, but ethical communities have been barely touched on at all. In what follows we shall make an initial attempt to remedy this omission by examining the communal and individual aspects of ethics separately, though it must always be borne in mind that they belong together in actual practice and can only be separated for analytical purposes.

An ethical community is a distinctive group of people that is committed to a given ethical way of life. Its members will often seek to distinguish themselves by outward symbolic means, such as special garb, markings, haircut, or beard, and so on. In these ways they declare that they belong together as a group and proclaim their seriousness of purpose, and that they seek the basic meaning of life in their particular commitment. It is the most important thing in life for them, in a way it is not for most others. They might be the initial creators or instigators of a new ethic, in which case they are a charismatic sect; or, as is more often the case, they are a traditional elite who are the carriers of an already well-established ethic. They are usually a much smaller and more exclusive group than the wider society of all those who subscribe to this ethic, those who as far as possible, given their other commitments and goals, try to regulate their lives by it. But these, so to speak, occasional practitioners also seek the meaning of their lives elsewhere, mainly in non-ethical activities; for this reason they will tend to be looked down on by the elect group. Thus, for example, though all the members of a given church or higher religion subscribe to its moral code, only those who live for it exclusively will make it their life's task to uphold it, and these might be a small group of religious virtuosi, such as mystics, monks, priests, or preachers. There will be good people among the mass of others, but even these will not be so constantly preoccupied in discussing, debating, and arguing about given moral issues as the inner core of the ethical community. Analogously so, it is most often a small court society that expounds and maintains an honor ethic, even though the whole aristocratic class is more loosely bound by it. To put it crudely, the setters of trends and keepers of standards in ethics, as in aesthetics, are few; their followers are many. Throughout the history of ethics there have been many very diverse types of ethical communities, involving people ranging from the lowest to the highest social standing, from plebeians to nobility, differing in wealth, power, and all other social attributes. Our previous historical account provides numerous instance of such diverse groups.

The role of an ethical community is crucial because all the functions of ethics are usually carried out within it. It is the community that deliberates and decides on general ethical matters, that teaches the ethic to others, and that might also theorize and philosophize about it. Those who are outside the inner core of the community, the common people, as it were, when they deliberate and act do so by reference to their community standards. At the back of a person's mind there is always the question, what will "they" say, the "they" being those to whom the person views as authoritative figures within a community.

Thus the community acts both externally and internally to sanction a person's conduct. Externally, it does so by means of various kinds of punishment and disapproval; internally, it inculcates psychological self-censoring mechanisms, such as, above all, the ethical emotions of guilt and shame. We have already examined in the first chapter the range of such sanctions and inducements as these operate in the four basic types of ethical systems, namely, in morality, the civic ethic, and the ethics of honor and duty. However, beyond such generalities, detailed studies are always called for to determine how a given community operates. At present few such are available.

Different kinds of ethical communities place different emphases on such outer or inner sanctions. They also differ in the way they affirm communal authority or individual autonomy in ethical matters. Even now some people always obey authority and unhesitatingly follow the instructions of their ethical guides, the father confessors of their souls, so to speak. These are the old-style "Catholic" types for whom moral authority is all important. In contrast to these, there are the old-style "Protestant" types who seek to decide everything in the absolute solitude of their individual consciences. Both of these are extreme positions, for in all ethics there is always some dialectical interplay between communal authority and individual conscience, the precise working out of which will vary from case to case. For without authority an individual is deaf to advice and reason, and without a conscience he is blind and must be led every step of the way.

An ethical community sets its own standards for what is true and false within its ethics. Through its internal, and often incessant, discussions, debates, and arguments, it arrives at what is right and wrong, good and bad, virtuous and wicked, or valuable and worthless. In this respect it functions analogously to an aesthetic community or a scholarly or scientific one. Those who are followers, not at the central core of their communities, usually simply accept the verdicts passed on to them as decisive and act on them as if they had set the standards themselves. However, this does not mean that communities of these kinds are elites colluding to dominate others or that they make arbitrary stipulations or reach a conventional consensus or that a winning position emerges after power struggles. Neither science, nor scholarship, nor art, and certainly not ethics are produced or "manufactured" in this manner, as some recent academic scholarship would make us believe. Communities in each of these practices follow their own quite distinctive procedures, their "methodologies," as it were, in arriving at their truth. Scientific methodology, relying on experimental results, is obviously different from that which operates in less objective branches of knowledge; and those that apply in the arts or in ethics are quite different again. But some such discursive procedure must always be in place, for otherwise the outcome would be an arbitrary assertion of collective will or victory in an ideological power struggle.

The way that communities function in establishing their ethical norms and values provides the most decisive argument against subjectivist or emotivist theories of ethics. The view that "nothing is good or bad but thinking makes it so," as Hamlet puts it, is countered by the realization that what is good or bad is not an individual subjective matter but a collective one, reached after a process of debate, according to a procedure acceptable within a community. It is the debate that establishes what is good or bad and not the feelings, wills, or desires of any of the participants before they enter it. How such a debate will go can never be predicted in advance, except, of course, where the decision is already a foregone conclusion, in which case the debate is constrained and spurious. An open debate often produces surprising results that none of the participants could have expected.

Such debates and deliberations within ethical communities regarding truth and falsity in ethics take a number of characteristic forms. Within the one community there are usually a number of divergent schools of thought and opposed leaders of opinion who are engaged in intense argumentation, following the methods, principles, and procedures of acceptable discourse for that particular community and its culture. One or another of these schools or leaders will eventually win out over the others, and its views will be instituted as authoritative, pronounced to be orthodox, rational, or commonsense, whereas the losing parties' views will be castigated as heretical, irrational, or absurd. In this way acceptable and accepted standards will be established. Countless examples of such processes can be given from all kinds of ethical communities throughout the course of ethical history. This is also the way in which what counts as valid reasoning, as knock-down rebuttal or proof, as evidence for and against, as special pleading and extenuation is determined. And what will be acceptable in one community might not be in another or might be in some respect but not in others. This is the reason that one ethical community finds it so difficult to debate with another; but within itself the criteria that apply are usually not in dispute. Even where there is such controversy, a final decision on any such matter can normally be arrived at in the context of the given community.

Often there will be but two main contending factions, the rigorists and the latitudinarians, as, for example, in the debates recorded in the Talmud where the school of Rabbi Shamai stood opposed to that of Rabbi Hillel.

The nature and diversity of such schools and differences of opinion depend crucially on the historical location of a community and the pressures and processes of change it is undergoing. Where there are strong incentives for adaptation to prevailing realities, then there will be compromisers eager to find a middle-ground reconciliation; but these will be opposed by zealots who will tend to purism, be resistant to such changes, and reaffirm the essential core principles of the ethic. These differences will become acrimonious when an ethical community has to confront a rival one within the same society and the choice is either to fight or to be reconciled. The issue will be debated within each community and the argument will be at its most intense and most heated. If the strain becomes too great, the community will split and divide into orthodox and heterodox parties, each accusing the other of heresy or treason. At such times violence can easily ensue and both parties will resort to every available means of persuasion, including cajolery, blackmail, the forging of documents, the creation of myths, and so on. Only in such circumstances does ethical disputation degenerate to become completely unethical and subject to the vagaries of power struggles.

Even in normal times, so to speak, the level of divergence permitted within the one community will differ, depending on how rigidly structured or firmly bound it is. However, in all such communities there must be some limits beyond which no adherent is permitted to go or will go for fear of complete exclusion and isolation. Some communities enforce authoritative decisions in a narrow and legalistic fashion; others are more tolerant and only insist on general guidelines that leave wide scope for differences in interpretation. When a community is so liberal and tolerant or weak to permit everyone to be, so to speak, "a law unto himself," to proceed as he or she sees fit, then this is usually symptomatic of the fact that it is in a state of dissolution. Many ethical communities are in this state at present.

Thus the relation between an individual and one or more ethical communities depends on his position in relation to them and on how exclusive or liberal they are. However, the individual never proceeds in total solitude, led only by the guiding light of his inner conscience or solely by dictates of reason or feeling, as if he were a kind of Robinson Crusoe of ethics. Nor does the responsible individual simply do what he is told by a superior ethical authority, a father confessor figure. An individual makes his own decisions, but a community and its traditions are always the source of reference for the individual when acting alone or in consultation with others. He might not be aware of this and act quite intuitively, but the background to this will always be some kind of upbringing in a given tradition that will reflect past debates and contentions within its ethical community.

All this is hard to gauge at present, because ethical communities are mostly in a debilitated state. Now when people act, they seem to do so without reference to any established ethical community, so it seems as if each individual has to decide for himself what is right and wrong. The traditional communities, such as the churches, universities, or civic bodies, now often focus on ritualistic inessentials or restrict themselves to vague general pronouncements on more important matters. Either way, they fail to provide proper guidance. On the other hand, new ethical communities, such as the movement for human rights, Amnesty International, the various ecology movements, or professional ethics groups are too specifically focused on one particular ethical interest; they are single-issue communities that do not provide a comprehensive ethical way of life. How to re-establish proper ethical communities is one of the key problems of ethics in a society in which people lack fundamental attachments to which they can adhere and through which they acquire a sense of belonging.

Having considered the communal aspect, we now turn to the individual side of the equation. Ethical action must always be individual action, not only in the tautological sense that groups are only collections of individuals so that whatever they do is actually carried out by their constituent members, but also in the substantive sense that it is the individual who carries primary responsibility for ethical acts. Ethics entails individual action in this strong sense. It is not always so in activities outside the ethical sphere, where the group, the organization, or the institution carries the primary responsibility and no one person is held to be individually accountable. As we have already shown, this is a situation so prevalent in contemporary society that it has become an ethos inimical to ethics. It was also quite characteristic of a pre-ethical ethos, where the collectivity of the clan or family took responsibility for the acts of its members who could not be directly blamed or punished for their misdeeds. But in ethics both of these conditions of individual non-responsibility are not available, especially so as it is not the act itself that counts as much as the intention with which it is done, which by definition is an individual subjective matter. The ethical community can advise and guide as to what is right and wrong, but it is ultimately the individual who must bear ethical responsibility for an act on his or her own behalf alone.

This is the reason that ethics and individualism are so closely bound up with one another, as we have already gleaned from our historical studies. From their earliest stages the four main types of ethics propounded more or less individualising definitions of what is a man and provided self-responsible models of the good man. And conversely, whenever this individualizing thrust has weakened so, too, has the disposition toward an ethical life. In modern European history the individualist trends have generally prevailed; the Reformation was a key turning point in the rise of modern individualism and it also brought with it the individualistic Protestant ethics, which was the basis for later Enlightenment individualism and a secular ethics. In the twentieth century the opposite tendencies have come to the fore. Anti-individualism emerged decisively with the onset of the totalitarianisms, all of which preached some variant or other of collectivism and a group ethos. In another form under capitalism it appears as so-called consumer individualism, an oxymoron that signifies an anonymous adaptation to the market. These developments, together with the prevalence of corporatism and "organization man" as the dominant type, have weakened any sense of individuality, which in so many different ways is essential for ethical action. For ultimately, only the individual is ethically responsible, so that where individuality wanes so does responsibility.

It is the individual, too, who must assess a situation as calling for an ethical response. This is the ethical predicament in which one finds oneself, and it is often a unique occurrence that one must perceive from one's own point of view. In this sense the ethical predicament is specific to the individual and the situation in which that person is placed on a given occasion. The individual must feel himself called upon to act by the ethical predicament as he perceives it. If he fails to grasp it as an ethical predicament or sees it differently, then no ethical action might be called for or perhaps a different kind of response altogether might be required. It all depends on the individual's sense of the predicament, for that elicits the action or fails to do so.

The ethical predicament might be either very obvious or very obscure. It is obvious, for example, when a drowning child cries for help, for almost everyone in our society will, under normal circumstances, realize that something needs to be done and try to save it. However, from this it does not follow that the person involved will know how to do it. Once again, it will be obvious if, for example, he is a good swimmer in good health and the accident occurs in a swimming pool; then he knows he is duty bound to jump in. On the other hand, it will be equally obvious that there is personally nothing for him to do if the accident occurs during a stormy night at sea and the child falls overboard from a fast-moving ship; the responsibility is then the captain's. However, it is not obvious what to do, though still obvious that something needs to be done, if the child might potentially be saved but the rescue attempt can only be undertaken at great hazard to oneself and others, which could lead to the loss of more lives. In such a predicament the brave, heroic, and resourceful people will distinguish themselves from others.

But the predicament is still ethically obvious, even though the decision to act is difficult for those involved.

However, there are ethical predicaments that are far from obvious, some so much so that most people do not even recognize that there is anything ethically amiss or questionable in the situation calling upon them to respond. This often occurs when what they are habitually doing is quite wrong. Such things are prone to occur in interpersonal relations. Thus there are many people who do not realize that what they are doing to another demeans, humiliates, or insults that person, or they do not recognize this when other people commit such outrages. These are the obtuse or callous people, the ones who find it difficult to put themselves into another person's shoes. The obtuse ones can realize what it is they are doing if it is explained to them by someone they trust and acknowledge as more perceptive. The callous ones will remain stubborn and insensitive, regardless of the amount of explanation or expostulation offered, for, as the Bible puts it, their hearts are hardened against it. Wrongs of this kind can be done to a specific single person on a unique occasion or they might be so habitually perpetrated by one group on another as to be accepted as normal. This can happen in matters of racial or social injustice, where one people or class dominates and exploits another. Thus owners of slaves or employers of foreign laborers could become so callous as to lose all moral sense of what they were doing to others, whom they eventually ceased to perceive as human beings like themselves. Not to perceive others as fully human is always a sure indication of gross moral dereliction toward them.

It is because an ethical predicament, such as the ones referred to previously, need not be obvious that ethical intelligence or sensitivity plays such a crucial role in ethical action. And this, too, is very much an individual matter, for some people have such discriminating capacities and some do not, and many only to a limited degree. What it involves is an emotional intelligence requiring an extensive cultivation and refinement of feelings, perceptions, and sensibilities.[2] Ethical discretion or tact is one example of such a quality. It is something essential in any act of extending charity to others more poorly placed, for without it one demeans the recipient and so defeats one's own charitable intent—one ends up taking away with one hand what one gives with the other. Much of ethical behavior in complex social situations is such a delicate matter. Sympathy and compassion are called for and other such qualities, which some people possess and others do not. To feel another's hidden pain, fear, or worry and adequately to respond to it is not equally given to everyone.

In fact, the exercise of all ethical virtues calls in most cases, except for the very obvious ones, for some measure of emotional intelligence, a point that philosophers of ethics have tended to obscure, and those that do recognize something like it—such as Aristotle, who invokes the term *prudence* (*sophrosyne*) to account for it—render it far too intellectually and rationalistically. Thus the exercise of proper courage requires more than just prudence or any such deliberative intellectual qualities, but rather the emotional intelligence of a sense of oneself in relation to the dangers facing one and what would ensue and how one would bear it if one did or did not act in the right ways. The obvious heroic courage of the soldier who wins medals might require prudence to know when and how to act but little in the way of emotional intelligence, for such a man behaves in approved and specified ways that are officially set down and apparent to everyone. However, the moral courage required to stand up against the authorities, perhaps in disobeying an order that one knows to be ethically wrong, requires qualities of another kind, such as self-possession, spirited pride, and instinctive self-affirmation, which are matters of emotional intelligence.

An ethical act such as this calls on qualities of the whole personality, among which the cultivated emotions are more central than any others. However, in drawing this close link between ethics and the emotions, we are not asserting any kind of emotivist theory of ethics. Ethical statements are not expressions of feeling, as crude positivistic theories of meaning maintain. To act ethically is not to be driven by one's passions; nor is there any inner struggle between reason and the passions involved, such that either the one or the other has to win out. Such views of the relation between ethics and the emotions, current at least since late-Stoicism, are based on a very partial and flawed understanding of the emotions and their role in action. The term *emotional intelligence* is intended to undercut any such simple-minded opposition of passion and reason or of feeling and intellect. For the feelings are not unintelligent and intelligence requires capacities of feeling. Unfortunately, the emotional side of life is that which is still least understood and at present most neglected.

The emotions and other qualities of character that are appropriate to ethics have all to be learned and culturally acquired. They are not innate, though they have a biological basis in crude urges and the feelings of basic social bonds. Certainly, the emotional intelligence required to grasp the ethical import of a situation has to be inculcated through the kind of education that is only available in the higher cultures. However, no amount of learning will guarantee that a person will come to possess these qualities of character, for they are not mere matters of indoctrination or training. They cannot be taught as habits, dispositions, or techniques, either in the way in which Aristotle conceived of it or in the way in which current exponents of so-called "social skills" perpetuate in an unthinking application of psychological stereotypes to character development. In matters of learning, ethics once again resembles aesthetics; some people have ethical talents just as others have artistic, and some are just ethically "unmusical," as Weber might have put it. Even brothers or sister subjected to the very same educational upbringing in ethics or the arts can mature differently as characters—one sensitive, the other unfeeling, like Cordelia and her sisters Goneril and Regan. In the arts a capacity to be creative or even appreciative cannot be acquired by teaching alone, but without any teaching it cannot be had at all; education is necessary but not sufficient, for there are other imponderables at work. To a large extent it is the same with ethical intelligence and many other ethical qualities. Thus, for example, ethical tact is a little like a sense of humor: some people grasp jokes immediately, others have to have them explained and so lose the point; just so, tactless people cannot grasp what they are doing and have to have it pointed out to them, usually when it is too late to matter. In the most extreme cases just as there are people who are blind to beauty, so there are those who are deaf to the voice of conscience.

Indeed, one of the fundamental traditional functions of literature was to teach people to see and understand ethical predicaments and thereby to aid in the development of their ethical intelligence. Depending on its quality as literature, a given work did this crudely and didactically as mere preaching or in an artistically compelling and moving way so as to make people discover such things for themselves through their own insights and emotional experiences and so be more inclined to re-shape themselves and their own behavior accordingly. In this way literature provides the supreme schooling of emotional intelligence. The great myths, epics, dramas, and novels of the past had this kind of educative function, apart from whatever else they exemplified of the great range of literary values. This is the reason that despite its profoundly shocking and disturbing nature, great tragedy has ultimately an educative role, for through its emotional impact it solicits people to be more sensitive and understanding and so become better beings. In such literature the relation between ethics and art is at its closest. This does not hold for all of literature and certainly not for all the arts. But insofar as all the arts mutually support and sustain each other within the one culture, they are interconnected; thus a literary culture is upheld by all the other arts, and it in turn upholds an ethical way of life. Plato might have been naive in believing that music inculcates virtue, but it is not wrong to see in the music of a society a pointer to the ethical state of its ethos. In that respect the music current in contemporary popular culture, that of drugs, sex, and rock-and-roll, is an alarming symptom of something pathological in our ethos.

Music, literature, and the arts in general of contemporary society disclose indirectly the state of ethics. A signal lack of cultivation and refinement characterizes all of them. This is at least partly due to the lack of proper education both in the arts and in ethics. The educative role of literature for ethics has largely been neglected in our schools and universities. Even the classics are taught in a purely scholastic manner, without much reference to the ethical predicaments of ordinary living. The whole educative task of cultivating the relevant ethical qualities of character, both of intelligence and feeling, has largely been abandoned. Outside the schools, literature is a mere commodity of the publishing industry, providing distraction and entertainment but little else of value. The results can be seen in the ethical obtuseness and crudity, not to speak of the incidence of criminality, current among the younger generation. The young are becoming as ethically desensitized by the regular fare of television and computer games that they imbibe constantly in much of their waking hours as they are aesthetically deadened by the mechanical pounding of the beat that accompanies these activities.

All this makes people incompetent in recognizing and in dealing with ethical predicaments where things are not simple or obvious, where it is not patently evident what needs to be done or how to go about doing it. Such people have little individual grasp of a situation or the capacity to respond to it in the urgency of the event. There are few active ethical communities they can appeal to, and even those available are usually not of much help where individual initiative is required. For nobody, except the person who is in that predicament, can fully grasp what it involves. This is the reason that we should not presume to judge others until we find ourselves in their shoes.

This is also the reason that the ability to know and do the right thing cannot be just a matter of acting according to rules or keeping to laws. The life circumstances in which ethical decisions have to be made are usually extremely complex. It is difficult, if not impossible, to enumerate all the factors that play a part in such a situation, usually one involving interactions among a number of people. Weighing up the relative importance of the relevant factors that are noted is always a matter of great uncertainty. The actor who is caught up in a predicament where an ethical act is called for suffers from the added uncertainty that he does not have full knowledge of the situation; for example, he does not know what the others in the case know, think, feel, or desire, and frequently, by the very nature of the case, he cannot know this prior to his own action. Complicating the fragmentary and partial knowledge he does have are his own feelings, desires, interests, and biases. The actor is often caught up in what in military parlance is called the "fog of war," where every participant only sees a small part of the action and nobody sees the whole while the battle is in progress. And yet decisions have to be made and actions performed in ethical as in military matters. Even where there are clear and unambiguous rules or tactical principles, it is never possible to know exactly how and where they apply. Life is not a game that can be played by the rules alone.

In the complexity of such a real-life situation, one in which decisions have to be unhesitatingly and quickly made, to know what to do and to do it calls for a personal response that brings into play diverse aspects of ethical character. Perhaps the most important of these is an intuitive grasp of what is at stake that is ethically relevant, the emotional motivation to be bound by it, and the will to act according to what is ethically called for in the case. The insight into the situation and the feeling toward it are not to be dissociated: one sees and thinks and feels at once, and the one would not be possible without the other. Thus, for example, one feels ethical indignation at what one sees to be an act of injustice, but the feeling is not a consequence of a prior seeing, for if one did not at the same time feel indignant, one would not see the injustice, since there are always so many other ways of perceiving the situation. Seeing injustice and feeling aroused about it provide the motivation for an ethical act, which might not necessarily follow since it might be frustrated by impediments of will, as, for example, such things as a lack of resolution or courage or inhibitions that one cannot overcome or some other such inner weakness. But where the act does ensue, then it is often a spontaneous outflow of the ethical insight and the emotion with which it is charged.

Very often the ethical person sees and acts in the one spontaneous gesture that is without hesitation or reflection. Thus, such a person might dive in at the risk of his life to save a drowning child or extend a helping hand to a fugitive in danger of being apprehended. Later, after the event, if asked why he did it, such a person might reply that at the time it seemed the natural thing to do, that there was something obvious and simple about it. Those who displayed great moral courage during the Second World War, such as those who saved Jews, characteristically explain themselves in these terms. It is in this sense that we can speak of knowing what one ought to do and doing it as a matter of ethical intuition.

Intuition plays an extremely important role in ethics. However, we take this word here in the simple sense where it is closely related to spontaneity, not in the theoretical one of ethical philosophy, such as, for example, the intuition of an extra-sensory quality of moral goodness that G. E. Moore invoked on purely speculative theoretical grounds. Real intuition, as it occurs in practical life, has nothing to do with such imputed non-natural qualities nor is there anything theoretic about it or anything non-naturalistic. It is the simple capacity of knowing without hesitation what to do, such as artists possess when they paint or compose or embroider a tale. It is instinctive, but not a result of any innate instincts, being wholly a learned matter—not nature, but second nature. So, too, in ethics people acquire an intuitive instinct for what to do or say, the outcome of upbringing and character formation that is acquired gradually over a very long period, but it is exercised immediately, often instantaneously so. Just so, the painter who has spent a lifetime mastering draughtsmanship might toss off a drawing in the one coordinated gesture of the pen.

The role of intuition in ethics and aesthetics also bears more extensive comparison. The intuitive grasp of life situations or ethical predicaments is very like the immediate grasp of works of art. Character qualities of perceptiveness, insight, imagination, and feeling are involved in both. Such capacities develop out of simpler "Gestalt" abilities to perceive wholes or structural complexes and to "see" connections between distinct fields of meaning. Motivation and feelings that determine interest, attention, and concentration play an even more crucial role in developed forms of seeing and understanding than they do in the simpler kinds. Hence, real-life situations, involving subtle personal relations in a complex social context, are in these respects not all that dissimilar to works of art, especially literary works. An ethical predicament that has to be understood in its intricate complexity, requires similar capacities to those involved in the appreciation of a book. Of course, seeing, understanding, and feeling are not necessarily acting as well, for the latter calls for firmness of will together with determination, courage, and resourcefulness, which might be absent and which are generally not called for in aesthetics.

It is for all these reasons that cultivation of intuitive capacities is one of the main goals of ethical education. Intuition in ethics is acquired, but it is not a matter of dispositions in the classical Aristotelian sense of ingrained traits. In most respects it is the opposite of that, being more a matter of flexible and fluid responsiveness somewhat akin to quick wit. An ethical character does not operate with stock responses; it calls for qualities such as tact and discretion, alertness and incisiveness, empathy and sympathy, and in general a nuanced rapport with others in situations that are not exactly like any encountered previously. This is what we mean by emotional intelligence, which requires both seeing, understanding, and feeling at once—that is, grasping what is at stake in a responsive way. In ethics, as in aesthetics, sensibility and sensitivity are not to be dissociated. The qualities of character that are a matter of such emotional intelligence are also acquired, but they are not learned as skills or techniques. The present emphasis in education on teaching social skills goes counter to any proper development of ethical character for it encourages manipulative abilities that are the very opposite of being emotionally in touch with others. Hence, it goes also against being an ethically responsive and responsible person.

The Disposition of Roles

The parallels between ethics and aesthetics go even further than we have so far indicated. There are crucial structural similarities in the way that ethical and artistic activities are practiced as social functions. Both involve practical and theoretical knowledge of many different varieties exercised by different people, frequently with specialized endowments. Such distinct practitioners play, as it were, different roles in the structural complex of each practice. They are mostly functionally differentiated and sometimes even distinct figures bearing generic names. To explain how the ethical and aesthetic fields are analogously structured as social practices, we shall outline five such constituent roles or partial practices. In some respects this is an arbitrary number, for even more distinctions could be drawn or still fewer but for our present heuristic purposes five is adequate as a basis for comparison.

In the arts we distinguish the following five characteristic figures: the artist or creator, the connoisseur or critic, the scholar or educator, the aesthetician or philosopher, and, finally, the artistic innovator or reformer. Each of these has a distinctive role and function in the practice of the arts and each appears in various historical guises in a more or less specialized capacity, for often the same person can exercise two or more of these roles at once. Briefly put, they can be distinguished as follows: the artist is the person producing the work of art; sometimes, as in filmmaking at present, this can be a collectivity rather than a single individual. The connoisseur or critic is that person who perceives, receives, and appreciates the artist's work, critically discussing, judging, and evaluating it in ways that the artist is frequently unable to do. The scholar or educator is the person who studies art in general, examining whole traditions or a corpus of works, and makes comparative studies frequently along historical lines. The aesthetician or philosopher is concerned with the most general features of aesthetic form or value and places these in relation to all kinds of other fields of value, such as ethics. Finally, the innovator or reformer is, as it were, the law-giver of art, the person who establishes new values and new standards that will result in new styles or even new arts. Obviously, this last function will be performed to some limited extent by every original artist, critic, or theoretician, but there are some people who are particularly renowned for this role even though they did not excel in any of the others. Thus, for example, Vincenzo Galilei, the father of the more famous son, was one of the most important musical innovators in history, though not himself a good composer.

There are five such distinct roles or figures in ethical practice as well. Comparable to the artist, there is the actor, the person who knows what to do and does it. Like the critic or connoisseur, there is the ethical judge of action, the wise or prudent person. The ethical scholar, historian, or educator is in an analogous position to the aesthetic counterpart. So, too, is the ethical philosopher. Finally, the ethical reformer or law-giver is like the aesthetic revolutionary or innovator.

The analogies in these roles or figures do not amount to exact correspondences for there are crucial differences as well. Ethics is not an activity productive of works, as art most often is; the good works of ethics are forms of conduct and not like objects or performances in art. Ethics is basically a regulative and directive activity and art a productive one. Hence, ethics is prone to regulating other activities, including the artistic ones, prescribing for them limits and restrictions, as well as directing them to realize certain kinds of values and goals. To its critics and opponents, ethics appears as a highly intrusive matter; the ethical man is castigated as a busybody who cannot mind his own business. And this is, strictly speaking, true for ethics has no special business of its own to mind but is concerned with all affairs. All attempts to restrict ethics to a specific field only narrow and stunt it. This has tended to happen of late, as only the two extremes of personal private life or universal human rights are admitted as ethical domains.

It is in keeping with its scope that ethical knowledge is a very special kind of knowledge; it is not like the practical know-how of the artist or like the theorizing of the scientist. It involves both practical and theoretical aspects but of a kind relevant to knowing what to do, not to how to make things or how to explain them. Yet despite all these differences, it is illuminating to concentrate on the analogies for that permits us to understand better how ethics as a conjoint activity of many types of constituent practices functions as a whole. To show this we now proceed to outline the five roles or figures in somewhat more detail.

Like the artist, the exemplary ethical actor, the good man, knows what to do and does it but is not necessarily able to critically justify why this and not any other course is the right thing to do or is capable of convincing other people that this is so. In normal circumstances such a person is the ordinary decent individual. In dangerous times such good people might act as heroes. But when asked why they did such risky things, all they could often say is that it seemed simply the obvious and intuitively evident thing to do, that it had required no deliberation or thought, and so on. Mostly such people were acting within an ethical tradition, such as that of Christian morality, or aristocratic honor, or communistic solidarity, which they had internalized completely so that its demands seemed natural to them.

By contrast, the judicious or wise person, one able to assess ethical issues and the actions of others, need not necessarily be a good man capable of acting heroically or even doing the right thing ethically when required. Such are people who are experienced in practical matters and have deliberative capacities that make them competent advisers with whom to take counsel about what to do. They are able to arrive at the right decision not only for themselves but also for others, taking all factors into account from another's point of view. They are good judges, but that does not mean that they are capable of action, for something different is involved in acting than in deliberating. The Nestors of this world are rarely its heroes.

The ethical judge and critic has ethical knowledge and is worldly wise in a way that need not call for any book learning about ethics as a whole. It is the scholar who has such knowledge, for it can only be gained through an educative process of study. Such a scholar or educator need not be particularly prudent or wise in practical affairs. Yet ethical education can make a practical difference. It can help one transcend the narrow parochialism of one's own ethical tradition and give one a perspective for understanding others. This is particularly useful in dealing with foreigners and strangers. It might also be helpful in cultivating tolerance toward those who espouse other ethics in one's own society and safeguard one from excessive narrowness or dogmatism in one's own ethics. As we have stressed before, education of itself does not necessarily make one good, but it does help to make one more understanding.

At its most general and abstract, ethical knowledge becomes philosophical. The ethical philosopher or sage is a distinctive figure in many ethical traditions. As we have seen from our historical studies, ethical philosophy served many purposes in the cultural economy of ethics; above all, it enabled syncretist fusions to be effected and it facilitated processes of rationalization to take place. Right throughout the history of the West philosophy has played a crucial role in ethics and in a similar way, though to a lesser extent, in the East as well. Unfortunately, however, at present ethical philosophy has become purely academic and there is not much that such philosophy can contribute to the urgent ethical problems of our time. We shall consider what is to be done about this presently.

The truly radical changes in ethical history were generally not produced by philosophers but by the revolutionary innovators called law-givers or great reformers. These are the rare charismatic individuals, frequently prophetic figures, who inaugurate a new ethical dispensation or radically transform an existing one. They usually give rise to ethical movements that bear their names. Thus people who follow such leaders call themselves by their names, as Franciscans, Lutherans, Calvinists, Rousseauists, St. Simonians, Tolstoyans, and so on. These individuals who bring about such radical transformations need not themselves be good or prudent or learned men and few of them had much knowledge of philosophy, but they were all men of ethical vision who could envisage a new way of life and advocate it with passionate intensity. If they could persuade others to believe in their message and follow them, then they inaugurated social movements with historically transforming potential.

The five roles or figures we have outlined are in actuality rarely discrete; they form a continuum in which there are no differentiating markers. Nor are they exclusive of each other, for the one person can simultaneously exercise two or more of these functions and, mostly, this is, indeed, the case. The good man can be prudent and critically astute, the prudent man can be learned, the learned philosophical, and the philosopher might be all of these at once, though this is very rarely the case. We have given an ideal-type presentation of these roles or figures; in reality they will always be mixed and apply in varying degrees to actual people.

In a fully developed and mature ethical culture, all five roles will be exercised in conjunction with each other to constitute an integrated ethical community. It is just the same with a developed artistic culture where artists are supported by critics and connoisseurs, frequently their patrons, and these in turn are enlightened by scholars and philosophers. An artist without such a supportive public cannot mature and soon comes to ruin. It is the same in ethics. It is not possible for people to acquire a sound ethical character and act rightly outside an ethical community where there is an ongoing concern with ethical matters, where people judge each other's actions scrupulously and examine them closely; where discourse and debate are carried on about ethical issues; where there is an ethical literature that is studied, among which there are frequently works of philosophy; and, finally, where those with a new ethical message are taken seriously and given heed, even if this only results in condemnation. And this also means that such an ethical culture cannot exist without genuinely good people, those willing and able to act on their ethical intuitions of rightness, for ultimately without such proof in practice, ethics becomes no more than idle talk or sermonizing. And without a basis in common everyday ethical life, learning and philosophy are no better than academic exercises. In a condition of failing ethical discourse in ordinary life and desiccated learning among the academics, there can be few prospects of any innovative ethical revolutions or even significant reforms. This is the situation we find ourselves in today.

It is now possible to restate the question we initially asked at the start of part 2—"Where does ethics stand today in our contemporary global civilization?"—in much more specific terms. We can rephrase it as, "How are the five roles of ethics being exercised at present?" This will provide an answer not merely in general historical and social terms, such as we have already given, but also in terms of the experienced actualities of ethical life. We need to know how ethical actions are actually performed in the context of real situations, such as are likely to occur in our time, how advice can be sought before the act and judgment rendered after it, how an ethical upbringing might be undertaken and to what extent this can still give rise to ethical character formation, how knowledge about ethics might be acquired, how it is theorized, and finally, whether there are people or movements capable of ethical innovation at present. Once we have specific answers to these questions, then we shall be in a position to assess where ethics stands today and how this might have altered over the course of the last century or so.

It is worth noting that there are analogous questions we can ask about the state of art in our culture. We can also separate for heuristic purposes of analysis the five roles or constituent practices of art and examine each one on its own. Such an assessment would soon reveal that in none of its roles is art in a very sound state. There is no coherent aesthetic culture anymore and what is left are fragments of artistic practices deriving from various discrepant sources, traditional and contemporary. This fact should make us very apprehensive about ethics as well. But this does not mean that we need give in to apocalyptic pronouncements of the "end of ethics" any more than to those of the "end of Art," which are already being thoughtlessly voiced in our time. That ethics suffers from what Adorno called "damaged life" is undoubtable; it is demonstrated in specific detail by his reflections on life in exile and it fits our preceding general sociological account of the conditions of life in contemporary society.[3] But that does not mean that the damage is so extensive as to be beyond any repair or that ethics is beyond recovery. Yet before we can make any such attempts, first we must gain a clearer sense of the damage that has been sustained.

We begin our assessment with the role of the ethical actor, the person called upon to act in an ethical predicament. Such a person will frequently now have great difficulty in being ethically decisive, sure, and confident of himself, so as to know unhesitatingly what is the right thing to do in the urgency of the ethical moment. He or she will no longer be able to rely on a fully formed and mature ethical character, for such is almost impossible to develop under the contemporary conditions of "damaged life." In particular, what is mostly likely to be lacking is emotional intelligence, which, as we previously pointed out, is so crucial to intuitive and spontaneous action. We no longer possess the ethical *nous* of tact and discretion that comes with emotional cultivation. Our emotional life is cruder and shallower and our character tends to be lacking in sophistication and complexity. One has only to compare the protagonists of the novels of a century ago with current ones to be struck by a difference that almost amounts to a change in human personality.

Our capacity for moral character formation and moral action has been particularly impaired; for morality is the aspect of our ethics that is under greatest attack. The onslaughts on individual conscience have, as we have seen, come from many quarters; the supports for it are weak and vacillating. Relatively speaking, morality is far worse situated than the other ethics because it is even worse off in respect of any viable ethical communities intent on maintaining a moral way of life. The churches and various other religious bodies still claim to be moral communities, but most of them have compromised with the powers of the world far too much and far too long to be taken seriously in this capacity. This does not mean that there are not many individuals who are upright moral beings within them. But, as events during the Second World War and subsequently in times of crisis have repeatedly proved, such people tend to be left in the lurch by the official authorities in emergency situations. Other social institutions that traditionally maintained moral standards, such as the universities or the press, have long ceased to have any moral significance. For them, the First World War and the chauvinism that it aroused were the decisive shibboleths that they failed to pass.

Hence, the moral actor, who is potentially anyone trying to be an autonomous individual in a law-regulated conformist society, faces exceptional difficulties that are often crippling. Such a society is given over to all those valuations that are antithetical to morality. Such are the values of the marketplace, of the state, of the educational institutions, of the media, and all the other dominant forces of our society. How under these circumstances anyone can become a moral being or survive with an intact conscience is only to be wondered at, though it happens more often than we have the right to assume. But even supposing that someone has somehow acquired the propensity of being a good man, then there are still the almost insurmountable problems of how this can be realized in the ordinary course of living at present.

There are no clear and simple answers as to what is the morally right thing to do, such as were provided by the old traditional moralities. The moral actor can no longer grasp a morally problematic situation with incisive insight and act with instinctive certitude, for at any one time in the ambiguous complexity of contemporary settings all kinds of other ethical demands, deriving from old and new fragments of civic or social ethics, are bound to arise and clash with the moral calls of conscience. In such a contradictory context even the individual with the best moral will is often in a quandary as to what to do, for the promptings of conscience cannot always be followed, as we shall show in the next chapter; sometimes they must be compromised for the sake of other ends. Anyone who follows an absolute moral course of pure intent and acts only on such an uncompromising conscience is more than likely to suffer defeat after defeat, of both an ethical as well as pragmatic kind. Thus, for example, the statesman who is never willing to sacrifice even one innocent person, no matter what the consequences, will very likely only end up by handing over the reins of power to dictators or terrorists, which is ethically far worse. The private person who always acts against what he takes to be the immoral demands of the state will inevitably end up a martyr, which is a self-defeating gesture looked at from an ethically more comprehensive point of view. When and how to compromise the moral demands of conscience, and when not to do so no matter what, becomes a painfully agonizing problem.

Contemporary beings cannot look to the integrity of ethical character that the ideal figures of the past provided as models. Nobody can be a gentleman anymore. Thus Polonius' maxim "only to thyself be true . . . and thou canst not be false to any man" no longer holds for there is no true Self. The Self has become so socially fragmented that self-identity as an integrated ethical character can no longer obtain. Society imposes on people far too many disparate and divergent roles for any kind of consistency and unity of character to be possible. Hence the prevalence of role-playing, which in the past was viewed as ethically dubious and frequently denounced as deception, hypocrisy, or at least insincerity. Now it has become the indispensable means of self-presentation. It is not surprising that as a theoretical concept it is promoted extensively in contemporary psychology and sociology. Role-playing is now necessitated as a practice, for society imposes so many diverse functions on the same person; home, office or factory, church, political arena, educational institution, leisure playground, and many others are the sites for a diversity of roles. And with these roles come all kinds of conflicting values and opposed ethical norms.

Under such confused and ethically ambiguous conditions even the best intentioned of moral actors, even someone who is a really serious individual, will not be capable of developing a coherent moral character. At best such a person will only succeed in performing many isolated and disjointed moral acts, "beau gestes" in a contemporary sense. These are, nevertheless, exemplary gestures whose importance is immense, for they affirm a moral stance that would otherwise be lost and forgotten. Such, for example, are the actions of the various kinds of "whistleblowers." But as this example demonstrates, the costs in personal terms of doing the right thing is invariably high; careers, friendships, spouses, as well as income, are often forfeited. In totalitarian or dictatorial societies such acts led inevitably to martyrdom. Thus the person who "in spite of all" is determined to make life morally meaningful must be realistically aware of the costs incurred and be prepared to meet them, for otherwise dejection will ensue at the first serious setback.

How can the conditions for a moral life be ameliorated? How can the capacity for moral action be repaired? The first of these questions places its emphasis on cultural factors, the second on individual ones, which seem distinct but actually must be seen together. Social and individual efforts for moral improvement must come together even though one attacks them from different directions, like the excavations of a tunnel through a mountain, which also begin from opposed ends but must come together in the middle. Cultural improvement is to be sought through the building of moral communities, no matter how limited and small these might be to begin with, perhaps no more than a few kindred souls coming together. Individual improvement is to be sought through the cultivation of emotional intelligence, which is a key aspect of maturation and character formation. This is what permits one to grasp ethical predicaments so as to know what to do on any given occasion. To have the strength of will and courage to do it is, of course, the crucial test for action and might not necessarily follow but is more likely to if one has a moral conscience. Such a conscience cannot be acquired in isolation but only through upbringing and interaction with others in a moral community. Hence, conscience and community are the individual and social facets of the one moral ethos and must be seen together in a balanced relation.

This brings us to the second of the basic ethical roles, that of judgment and criticism, which is involved in deliberating or reflecting on one's own acts or advising those of others. The main difficulty facing the exercise of moral judgment at present is the lack of contemporary moral communities given to practicing a deliberative moral discourse. This is analogous to the decay of artistic communities of connoisseurs, among whom critical discourse flourished and aesthetic judgments were debated. What is left of traditional groups of moralists within churches or universities are under assault, both from outside and inside forces. In other newer institutions such discussions are discouraged and avoided. Thus in the helping professions, moral deliberative discourse is considered "judgmental" and substituted with non-ethical term and ways of judging, so that instead of considering what is right and wrong, only issues of health, adjustment, efficacy, or efficiency are ever raised. But often these are merely disguised euphemisms for implicit non-ethical judgments whose standards remain tacit and so cannot be openly questioned or disputed.

The same thing takes place in the arts, where the avoidance of critical aesthetic discourse makes for an absence of connoisseurship and thereby for an inability to make evaluative judgments. Such judgments tend to be discouraged, and instead issues of quality are reduced to matters of taste or, even worse, to ideological propriety or political correctness. The upshot of this anti-aesthetics is that the value of works of art is completely relativized. One is now taught even in some universities that there are no distinctions between the works of Shakespeare and those of Ian Fleming, for as a character James Bond is just as "interesting" as Hamlet. Thus in the arts there is a debasement of judgment that is very like the relativisation of judgment in ethics.

Judgment is a critical faculty that requires its own cultivation. On many occasions judgment follows action as a reflection on what someone else has done or what one has done oneself. The ethical judge is then in the same position as the legal judge, who adjudicates on an already committed deed that is charged with being an offence or impropriety. Such a judge can call all participants and witnesses to account and so gain an overall perspective of the act that would not have been available to the actors at the time. He is also aware of the consequences that ensued, such as how much harm or benefit resulted to everyone involved, which is also something that might have been unforeseeable or only imperfectly predictable before the act was done. Thus the further the judge is removed from the act, in time, mood of the moment, and pressure of events, the more he is able to deliberate upon it impartially and in that sense objectively.

However, between the uninvolved and disinterested stance of the judge and that of the actor himself there is a whole range of intermediate positions. For the closer someone comes to the act in propinquity of interest and concern, the more that person is a participant himself. If he is totally involved, then his role becomes ultimately only barely distinguishable from that of the actor; he becomes an accessory to the act. All kinds of counselors and helpers who are called upon for advice by the actor before he acts are in such intermediate positions. Some degree of responsibility always devolves upon them if they are complicit with the actor in what he does. For where ethical advice is sought, given, and acted on, responsibility for the act, at least partially and indirectly, also falls on the adviser; thus one can also incur guilt for giving someone else the wrong or misleading counsel. The person who constantly and habitually advises others takes on the role of ethical teacher and his responsibility for what his charges do is even more pronounced. Parents are normally assumed to be the primary ethical teachers of their children and can be blamed when these go astray, at least in their young years. Though even this degree of parental responsibility tends to be abjured these days.

The qualities of character enabling one to perform any of these functions of ethical criticism, ranging from advice before the act to judgment after it, have traditional appelations that are but rarely used now. These are terms such as *wisdom, prudence, scrupulousness, dispassionateness, integrity, judiciousness*, and many others, which now sound old fashioned and when applied to someone often carry an ironic edge. This is itself an indication that ethical criticism and discussion are no longer accepted activities of everyday life. If utilized at all, they are reserved for special occasions or, worse still, used as propaganda by moralistic conservatives to browbeat their liberal opponents.

The social reality behind these sad facts is that the practices in which the qualities of ethical criticism need to be acquired and constantly rehearsed to remain in use are no longer a prominent part of the everyday ethos of our culture. These activities were mainly carried out within ethical communities. They consisted of constant and continued ethical debates and discussions about general and particular acts. Dialectical confrontations between communities involving more contentious differences concerning norms and values would also take place. In all these ways a critical culture of ethics was maintained. The people of such a culture were constantly intent on viewing every possible kind of act from an ethical point of view: acts that were done or might be done, real actions or those in fiction, individual ones or those of a group kind, and so on. And just as a critical culture in the arts, in which much talk about works of art goes on, promotes the aesthetic qualities of character that endow people with the capacities to appreciate and evaluate, so an analogous critical culture in an ethical ethos produces individuals who are able to judge and justify.

Where does our contemporary ethos of a global civilization stand in respect of these activities of ethical criticism? Are we now intent on the scrupulous examination of acts? Do we examine our own consciences as a habitual practice? Do we probe our own motives and those of others, even when there is nothing wrong with the act itself? Do we engage in continual discussions and debates upon such matters? Do we normally solicit ethical advice from others before acting? Are there institutionalised fora for public debate on ethical issues? Is the teaching of ethics a normal part of upbringing? Is there a literature of various kinds of texts to which all such matters are referred? Are such texts used in teaching and do people take them seriously in conducting their lives? Do people look to exemplary ethical individuals, either in fiction or in reality? Are there people who are lauded and taken as role models? Even in raising these questions, it is patently apparent that they are derived from and apply to a much more traditional culture than our own. They do not fit contemporary conditions of our ethos, which is not fundamentally ethically inclined. Ethics, in so far as it is still operative, is effective in quite different ways than it used to be. Much has happened, as we have already shown, to displace it from its central place in the ethos.

What might be done to repair our capacity for ethical judgment? The first priority in this is simply to reintroduce ethical discourse. People should allow themselves to judge and practice judgment wherever this is called for—that is, to view and talk about life situations from an ethical perspective. In this way something like a culture of ethical connoisseurship might begin to be reconstituted. It is the same with respect to the arts, where a critical discourse that judges must be recovered, for without that there is no discrimination; there are no standards and no way of valuing some works over others. Those who denounce aesthetic judgment are the unwitting advocates for market valuations instead of proper values, for it is price that then establishes by default any sense of distinction and worth. It is analogous with those who argue against moral judgment; they, too, permit the encroachment of non-ethical and even immoral standards of value, usually those to do with status, power, and money, to obtain instead. The so-called realists who advise us not to be "judgmental" but to accept things as they are, not to look for guilt or to blame but to learn to "handle" people and situations—namely, to manipulate them—those professionals who urge us to be impartially "objective," all such people who try to dissuade us from exercising judgment are simply working for the demoralization of society. What they have succeeded in inculcating in many ordinary people is a new kind of shame, the shame of appearing unsophisticated, naive, old-fashioned, and moralistic in making judgments. Thus people have become inhibited from using any of the old and simple expressions that are now almost banned from official discourse; liars and thieves in public places are no longer called that; rather new euphemisms such as "credibility gap" and "misallocation of resources" have appeared, which disguise the fact that someone is morally guilty. All such immoralities that come to be generally condoned hide behind smoke-screens of euphemism. The Nazis, even among themselves, did not speak of killing Jews, only of implementing the measures of a Final Solution, resettlement, disinfection, and so on. All regimes resort to such talk when they need to hide their misdeeds. One of the ways of guarding against this obfuscation is simply to return to the simple and direct discourse of moral judgment.

However, we should not rush to judge or use the language of judgment without restraint. An excess of judgment can lead to self-righteousness and maliciousness. This has always been traditionally recognized in all those sayings that urge discretion in judgment. "Judge the deed and not the doer" is invoked, in order to avoid blanket condemnation of a person guilty of one wrong act. "Never judge a man until you are in his shoes" acts as a warning against cold disapproval and rejection devoid of imagination and sympathy for the person in a difficult situation. And, finally, there is the gospel saying "judge not that ye shall not be judged," which seems to abjure all moral judgment but is actually only a warning against complete condemnation and leaves open the ever-present possibility of forgiveness.

To render judgment is a matter of discourse, and discourse has to be learned. The discourse of morals, as of the other branches of ethics, depends to some degree on moral knowledge, and this in turn is to some extent bound up with formal education. Hence, the educative role of ethics is the next that we must consider. Education is essential to ethics—not in the obvious sense that it makes people ethically better; it rarely in fact does that; rather in a more round-about way, in that it upholds an ethical culture. It teaches one how to conduct ethical discourse, and though there is a large gap between talk and action, yet discourse is essential for the cultural continuity of ethics that makes action possible.

At present there is an urgent need to introduce the teaching of moral discourse into the educational program for young people. But doing it through schools as they are constituted at present has not proved very productive. Imposing moral lore on unwilling students as part of religious instruction in a classroom setting has repeatedly shown that at best they treat it as a marginal curriculum subject of no great importance and at worst as an opportunity to misbehave. Some better way must be found to make students, especially the younger ones in the lower grades, take morality and ethical instruction generally with greater seriousness. We have some suggestions to offer as to how this might be initiated at the higher levels of university study. But much greater and more committed pedagogic thought and research are called for than are at present available into this whole question of ethical education.

The purpose of ethical education is to make ethical knowledge available, generally of one's own ethical system, but where this is undertaken in a more enlightened spirit, then it will also teach about other ethics as well. As we have already indicated, to have ethical knowledge in this sense is different from being able to act or judge correctly. Knowledge is a much more intellectual matter, normally acquired from texts. Such knowledge might not of itself be very effective on an individual level, yet it has great importance for an ethical ethos as a whole. A culture in which ethical knowledge is extensively cultivated is a much more ethically mature and sophisticated one than a culture without it. In some cases it might even be a more enlightened and tolerant culture. Every culture develops its own type of ethical knowledge and the discourse that goes with it, and it nurtures its young accordingly. We shall briefly outline a few of the main types of Western educative practices.

The classical Greco-Roman tradition of ethical education was focused on rhetorical training directed to oratory and public debate. For this purpose the works of the poets—above all, Homer—were studied. A small elite graduated to a philosophical education, utilizing texts of the canonic schools of philosophy. Mostly, however, this was a literary education. The arrival of Christianity, as we have seen in our historical account, at first made little difference to this educational program; nearly all the pagan classics continued to be studied. However, gradually, an alternative Christian moral education developed, based on the Bible and the Church Fathers. Eventually, this displaced the humanistic traditions, especially during the so-called Dark Ages, when the monasteries became almost the sole educational institutions.

A humanistic ethical education only revived with the Renaissance, when more of the ancient texts were recovered and taught and new textbooks were written with an expressly ethical purpose by such authors as Erasmus, Vives, Castiglione, and others. In the modern period the humanistic trend culminated in the nineteenth-century German conception of *Bildung*. Institutionally, it was based on the newly founded *Gymnasium* at the secondary level and the newly reformed medieval university at the tertiary. These reforms originated from the circle of officials around Wilhelm von Humboldt, the founder of Berlin University, who based himself on the literary authors of Weimar and the philosophers of Jena—that is, on the new *Dichter und Denker* of the German cultural revival. Educationally considered, *Bildung* was a very impressive program that aimed to produce a highly refined, all-rounded, mature, and culturally knowledgable character. It combined the literary ideal of the *Schöne Seele* with the philosophic and scientific ideals of the *gebildeter Mann*. Goethe, so proficient in both these respects, was its cynosure.

Ethically considered, however, *Bildung* had weaknesses and these became more evident later in the nineteenth century, when the *Reich* was founded as Germany was unified. It did not translate too well into practical action and critical judgment, remaining far too idealistic, intellectual, and aesthetic. It promoted elevated thoughts and fine feelings that could be given no practical expression in ordinary life, especially during the Wilhelmine period when habits of obedience to authority and conformism in opinion were promoted. These weaknesses led directly to the German tragedy of the twentieth century, the First World War and the Nazi regime. Traditional *Bildung* was not able to counteract the chauvinistic tendencies that led to these disasters; on the contrary, a deformed notion of German *Bildung* encouraged and sustained them. The gradual infusion of nationalist sentiments into the German educational curriculum at all levels meant that, eventually, support for the Nazis among students, teachers, and professors was higher than among any other segment of society.

At present, *Bildung* is no more than a distant memory even in Germany. Education has tended to become largely professional and technical. Its main purpose is to foster professional competence and technical specialization. It does not have much to do with the promotion of ethics or character development. The ethical dimension has even been lost in disciplines such as literary studies where it used to be pronounced until very recently. The belated recognition that something is seriously wrong with this situation, deriving from the numerous ethical scandals in society, especially in business affairs, has led to the hurried creation of courses on ethics in all kinds of professional contexts; medical, legal, technological, scientific, and so on. But the idea that a problem so deep-rooted in our culture can be repaired by such quick-fix methods itself reveals an extraordinary level of ignorance and naiveté about ethics. One of the main aims of this work is to help correct such misconceptions by revealing the full scope of what an ethical culture involves. Once such a culture has been as deeply corrupted and disturbed as it has in our societies, there are no easy solutions. The process of repairing it must be undertaken at all kinds of levels—social, cultural, and individual— and though education is one aspect that must be promoted, this cannot be done through the kinds of educational practices currently in force.

One of the most important unsolved problems of educational theory at present is how ethics might be brought back into tertiary studies. The sorry state of ethical education in the universities is institutionally indicated by the absence of any department of ethics or morals. It is highly significant that by contrast to ethics, the allied fields of law, politics, and economics, which traditionally were held to be of lesser importance, have established themselves as major disciplines. Not only have they reached the academic status of departments, but in most universities they are faculties with many specialized disciplines. This is indicative of their relative importance not only as academic studies but also for society in general. People with legal, political, and economic or business knowledge are needed and valued; those with ethical knowledge are not. How and why this happened in society, we have already indicated in our historical account. How it came to reflect itself in university curricula is also a long and intricate story that cannot be told here. Remains it to be said that first law (already from the medieval universities onward), then politics (from at least the cameralistics of the eighteenth century) and, finally, economics (as political economy from the middle of the nineteenth century) became autonomous disciplines of study, whereas ethics remained under philosophical tutelage and was relegated to the status of a minor sub-discipline. As a result, the whole subject was never able to free itself and has remained stunted.

The issue that ought to be debated now concerning proposals to introduce ethics into university studies is whether it is better to try to build ethics into a major discipline comparable to politics and economics or whether to develop specialized ethical aspects of some existing subjects separately. At present, it is the latter approach that is being pursued and no thought is being given to the former; there are no proposals afoot to establish ethics as a comprehensive area of study, such as is advocated in this work. But without that, there can be no proper ethical knowledge and, therefore, no understanding of the role of ethics in specialized fields. What is left of ethical philosophy as a mere sub-specialty of academic philosophy cannot possibly provide such an understanding and is not even very conducive to ethical knowledge. Ethical philosophy itself needs to be totally reconceived.

Traditionally, ethical education used to culminate in ethical philosophy, at least in the Western classical educational regimen. But this was when philosophy played a quite different role in knowledge—as the so-called queen of the sciences—from the one it has at present. Since it is doubtful whether philosophy can ever again recapture this status, it is obvious that ethical philosophy must assume a much more modest function in relation to ethics. Historically considered, philosophy is not essential to ethics; not all the ethical traditions were philosophically based. The Judaic and Persian traditions had not much use for philosophy and only the Greek and Chinese made it into an integral part of their ethical education. What role philosophy will have in relation to ethics in the future depends very much on whether it can address the major ethical problems of our time, which at present it does not seem able to do; though in this respect there are a few exceptional philosophers whose work we will presently consider.

As we have already intimated in previous chapters, philosophy has had many and diverse functions in the history of ethics. The primary one is intellectual, to elaborate theories that contain ideal principles of great generality and rational consistency. Such principles or ideals are very useful in mediating between opposed ethics that have to co-exist with each other and thereby in helping to bring about syncretic hybrid forms of ethics. They also have important legal and theological functions, principally in the codification of laws and in the rationalization of religious ethics. The role of the Greek philosophies in the history of Christian morality, almost from the start of this religion, is particular rich in numerous examples of such functions. In the modern period, the intellectual function of philosophy has been exercised through what Kant called the "metaphysics of morals," that is, the rational justification and elucidation of fundamental principles that are to serve as the basis of modern ethics. The modern contest between religion and science on the ground of ethics has to some degree been mediated by this philosophical means, as the prevalence of neo-Kantianism in the nineteenth century demonstrates.

However, for philosophers themselves any such external function of philosophy was always seen as secondary to its primary role of propounding a philosophical way of life. Ethical philosophy was taken to be in the first place a practical mode of living and only incidentally a theoretical mode of thought as well. Though, of course, theory and practice were not dissociated: theory meant an intellectual insight into life's purpose, and practice was simply the effort to realize this in practical activities. The modern scientific concept of theory as a mere intellectual construct of ideas, entailing nothing in the way of personal conduct, was foreign to any traditional conception of philosophy. To elaborate a theory of ethics and not to have to live up to it oneself, as is taken for granted among contemporary ethical philosophers, would have been considered a form of hypocrisy.

In the Greco-Roman tradition, according to Pierre Hadot, "philosophy did not consist in teaching an abstract theory—much less in the exegesis of texts—but rather in the art of living."[4] He explains this as follows:

> It is a concrete attitude and determinate life-style, which engages the whole of existence. The philosophical act is not situated merely on the cognitive level, but on that of the self and of being. It is a progress which causes us to *be* more fully, and makes us better. It is a conversion which turns our entire life upside down,

changing the life of the person who goes through it. It raises the individual from an inauthentic condition of life, darkened by unconsciousness and harassed by worry, to an authentic state of life, in which he attains self-consciousness, an exact vision of the world, inner peace, and freedom.[5]

All the canonic six schools of philosophy of the Roman higher educational establishment—namely, the Academic, Peripatetic, Stoic, Epicurean, Skeptic, and Cynic—practiced a version, each peculiar to itself, of this basic program of philosophy. Christianity took it over in its entirely in embracing some of those ancient schools, particularly the Stoic and neo-Platonic, and incorporated them within its own outlook. This view of philosophy as an art of living persisted right throughout the tradition; it was only severely tested and challenged in the modern period and at present has almost disappeared.

The idea of ethical philosophy as mere theory of ethics, and no longer as a way of life, began to gain currency in the medieval universities with the rise of scholasticism in philosophy. From then on, according to Hadot, it was institutionally linked to the university and so to the theoretical academic attitude. Modern philosophy, which arose outside the university on the basis of the new sciences, made no attempt to break out of this theoretical orientation to ethics, but further reinforced it.

> Philosophy—reduced as we have seen to philosophical discourse—develops from this point on in a different atmosphere and environment from that of ancient philosophy. In modern university philosophy, philosophy is obviously no longer a way of life or form of life—unless it be the form of life of a professor of philosophy. Nowadays, philosophy's element and vital milieu is the state educational institution.[6]

Taught by salaried professionals, the professors, within state-sanctioned institutions, the universities, ethical philosophy lost completely any relevance for life. It became a minor sub-speciality of departments of philosophy, which themselves broke up into numerous specialisations. Even as theory, ethical philosophy suffered, becoming ever more etiolated, hair-splitting, and trifling. The full-blooded theories of the nineteenth century, such as Intuitionism, Utilitarianism, Kantianism, and Hegelianism, were, in the twentieth, displaced by so-called meta-ethical analysis of ethics "values," the "language of ethics," and "ethical concepts." Positivism exerted its intellectually deadening and inhibiting restrictions over ethics, as it did over other disciplines; its so-called logical separation of Fact and Value left ethics stranded high-and-dry on the side of Value, together with other supposedly subjectivist and emotivist detritus. After the Second World War a nadir of ethical thought had been reached in philosophy, from which a few philosophers are now desperately trying to recover.

But there have always been exceptions to this stranglehold of theory; there have been a few philosophers for whom ethical thought was linked to a way of life. It is to these we must now turn for inspiration. Spinoza's ethics, despite its high intellectuality and logic-driven rationalism, does elaborate an ethical way of life, one that he himself followed and for the sake of which he abjured all worldly favor and fame. Rousseau, perhaps the greatest moralist of modernity, though less of a philosopher, is also an exception in elaborating an ethical way of life that summed up many modern trends but also had close affinities to some of the ancient philosophies. He did not himself altogether practice what he preached, but he was aware of the disparity and tried to apologize for it in his autobiographical writings. Since then, only the rare philosopher has tried to lead an ethical life in conformity with his own prescription; two such, at least partial, cases were Schopenhauer and Nietzsche, who were also not academics.

Perhaps the last historic instance of an ethical philosophy that is also a way of life was Existentialism. In its various versions this took many forms that we cannot elaborate in detail here; we will merely mention one of the last, that of Sartre. In his hands it became less of a way of life but instead gained brief notoriety as a style of fashion. Sartre, too—a little like Rousseau, though with even greater bad faith—is now known not to have practiced what he preached. After a while he even stopped preaching it, as he drifted into the Marxist camp and abandoned ethics altogether for politics. As he himself belatedly confessed:

> There was a moralising period before the war, with demystification of certain moral concepts and ideas. But not morality itself. At that period I always wanted to show . . . that no matter what we do, we do it within some moral frame of reference. . . . Anyway the idea was a kind of moralism. And from the time I became more involved politically, this moralism began to yield to realism, if you like. In other words, it began to give way to the political realism of certain Communists or of a great number of Communists: all right, you do it because it works, and you check it out, you evaluate it according to efficiency rather than some vague notions having to do with morality. . . . I finally arrived at pure realism: what's real is true, and what's true is real. And when I reached that point, what it meant was that I had blocked out all ideas of morality.[7]

In blocking out morality for the sake of political realism, in this case a kind of *raison de Revolution*, Sartre had in effect abandoned ethical philosophy for the ideology of extremist politics. In this he was, whether consciously or not, following the example of one of his mentors, Heidegger, who had previously also moved from a kind of Existentialism of authenticity to Nazi ideology. Gentile and Lukacs had even earlier undertaken a similar exodus from ethical philosophy, respectively to Italian Fascism and Stalinist Bolshevism.[8]

In one way or another, either through academic sterility or through a politics of commitment, philosophy seems to have become ethically bankrupt. If anything of the philosophical role is to be won back for ethics, a difficult recovery is called for. The task is one of actually developing an ethical philosophy in the full sense—that is, a philosophy according to which one can live. This is a task that some contemporary philosophers are attempting to accomplish. Perhaps the most renowned of these is Emmanuel Levinas, whose ethical philosophy has a religious basis and is mainly oriented to morality. Since it is also of a highly abstruse and conceptually elusive character, following on from Husserl and Heidegger, it is futile to try to discuss it here.

A much more approachable ethical philosophy in an analogous vein has recently appeared in the work of Gernot Böhme. In his book *Ethik im Kontext*, he has taken up Hadot's traditional topos of philosophy as an ethical way of life and sought to give it a contemporary relevance.[9] His key notion is the concept of "seriousness" (*Ernst*), and he defines moral issues as those things we treat with the fullest possible seriousness, ones that determine what kind of a being one is and in what kind of society one lives. He addresses himself specifically to the practical problems of ethics that arise from living in a technological society. His work is a most timely and welcome philosophical initiative, one that departs from the formalistic generalities of the various academic schools of philosophy but yet does not fall into the specialist narrowness of so many current "practical ethics" approaches.

What can philosophy do for ethics? On its own, philosophy never did and never can establish an ethical way of life for a whole society, only one for philosophers. Philosophy cannot even provide general principles from which what is right and wrong or good or bad can be deduced. Gernot Böhme is quite clear that that is not its role, and Pierre Hadot gives the reasons why this is so:

> Does the philosophical life, then, consist only in the application, at every moment, of well-studied theorems, in order to resolve life's problems? As a matter of fact, when we reflect on what the philosophical way of life implies, we realize that there is an abyss between philosophical theory and philosophizing as living action. To take a similar case: it may seem as though artists, in their creative activity, do nothing but apply rules, yet there is an immeasurable distance between artistic creations and the abstract theory of art.[10]

Philosophical theory, too, is far removed from action, and even "philosophizing as living action," as a philosophical way of life, at best applies to a few individuals in any one society. Of what use then is philosophy for ethical life in general?

The philosophical role is conducive to general ethical culture in many indirect ways, as the history of ethical philosophy has repeatedly exemplified. We have already discussed many of these uses of philosophy. Among the most important is to provide the intellectual justifications and rationales for ethics. In contemporary philosophy the various attempts to develop theories of existential meaning and of the meaningful life are most conducive to this effort. We shall take up this point in the next chapter.

Given the restricted role of philosophy in the overall disposition of ethical life in general, the present difficulties of ethical philosophy are not all that serious for society. What is of far greater consequence is the lack of significant movements of ethical innovation. In the ethical tradition this role was not carried out by philosophers but by prophets, law-givers, and other such charismatic figures, both religious and secular, whose influence on the course of ethical history was far more decisive than that of intellectuals. Such were the founders of religions and sects, the leaders of the great social and political movements, the great reformers and others who brought about social upheavals in the ethical life of societies. These were the societies among which, as Weber puts it, there pulsated "the prophetic *pneuma* which in former times swept the great communities like a firebrand welding them together."[11] Obviously, as well as such spectacular manifestations of ethical innovation there were many that only succeeded in small ways in changing the course of ethical life and still many more that were relative failures. But the impulse to ethical change and to charismatic reinvigoration was there. Now it has largely waned.

It is true that until recently in the modern period, there were all kinds of ethical reformers, both genuine and spurious. Among the more genuine were relatively lesser figures: various pacifists, such as Thoreau, Tolstoy, and Ghandi, and all kinds of educators, such as Froebel, Dewey, and the more erratic Rudolf Steiner. Unfortunately, their influence has almost completely dissipated now, as any such educative projects have been displaced by the new pseudo-scientific methodology based on psychological theory and skill-training methods. The greatest impact, both for good and ill, was brought about by the great political ideologues who were the founders of the major political movements of the nineteenth century. Thus, for example, among the founders of socialism—perhaps the most ethically innovative political movement during the last two centuries, despite its present eclipse—were such varied figures as St-Simon, Owen, Fourier, Proudhon, Marx, and Engels, who must be considered among the radical ethical prophets of their time. It is one of the great tragedies of history that out of these idealistically sincere, but perhaps on hindsight pragmatically flawed, ethical impulses there should have emerged the totalitarian regimes that became the most destructive forces against ethics in history. We have still not recovered from this disaster and many of our ethical problems can be attributed to it, as we indicated in our historical account. How it happened is well known, but why it took this anti-ethical turn is still not well understood. The consequences of this ethical betrayal by extremist socialist parties and their totalitarian progeny is one of the main reasons that ethical innovation as revolutionary radicalism is so distrusted and resented at present. This disenchanted "end of ideology" mentality has also brought with it the end of ethical idealism. The last idealist upsurge proved itself to be definitively spurious. This was the student activism of the late 1960s, which flared up spectacularly, fanned by media publicity, and disappeared just as abruptly, leaving little but a residue of youthful cynicism.

The age of ethical prophecy is past. The totalitarian dictators and the destructive movements they launched in this last century have discredited any kind of secular prophecy for a long time to come.. All such figures—for they do not fail to present themselves ever anew—are now seen as false messiahs, usually not without good reason. There is even suspicion of anyone who preaches any radical message of ethical renewal or puts forward a new educative panacea to make people better. Intellectuals with any such pretensions are also distrusted, given their record of *trahison des clercs* during this century. As Weber put it at the start, "Academic prophecy, finally, will create only fanatical sects but never a genuine community."[12] And he was proved right by the many malign masters who subsequently preached messages of salvation.

It may be objected against this seemingly overly pessimistic assessment that a number of genuine movements of reform and renovation have only very recently successfully transformed society. The environmental movement is the most obvious one that comes to mind. It is true that environmentalism is a mass movement that has had a significant impact on the treatment of animals, flora, and fauna habitats and Nature in general. It has in this respect changed people's attitudes to natural phenomena and altered some social practices and even manners. However, it is doubtful whether it can be considered an innovative ethical movement. It is akin to the movement for public hygiene that had taken hold during the course of the nineteenth and twentieth centuries through legislation for the protection of public health and through the inculcation of new hygienic habits, such as hand-washing and the eradication of flies from kitchens. The environmentalist movement, insofar as it has been socially successful, is to a large extent an extrapolation from medical salubrity to a general clean environment, one without pollution or contamination where human uses are concerned. Thus people demand, and have to some extent received, clean water, air, and an uncontaminated soil and its produce.

It is true that there is also a radical wing to this movement with a much more all-embracing conception of environmentalism, even a philosophy going under the name of "deep ecology," and this does have an ethical aim. It is that of living in accordance with Nature and caring for all species equally, because in the eyes of Nature all species have equal worth. In some respects this is reminiscent of Stoicism with its emphasis on a simple, natural lifestyle that only caters to basic needs and not to luxuries and superfluities. In other respects, particularly in its attitude to animals, it is reminiscent of Buddhism, and it also tends to favor vegetarianism. Whether a complete ethical life could be based on these principles is yet uncertain. But even if it were possible, it could only give rise to small communities or sects. The large population of a modern society as a whole could not adopt such a project of natural living *in toto*, though obviously limited aspects of it could and should be institutionalized; in some small respects they have been so already, as, for example, in more considerate practices of waste disposal. But otherwise, the environmentalist ethic has not had any general effect on people at large and it is doubtful whether it could, given the nature of modern societies, whose needs can no longer be met in any "natural" way but only through large scale industry and mechanized agriculture.

Something similar also holds for the other partly successful social movement of our time: feminism. It is undeniable that the treatment and place of women have drastically improved as compared to all earlier societies. Partly this has been due to sheer medical means, such as the invention of more safe and sure methods of contraception, which has lifted the burden of constant child-bearing, but more so from changes in social mores, such as the provision of equal educational opportunities for girls and the availability of work for women, though still not on a completely equal basis to men. For these reasons and many others, feminism has been partly successful and has promoted a spate of legislation designed to ensure the equality of women in all formal respects. Now there is almost nothing that a man can do to which a woman is not formally entitled, even in areas of military service that have traditionally always been denied to women. Legislation to safeguard the dignity and respect of women has not been so successful and has even been partly counterproductive, as sexual-harassment cases reveal. In any case, legislative measures by themselves cannot bring any lasting ethical benefits.

Undeniably, feminism has been conducive to important social adjustments in the ethos of society. But it has not been much of an ethical improvement and certainly not one in respect of morality. Thus sexual morality during this period has suffered, as the so-called sexual revolution so glaringly revealed, for as a result of it women came to be regarded more as sexual objects of desire than as partners in love and companionship. There has since been a retreat from the 1960s and 1970s era of uninhibited promiscuity, partly for medical, rather than moral, reasons having to do with the AIDS epidemic, but also because few women any longer wish to make themselves freely available for they tend to end up as the victims of sexual predators. One might sum up the change in sexual mores in general by saying that women are now less abused but more used. Any genuine sexual ethic of erotic love is nowhere in evidence.

Feminism as an ideology has as large pretensions as environmentalism. At its most radical it looks toward a total social transformation through the elimination of patriarchal culture, from which, supposedly, all the past evils of society have come. If only the domination of men was eliminated and society feminized, then, so the argument goes, all the characteristically feminine virtues of caring, nurturing, conciliation, and peace without resort to violence would come to the fore. One cannot but look on this as another utopian hope that is destined to be unfulfilled, like so many others of the recent past. Any attempt to bring it about, even if successful, would be bound to result in something quite other than anticipated, for there would be all kinds of unintended consequences that would militate against the worked for aims.

Radical ethical improvement in our time is unlikely, for that calls for the kind of radical innovation that has been rendered impossible for reasons that Weber set out at the very start of the century:

> The fate of our times is characterized by rationalisation and intellectualisation and, above all, by the "disenchantment of the world." Precisely the ultimate and most sublime values have retreated from public life either into the transcendental realm of mystic life or into the brotherliness of direct and personal human conduct.[13]

Since Weber wrote this, rationalization and intellectualization have taken even more all-embracing and rigid forms, as exemplified by the mechanical rationality of computers and ever larger systems of organization, making any kind of charismatic irruption productive of new ethical ways of life highly unlikely. The retreat to "ultimate and most sublime values," ever further removed from public life, has continued; now such values, or the little that is left of them, are only to be found in the narrowest of circles or even in individual isolation.

What has taken place in ethics has also happened to serious art. Weber had seen that "it is not accidental that our greatest art is intimate and not monumental," and he warned that "if we attempt to force and to 'invent' a monumental style in art, such miserable monstrosities are produced as the many monuments of the last twenty years."[14] This, spoken in 1919, prophetically anticipates the even worse monstrosities of art and ethics that attempts, by force, to forge a "monumental style" would produce in the ensuing twenty-year era of the great totalitarian dictators. The monstrosities have since changed their character; they are no longer monuments to the great leaders and *Führers* of "social revolutions" and heroic tributes to the new Man that these would produce; now they are more likely to be projects of social engineering for urban renewal produced by anonymous committees of planners and architects. The results, both aesthetic and ethical, are the same—human sterility in a concrete wasteland.

Weber's admonition "to bear the fate of the times like a man"—or woman, as we would now say to avoid so-called sexist language—is now even more daunting and difficult to meet. Yet his basic prescription, "to set to work and meet the 'demands of the day' in human relations as well as in our vocation,"[15] unheroic and unglamorous as it sounds, still holds good for our time. It is ethics in adversity. It enjoins us to maintain what can be kept of an ethical life, to hold on even if only "to shore up the fragments against ruin" (T. S. Eliot). Such a task has an exemplary role to play; it shows that an ethical life is worth living for it makes for a meaningful life.

On this note the whole focus of our investigation shifts from the general cultural considerations of this chapter to the individual perspective of the next. All the main issues thus far discussed reformulate themselves in personal terms on the level of individual existence. Instead of asking, "What kind of ethical culture do we wish to create?" ask "What kind of person do I wish to become?" And even prior to that question is the still more basic one, "Should I choose to lead an ethical life?" Why be ethical at all? This used to be considered a theoretical question for philosophers; now it has become a practical one for everyone. One can now choose not to be ethical in ways that such a choice was not available previously in more traditional times. Before, it was only possible not to be ethical by leading the life of a criminal or by being evil, and this had to be done in secret and could not be publicly declared. Now it is possible to lead a non-ethical lifestyle in which one openly ignores basic ethical precepts and flaunts this in public without incurring any problems with either the police or one's neighbors. Thus ethics has come into question not just in theory but in the ordinary course of living. Those who wish to persist in being ethical now need to justify themselves, explicitly or implicitly, by giving reasons why it is still worthwhile to do so. Ethics can no longer be taken for granted.

CHAPTER 5

~

Ethics and the Individual

Why Be Ethical?

Either at the start or at the conclusion of every serious treatment of ethics, there are two fundamental questions that must be answered: Why should one be ethical and how should one be ethical? If these two questions are not tackled, either explicitly or implicitly, then much of the point of writing on ethics is lost; it becomes a mere academic exercise. At the very start of ethical philosophy Aristotle had already indicated this when he warned against mere theoretical curiosity in ethics: "The branch of philosophy on which we are at present engaged differs from others in not being a subject of merely intellectual interest—I mean we are not concerned to know what goodness essentially is, but how we are to become good men, for this alone gives the study its practical value. . . ."[1] In raising the two basic questions, we intend to live up to the spirit of Aristotle's injunctions in a contemporary context.

This must not be taken to mean, of course, that we can give satisfactory answers to these basic questions. On the contrary, it is part and parcel of our difficult ethical condition and our damaged ethical lives that we can no longer answer these questions in a fully satisfactory and coherent way. That is to say, we can no longer justify ethics in the way that this could be done with certitude and assurance in more traditional societies. Nor can we any longer judge what is right and wrong or how to lead an ethical life in general with that traditional degree of confidence. Nevertheless, we are bound by intellectual honesty to explore the issues prompted by these questions and to give the best answers that we can muster at present, no matter how inadequate these might seem when compared to those traditionally given. Since we did not raise these questions at the start of our inquiry, we are duty bound to turn to them now toward the end.

It is symptomatic of the state of thought about ethics in our time that the very question, "Why be ethical?" has been dismissed by positivistically minded philosophers as meaningless. Hence, there is, on this view, no need even to attempt to answer it. In other words, ethics is in no need of justification; it can simply be assumed as a given value presupposition or be taken for granted as part of common sense. What we have shown is that this is far from the case at a time when the whole ethical enterprise is so much under threat. To us, it is apparent that not only is the question meaningful, it has become an urgent practical issue; it is, perhaps, the most meaningful question of all in this respect, for on it depends the very meaning of ethics.

"Why be ethical?" some will ask cynically, well aware that there is now a choice not to be so. In fact, it is of great practical advantage not to be ethical. This does not mean that to give up on ethics one needs must become a criminal; one can well keep to all the laws and never get into any trouble with the police. One need merely act in such a way that outside the limits of the law, one pleases oneself in what one does or always acts to one's own advantage. One is simply no longer bound by the old, outmoded ethical scruples or feels any of the old inhibiting ethical emotions. Hence, one need have no compunction about betraying those who trust one (in the general currency of personal relations, trust is not even at issue since genuine friendship is so rare), lying when this proves necessary (who ever expects the truth in any kind of deal?—and life is more and more a matter of deals), promising what one has no intention of performing (this is something that politicians practice with such regularity that it is not even possible to call it promising), showing hypocritical regard for those one despises (also such a normal occurrence in academic life that it can no longer be considered hypocrisy, for everyone knows what this sycophantic game is all about) and, in general, doing whatever is required to gain one's ends. In the process why should one not take advantage of moralistic fools, those who stupidly or perversely still stick to the old ethical norms? Being constantly on the receiving end, such "fools" will soon enough also learn wisdom and not pursue their ethical follies for much longer. Eventually, no ethical expectations will be entertained by anyone from anyone. The whole society will become demoralized in the strict literal sense of losing its moral sense, such that anything that is not explicitly forbidden by law is allowed.

In such conditions of ethical degeneracy the question "Why be ethical?" is not only the most meaningful question of all to be asked about ethics, but it is one that assumes a personal existential urgency. To be or not to be ethical, that is the question of life and death as far as ethics is concerned. It is no mere matter of intellectual interest or theoretical curiosity. And no mere intellectual or theoretical answer is ever sufficient. It has to be answered practically in the course of living. Nevertheless, intellectual and theoretical answers, too, must be sought and these assume a practical significance when translated into common discourse and educational syllabuses. This was also how such answers figured in more traditional societies.

Traditionally, the justification of ethics was given by elaborating a comprehensive religion or philosophy or some other worldview in which ethics had an integral part to play. Insofar as such a comprehensive paradigm or intellectual rationale could not be gainsaid—for it mediated everyone's conception of what is Reality, Nature, Man, Society, and so on—so the ethical system that went with it could also not be refuted, rejected, or refused. In this way ethics was justified on the basis of ultimate considerations. There were a number of set ways of doing this that were more or less pronounced in different cultures. Ethics could be justified religiously by reference to a God or a transcendent Reality and some soteriological scheme of individual salvation; or naturalistically by reference to some order of Nature, the cosmos, or the rational nature of things and beings; or, as we would now say, psychologically by reference to the nature of the soul (*pneuma*) and the proper state of spiritual being and how this might be attained; and, finally, in a pragmatic utilitarian way by reference to the preferred state of society and what was held to be conducive to human happiness. Obviously, these are only the most general types and all other kinds of variations and combinations were also utilized in the actual justifications invoked. Such rationales first arose together with ethics during the Axial Age (700–300 B.C.) and they have been extant ever since. We have inherited them as part of our intellectual traditions, both those of the West and the East.

For reasons that are only too well known and need not be elaborated here at any length, all the traditional justifications of ethics have collapsed and can no longer be upheld with strict intellectual honesty, except by those who are diehard traditionalists or really, when it comes down to it, fundamentalists. We shall very briefly review the reasons for this and give the gist of the basic problems with the traditional justifications.

The old religious cosmological justifications have broken down because ethics can no longer be seen as having anything inherently to do with our present conceptions of Reality, Nature, Man, or Society. For the most part, these are now scientific and science is currently held to be value-free, which means that it is believed to be impossible to derive evaluative conclusions from its theoretical or factual premises. This positivistic conception of science, which most scientists accept, militates against any scientific basis for ethics. But science is not alone in its divorce from ethics; most other aspects of intellectual and cultural life are also separated from it. This means that ethics has been severed from Reality, which could not possibly happen in traditional society.

In religious societies there was an inextricable bond between ethics and a religious conception of Reality. Those who believed in God also believed in upholding God's commandments; those who had faith in a Savior also accepted His path of salvation. Even today, such strict believers have no problem justifying ethics. But increasingly they can only remain strict believers by turning their backs on all the secular currents of modern thought, especially of science. Religious belief can only be maintained as a separate sphere isolated from all other dispensations, a marginal area of traditional concerns. If ethics is justified on religious grounds alone, then it, too, falls into that marginal predicament. However, for most people ethics can no longer be thus religiously justified. And it would be gratuitous to have to convince them to believe in God and be religious first before arguing for them to be ethical. Some other more intellectually acceptable way will have to be found for justifying ethics.

Similar problems arise with the traditional naturalistic way of giving a rationale for ethics. On this view ethics was justified by being shown to be in accord with Nature and Reason, above all, with human nature and the rational order of human society. To live ethically meant to live in conformity with the laws of Nature as these are discovered by Reason; not to live ethically meant to go against one's own nature and the whole order of the universe. As we have already seen in our previous historical studies, there were many versions of this basic view, both in the West and the East, such as among the Stoics and the Confucians. All of them have more or less been intellectually discredited under the impact of modern science and its quite different conception of Nature and Reason. The universe is no longer seen as a cosmos but a chaos of exploding energy and the world, our little living planet earth, is but an insignificant planet circling a minor star in one of the billions of galaxies. Nor is the scientific conception of human nature any better basis for ethics. There is nothing in the evolutionary view of the origins of the human species that would lead to the supposition that these ape-like creatures need to be ethical or even social beyond the barest essentials sufficient to maintain the human pack. Any such anthropological conception of human nature is quite unable to account for ethics as the product of civilization and the high cultures; at best, it can only explain the rudiments of ethos.

The traditional "psychological" way of justifying ethics is also no longer tenable. On this view the soul is so constituted that it needs ethics for its full development and the happiness of its being. Virtue is happiness, as Plato maintained; or virtue is necessary, though not sufficient, for happiness, as Aristotle held. According to the Stoics, the virtuous man could be happy regardless of the outer circumstances in which he found himself. This view flies completely in the face of contemporary experience, for we now know that nobody, no matter how virtuous, could be happy in Auschwitz. The Stoic view, shared by all metaphysical philosophers, presupposes a dissociation of soul from body, such that the former can remain in virtuous equanimity no matter what the latter is suffering. We now know that the state of the soul depends intimately on the body—hence, that the state of the body determines that of the soul. Happiness is much more bound up with the satisfactory state of the body than with the virtuous disposition of the soul. Thus someone in a comfortable bodily condition in successful outward circumstances might well be happy, regardless of that person's ethical standing. The wicked can also be happy. No necessary nexus can be maintained between virtue and happiness, unless one were to define the terms in such a way as to make it tautological that only the virtuous person can be happy. If one does not resort to this expedient, then no justification of ethics can be given in terms of happiness or any such state of personal well-being.

Finally, that only leaves the pragmatic utilitarian justifications of ethics, the various views that hold that ethics is essential to social well-being. These justifications vary from the full Utilitarian philosophy that ethics makes for the greatest happiness of the greatest number, to more restricted considerations such as that some ethical substructure is necessary for social order and peace. Many such arguments have been current since the Sophists; they were particularly prominent during the Enlightenment, when all the previous justifications usually associated with religion and metaphysical philosophy became less convincing. The rise of the new social sciences, such as economics, psychology, and sociology, and the prevalence of utilitarian social reform movements all gave added weight to the utilitarian justifications of ethics. But the whole problem with these views is that society *per se* does not depend on ethics for its functioning or for its basic social well-being, since there were societies prior to the historical rise of ethics and there will be societies after its demise. The argument relies on a confusion between ethics and ethos: society requires an ethos but not necessarily an ethics. Nor would it even apply if one held that ethics is necessary for social order, tranquility, happiness, or other such desirable social virtues. It can also be argued on historical grounds, to the contrary, that ethics makes for conflict and war; one need only consider the history of Christian morality, the ethics of love *par excellence*, to see how much hate and strife were engendered by it. Perhaps a better ordered and more peaceful world would eventuate if ethics was removed as an arena of contention. This might not be very desirable for other reasons, but utilitarian considerations need not necessarily be among these. Ethics has to be justified apart from any utility it might be shown to have for society in general.

It is clear from all the previous counter-arguments that the traditional justifications of ethics can no longer be maintained. The answers they give to the question "Why should one be ethical?" are either not true or no longer applicable. This does not mean, as the Positivists suppose, that the question has to be abandoned as unanswerable, for then the ethical life could be given no intellectual justification and would simply become a matter of irrational choice. The view that being ethical is some kind of an arbitrary desire, a decision for some values as against others or an existential commitment, is not one that will satisfy those for whom it is a genuine matter of doubt and indecision whether an ethical life is worth living. Much more intellectually persuasive and emotionally compelling reasons than that need to be given. Perhaps any that we can now produce will not be as satisfying as the traditional ones, and some people will be inclined to stick to those and try to elaborate modern variants of them. In the light of the previous objections, we consider this to be futile and are, therefore, bound to seek for other, more germane justifications of ethics. Even if the ones we can now adduce are not as conclusive as the traditional ones were for past generations, they are certainly more acceptable to most thinking people now.

The problem of justifying ethics at present presents itself in the form of this simple question: Can it be shown that the ethical life is worth striving for, despite all the difficulties it is bound to bring the individual under contemporary adverse conditions of society? As a practical issue this question should concern every person and most urgently every parent, who must ask himself or herself: Should I bring up my children to be ethical beings or allow them to adjust to the ethos current in their society and teach them to practise only that which the law demands of them and no more? And if a given society, either now or in the near future, makes no ethical demands whatever, then perhaps it were better to bring up one's children to conform to that and not burden them with excessive restraints that will only hamper their pursuit of happiness or whatever personal predilection goes by that name. If one's intent as a thinker is to uphold ethics, then it must be possible to say something at least to perplexed parents as a guide to nurturing practice.

The most we can say at present, and it is perhaps not much, in justifying the ethical life is that it is worthwhile bringing up children to be ethical for that is the best chance one can give them of leading a meaningful life. Ethics has to be defended in terms of the quality of life it affords in itself, rather than in terms of other things that are its rewards; it is that life itself that is worthwhile regardless of its fruits, which are sometimes bound to be tragically bitter. Ethics has to be argued for in the same way and justified on analogous grounds as we uphold other diminishing and impoverished cultural concerns, such as art or religion.

The justification of art can be given in similar terms to that of ethics: a life without art is qualitatively poorer than one with art. A person without much aesthetic appreciation, with little sense of beauty, and with not much perceptiveness, imagination, or wit leads a less desirable life than one with those qualities. We should value such aesthetic capacities in a person even if they do not add to health, wealth, status, or power. An aesthetically impoverished society, such as our present one, which cultivates only a narrow range of crude arts, is poorer in the cultural quality of its life than the past more artistically endowed societies. An anaesthetic and dull society might function much better in utilitarian terms than one that devotes its resources to art; it might attain a more affluent lifestyle through an economically more rational policy of investment. This, indeed, has been a constant tendency in capitalism, not to waste money on the arts or, if need be, only to produce those arts that can command a market value. The result has been the anaesthetic wasteland of commercial art. Society has suffered accordingly and people are worse off precisely in those respects that cannot be given an economic valuation. Life can be lived without much art, but it is a reduced and diminished life.

Ethics does not lend quality to life in quite the same way as art, religion, the quest for esoteric knowledge, or any of the other high but useless endeavors, but like these it is also a matter of endowing life with meaning. "Meaning of life" is an expression that is often invoked and seems not to mean much itself, but it is not a mere pious sentiment; it does refer to something of great and universal human importance. Man does not live by bread alone. As well as satisfying their needs and wants, human beings have from primitive times always sought to endow their lives with meaning, though that has kept on changing in line with cultural developments. In the face of the meaninglessness of death, which is the most basic certitude of life, human beings have sought to elaborate various kinds of religious meanings. Traditionally, such meanings were based on mythological conceptions of gods and spirits, of the fate of the soul after death, of last judgment and immortality, and eventually, later in history, on the idea of a supermundane God who makes ethical demands. In whatever way ethics was historically introduced into the different societies in which it made its first appearance, it was always accompanied by a worked-out scheme making explicit the meaning it held for those who maintained it. One can interpret the various traditional justifications of ethics that we previously examined as sophisticated and intellectualized ways of expressing such basic meanings with which life was traditionally endowed.

Most people today no longer endow their lives with such meanings; hence, the traditional justifications of ethics are not acceptable to them, except, of course, for those who are very conservative in such things. For most others a different kind of meaningfulness must be invoked in order to justify ethics. Transcendent, rational-naturalistic, spiritualist, or optimistic utilitarian meanings will no longer do; instead cultural purposes must be invoked, as we also do for art. Ethics, like art, is a cultural creation that human beings cultivate to endow their lives with meaning. In other words, the meaning of ethics for life does no longer lie in any supernatural, transcendent, or other exterior realm of meaning but is intrinsic to itself; the ethical life is inherently a meaningful life in and for itself.

This might seem a very disenchanted meaning of meaning. Yet its compellingness is affirmed when the necessity of such meaning is realized and the harm of not pursuing it is grasped. The necessity of meaning for life is a human universal; some kind of meaning must always be sought, for otherwise anxiety and anomie ensues. As Nietzsche put it, human beings would rather will Nothing than nothing will, and this can be rephrased in terms of meaning rather than will: humans would rather find meaning in nothingness than have no meaning at all. Nobody can lapse into an utterly purposeless and pointless life short of committing some kind of suicide, either a slow death of spirit or a quick bodily death. The meaninglessness of contemporary life for many is revealing itself in the heightened incidence of both kinds of suicide, especially among the young. If we are compelled to seek for meaning on pain of death, then the sole question is what kind of meaning should we strive for and which is best?

On many counts the ethical life commends itself as a superior form of meaning—that is its most basic justification. Of the many kinds of meanings in terms of which people can order their lives, such as striving for power, status, wealth, and other such worldly successes, ethics presents itself as among the most constant and permanent. It is a meaning that informs the whole of one's life. Once attained, it cannot be lost except through self-betrayal; in this respect it is like knowledge. It is open to nearly all at almost all times: the richest and poorest, the most powerful and weakest, the able and incompetent, the intelligent and to some extent even the stupid—nearly all can lead an ethical life. Under almost all conditions of life some ethical significance can be affirmed and meaning found, even in Auschwitz. Indeed, as Primo Levi and other survivors of the concentration camps have revealed, it is precisely under such inhumane circumstances that the genuinely ethical human beings stand out. Acting ethically might not have markedly improved their own chances of survival, but it had extraordinary exemplary significance in affirming the meaningfulness and worth of living ethically for all others and in uplifting their spirits.

Ethics is not the only supremely meaningful life; the life of art, religion, and knowledge is also of a higher meaning. It is not to our purpose here to enter into the age-old controversy as to what kind of life is superior. Nor do we wish to insist, as was so often done by traditional philosophers, that these other kinds of endeavors must entail an ethical life. This was, as a historical matter of fact, often not so among the supreme exponents of these activities. Great artists have sometimes been indifferent to ethics and some in recent times have claimed the right, in the name of their art, to step beyond good and evil. Religious mystics, who have found union with the divine, have also thought themselves beyond sin. Scientists dedicated wholly to knowledge and truth have sometimes paid no heed to the means involved in making their discoveries. There have always been Faustian individuals who were willing to sacrifice their ethical souls for other types of supremely meaningful achievements. It would be invidious to try to prove them wrong.

We can grant that ethics need not be considered the *summum bonum*, the be-all and end-all of human endeavor. We need no longer insist that on ethics alone depends the salvation of the soul, or that it is the one thing needful in life. We can allow for a certain degree of relativism in these ultimate concerns of meaning. What is important, however, is to establish that meaning matters, that life without some meaning can hardly be lived, and that there are better and worse ways of finding it. Ethics provides a better form of meaning than most others and perhaps as good a one as any other. That is its initial and most fundamental justification.

Ethics provides not only a more meaningful life but also a more serious life. The capacity to take one's life and oneself seriously is one of the key endowments of an ethical upbringing. This is another of the main reasons why it is desirable to bring up one's children on some ethical basis. For this will enable them to treat personal relations seriously, to be serious about their choice of work and career, to undertake serious public commitments, and to seriously review their beliefs and aspirations. Seriousness is a basic attribute of ethics, and Gernot Böhme has made it the key criterion: "Moralische Fragen sind solche Fragen mit denen es für den Einzelnen ernst wird."[2]

Someone who does not take himself or herself seriously cannot be an ethical person, because for such a person nothing really matters deeply. Such can be a very easy-going and charming person, one who allows life to drift, perhaps all the better to take advantage of every opportunity that fortune offers for benefit or enjoyment, whose life thereby might become an exciting sequence of picaresque adventures. For most ordinary people, however, the unserious life is one of banausic routine and dull conformity, that of the person accepting whatever social fate hands out. To be a serious person does not mean being an ageless puritan; it does not prevent one being light-hearted and jovial. To be serious and playful are not incompatible, and some of the best people have been both at once. This is what Goethe alluded to when he thanked his parents for his inherited endowments:

> Vom Vater hab Ich die Statur
> Des Lebens ernstes Führen,
> Vom Mütterchen die Frohnatur
> Und lust zu fabulieren.[3]

Those artists, such as Oscar Wilde, who denied the importance of being earnest and made all of life a matter of aesthetic *"fabulieren,"* lacked the qualities of seriousness to lend ethical weight to their work or their personality.

The ethical life can thus also be justified as that life that gives a person the capacity for seriousness. This does not necessarily redound to one's success or happiness; on the contrary, it can, under unfortunate circumstances, lead to tragic failure and misery. Only those who take things with full seriousness can, strictly speaking, suffer a tragic fate. Ethics itself sets the stage for tragedy, in that ethical conflict is always liable to take a tragic course. Hence, anyone committed to an ethical life must be prepared for the unfortunate eventuality of a tragic fate. Such a person can only hope or pray that fortune or fate or Providence will spare him or her from being tested in a tragic predicament. To be liable to tragic suffering might not seem like much of a recommendation for the ethical life, but if it is coupled with the realization that this is so because a tragic being is one capable of taking life seriously, then it reveals the kind of inner-Self that ethics promotes.

Our third justification of ethics is precisely on this score: The ethical life develops a Self that has character, in the sense that it is capable of autonomy, freedom, and individuality. In some ways this is related to an old *topos* that goes back to the very origins of philosophy. The ethical life, taken by philosophers as supremely the life of philosophy, was seen as uniquely able to form character in this sense. As Pierre Hadot explains:

Philosophy presented itself as a method for achieving independence and inner freedom (*autarkeia*), that state in which the ego depends only upon itself. We encounter this theme in Socrates, among the Cynics, in Aristotle—for whom only the contemplative life is independent—in Epicurus, among the Stoics. Although their methodologies differ, we find in all philosophical schools the same awareness of the power of the human self to free itself from everything which is alien to it, even if, as in the case of the Skeptics, it does so via the mere refusal to make any decisions.[4]

Variants of this theme are still to be found in some modern philosophers, even when philosophy ceased being a way of life. Applied to ethics specifically such ideas can be found above all in Spinoza and Kant, but to a lesser degree also in Schopenhauer and Mill, as well as some others. Even though we recognize in this an age-old philosophical velleity—an unrealizable wish to escape from the constrained world of the body into the free world of the soul—yet there is much to be said for it when it is referred to ethics. In some much more restricted sense than that favored by philosophers, the ethical life is an autonomous, free, and individual life.

Ethics can be justified in terms of autonomy, freedom, and individuality, provided these terms are realistically defined and qualified. They must not be taken in any absolute sense. The ability to lead an ethical life does not mean that one has also the capacity to stoically endure and be indifferent to the external circumstances and conditions of bodily life, no matter how difficult these might be. Ethical freedom does not mean having total command over oneself. But it does mean that one has greater self-possession and control, especially over one's impulses and fears. The person of ethical character is able to decide to a greater extent—never absolutely—what he or she will or will not do. As we shall see, this capacity to refuse something on ethical grounds is one of the main ways that the individual in contemporary societies has of affirming a sense of Self as against the pressures to succumb to the ways of the world and become "like everybody else." In this way ethics permits a modicum of individual freedom from the fetters of social conformity, at least in non-totalitarian states. Thus under contemporary conditions of social life there is a close connection between being a self-directed being—that is, an individual in that sense—and leading an ethical life. Such ethical individualism is the very opposite of the consumerist individualism of the marketplace, the conformism of people who always choose what they are expected to and submit to the buffeting influences of every mass current that pulls them hither and thither.

The ethical individual has also a greater capacity to make life more coherent. Under contemporary conditions of role segregation and functional differentiation, this is perhaps only possible to a very limited extent. Nevertheless, the ethical being is best placed to realize in this respect the little that is achievable. This will enable such a person to evince a greater reliability in relations with others and promote trust and clarity of purpose in ordinary dealings. Mutuality and love are frequently only possible where there exists such a basis of integrity. Without the nurturing of an ethical life, most of our reliance on each other, one that permits close intimate relations to be developed, could not strike root and flourish. Hence, without ethics life becomes barren in all its intimate personal and social respects.

To embark on an ethical life, however, does not promise a safe and happy outcome. On the contrary, it exposes the person who is bound to it to the ever-present possibility of failure and tragic suffering. Of course, contingent circumstances play a major role in this, especially the kind of society in which one happens to find oneself. As history has recently shown, there are some societies where the honest person cannot survive for very long. And even in law-abiding, liberal-democratic societies, honesty is not always the best policy. Inevitably, even in favorable circumstances, all kinds of sacrifices have to be made for one's ethical self-respect. But frequently, too, such losses bring their own rewards. A sense of having done the right thing despite the cost can be a source of dignity and inner satisfaction that outweighs what one has lost. The composure of ethical virtue should not be cynically disparaged. It can give one a quiet and steady self-assurance that is the opposite of either self-assertiveness or self-righteousness.

Thus even under difficult conditions the ethical life is worth pursuing. It brings with it the potentiality for a more meaningful existence than those spent in strivings for worldly success, wealth, status, and power. It endows one's life with seriousness, self-respect, and dignity and gives one a measure of individual autonomy and personal freedom. To what extent one can realize these potentialities and actually achieve an ethical life depends not only on oneself but also on one's society. Under adverse social conditions the ethical individual who is true to himself faces only inevitable tragedy. This is the reason that it is politically crucial to struggle for a society that allows some scope for the realization of an ethical life.

Thus the ethical life can be justified intellectually on rational grounds, but this does not mean that it will be motivated by these means. Nobody is ethical solely for good reasons. The incentive to be ethical must be there to start with before such reasons can begin to have a persuasive and compelling effect on one's practical life course. The desire to be ethical must come from other sources, mostly from upbringing, crucial relations, and role-models;

decisive experiences such as falling in love or religious conversion also play a significant part for some people. But the intellectual and rational aspect is not to be disparaged as mere rationalization in the Freudian sense. Reasons matter and have an influence on people, especially on those who are intellectually inclined, and most intelligent people are to some extent. If there are good reasons to be ethical and if the ethical life can be rationally justified and explained, then this will make a difference to such people. To most, who have no inherent interest in ethics, it will mean nothing, and to those who are already ethical without the benefit of rational justification, it will make no difference. But to some it will matter, those for whom rational persuasion can tilt the balance and prompt a firmer adherence and more staunch commitment to a given life course.

How to Be Ethical?

If one has the need and inclination to be ethical, then the next issue that confronts one is how to do so—namely, what kind of an ethical life to lead. This is not a completely open choice made on a *tabula rasa* of infinite possibility, starting from scratch. Rather, it is a highly conditioned and constrained process of modification and adjustment made on the basis of what one already is and what one strives to become. The crucial limiting factor in this is what one's society allows and facilitates or what it restricts and frustrates. The nature of one's society is decisive, for that has already determined one's upbringing. The historical circumstances in which a society finds itself are also very important in this respect, especially conditions of peace or war, economic plenty or scarcity, and so on. Under such conditions of restriction, one has to decide how to be ethical in the light of the opportunities and the potentialities available to one in the given social situation. Hence, it is not a completely willed matter in which one's ideal wishes can be given unlimited scope. One must play the ethical game with the cards dealt one by one's fate, for to try to select a perfect hand leads to cheating on life.

The problem of how to be ethical faced at the end of the twentieth century is much more difficult than that faced at the end of the nineteenth. Then there were many more possibilities open, some of which were attained and others that might have been achieved if people had been more intent on the possible rather than striving for the ideal. At that time most of the ethical traditions were still viable and sustained intact forms of social life. In Europe there was still at least one coherent ethical ethos, the so-called Victorian morality or "bourgeois" ethic, which retained aspects of many past Western ethics. The figure of the gentleman was still a representative ethical model. As well as these traditional survivals, there were also forward-looking moderate ethical movements of many kinds striving for reforms in all dimensions of society, as well as extremist ones agitating for a total revolutionary break with the past. Much that was positive was achieved and more could have been had they not been intent on unrealizable ethical dreams whose flawed idealism led to the crimes and follies of the twentieth century.

Now all that is left of all such traditionalist and progressivist trends of the recent past are no more than fragmentary remains. Our initial problem in deciding how to be ethical is what to do with these survivals, many of which are inherited through upbringing and some are still inherent in institutions. Thus, for example, those who derive from religious families will most probably have imbibed the rudiments of morality. Those of aristocratic origin will have acquired some quirky notions of honor and personal dignity. To some, a commitment to public life might have been passed on and public spiritedness or group solidarity inculcated. Schooling of a more discerning kind might have taught many something about duties and responsibilities. Even revolutionary traditions of idealism were until very recently still maintained in a few radical circles. All such acquired ethical characteristics or virtues have suffered from various kinds of perversions and debasements and have frequently remained stunted at a childish level or been reduced to inhibitions and rituals in later life. Frequently, they are outgrown altogether and thrown off as a useless burden from the past that only impedes one in attaining one's ambitions or freely engaging in new lifestyles.

But they could also be the basis for a more mature ethical life, to the degree that one's society still allows this. There are many societies where any kinds of ethical integrity is so difficult as to be well nigh impossible. There are even worse societies where truthfulness is punished, where civic mindedness only leads to frustration, where honor is quixotic and sure to provoke ridicule, where dutifulness is identified with obeying authority, and where scrupulous conscience is condemned as self-stultification. In all societies, practicing the old ethical virtues calls for great care and caution or it is bound to bring one grief.

The problem of maintaining a proper moral conscience is particularly difficult at present. Such a conscience is generally the legacy of a religious upbringing or one that is not too many generations removed from its religious sources. In its religious context it still tends to be encumbered with all kinds of ethically extraneous religious beliefs that from any enlightened point of view must be condemned as irrational. Religion frequently has recourse to irrational fears (hellfire); it requires unquestioning submission to authorities (threat of excommunication); it imposes arbitrary beliefs (dogmas) and makes irrational demands on behavior (ritual proprieties). The mature conscience of an ethically serious person must free itself from such fundamentalist impositions or it must distance itself from them by regarding them as doctrinal conventions or strictly theological requirements that are not ethically significant.

However, once such a process of enlightenment begins and moves in a secular direction, then this brings other kinds of problems with it. For completely removed from any religious context it becomes increasingly more difficult for a moral conscience to be passed on from generation to generation. It has yet to be shown that a purely secular conscience can reproduce itself over many generations. The more it is remote from its religious roots, the weaker it tends to get. How to inculcate it without religiously derived supports is a problem that has as yet not been overcome.

The dilemma of conscience, caught between fundamentalism and secularism, reflects that of morality altogether. A purely secular enlightened morality is derivative from a larger religious tradition, and it might not be capable of surviving for very long on its own. But to seek to reinstate it into its traditional context is to be driven back to fundamentalism. It is understandable that many people should reach for traditional answers to their present problems, but it is also apparent that this move will at best defer, not solve, these problems, which derive from unavoidable changes in the way of life of most people in the world. The ethically serious person must confront this dilemma without any subterfuges and find a way of retaining inherited morality without falling back into a traditionalist stance, yet with the obligation of ensuring that such traditions can be passed on to future generations, for otherwise morality will die out.

There are analogous dilemmas with all our ethical traditions. It is not possible to maintain them in their traditional forms for contemporary conditions of society have altered too much, but it is not possible to abandon them either, for then ethical life is reduced to a minimalist residue of laws and precepts. This, as we have seen, is not unlike the problem encountered in other spheres of culture, such as the arts, where there is also the difficulty of knowing what to do with surviving fragments of once-intact and coherent cultural styles. Such problems of culture result from the intrusion of a global technological civilization into all areas of traditional life, which results in the breakdown and dissipation of traditional forms.

On a personal level one can only deal with the problems of ethics piecemeal, as and when they come up and require urgent resolution. General decisions or commitments as to what kind of an ethical life one ought to lead or what kind of a person one desires to become are frequently no better than New Year resolutions. At best, they are efficacious in choosing a lifestyle or a new role. The real ethical choices one has made in abandoning one kind of life for another, and in becoming the kind of person one is, usually reveal themselves *ex post facto* when one looks back on how one has acted on many specific occasions over a period of time and realizes that a pattern has emerged that defines one. The specific actions one performs in response to each concrete ethical predicament are what determine who one is—they shape one's ethical identity. As we have already discussed previously, no general prescriptions can be given for how a person ought to respond in each ethical predicament whose precise contours are unforeseeable. Such a predicament can present itself as a problem concerning what kind of an ethic is relevant to the given case. Though no general solutions to such problems can be given, nevertheless, the form they assume can be discussed in general terms, as we proceed to do in what follows.

The ethical problems that arise under contemporary conditions fall more or less into the three functionally separate dimensions of contemporary life: namely, political life, social life, and private life, or, better put, individual life. These are the three separate spheres of living that tend to be dissociated and frequently so much without relation to each other that people might be said to lead three separate lives. Political life is that sphere where people act as citizens or members of some compulsory political association such as the state or the national and international organizations involved with the state. Social life concerns one's group memberships, such as ethnic and religious affiliation, class and status-group position, vocational and voluntary organizations, cultural belonging through educational background and self-cultivated accomplishments, and so on, or all the other factors that make for social identity. Individual life governs another kind of identity, that of private life, which determines the kind of individual being one is; on this depends what attitudes, beliefs, feelings, and predispositions one evinces; what aspirations, hopes, and fundamental values one lives out; what relations one is capable of entering into with others; and how one treats one's neighbors, that is, people who are close to one or those in one's immediate vicinity—all in all, it is that which used to be called individual character. Political, social, and private identities have perhaps never before been so dissociated as they have become under contemporary conditions of living. What one does in one sphere of life need have little, if any, relation to what one does in the other spheres. As Adorno put it, "Atomization is advancing not only between men, but within each individual between the spheres of his life."[5] Out of this inescapable fact arise many of the difficulties and incoherencies of contemporary ethics.

Hence, unavoidably, providing answers to the ethical problems that arise in the various spheres will have to differentiate between the many different ethics that correspond to them. For the sake of simplicity we can roughly group these together into three categories, corresponding to the basic divisions of contemporary life: political, social, and personal. There will have to be an ethic of the good citizen, an ethic of the good person, and an ethic of the good man or an individual ethic. We need to expound and explore each of these ethics separately and later determine whether any coherence can be established between them.

Being a good citizen no longer means participating effectively in the affairs of a polis or even nation state; now in a global world it also means being a member of all the other political associations that are larger than or smaller than the state. Thus in its ultimate extension, being a good citizen means being a world citizen, a true cosmopolitan, and below that, it might also entail being a citizen of the regional grouping to which one's state belongs, such as, for example, being a good European. At its politically narrowest, it might mean participating in the local politics of one's city, province, or ethnic region as, for example, being a good Welshman or a citizen of Great Britain.

At each of these levels of political belongingness there are characteristic ethical duties, responsibilities, goals, aspirations, ideals, and values to which the citizen is bound and for which he or she will act with varying degrees of commitment, depending on circumstances as well as individual disposition. Obviously, the level of personal sacrifice and dedication acceptable to masses of citizens in war-time will only be assumed by the rare few in peace-time. The extent to which people are willing to act as world citizens also varies from place to place and person to person. In general, however, at least in liberal democratic Western societies many people are willing to assume a fundamental cosmopolitan responsibility and act, more or less desultorily, for the defense of the rule of law, basic human rights, and some elements of democratic participation throughout the world. Such people are usually also dedicated to principles of non-aggression and solidarity between states and are willing to work for disarmament, aid for poorer countries, and protection of the global environment. Such activists will be also devoted to the furtherance of an ethic of universal law, such as that promulgated in numerous United Nations declarations.

In contradistinction, and sometimes in contradiction, to such goals of universal justice for the whole of mankind stand the ethical demands of justice within one's own society. For what is good for one's country need not be necessarily good for the world and vice versa. But one has an ethical duty to work for both, which sometimes creates difficult, even irresolvable, predicaments. A just and decent society within one's own state can sometimes be only achieved at the expense of other people in other states. Thus, for example, to provide employment and the means for a dignified life for everyone in one's own country might mean having to restrict the free importation of goods, which denies the livelihoods of the people in other countries. There are equally difficult issues of justice even among the various groups and classes whose interests conflict in the one society. All these are matters of the application of ethics to politics. Political differences, such as are typically found among the exponents of the various ideologies and political parties, have also an ethical dimension. They result in varying conceptions of a civic ethics, the ethics of the good citizen.

At all levels of citizenship, at both the cosmopolitan extreme of universal ethics and the local particularity of civic ethics, the realization of ethical ends takes a similar political cum legal form. Citizens compete with each other in one kind of political arena or another—usually through parties, organizations, and other institutional bodies—to have their ethical demands accepted by their society as a whole and sometimes by other societies as well. Victory in such a political struggle leads to authoritative enactment of the ethical principles involved in the form of law, which is then coercively enforced on everyone in all kinds of ways. Thus both universal and civic ethics are largely matters of good laws; their enactment involves a political-legal contest that most frequently requires politicians to play a decisive part.

Hence, a special and particularly important form of ethics in the political domain is that guiding the policies and actions of politicians—that is, rulers, statesmen and leaders in general. This is the ethics of power that comes into play when a person does not act on his or her own behalf but on that of a political entity, typically a state or nation or some international body responsible for the whole of mankind. This brings with it all kinds of problems. The history of the relation between ethics and politics is full of such issues and cannot be expounded here in any detail. However, a few salient points might be mentioned. In the Christian moral tradition the attempt was made from early on to provide moral guidelines and restrictions on the exercise of power and the use of violence, such as, most characteristically, the just war theory, which goes back to St. Augustine. But this did little to prevent war. A contrary secular current stemming from the Italian Renaissance and articulated in the work of Machiavelli, Guicciardini, and others was designed to free the exercise of power from moral trammels and provide an autonomous doctrine of the uses of violence that eventually went under the name of raison d'état. This justified aggressive wars. It became discredited after the carnage of the two World Wars, when the right to go to war in pursuit of state interests became ethically intolerable and far too dangerous for mankind when the nuclear armed superpowers were involved. The world returned to a modified version of just war theory, which, as embodied in United Nations declarations, only permitted wars of self-defense against aggression, though in practice that has tended to be loosely interpreted.

An ethics of power governing relations between the states of the world community has yet to be developed. However, some pointers regarding the actions of statesmen and politicians in general might be ventured. The ethic incumbent on statesmen and politicians in all their dealings is an ethic of responsibility in Weber's sense. Such a person must take the consequences of his or her decisions and acts into account, not only those that impinge on his or her own state or nation but on others as well, including ultimately the whole of mankind. All such rulers have sometimes to resort to the means peculiar to politics, which in the last resort entails violence and war. The use of violent means for good ends can be ethically justified even in the contemporary political world under certain conditions. It is not allowable to pursue *raison d'état* or the interests of state in a blanket way, but it is permissible to defend, by war if necessary, the existence of a state and the welfare and freedom of its citizens where these are under attack or internationally to defend the human rights and freedoms of people in other societies. In other words, even evil means can be resorted to for good ends.

The use of violence or other such ethically dubious means of politics to achieve good ends is, however, fraught with all kinds of paradoxes. The ends do not always justify the means, but sometimes they do. It is impossible to determine *á priori* in any formal way when they do and when they do not; no rules or principles can be given for deciding this in a given concrete case. However, in a very general way, which is of some use in practice, it may be said that the ends do not justify the means when the means are such as to negate and to cancel out the ends. Thus, for example, to destroy a people in order to liberate them, as the American military authorities were prepared to do in Vietnam, is obviously to defeat one's own purpose, so that in such cases the ends do not justify the means. However, when the consequences of not using certain means to achieve a good end far outweigh in evil effect the use of those means, then they are justified. If it could be shown that not fighting in Vietnam would lead to the totalitarian enslavement of all the people in that whole South East Asian region—namely, if the so-called "domino theory" were true—then it would have been justified to fight even at the cost of the destruction of Vietnam itself. It calls for the acute insight of the statesman—which is not just an objective rational faculty but an emotional intelligence—to make such a decision and determine when the ends do or do not justify the means necessary to bring them about in any one specific case. This is the ethical predicament as it presents itself most paradoxically to the statesman or politician.

As we have already stressed repeatedly in this work, ethics that is tied to politics and law is also encumbered with other characteristic paradoxes, at no time perhaps more so than in contemporary settings, for this form of ethics is perhaps more predominant than perhaps ever before. The more this kind of ethic comes to the fore, the more are the other types displaced and their currency devalued. As the rule of law comes to prevail, so any other ethical requirement that does not have legal backing becomes an arbitrary matter of personal discretion. Social ethics, in particular, is no longer what it was when Hegel treated it under the rubric of *substantielle Sittlichkeit*. Nevertheless, it is by no means negligible even in our present conditions of social alienation and vacillating person identity. Social ethics is that of the good person, the upright person of good character. It is a matter of one's social roles, hence the term *person* can here be taken in its original etymological sense of *persona* (*prosopon* in Greek), the masks one wears as the protagonist in the play of social intercourse. As a social being one fulfills many roles, depending on one's membership in the various groups, associations, and organizations of one's society, into some of which one is born, others one acquires by inheritance, and still others one chooses by personal predilection. It is through this kind of belongingness that a person achieves a social identity—that is, becomes who he or she is and develops as a distinct personality with a specific character in a given social context.

This is an ethical character when it internalizes the ethical requirements of the roles that the person enacts. Such role-ethics are of many kinds, corresponding to the various roles one has chosen or is normally called upon to play in society. The most common types are the various vocational ethics, such as professional ethics, the ethics of business dealings, and scientific research; family ethics in all its various ramifications belongs to this general category, as do the ethics of relations to friends and associates, as well as the various kinds of religious ethics that have a purely social function. The exercise of such ethics depends on the development of the characteristic virtues that pertain to good character. Thus, for example, honesty and truthfulness are the general predispositions behind all kinds of social ethics. The more roles one is endowed with or adopts, the more such virtues one must exercise if one seeks to lead an ethical life. Not all of these will be consistent with one another, for many such social ethics are incompatible with each other. Such are the well-known clashes between the duties to one's vocation and those to one's family—that is, between the virtues of conscientious devotion to work and those of caringness in one's intimate relations. Many other types of social ethics are in similar kinds of ways at odds with one another.

The main difficulties in being a person of good character lie in mediating and reconciling the various clashing or even contradictory demands that one's role-ethics impose on one. The way one does this determines the nature of one's character and one's social identity. There are various strategies that different types of personalities adopt: there are the steadfast, single-minded types who identify themselves predominantly with one role and try to subordinate all the others to this supreme requirement; and there are the all-round types who seek to be something of all things and work for adaptive compromises—as it were, the ethical hedgehogs and foxes. Each person must thus work out his or her ethical fate and shape his or her character accordingly. Emotional intelligence of a particularly high order is required to do this well, in the light of the always very limited and constrained possibilities that one's circumstances, as determined by one's position in society, permit. There are pitfalls in every strategy; each can bring one to the brink of tragic ruin. There are no recipes or prescriptions for molding one's character, nor can one plan or decide this in advance. One learns what kind of a person one is in testing situations that sometimes reveal that one has become what one never wanted to be. And even such self-knowledge is not given to everyone, for most people do not know who they are and are sometimes unwilling to accept it even when shown by others. To what extent one is honest with oneself about oneself goes beyond social character and depends on what kind of a moral individual one is.

Thus we finally come to the third major ethical dimension, that of the ethics of the good man as opposed to the good citizen or good person. This is the area of ethical endeavor that is neither legally and politically mandatory nor that which is obligatory because of group membership and social involvement. It is the self-imposed and maintained ethics of conscience. Neither state nor society can make such ethical demands on the individual; they must come from within. Of course, as we have already stressed, this is not anything innate; it is acquired in the course of socialization, enculturation, and education. But it is an individual and not merely a social endowment, in that it enables the single man or woman to stand firm against the demands of society or state. "Here I stand, I can do no other" is its motto, theme, and characteristic expression, from which it is readily apparent that its source and historical origin are that facet of religious ethics that we previously defined as morality.

Contemporary morality has its locus in the individual, for it only exists where someone has succeeded in developing and sustaining an individual conscience. As we have already seen, that is no mean achievement under contemporary conditions of social uniformity and conformity. Cultivating the feelings of refined guilt on which a conscience depends is almost a kind of ascetic luxury that most people feel they can ill afford. Under the totalitarian conditions that so often prevailed in the last century, it was almost suicidal to do so. And even now, under conditions of formal freedom, this kind of moral attitude and its associated moral emotions are a great handicap in transacting one's life chances to best advantage.

Morality is that dimension of ethics that is most under threat in contemporary societies. It faces the same dangers as beset the individual as an autonomous being in general. The social forces that sustained it in the past, such as, above all, the institutions of the established religions and sects, are no longer as effective in this respect as they used to be. Besides, any religious justification of morality has lost its efficacy for many people. For such people, if it exists at all, it has assumed a secularized version. Whether it can be maintained in this form over many generations is, as we have previously stated, still a largely unsolved problem of secular society. At present, keeping it intact is part of the effort that some undertake to preserve traditions whose existence is becoming more and more precarious.

Those who have inherited morality in its non-religious secularized forms have done so largely from the social movements and moral reformers and writers of the nineteenth century. In this form it has generally taken the guise of an enlightened humanism. Its prescripts mainly concern the treatment and regard for human beings as moral subjects. Out of it arises a generalized sense of humanity, of humane behavior and human solidarity, which is focused on individual human beings as these happen to be encountered in moral predicaments that call for a moral response. Morality is not primarily a matter of general principles, laws, rules, beliefs, ideas, or values, though these are not absent. Rather, it tends to be more a matter of how the individual reacts in concrete situations and this depends on moral intuitions and habits of feeling as much as anything else. George Eliot's dictum emphasises this with particular force: "There is no general doctrine which is not capable of eating out our morality if unchecked by the deep-seated habit of direct fellow-feeling with individual fellow men." This is clearly a secularized humanistic version of the Torah commandment to love one's neighbor, which stands at the origin of Western morality. In this Judeo-Christian tradition the concept of the neighbor is extended to all people. What this means is that anyone might in certain circumstances become the subject of one's moral concern and call on one to act appropriately. This is also what Eliot means by the expression "individual fellow-men," which potentially embraces the whole of mankind but in practice refers to those to whom "direct fellow feeling" is owing.

Morality is at once general and specific. A moral norm applies to everyone, but it is only invoked in concrete situations or moral predicaments where it applies only to those concerned and nobody else. Or, to take a simple example, though one is morally obliged to save the lives of all who are in danger, one need only respond to the call to save someone's life if and when one happens to meet it in one's normal course of living; one is under no obligation to seek out people in danger wherever they might be found. There is moral virtue in saving the life of a drowning child, but this ought not oblige one to become a life-saver constantly on the lookout for drowning children. It is somewhat analogous for all moral demands—one has to meet those demands that one encounters in ethical predicaments that call on one's "direct fellow feeling." Like the Good Samaritan, one has to come to the aid of those one encounters on one's way or those who in one sense or another are close to one and can be considered "neighbors"; one is not required officiously to look for people in need wherever they might be found. If one has embarked on such a supererogatory moral quest, then one has to abandon an ordinary life, and with it all other ethical demands, and undertake only the one thing needful; and that is the vocation of a saint, which, though morally supreme, has all the shortcomings of exclusiveness and all kinds of other ethical drawbacks. It is certainly not an all-rounded ethical life but that of the aspiring moral virtuoso.

For ordinary people, morality best reveals itself and can be most clearly seen in situations of danger, where risk is incurred and sacrifice is involved. One acts morally in a truly significant way when one has something to lose. Acts performed in safety and security can but rarely be truly moral, though they might be virtuous according to other ethical criteria. Hence, morality comes most frequently to the fore when the individual has to oppose society, state, religious and professional authorities, or even family, for in such predicaments he or she always has much to lose. The individual will tend to have most to lose when, by acting morally, he or she also has to go against the legal and ethical norms that govern membership in the associations of society and citizenship of the state. In such cases morality can go against social ethics, civic ethics, and conventional religious ethics.

It is a commonplace to recognize that acting on one's conscience can involve one in breaking the law, and it is frequently also acknowledged that acting morally might entail transgressing the normal ethical norms of one's state, society, and religion. Thus, for example, saving the life of someone who has been unjustly condemned as an enemy and is politically persecuted might involve one in lying on oath; stealing; being disloyal to nation, friends, and family; and in general acting as a bad citizen and a bad person. Morally, one might be justified in doing so, though it could scarcely be defended on other ethical grounds. In such cases we tend to say that the call of conscience prevails over everything else.

It is part of the tragedy of ethics that all the ethical prescriptions and requirements do not consistently back each other up, such that together they provide clear and non-contradictory answers to all of life's quandaries. We most often encounter the opposite situation, where upholding one ethical demand means going against other, no less stringently obligatory, ones. It has often been recognized that "oughts" clash, "goods" are in conflict, values contradict and ends negate each other, duties oppose, obligations cancel out, and so on, for all the ethical terms. Such ethical conflicts have been the standard fare for theatrical tragedies throughout the ages, and this is no mere artistic convention, for tragedy best plumbs and explores the contradictions inherent in cultural and social life and which are often exemplified in real life conundrums. It is an aspect of what Weber has called the ethical irrationality of the world.

The three basic ethical spheres of civic ethics, social ethics, and individual ethics or morality are, thus, frequently in a contradictory relation to each other. This often means that being a good citizen requires one not to be a good human being, or being a good human being will entail not being a good individual man or woman. The patriot who sacrifices all for his country might be an excellent citizen, but he is bound not to be a good human being in relation to his family obligations or perhaps not even a good individual, by reference to his moral conscience, if he is willing to kill his friends if they become enemies of his country. On the other hand, someone who refuses to fight for his country for the sake of his duties to his family will be a bad citizen, one who might also end up as a bad individual if he is prepared to send others to fight and be killed in his stead. It is also possible to conceive of someone who is morally a good individual but a bad citizen and bad individual to boot; the celebrated case of Oscar Schindler, the German scoundrel who, nevertheless, saved Jews during the Second World War, exemplifies a man who came close to this condition. It is difficult, if not impossible, even with the best ethical will in the world, to be all three at once; the aforesaid ethical irrationality of the world does not permit this. People of good will try to cope with this most insoluble of all ethical problems in various ways: Some tend to emphasize one ethical dimension at the expense of the others, some try to balance them as far as possible, some adopt one ethical stance at one time and another later to suit the circumstances. There is no optimal solution. This struggle continues as long as one strives to lead an ethical life.

Religious ethics tends to insist that conscience must predominate as against everything else; namely, that morality must be the ultimate standard. This, however, produces all the paradoxes of acting always with purity of conscience or good intent that Weber opposes and so passionately argues against.[6] The paradox of consequences is the one that particularly troubles Weber. He points out that to act on the principle that the virtuous Christian does what is right and leaves the consequences to God means that evil often wins out. Thus the Christian pacifists, such as the Quakers, who refuse to kill under any circumstances, sometimes might contribute by their inaction to the victory of evildoers. The principled Kantian who refuses to lie, no matter what the consequences, might promote a worse evil than mere lying. The principle inherent in the adage "fiat justicia, pereat mundus" is not a very responsible one and people who subscribe to it unconditionally become dangerous ethical fanatics. The upshot of this line of argument is that one must take consequences into account and act upon the basis of what Weber calls the "ethic of responsibility." This, of course, has nothing to do with any consequentialist theories of ethics, such as Utilitarianism, according to which every act is supposedly judged on its results by the one standard of pleasure or happiness. It is more of a Kantian formal principle for balancing means, ends, and consequences.

However, acting on such an ethic of responsibility has itself the paradoxical consequence that sometimes one is ethically compelled to act against one's conscience. What this means is that sometimes, usually on rare occasions, in order to avoid worse ethical consequences, such as the total triumph of evil, one must forsake morality for the sake of other ethical ends. Thus on such occasions a clearly immoral act has to be perpetrated for the sake of avoiding civic or social evils or achieving humanitarian results that are overwhelming. Such acts are ethically extremely dangerous and fraught with the ever-present possibility of abuse. One must be what Weber calls a "mature man" to transact them without succumbing to blatantly unconscionable conduct and becoming corrupt and immoral. For acting in the light of the consequences against morality does not make the act morally right. It remains wrong even though one is compelled to do it for other weightier ethical considerations. A person who has to act in such a tragic predicament will suffer and bear the guilt of the act, even though knowing it had to be done.

This is one of the most poignant instances of the tragedy of ethics. There are many such celebrated historic cases, where morally good people have had to act against their conscience and suffered the inevitable self-torments of guilt. It is also the subject of literary treatment, as notably in Herman Melvil-

le's tale *Billy Budd*. The gist of the story is that Captain Vere has to arraign
and condemn under martial law the good and innocent sailor Billy Budd for
striking and accidentally killing the evil Claggart. As the narrator makes
clear, what is at stake is a "clash of military duty with moral scruple, scruple
vitalized by compassion." Though himself a man of conscience and compassion, Captain Vere, "prompted by duty and the law," as he himself puts it,
argues against conscience and compassion: "But tell me whether or not,
occupying the position we do, private conscience should not yield to that
imperial one formulated in the code under which alone we officially proceed?" Even though he knows that Billy is innocent, he also knows that he
is duty bound to enforce the law. Hence, his agonized cry immediately after
the blow is struck: "Struck dead by an angel of God! Yet the angel must
hang!" After pronouncing sentence, Captain Vere is mortified, his face is
"expressive of the agony of the strong," and we are told explicitly by the
narrator "that the condemned one suffered less than he who had mainly
effected the condemnation." This story is not just contrived fiction but the
representation of a recurring tragic ethical dilemma.

In the light of this consideration, it follows that morality does not always
have priority over all other ethics. Though under contemporary conditions,
where morality is the most endangered and the least secure facet of ethics,
it is essential not to allow one's conscience to be overridden except on the
most exigent of grounds, for given up too easily or too often it might weaken
and be lost. The corruptions of conscience are among the most prevalent
ethical diseases of the whole twentieth century. And very frequently such
corruptions begin for the very best of ethical reasons, appealing to the most
elevated motives, idealistic causes, and general ethical doctrines, which, as
George Eliot sagely predicted, proved all too "capable of eating out our morality."

Anyone who seeks to lead a full ethical life is subject to all of the three
basic types of ethics—civic, social and individual—and so is bound to encounter sooner or later the tragedy of ethics. For due to the ethical irrationality of the world, there is no way of avoiding or overcoming the clashes and
contradictions that will inevitably arise. When someone is caught up in such
a tragic predicament, then the individual must decide what kind of an ethical being he or she wishes to be, whether a good citizen, a good human
being, or a good individual man or woman. Some people in such cases decide
to be exclusively the one at the expense of the other possibilities, but most
tend to seek a middle course between exclusive alternatives and try for compromises. If one upholds morality at all costs, then one is bound to end up
compromised in respect of one's civic or social duties and responsibilities.

Taken to its utmost, it is a stand that only a saint or secular altruistic philan-thropist can maintain, someone who is willing to give up on most of life for the sake of "the one thing needful." This is not always an ethically intelli-gent or generally praiseworthy position to take. Thus a contemporary saint, such as Mother Theresa, can be criticized on more general ethical grounds for neglecting any civic stand she might have taken, but studiously avoided, to ameliorate through political means the very poor and destitute whom she chose to succor, but only at the point of death, with such touching moral solicitude. On the other hand, those who are willing to sacrifice themselves for political causes that might bring economic justice to the poor yet never exert themselves to help any specific poor person can also be ethically criti-cized as idealist do-gooders who love humanity but show no regard for any man or woman. As we have learned during the century to our cost, such people, endowed with unchecked political power, can be extremely dan-gerous.

However, this must not be taken as a plea for moderation and the mean, for in many situations it is the moderates who vacillate and hesitate, whereas it is the extremists who unerringly decide on the necessary course to follow. Where the fate and well-being of a whole society or a large group is at stake, then it might well be necessary to act ruthlessly. The statesman who decides to sacrifice innocent children rather than give in to terrorist blackmail might well be morally wrong but ethically right, seen from a larger point of view. Even the morally dubious, if not immoral, principle of *raison d'état* has some-thing to be said for it ethically and not just prudentially. The ends sometimes justify the means, provided the results are such as can be defended on ethical grounds that go beyond pragmatic considerations. To save the state and avert civil war or totalitarian dictatorship or any other such unmitigated evils, it is sometimes justified to resort to obviously immoral means. To avert nuclear war, almost anything is allowable—better Red than dead, as the old saying goes.

How people decide in such cases of ethical conflict where no compromise is possible determines their character as ethical beings. In making their deci-sion, they cannot appeal to any overarching ethical theory or to any funda-mental ethical principles. There is no *à priori* way of resolving ethical tragedies. Such tragedies occur in highly specific and unique situations that generally cannot even be envisaged in advance. Only when they adventi-tiously occur and present themselves as overwhelming dilemmas can they be confronted. They are only then subject to all the processes of ethical deliber-ation and decision making that we previously outlined. There must be people who are perceptive enough to fully grasp what is involved. Those faced with the burden of acting and their counselors or advisers must be capable of discussing the ethical issues involved so that the problem is fully understood in ethical terms, for only then can deliberation proceed on a sound rational basis. The judgments that are finally arrived at are as unforeseeable as are the situations that prompt them. These are not matters of applying general principles to specific cases. Applied ethics in this sense does not exist.

The general principles that we do utilize, such as the basic norms of the Decalogue: Do not steal, do not lie, do not kill, do not commit adultery, and so on, can only rarely be unambiguously applied. Their very meaning and significance changes, depending on the ethical sphere where they might be invoked. Stealing, lying, and killing mean something clear and simple when personal relations between people as individuals are involved; it is easy to know what it means to steal from, lie to, or kill one's neighbor, friend, or any human being one encounters face-to-face. But what does it mean for those who act on behalf of the state, when stealing can take the form of compulsory expropriation or even high taxation, lying the form of propaganda, and killing that of bombing cities from the air? What such basic principles amount to outside the personal moral sphere is much more uncertain and has to be continually reinterpreted to take into account the political and legal realities of a given society at a specific period of historical time. Does a socialist program of nationalization of private property amount to large-scale theft? Is it more permissible when it is the property of multinational companies with anonymous shareholders than if it is the land owned by peasants? And similar issues arise with respect of lying and killing, and even with committing adultery. The person who wishes to act in an ethically responsible way as a good citizen will not find it as easy to apply the basic ethical rules as if she merely wishes to act as a good individual in a private setting.

Traditional moral prescriptions are not easy to apply outside very narrow dimensions of contemporary life, which are no longer even the most important ones as far as contemporary mores and their attendant valuations are concerned. Private and individual life no longer has the supreme importance it had when so many were concerned with the salvation of their souls or with their probity and conscientiousness as upright gentlemen and ladies. This is a reflection of the general sociological fact that morality has fallen on hard times. But it is not only traditional morality that is no longer obviously applicable; the other traditional ethics have also suffered a similar fate. What is now the relevance of an ethic of honor when few of the claims of honor can now be asserted or demanded of others? Anyone who still seeks to engage in affairs of honor will soon discover how ridiculous that is now considered. A civic ethic in the old classical sense of "dulce et decorum est pro patri mori" is murderously dangerous when invoked in contemporary nationalism or irrelevant when referred to the cosmopolitanism of world citizenship. What can it now mean to be a good European patriot? An ethic of duty in anything like its original Confucian mandarin sense cannot be applied to contemporary officials in China or elsewhere. Could such cadres stand up against the new emperor, the Party, when it transgresses against the customary norms? What does the self-respect and dignity of office mean under present conditions of bureaucratic civil service?

Nevertheless, this must not be taken as an argument for abandoning what is left of the fragments of our ethical traditions. What now survives of these is often so partial and so stunted as to be a grotesque reflection of its own past. But even in this form the ethical past has still a contemporary relevance. It has an educative role, especially for children and the young in general. Obviously, it needs to be reformed and improved wherever possible, but it must not be abandoned. For only someone brought up, at least initially, in something like the old ways can mature into an ethical being in any new way.

What is still of great importance now and not to be neglected is an upbringing in ethics that enables one to know and understand the ethical traditions of the past. Only such an ethically educated person can fully appreciate what of these past traditions can be preserved and reapplied and what is no longer relevant and must be consigned to history. Thus without some kind of traditional moral upbringing, one cannot mature to a more sophisticated morality that can be invoked to cope with current difficulties of living. Without an acquired sense of honor and pride, such as some schools and military academies still seek to inculcate, though most often in crude and crass traditional ways, it is difficult to develop a proper level of self-respect. Without traditions of civic virtue, such as some democracies still maintain, it is not possible to fulfill a participatory role as a good citizen even partially. Without a whole panoply of inculcated duties that derive from the still-functioning traditional institutions, it would be beyond the capacity of any person to build up the character virtues necessary for any of the present social ethics. Tradition is the vast storehouse of teaching resources, without which an ethical education is unthinkable.

The problem of what to retain of the ethical past as worth holding on to and keeping and what to abandon as now useless baggage cannot be answered in the abstract or in general terms. It must be tackled in the concrete specificity of the real problems of contemporary life. There are no rational *à priori* decisions to be made about this according to some general scheme of a communicative ethics or any other such overarching philosophical theory.

Deducing specific precepts from general principles will not serve the purpose. On the contrary, we can only build up general principles, as it were, by induction from the numerous specific solutions in given cases, the ethical answers we decide on in all the various problems we happen to encounter as they arise. We frequently argue from case to case. Such procedures will always be restricted, changeable, imperfect, and never completely adequate, for no serious problem is susceptible to an obvious and simple solution. From such limited cases we build up the general structure of a comprehensive ethical standpoint. Thus, we constitute a temporarily more adequate ethic by making continual alterations and running repairs to the ethics we already possess, in the light of the difficulties and breakdowns we experience in the practical course of living. An ethic is constructed not in the way a ship is built, on the basis of pre-prepared plans and components, but more in the way that a ship might be fitted out or repaired while still at sea. There is no safe harbor or dry-dock where it can be laid up and completely redesigned and overhauled.

Thus far we have discussed the general form of the field of ethics in overall terms, but that in itself will not determine anything of the content of any one of the specific ethics. What should civic ethics, social ethics, and morality at present be primarily concerned with? To answer that requires reviewing the fundamental problems that tend to arise in these spheres of contemporary life, those that most frequently and urgently call for ethical decisions. On the average, collective response to such problems depends on what kind of society we are prepared to tolerate and ultimately what kind of world we will create. In what follows, a few such ethically salient problems will be outlined in brief, though these are far from being exhaustive.

On the level of civic ethics there are three kinds of problems: those of a global dimension that potentially should concern everyone on earth, those that touch on given countries or states; and those that are local and only involve affected groups. On the global level there are, first, the well-known problems of peace and war, above all, that of nuclear war; second, there are the problems of the degradation of the environment, which potentially embrace the whole of earthly Nature; and third, there are problems of human population and how to produce and distribute the resources necessary to sustain such ever-growing numbers of people and, if possible, to reduce their rate of increase. All three of these problems are interconnected issues of human well-being and justice on a global level that demand an ethical response from us as citizens of the world. Obviously, what this response should be is a disputed matter to which many kinds of answers in contradiction to each other have been given and will continue to be given. For example, should population be reduced by measures that might be considered morally dubious, such as forced sterilization and abortion, or should instead only voluntary means be used, in which case such policies might fail in the face of religious and traditional intransigence? How should the world's food stocks be apportioned? Should supplies be distributed mainly to those in greatest need or mainly to those who make an effort to help themselves? Sooner or later, such dilemmas and many more like them have to be confronted on an international level.

Citizenship of given states brings with it more specific problems that each country will have to answer for itself. For the wealthy industrialized countries there is the prevalent problem of immigration from poorer countries. Should we admit all who might wish to come for economic reasons or only select groups, such as political refugees? And among the latter, should we admit those who are prone to cause political troubles in their host country and country of origin, such as various kinds of dissidents given to terroristic activities? Then there are innumerable problems to do with employment and unemployment. Is it ethically right to maintain the majority on high levels of income at the expense of a minority of unemployed or would it be better to lower the income of everyone so as to employ everyone? All such problems and many more are ethical issues of concern to citizens. How they collectively answer them will determine their common civic ethics and, *ipso facto*, the level of social decency in their societies.

In these matters the ethical debate is public and it nearly always takes a political form. Those who in common share a given solution and make joint proposals to instantiate their ethical goals will have to organize themselves in the framework of a political party or pressure group or become a mass movement in order to realize their aims on a state level. If they are successful, then their campaign will result in legislation that is enforced by the courts or some other such agencies, some of which might be international bodies. Thus with most such matters there occurs a political implementation of civic ethics in the form of law.

But in acting ethically to implement new laws, one is confronted with another difficult dilemma, for through such ethical action and its political results, the tightly knit web of law and regulation will continue to expand and strangle in its meshes the very life of the ethics that produced it in the first place. Thus the enactment of ethics on an international level will simply continue the process of legislative encroachment that has already been taking place nationally for many centuries. Now as in the past the dilemma is inescapable: ethics must sometimes unavoidably act against itself. We have no choice but to demand more legislative intervention for the sake of the higher ends that must be safeguarded. Thus, for example, for the sake of environmental protection the network of legal restraints will continue to proliferate until it will be difficult to do anything out of doors without a license or without infringing on one law or another. At present this process is necessarily unavoidable, for if delayed, as it is in some Third World countries, there will soon be little of the environment left to protect.

It is possible that in some future world society such matters will be dealt with in an ethical way without strict law and enforcement procedures. Thus it is possible to imagine that, eventually, people will be brought up so as not to wish to harm the environment, that they will have an environmentally protective conscience and the kind of love of Nature that primitive people display. Analogously so, it is possible to suppose that people will become peace-loving and magnanimous and look on any aggressive act as if it were the violation of a deeply held taboo and be generous in sharing their personal resources with others in distant lands. Yet at present these are merely utopian dreams, even though there are some small minority groups, like the Quakers and a few others, who actually live according to such an ethics. But it is not something to be relied on at present or expected from everyone. Now we must still look to the state and its legislative powers to achieve many basic ethical goals, especially so in international affairs. Hence, the conflict between ethics and law is with us to stay as a permanent dilemma.

Such dilemmas also arise within various areas of social ethics, where the problem is one of either instituting formal regulations and rules or allowing things to be settled by informal means without the backing of coercive measures. We have already given many instances of such issues. The problem arises in nearly all social relations at present where legislative or regulative measures have been introduced in order to correct a perceived ethical wrong. As we have seen, it arises in the context of family matters, of gender relations, of ethnic and racial relations, and so on. Such laws have already proved themselves in some respects counterproductive. But the question remains whether it is better to tolerate some degree of social evil or to act legislatively against it and risk the consequences of excessive social repression. These matters need to be settled on a case-by-case basis, for there are usually good ethical arguments on both sides. Such issues arise also in regard to the various kinds of group ethics, where there are typical problems of internal and external regulation and to what extent either of these should be explicitly spelled out in terms of rules of behavior or left to the unspecifiable conventions of good manners and a spirit of solidarity, trust, loyalty, and fair play. All this is of particular concern where power is at stake, as in political parties, labor unions, and business associations.

A fundamental issue of social ethics in all societies concerns the ethics of the professions. This is becoming more of a problem, as much of working life is becoming professionalized—that is, subject to certification and specialized competence. The number of new professions is rapidly increasing, for every major change in the economy, especially due to new technology, gives rise to new specializations. The new information technologies, for example, have brought about a great proliferation in new skills and types of jobs. Few if any of these professions have any ethics to regulate them nor are their members in any way ethically educated or prepared to face the ethical problems of their work. They have few traditions of acceptable behavior or norms of responsibility to fall back on, so they tend to be unscrupulous and indiscriminate. Ethics plays little part in their consciousness of their role.

This was not so with the older vocations, which had well established professional ethics. Such ethics were variants of a general ethics of duty with specifications of responsibility and a sense of vocation appropriate to the given work. The two main professions with distinctive ethical codes were medicine and law, for these required special university educational qualifications and considered themselves of a higher status. But a number of other professions for which degree certification was called for, such as teaching and civil service, were also intent on cultivating an appropriate professional ethics. Now that nearly all professionals have university or tertiary qualifications of one kind or another but have undergone an educational training to qualify them for their job in which ethics played no part, the issue of ethics for such people should be of great concern.

There are some very difficult ethical problems that have to be confronted in formulating ethics for these new professions that are not generally recognized. There is invariably a conflict of interest between the professionals or their association and their clients or the public whom they serve. What is good for psychologists is not necessarily good for their patients, what suits teachers need not help their students, and so on for many others. There are also conflicts between the interests of the employers of professionals, those who provide them with the means to exercise their competence, and the interest of the public or the society at large. Thus those who are employed by business firms have constantly to reconcile the profitability of their work as against its actual or potential harmful consequences. For example, scientists working in such industries as tobacco, alcohol, and other drugs are faced with the ethical difficulty of either disclosing the effects of what they help produce and so in effect betraying the trust of their employers, or vice versa, not disclosing it and so deceiving the public. The ethical predicament becomes even more difficult to resolve when their employer is the state and when they are engaged on projects of vital national importance, such as arms production, carried out under stipulations of sworn secrecy. Physicists engaged on nuclear weapons research have had to grapple with such ethical issues from the very start and they have not succeeded in resolving them. They have faced the stark choice of either walking away from such work, an option taken by very few, or, as the great majority have done, doing the state's bidding without question.

There has always been the temptation for professionals and experts to abjure responsibility for their work and to maintain a very narrow and restricted code of ethical conduct. Thus most scientists have tended to argue, and to act as if they implicitly accepted the argument, that responsibility for the consequences of their work on arms production is in the hands of the politicians in the first place and ultimately in those of the people who elect them. Those engaged in commercial work argue analogously that whether their products are available for sale or not is a matter of the law or, at least, of business practice and so is none of their professional responsibility. Even in what were once the traditional professions there are now strong tendencies to evade or disclaim responsibility and so weaken what is left of the traditional ethics. Medicine and its ancillary branches, such as psychiatry, are in some respects now being purveyed as marketable commodities and are succumbing to the ethos of the marketplace. Legal practice is in some countries, such as the United States, assuming in certain of its processes the aspects of a competitive sport, frequently played for very high stakes. For professionals to operate within the limits tolerated by the law is no substitute for satisfying the ethical requirements of their professions.

How to establish and strengthen professional ethics is thus a crucial matter in determining how to be ethical in contemporary working situations. The role of the individual is often decisive in alerting the general public and fellow workers about ethical inadequacies and abuses. Such people are commonly known as "whistleblowers." Almost invariably, their fate used to be that they were punished for their exposures by loss of position or demotion. Now they are generally protected against reprisals by law and sometimes even rewarded. This has in turn prompted the emergence of opportunistic denouncers who are driven by greed or the desire for notoriety.[7] Yet despite such abuses, the genuine whistleblower, exposing a demonstrable ethical fault, must be encouraged and protected, for in that lies one of the last hopes for individual ethical initiative in our working ethos.

The act of "whistleblowing" is an emblematic instance of moral action in general, for just as the whistleblower is faced with the unenviable choice of having to act against an organization or profession to which he or she belongs, so is the moral individual most often called upon to act against society or, at least, against an entrenched social interest. In our kind of society, moral action very frequently involves the individual setting himself against one or another social force in an act of resistance against that which is imposed on everyone. We have already noted many instances of such social pressures and examined the social forces that exert them. The law and the whole panoply of regulative measures carried out by the state and its agencies are powerful forces that work against any sense of individual moral responsibility, and to act against them, where this is called for, is difficult and dangerous. Similarly, the major forces of civil society can only be counteracted at considerable personal risk. To go against the market, the Culture Industry, the media, the technological infrastructure and the kind of work routine it promotes, and the powerful organizations is to go against the current of contemporary civilization. And yet this is called for if any sense of a moral Self and individual conscience is to be maintained, for these are social forces that are inimical to any such integrity.

Thus the moral life is bound to be a difficult life in our society, for it will mainly be led in opposition. The most characteristic moral act in such a conformist society is the act of refusal and non-compliance to what society imposes through its imperatives of law, schooling, or market success. To say *No*—this I will not do, this I will not accept, this I will not tolerate, this I will not swallow—is the typical form that moral self-affirmation through negation takes. But such a stand of non-conformity or non-adjustment will be bound to arouse all kinds of negative reactions and bring painful consequences. The moral individual today risks continually being branded an enemy of the people. Nevertheless, it is only through such acts of refusal and rejection that moral autonomy can be affirmed and, *ipso facto*, moral individuality maintained.

Moral individuality is a kind of positive capability of being oneself and not merely what society strives to make of one. It is a capability that is indispensable to any moral life at present, for through it the individual can stake out a space of inner freedom in which moral choices can be made. Such choices are never willful and arbitrary decisions, such as the Existentialist theory of commitment envisages. They are not made in pure and perfect freedom but under the pressure of events in constrained circumstances, allowing only a few options. It is from such imperfect and often flawed actions that an always-precarious moral life is constituted.

Under contemporary conditions, the relation between morality and personal happiness has become more problematic than ever before. Virtue is today as liable to be conducive to unhappiness as to happiness. The ever-present ethical irrationality of the world—namely, that one can suffer for being virtuous and just—haunts one in new guises. Traditionally, this was seen as the tragedy of a Job; today it is more likely to be the tragedy of a job. For a job of one kind or another alone grants one a position and public presence, and without it personal social well-being is very difficult to attain. And yet if one acts morally, the first thing one is liable to lose is one's job and so be denied any accredited standing. But keeping one's job means that one cannot call into question whatever it is that one's employers happen to be doing. If one does, then this is bound to have dire consequences for one's personal happiness, as so many of the early whistleblowers discovered.

Of course, it is always possible to withdraw from the job treadmill and to some extent from society altogether, provided one has the financial means to support oneself in isolation. This is today an option akin to the traditional retreat to monasteries and convents, though it is without any of the traditional supports of a community of fellows and of general public approval. It is doubtful if such a life is tolerable under present conditions for very long to any but the hardiest exceptions. Most of the countercultural experiments in social withdrawal seem to have come to nought. In any case it is an escape from the problems of the world, which is hardly a moral response to the troubles of one's neighbors. It is morally more worthy to face the difficulties that others confront but to cope with them differently. If nothing else, this has an exemplary value.

Under contemporary conditions, the moral life faces far greater difficulties than the other major ethical spheres, civic ethics or social ethics. The reasons for this have already been extensively explored and explained. Mainly, it has to do with the lack of effective ethical communities upholding morality and with the parlous state of the autonomous individual in a conformist society of consumerism. In the other ethical spheres there are still some viable communities at work. In civic ethics there are numerous organizations devoted to upholding human rights and other civic causes at an international or national level. In social ethics there are all kinds of bodies, such as, for example, professional associations, given to maintaining vocational codes. Morality is relatively bereft of such supports because the religious or secular authorities that used to sustain communities have tended to abandon this role under political and social pressure.

Hence, the task of rebuilding moral communities is of utmost urgency at present, for without some public sustenance the moral individual cannot survive for very much longer. Sooner or later, if things go on in the next century as they have done in this last one, such people will disappear. With them will go a whole dimension of what used to be called spiritual life. The dessication of the moral spirit will have dire consequences for creative life in general. For without the moral courage to stand up against all odds, the creative spirit in all activities withers. That is the measure of the moral challenge facing us as we start this millennium.

~

Notes

Introduction

1. Friedrich Nietzsche, *The Will to Power*, trans. W. Kaufmann and R. J. Hollingdale (New York: Vintage Press, 1964), sec. 868, p. 465.

2. George Eliot, *Middlemarch,* chap. 61 (Harmondsworth: Penguin, 1977), p. 561.

3. Adam Smith, *The Wealth of Nations* (7th ed., London, 1793), book I, chap. 2, p. 19.

4. Max Weber, *The Sociology of Religion*, trans. E. Fischoff (London: Methuen, 1965), p. 217.

5. Theodor Adorno, *Minima Moralia,* trans. E. F. N. Jephcott (London: NLB, 1974), p. 24.

6. Max Horkheimer, *Dawn and Decline*, trans. M. Shaw (New York: Seabury Press, 1978), p. 226.

7. Ralph Waldo Emerson, *The Collected Works,* A. R. Ferguson and J. F. Carr, eds., vol. 3 (Cambridge, Mass.: Harvard University Press, 1983), p. 124.

8. Emerson, *Collected Works,* p. 126.

9. Quoted in John Ralston Saul, *Voltaire's Bastards: The Dictatorship of Reason in the West* (New York: Free Press, 1992), p. 324.

10. For example, see the now classic works of George Orwell, or for something more topical, see Jean-Francois Revel, *The Flight from Truth: The Reign of Deceit in the Age of Information*, trans. Curtis Cate (New York: Random House, 1991).

11. Max Weber, in "Science as Vocation," *From Max Weber,* ed. H. H. Gerth and C. Wright Mills (New York: Oxford University Press, 1946), p. 149.

12. Weber, *From Max Weber,* p. 149.

Chapter 1

1. For a full account of representation, see Harry Redner, *A New Science of Representation* (Boulder: Westview Press, 1994).

2. Redner, *New Science*, chap. 1.

3. Clifford Geertz, *The Interpretation of Cultures* (New York: Basic Books, 1973), p. 129.

4. C. Stephen Jaeger, *The Origins of Courtliness, Civilizing Trends and the Formation of Court Ideals 939–1210* (Philadelphia: University of Pennsylvania Press, 1985), p. 109.

5. See Redner, *New Science*, chap. 2.

6. Arnold Toynbee, *A Study of History*, vol. 12 (New York: Oxford University Press, 1964), p. 56.

7. However, see Redner, *New Science*, chap. 2.

8. Baron Secondat de Montesquieu, *The Spirit of the Laws*, trans. A. M. Cohler, B. C. Miller, and H. S. Stone (Cambridge: Cambridge University Press, 1989), p. 36.

9. J. Lindblom, *Prophecy in Ancient Israel* (Oxford: Blackwell, 1962), p. 348.

10. Quoted in E. R. Dodds, *The Greeks and the Irrational* (Berkeley: University of California Press, 1956), p. 35.

11. Quoted in S. G. F. Brandon, *The Judgement of the Dead* (London: Weidenfeld and Nicolson, 1967), pp. 34–5.

12. Dodds, p. 36.

13. Brandon, *Judgement*, p. 37.

14. Brandon, *Judgement*, p. 40.

15. Dodds, p. 36.

16. Dodds, p. 36.

17. Martin Buber, *Good and Evil* (New York: Charles Scrivener and Sons, 1952), p. 51.

18. Buber, p. 86.

19. Buber, p. 87.

20. See R. J. Zwi Werblowsky, *Magie, Mystic, Messianismus, Vergleichende Studien zur Religionsgeschichte des Judentum und des Christentum* (Hildesheim: Georg Olms Verlag, 1997).

21. Max Weber, *Ancient Judaism*, trans. H. H. Gerth and D. Martindale (New York: Free Press, 1952), p. 242.

22. Weber, *Ancient Judaism*, p. 254.

23. Weber, *Ancient Judaism*, p. 254.

24. Weber, *Ancient Judaism*, p. 254.

25. Weber, *Ancient Judaism*, p. 254.

26. Weber, *Ancient Judaism*, p. 254.

27. Weber, *Ancient Judaism*, p. 254.

28. Weber, *Ancient Judaism*, p. 255–6.

29. Weber, *Ancient Judaism*, p. 256.

30. Weber, *Ancient Judaism*, p. 386.

31. Hans Küng, *On Being a Christian*, trans. E. Quin (London: Fontana/Collins, 1978), p. 255.

32. Küng, p. 255.

33. Küng, p. 255.

34. Küng, p. 255.

35. Küng, p. 255.

36. Arendt writes as follows: "There is certainly no denying the statements of Karl Holl (in 'Augustines innere Entwicklung' *Preussische Akademie der Wissenschaften* [1918]: 47) that 'this brief outline confirms, to begin with, that the influence of Saint Paul did not extend into Augustine's ultimate depths. It did not touch the basic eudaimonistic trait of his ethics, nor, for all the talk about *caritas*, the endeavour's concentration upon the self.' Holl claims that 'this has to do with the fact that Augustine knows how to grasp the commandments of the Sermon on the Mount from their negative side only. The innermost essence of neighbourly love, its will to self-sacrificing community, remained hidden from him' (19). However, it can be shown that even in Saint Paul's case (though not in Jesus' own words) love of neighbour remains consistently tied to the individual, i.e. that the fundamental question of an understanding of neighbourly love, as commanded by Jesus, reads as follows: As one seized by God and detached from the world, how can I still live in the world?" Hannah Arendt, *Love and Saint Augustine*, J. Vecchiarelli Scott and J. Cheliuk Stark, eds. (Chicago: University of Chicago Press, 1996), p. 91.

37. E. Washburn Hopkins, *Ethics of India* (Port Washington, N.Y.: Kennikot Press, 1924), p. 136.

38. Quoted in Hopkins, p. 153.

39. Hopkins, p. 153.

40. Max Weber, *The Religion of India*, trans. H. H. Gerth and D. Martindale (New York: Free Press, 1958), p. 208.

41. Weber, *Religion of India*, p. 208.

42. Weber, *Religion of India*, p. 212.

43. Weber, *Religion of India*, p. 208.

44. Weber, *Religion of India*, p. 210.

45. Weber, *Religion of India*, p. 208.

46. Weber, *Religion of India*, p. 213.

47. Weber, *Religion of India*, p. 218.

48. Weber, *Religion of India*, p. 238.

49. Obeyesekere writes as follows: "Niemand wird der Auffassung widersprechen dass buddhistische *maitri* und christliche *caritas* idealtypisch gesehen verschieden sind; doch Webers psychologische Charakterisierung der buddhistischen "Liebe" ist voll und ganz aus seinen Verständnis der Psychologie des *arhat* erschlossen. Sie ignoriert die praktische Ethik des Buddhismus, die in der *suttas* und insbesondere in den *jataka* verkörpert ist. In den *jatakas* gibt es zahlreiche spezifisch buddhistische Vorlesungen von feindesliebe und Liebe zum Mitmenschen, die fast ausnahmslos dem Laien zum Vorbild und zur Erbauung dienen sollen. Webers Voreingenommenheit resultiert hier in der unrealistische Vorstellung, der frühe Buddhist sei ein einsamer sucher der persönlichen Erlösung gewesen." Gananath Obeyesekere, "Exemplarische Prophetie oder ethisch geleitete Askese?" Wolfgang Schluchter, ed., *Max Webers Studie Über Hinduismus und Buddhismusr* (Frankfurt: Suhrkamp, 1984), p. 268.

50. Schluchter, p. 250.

51. Schluchter, p. 250.

52. Max Weber, *"Science as Vocation,"* pp. 148–9.

53. See Harry Redner, *The Ends of Philosophy* (London: Croom-Helm, 1986), chap. 5.

54. Friedrich Nietzsche, *Beyond Good and Evil*, trans. R. J. Hollingdale (Harmondsworth: Penguin, 1973), sec. 202.

55. Friedrich Nietsche, *On the Geneaology of Morals*, K. Ansell-Pearson, ed., trans. C. Diette (Cambridge: Cambridge University Press, 1994), p. 66.

56. Nietzsche, *Genealogy*, p. 66.

57. Ruth Benedict, *Patterns of Culture* (Boston: Houghton Mifflin, 1934), p. 276.

58. Plato, *The Laws of Plato*, trans. Thomas L. Pangle (New York: Basic Books, 1980), p. 24.

59. Quoted in Arthur Adkins, *Merit and Responsibility* (Oxford: Clarendon Press, 1960), p. 75.

60. Max Weber, *The City*, trans. D. Martindale and G. Neuwirth (New York: Free Press, 1958), pp. 170–1.

61. Weber, p. 171.

62. E. R. Dodds, *The Greeks and the Irrational* (University of California Press, Berkeley, 1951), p. 35.

63. Dodds, p. 35.

64. Dodds, p. 40.

65. Adkins, p. 83.

66. Adkins, p. 75.

67. Adkins, p. 74.

68. Adkins, p. 78.

69. Adkins, p. 78.

70. Francis Sparshott, *Taking Life Seriously* (Toronto: Toronto University Press, 1996), p. 394.

71. Sparshott, p. 190.

72. Adkins, p. 30.

73. Adkins, p. 32.

74. Adkins, p. 73.

75. Adkins, p. 198.

76. Adkins, p. 239.

77. Adkins, p. 227.

78. Adkins, p. 270.

79. Julia Annas, *The Morality of Happiness* (New York: Oxford University Press, 1993), p. 17.

80. Sparshott, p. 226.

81. Sparshott, p. 182.

82. Sparshott, p. 182.

83. Sparshott, p. 356.

84. Adkins, p. 32.

85. Quoted in Adkins, p. 73.

86. Adkins, p. 73.

87. Adkins, p. 78.

88. Adkins, p. 74.

89. Thucydides, *The Pelopponesian War*, book II, trans. Rex Warner (London: Penguin Classics, 1954), pp. 118–19.

90. Adkins, p. 230.

91. Adkins, p. 227.

92. See Redner, *New Science*, chap. 3.

93. Annas, p. 126.

94. Annas, p. 126.

95. Sparshott, p. 439.

96. Dodds, p. 18.

97. Dodds, p. 45.

98. Adkins, p. 88.

99. Friedrich Nietzsche, *On Genealogy*, p. 70.

100. Thucydides, p. 122.

101. Thucydides, p. 122.

102. Sparshott, p. 142.

103. Max Weber, *The Religion of China*, op. cit., p. 157.

104. Weber, p. 236.

105. Weber, p. 241.

106. Weber, p. 111.

107. Weber, p. 122.

108. Weber, p. 162.

109. Weber, p. 156.

110. Weber, p. 234.

111. Quoted in H. H. Rowley, *Prophecy and Religion in Ancient China and Israel* (London: Athlone Press, 1956), p. 64.

112. Karl Bürger, "Das Chinesische Rechtsystem und das Prinzip der Rechtesstaatlichkeit." In Wolfgang Schluchter, *Max Webers Studie über Konfuzianismus und Taoismus* (Frankfurt: Suhrkamp, 1983), p. 164.

113. Quoted in Heiner Roetz, *Confucian Ethics and the Axial Age* (Albany, N.Y.: SUNY Press, 1944), p. 261.

114. Roetz, p. 261.

115. Roetz, p. 261.

116. Peter Weber-Schäfer, "Die konfuzianischen Literaten und die Grund werte des Konfuzianismus." In Schluchter, p. 226.

117. Quoted in Roetz, p. 49.

118. Weber, *Religion of China*, p. 235.

119. Weber, *Religion of China*, p. 248.

120. Schluchter, p. 32.

121. Weber-Schäfer, p. 222.

122. Max Weber, *Religion of India*, p. 180.

123. Weber, *Religion of India*, p. 184.

124. Christopher Isherwood, ed., *The Bhagavad Gita*, trans. Swami Prabhavananda (New York: Mentor Religious Classics, 1953), p. 40.

125. *Bhagavad Gita*, p. 45.

126. *Bhagavad Gita*, p. 48.

127. *Bhagavad Gita*, p. 217.

128. Max Weber, *Religion of India*, pp. 185 and 189.

129. Weber, *Religion of India*, p. 189.

130. *Bhagavad Gita*, p. 40.

131. *Bhagavad Gita*, p. 48.

132. *Bhagavad Gita*, p. 40.

133. *Bhagavad Gita*, p. 56.

134. *Bhagavad Gita*, p. 62.

135. James Francis, *Subversive Virtue: Asceticism and Authority in the Second-Century Pagan World* (University Park, Pa.: Pennsylvania State University Press, 1995), p. 4.

136. Francis, p. 4.

137. Francis, p. 2.

138. Francis, p. 2.

139. Francis, p. 2.

140. Quoted in Annas, p. 107.

141. Quoted in Francis, p. 18.

142. Pierre Hadot, *Philosophy as a Way of Life*, trans. M. Chase (Oxford: Blackwell, 1995), p. 193.

143. Annas, p. 302.

144. Pierre Hadot, p. 193.

145. Quoted in Annas, p. 302.

146. Louis Dumont, *Essays in Individualism* (Chicago: Chicago University Press), p. 33.

147. C. Stephen Jaeger, *The Origins of Courtliness* (Philadelphia: University of Pennsylvania Press, 1985), p. 117.

148. Jaeger, p. 117.

149. Jaeger, p. 119.

150. Jaeger, p. 101.

151. Jaeger, p. 126.

152. Jaeger, p. 101.

153. Jaeger, p. 101.

154. Max Weber, *Religion of China*, p. 215.

155. Weber, *Religion of China*, p. 176.

156. Jaeger, p. 46.

157. F. J. C. Hearnshow, "Chivalry and Its Place in History." In Edgar Prestage, ed., *Chivalry* (New York: A. Knopf, 1928), p. 21.

158. Hearnshow, p. 32.

159. Hearnshow, p. 24.

160. Georges Duby, *The Chivalrous Society*, trans. C. Postan (London: Edward Arnold, 1977); Maurice Keen, *Chivalry* (New Haven: Yale University Press, 1984).

161. C. Stephen Jaeger, *The Origins of Courtliness*, op. cit., p. 257.

162. Jaeger, p. 262.

163. Jaeger, p. 262.

164. Jaeger, p. 242.

165. Jaeger, p. 268.

166. Christiane Marchello-Nixia, "Courtly Chivalry." In *A History of Young People in the West*, vol. I, Giovanni Levi and Jean-Claude Schmitt, eds.; trans. Camille Naish (Cambridge, Mass.: Harvard University Press, 1997).

167. Marchello-Nixia, p. 153.

168. Hearnshow, p. 18.

169. Joachim Bumke, *Courtly Culture, Literature and Society in the High Middle Ages*, trans. Thomas Dunlop (Berkeley: University of California Press, 1991), p. 377.

170. Quoted in Bumke, p. 378.

171. Quoted in Marchello-Nixia, p. 151.

172. Quoted in Marchello-Nixia, p. 165.

173. Renata Ago, "Young Nobles in the Age of Absolutism." In Levi and Schmitt, p. 297.

174. Bumke, p. 309.

175. Bumke, p. 309.

176. Quoted in Bumke, p. 310.

177. Bumke, p. 311.

178. F. J. C. Hearnshow, p. 32.

179. Richard W. Kaeuper and Elspeth Kennedy, *The Book of Chivalry of Geoffroi de Charny* (Philadelphia: University of Pennsylvania Press, 1996), p. 12.

180. See Norbert Elias, *The Civilizing Process*, vol. I, trans. E. Jephcott (Oxford: Blackwell, 1982).

181. Reinhold Merkelbach, *Mithras* (Köln: Hain, 1984), p. 23.

182. Merkelbach, p. 37.

183. Merkelbach, p. 37.

184. Merkelbach, p. 23.

185. Merkelbach, p. 24.

186. R. C. Zaehner, *The Dawn and Twilight of Zoroastrianism* (London: Weidenfeld and Nicholson, 1961), p. 98.

187. Zaehner, p. 110.

188. Zaehner, p. 98.

189. Josef Wiesenhöfer, *Das Antike Persien* (Zurich: Artemis & Winkler, 1993), p. 124.

190. J. M. Cook, *The Persian Empire* (New York: Schoeken Books, 1983), p. 231.

191. Cook, p. 231.

192. See Edwin M. Yamauchi, *Persia and the Bible* (Grand Rapids, Mich.: Baker Book House, 1990), pp. 458–67.

193. Margaret C. Miller, *Athens and Persia in the Fifth Century B.C.: A Study in Cultural Receptivity* (Cambridge: Cambridge University Press, 1997), p. 252.

194. Miller, p. 257.

195. Miller, p. 256.

196. Wiesenhöfer, p. 212. For the Parthian antecedents of Sassanian feudalism and

the cult of honor, John Ellis has this to say: "They lived in small castles and block-houses, and evolved a typical feudal culture centered round jousting, hunting, war, and a chivalric code that emphasized the virtues of personal honour and the protection of women. The grandees, on the other hand, supplied a new type of horseman, a development of the Sarmatian and Saka knight, who encased both himself and his horse in mail armour and armed himself with a great bow, lance and sword. Here, upward of a thousand years earlier, are most of the basic elements of western European feudalism." John Ellis, *Cavalry: The History of Mounted Warfare* (New York: Putnam's, 1978), p. 38.

197. Ellis, p. 293.

198. Zaener, p. 296.

199. Zaener, p. 284.

200. Zaener, p. 297.

201. Zaener, p. 297.

202. Rudolf Fahner, *West-Östliches Rittertum* Stefano Bianca, ed. (Graz: Accademisches Druck, 1997).

203. See Denis de Rougement, *Passion and Society*, trans. M. Belgion (London: Faber and Faber, 1940).

204. Julie Scott Meisami, *Medieval Persian Court Poetry* (Princeton: Princeton University Press, 1987), p. x.

205. Meisami, p. x.

206. de Rougemont, p. 102.

207. de Rougemont, p. 102.

208. de Rougemont, p. 102.

209. Max Weber, *Basic Concepts of Sociology*, "Types of Legitimae Order," from *Wirtschaft und Gesellschaft*, part I, chap. 1, sec. 6. (Tübingen: C. B. Mohr, 1956).

210. Max Weber, *Protestant Ethic and the Spirit of Capitalism*, trans. Talcott Parsons (London: Unwin, 1930), p. 97.

211. Quoted in Ruth Benedict, *Patterns of Culture*, op. cit., p. 95.

212. Max Weber, *Sociology of Law*, M. Rheinstein, ed. (New York: Simon and Schuster, 1967), p. 20.

213. Agnes Heller, *General Ethics* (Oxford: Blackwell, 1988), p. 33.

214. Heller, p. 33.

215. Weber, *Ancient Judaism*, p. 235.

216. See Redner, *Malign Masters: Gentile, Heidegger, Lukacs, and Wittgenstein* (London: Macmillan, 1997), chap. 3.

217. Weber, *Religion of India*, p. 251.

Chapter 2

1. See Harry Redner, "Ethics in Unethical Times." In M. Dascal and A. Cohen, eds., *The Institution of Philosophy* (Illinois: Open Court, 1989).

2. Aristotle, *Poetics* (1459b), part 3 (London: J. M. Dent, 1949), p. 47.

3. See Jean Marie Salamito, "Christianiserung und Neuordnung des gesellschaftli-

chen Lebens." In Charles and Luce Piètri et al., eds., *Die Geschichte des Christentums*, vol. II, trans. From French by N. Broch and O. Engels (original French edition Paris: Declée, 1995, German edition Freiburg: Heider, 1996), p. 801.

4. Salamito, p. 801.

5. Charles Norton Cochrane, *Christianity and Classical Culture* (New York: Oxford University Press, 1957), p. 226.

6. Timothy D. Barnes, *Athanasius and Constantius* (Cambridge, Mass: Harvard University Press, p. 12.

7. See Piètri, "Christianisierung."

8. Pierre Riché, *Education and Culture in the Barbarian West, Sixth through Eighth Centuries*, trans. J. J. Contrini (Columbia: University of South Carolina Press, 1976), p. 7.

9. Quoted in James Bowen, *A History of Western Education, vol. 1 The Ancient World: Orient and Mediterranean* (London: Methuen, 1974). P. 265.

10. Bowen, p. 266.

11. Bowen, p. 267.

12. Bowen, p. 282.

13. Bowen, p. 282.

14. H. I. Marrou, *A History of Education in Antiquity*, trans. G. Lamb (London: Sheed and Ward, 1956), p. 350.

15. Karl Marx, *The Eighteenth Brumaire of Louis Bonaparte* (New York: International Publishers, 1987), p. 121.

16. Max Weber, *On Law in Economy and Society*, trans. M. Rheinstein and E. Shils (New York: Simon and Schuster, 1967), p. 250.

17. Weber, *On Law*, p. 252.

18. Weber, *On Law*, p. 253.

19. Weber, *On Law*, p. 253.

20. Weber, *On Law*, p. 253.

21. Weber, *On Law*, p. 274.

22. Piétri, "Das Scheitern, p. 242.

23. Max Weber, *The Protestant Ethic and the Spirit of Capitalism*, trans. Talcott Parsons (New York: Charles Scribner, 1958), p. 126.

24. Weber, *Protestant Ethic*, p. 80.

25. Weber, *Protestant Ethic*, p. 117.

26. Weber, *Protestant Ethic*, p. 270.

27. Max Weber, *Religion of China*, p. 241.

28. Weber, *Protestant Ethic*, pp. 180 and 182.

29. Weber, *Protestant Ethic*, p. 182.

30. Weber, *Protestant Ethic*, p. 182.

31. See Harry Redner, *The Ends of Philosophy* (London: Croom-Helm, 1986), appendix 1.

32. Weber, *From Max Weber*, p. 293.

33. Weber, *From Max Weber*, p. 294.

34. Weber, *From Max Weber*, p. 274.

35. Weber, *From Max Weber*, p. 293.

36. Max Weber, *Religion of China*, p. 248.

37. Weber, *Religion of China*, p. 127.

38. Weber, *Religion of China*, p. 127.

39. Weber, *Religion of China*, p. 247.

40. Weber, *Religion of China*, p. 225.

41. Weber, *Religion of China*, p. 335.

42. Weber, *Religion of China*, p. 226.

43. Weber, "Science as a Vocation," p. 148.

44. See Richard Sennett, *The Fall of Public Man* (Cambridge: Cambridge University Press, 1974).

45. Eliot, *Middlemarch*, p. 561.

46. See Redner, *Malign Masters*.

Chapter 3

1. Jean Leca, "Individualism and Citizenship." In Pierre Birnbaum and Jean Leca, ed., *Individualism*, trans. J. Gaffney (Oxford: Clarendon Press, 1990), p. 182.

2. Saul, *Voltaire's Bastards*, p. 326.

3. Saul, p. 326.

4. Peter W. Morgan and Glenn H. Reynolds, *The Appearance of Impropriety* (New York: Free Press, 1997), pp. 170–1.

5. Morgan and Reynolds, p. 171.

6. Morgan and Reynolds, p. 171.

7. Morgan and Reynolds, p. 160.

8. Morgan and Reynolds, chap. 2.

9. Jürgen Habermas, *Legitimation Crisis*, trans. Thomas McCarthy (Boston: Beacon Press, 1973).

10. George Soros, *The Crisis of Global Capitalism* (Boston: Little, Brown & Co., 1999), p. 11.

11. Jean Chesneaux, *Brave Modern World*, trans. D. Johnstone (London: Thames and Hudson, 1992), p. 157.

12. Chesneaux, p. 156.

13. Saul, p. 384.

14. Weber, *Sociology of Religion*, p. 217.

15. Weber, *Sociology of Religion*, p. 216.

16. Weber, *Sociology of Religion*, p. 217.

17. Robert E. Lane, *The Market Experience* (New York: Cambridge University Press, 1991), p. 260.

18. Lane, p. 263.

19. Richard Sennett, *The Corrosion of Character: The Personal Consequences of Work in the New Capitalism* (New York: Norton, 1998).

20. Sennett, p. 26.

21. Sennett, p. 98.

22. Sennett, p. 106.

23. Sennett, p. 116.

24. See Harry Redner, *The Ends of Science* (Boulder: Westview, 1987), chap. 5.

25. Redner, *Ends of Science*, chap. 3.

26. Max Horkheimer, *Dawn and Decline*, trans. M. Shaw (New York: Seabury Press, 1978), p. 160.

27. Peter Sloterdijk, *Critique of Cynical Reason*, trans. M. Eldred (Minneapolis: Minnesota University Press, 1987), p. 88.

28. Gernot Böhme, *Ethik im Kontext* (Frankfurt a.M.: Suhrkamp, 1997), p. 53.

29. Böhme, p. 116.

30. Chesneaux, p. 142.

Chapter 4

1. This work on ethics is to be accompanied by an analogous study of aesthetics that will make these comparisons more explicit.

2. For a psychological study of this, see Daniel Goleman, *Emotional Intelligence* (London: Bloomsbury, 1996).

3. See Theodor Adorno, *Minima Moralia: Reflections from Damaged Life*, trans. E. F. N. Jephcott (London: NLB, 1974).

4. Pierre Hadot, *Philosophy as a Way of Life: Spiritual Exercises from Socrates to Foucault*, A. I. Davidson, ed.; trans. M. Chase (Oxford: Blackwell, 1995), p. 83.

5. Hadot, p. 83.

6. Hadot, p. 271.

7. J.-P. Sartre, *Sartre by Himself*, trans. Richard Leaver (Sydney: Urizen Books and Outback Press, 1968), p. 122.

8. See Redner, *Malign Masters*.

9. Gernot Böhme, *Ethik im Kontext*.

10. Hadot, p. 268.

11. Max Weber, "Science as Vocation," p. 155.

12. Weber, "Science as Vocation," p. 111.

13. Weber, "Science as Vocation," p. 155.

14. Weber, "Science as Vocation," p. 155.

15. Weber, "Science as Vocation," p. 156.

Chapter 5

1. Aristotle, *The Ethics of Aristotle*, book 2, chap. 2, trans. J. A. K. Thomson (Harmondsworth: Penguin, 1955), p. 57.

2. Böhme.

3. From father I got my figure, / And my serious bearing; / From mother dear my blithe spirit / And my yen for storytelling.

4. Hadot, p. 266.

5. Adorno, *Minima Moralia,* p. 130.

6. Weber, "Politics as Vocation."

7. See Morgan and Reynolds, pp. 112–115.

Index

~

About the Author

Harry Redner is the author of a number of books on various subjects: *In the beginning was the Deed* (1982), *The Ends of Philosophy* (1986), *The Ends of Science* (1987), *A New Science of Representation* (1994), *Malign Masters* (1997) and with Jill Redner, *Anatomy of the World* (1984), as well as editor of *An Heretical Heir of the Enlightenment* in honor of C. E. Lindblom. For most of his academic career he was at Monash University in Melbourne, but during this time he was also Senior Fulbright Fellow in the United States with visiting positions at Yale, Berkeley, Boulder and Harvard. Since his retirement from Monash in 1996 he has held visiting appointments at Haifa, Darmstadt and Paris at the Ecole des Hautes Etudes en Sciences Sociales.